International Perspectives on Education Reform
Gita Steiner-Khamsi, Editor

Educating Children in Conflict Zones: Research, Policy, and Practice
for Systemic Change—A Tribute to Jackie Kirk
Karen Mundy and Sarah Dryden-Peterson, Eds.

Challenges to Japanese Education:
Economics, Reform, and Human Rights
*June A. Gordon, Hidenori Fujita,
Takehiko Kariya, and
Gerald LeTendre, Eds.*

South–South Cooperation in Education and Development
*Linda Chisholm and
Gita Steiner-Khamsi, Eds.*

Comparative and International Education:
Issues for Teachers
*Karen Mundy, Kathy Bickmore, Ruth Hayhoe,
Meggan Madden, and Katherine Madjidi, Eds.*

Educating Children in Conflict Zones

Research, Policy, and Practice for Systemic Change— A Tribute to Jackie Kirk

KAREN MUNDY

SARAH DRYDEN-PETERSON

Editors

Teachers College, Columbia University
New York and London

Chapter 2 is an abridged version of Kirk, J. (2007). Education and fragile states. *Globalisation, Societies and Education*, 5(2), 181–200. Used with permission.

Chapter 5 is an abridged version of Kirk, J. (2008a). Addressing gender disparities in education in contexts of crisis, postcrisis and state fragility. In M. Tembon & L. Fort (Eds.), *Girls' education in the 21st century: Gender equality, empowerment, and economic growth* (pp. 153–180). Washington, DC: The World Bank. Used with permission.

Chapter 7 was originally published as Winthrop, R., & Kirk, J. (2008). Learning for a bright future: Schooling, armed conflict, and children's well-being. *Comparative Education Review*, 52(4), 639–661. Used with permission.

Chapter 12 draws extensively from Sigsgaard, M. (Ed.). (2011). *On the road to resilience: Capacity development with the Ministry of Education in Afghanistan*. Paris: IIEP.

Published by Teachers College Press, 1234 Amsterdam Avenue, New York, NY 10027

Library of Congress Cataloging-in-Publication Data

Educating children in conflict zones : research, policy, and practice for systemic change: a tribute to Jackie Kirk / Karen Mundy, Sarah Dryden-Peterson, editors.
    p. cm. — (International perspectives on education reform)
Includes bibliographical references and index.
ISBN 978-0-8077-5243-2 (pbk. : alk. paper)
    1. War and education—Cross-cultural studies. 2. Refugees—Education—Cross-cultural studies. 3. Postwar reconstruction—Cross-cultural studies. I. Kirk, Jackie, 1968–2008. II. Mundy, Karen E. (Karen Elizabeth), 1962– III. Dryden-Peterson, Sarah.
LC71.E282 2011
371.826'914—dc23   2011021265

ISBN 978-0-8077-5243-2 (paper)

Printed on acid-free paper
Manufactured in the United States of America

18 17 16 15 14 13 12 11   8 7 6 5 4 3 2 1

This volume is dedicated to **Jackie Kirk**, friend, colleague, inspiration to all of the contributors to this book, and lifelong advocate of the right to education for children and youth in conflict-affected settings.

JACKIE KIRK (1968–2008)

Contents

Acknowledgments xi

List of Abbreviations xiii

1. **Educating Children in Zones of Conflict:**
   An Overview and Introduction
   Karen Mundy and Sarah Dryden-Peterson *1*

PART I:
DEFINITIONS, CONCEPTS, AND KEY ISSUES **13**

2. **Education and Fragile States**
   Jackie Kirk *15*

3. **Can Education Interrupt Fragility?**
   Toward the Resilient Citizen and the Adaptable State
   Lynn Davies *33*

4. **Are We All Soldiers Now?**
   The Dangers of the Securitization of Education and Conflict
   Mario Novelli *49*

5. **Addressing Gender Disparities in Education**
   in Contexts of Crisis, Post-Crisis, and State Fragility
   Jackie Kirk *67*

PART II:
LISTENING TO THE VOICES OF CHILDREN AND TEACHERS **83**

6. **Refugee Children Aspiring Toward the Future:**
   Linking Education and Livelihoods
   Sarah Dryden-Peterson *85*

7. Learning for a Bright Future:
   Schooling, Armed Conflict, and Children's Well-Being
   Rebecca Winthrop and Jackie Kirk   101

8. Understanding the Diverse Forms of Learning Valued
   by Children in Conflict Contexts
   Rebecca Winthrop   123

9. The Multiple Relationships Between Education and Conflict:
   Reflections of Rwandan Teachers and Students
   Elisabeth King   137

PART III:
UNDERSTANDING INTERNATIONAL
PROGRAMS AND INTERVENTIONS   153

10. Alphabet Soup:
    Making Sense of the Emerging Global Architecture of Aid to
    Education in Fragile and Conflict-Affected Situations
    Peter Buckland   155

11. Aid and Education in Fragile States
    Victoria Turrent   169

12. On the Road to Resilience:
    Capacity Development for Educational Planning
    in Afghanistan
    Lyndsay Bird, Dorian Gay,
    Morten Sigsgaard, and Charlotte Wilson   183

13. "Helping Our Children Will Help in the Reconstruction of
    Our Country": Repatriated Refugee Teachers in Post-Conflict
    Sierra Leone and Liberia
    Susan Shepler   199

PART IV:
NEW DIRECTIONS IN
RESEARCH ON EDUCATION AND CONFLICT   219

14. Picturing Violence:
    Participatory Visual Methodologies in Working with Girls to
    Address School and Domestic Violence in Rwanda
    Claudia Mitchell   221

15. **From Child-Friendly Schools to Child-Friendly Research Methods: Lessons Learned on Child-Centered Research from UNICEF's Learning Plus Initiative**

Stephanie Bengtsson and Lesley Bartlett 235

16. **Innovative Methods in Education in Emergencies Research: A Randomized Trial Assessing Community-Based Schools in Afghanistan**

Dana Burde 255

References 273

About the Contributors 297

Index 301

Acknowledgments

The authors of this book wish to acknowledge the communities and children that worked with them to make their research possible.

Editorial assistance for this volume was provided by Caroline (Carly) Manion, without whom the volume would not have been possible. Francine Menashy provided a keen and thorough copyediting eye.

Funding for this book project came from the grants of Karen Mundy, through her Canada Research Chair and the Comparative, International and Development Education Centre (CIDEC) at the Ontario Institute for Studies in Education of the University of Toronto.

In addition, we would like to acknowledge the support received by Elisabeth King for this research from the Earth Institute at Columbia University, the School of Graduate Studies at the University of Toronto, the Social Sciences and Humanities Research Council of Canada, and the Canadian Consortium on Human Security; and the support received by Sarah Dryden-Peterson from the Mellon Foundation through the Migration and Urbanisation Node of the University of the Witwatersrand, the Fulbright Scholar Program, and the Social Sciences and Humanities Research Council of Canada.

List of Abbreviations

ANDS	Afghan National Development Strategy
AREU	Afghanistan Research and Evaluation Unit
AusAID	Australian Agency for International Development
BiH	Bosnia-Herzegovina
CAF	Conflict Analysis Framework
CAP	Consolidated Appeals Process
CBS	Community-Based School
CCA	Common Country Assessment
CDF	Comprehensive Development Framework
CERF	Central Emergency Relief Fund
CFS	Child-Friendly School
CG on ECCD	Consultative Group on Early Childhood Care and Development
CHAP	Common Humanitarian Action Plan
CIDA	Canadian International Development Agency
CPIA	Country Policy and Institutional Assessment
CRC	Convention on the Rights of the Child
CRS	Catholic Relief Services
CRS	Creditor Reporting System [see Chapter Eleven]
DAC	Development Assistance Committee
DfID	Department for International Development (UK)
DoPE	Department of Planning and Evaluation
DRC	Democratic Republic of Congo
ECCD	Early Childhood Care and Development
ECD	Early Childhood Development
EDB	Education Development Board
EDF	Education Development Forum
EFA	Education for All
EFA FTI	Education for All—Fast Track Initiative
EFA HLG	Education for All High-Level Group
EMIS	Education Management Information System
FTI	Fast Track Initiative

FTI PF	Fast Track Initiative Progressive Framework for Fragile States
FRESH	Focused Resources for Effective School Health
GBV	Gender-Based Violence
GDI	Gender-Related Development Index
GoC	Government of Canada
GTT	Gender Task Team (INEE)
GTZ	German Development Agency (Deutsche Gesellschaft fur Technische Zusammenarbeit)
HCI	Healing Classrooms Initiative
HRDB	Human Resource Development Board
HRE	Human Rights Education
IASC	Inter-Agency Standing Committee for Humanitarian Assistance
IAWG	Inter-Agency Working Group
IDP	Internally Displaced Person(s)
IIEP	International Institute for Educational Planning
INEE	Inter-Agency Network for Education in Emergencies
INGO	International Nongovernmental Organization
IPS	International Policy Statement
IRC	International Rescue Committee
MDGs	Millennium Development Goal(s)
MoE	Ministry of Education
MoHE	Ministry of Higher Education
NATO	North Atlantic Treaty Organization
NER	Net Enrollment Ratio
NESP	National Education Sector Plan
NGO	Nongovernmental Organization
NWFP	North-West Frontier Province
OCHA	Office for the Coordination of Humanitarian Affairs
OCHA FTS	Office for the Coordination of Humanitarian Affairs Financial Tracking System
ODA	Official Development Assistance
OECD	Organisation for Economic Co-Operation and Development
OECD-DAC	Organisation for Economic Co-Operation and Development—Development Assistance Committee
PACE-A	Partnership for Advancing Community Education in Afghanistan
PETS	Public Expenditure Tracking Surveys
PRA	Participatory Rural Appraisal
PRSPs	Poverty Reduction Strategy Paper(s)
PTA	Parent Teacher Association
PVRM	Participatory Visual Research Methodologies

RPF	Rwandan Patriotic Front
SIP	Sector Investment Program
SMC	School Management Committee
SWAp	Sector-Wide Approach
SWG	Sub-Working Group (IASC)
TVET	Technical and Vocational Education and Training
UN	United Nations
UNAIDS	Joint United Nations Programme on HIV/AIDS
UNDAF	United Nations Development Assistance Framework
UNDG	United Nations Development Group
UNDG EXCO	United Nations Development Group Executive Committee
UNDP	United Nations Development Programme
UNESCO	United Nations Education, Scientific, and Cultural Organisation
UNGEI	United Nations Girls' Education Initiative
UNHCR	United Nations High Commissioner for Refugees
UNICEF	United Nations Children's Fund
UNSCR	United Nations Security Council Resolution on Women, Peace, and Security
USAID	U.S. Agency for International Development

CHAPTER 1

Educating Children in Zones of Conflict

An Overview and Introduction

KAREN MUNDY

SARAH DRYDEN-PETERSON

Over the past decade, researcher and practitioner interest in the challenges of educating children affected by conflict has grown enormously. Shaped by high-profile conflicts in countries such as Iraq and Afghanistan, and by the large number of internal conflicts affecting the world's poorest countries, this interest has led to a wide and at times bewildering proliferation of interventions, as well as academic and professional publications and reports.

This book was developed as a tribute to Jackie Kirk (1968–2008), a scholar and activist whose publications were among the first to try to bring attention and organization to the study of education in conflict zones. Jackie's commitments were expansive: She was devoted to using human rights as a frame for understanding the educational needs of children affected by conflict; to developing strong codes of conduct and coordinating frameworks to guide the activities of international organizations active in conflict zones; and to infusing the voices of those on the front line of conflict—children, teachers, and parents—into all efforts to support children's learning in situations of conflict and fragility.

Jackie would have understood well the need for a solid introduction to the study of education in conflict-affected situations. To honor her, this volume brings together 16 chapters by some of the world's leading scholars and practitioners in this field. Each chapter provides an accessible and current discussion of an important issue or set of issues related to the scope, challenges, and key opportunities for addressing the educational needs of children in conflict zones. The volume is organized into four main sections: definitional and conceptual issues; the voices of children and teachers; international programs and interventions; and new directions in research.

In what follows, we provide an introduction to the study of education in conflict zones, to help readers situate the individual chapters in broader debates and challenges. We begin by describing the scope of the problem and the tricky definitional question: Which countries should we consider conflict-affected? Next we discuss some of the key conceptual and practical debates in the field; the needs of children and teachers in different phases of conflict; and the roles played by international actors. Finally we look at the need for more and better research, situating the chapters of this volume at the cutting edge of a call for new methods and approaches to understanding the needs of children affected by conflict.

THE SCOPE OF THE PROBLEM:
OUT-OF-SCHOOL CHILDREN IN ZONES OF CONFLICT

In recent years, remarkable progress has been made in meeting the international Education for All (EFA) goals and the Millennium Development Goal (MDG) for universal primary education. Globally, the number of children decreased from 115 million to fewer than 70 million between 2000 and 2010 (UNESCO, 2011, p. 40). However, in conflict-affected countries, progress has been less robust. As compared with children in other low-income countries, children affected by conflict are less likely to survive to school age; more rarely attend school and complete a full basic education; and are much less likely to gain access to secondary education. Children in conflict zones receive a poorer quality education and face greater marginalization in education due to poverty, gender, and ethnicity than do children in countries not affected by conflict.

To understand the scope of the problem, we must begin with a broad description of conflict zones themselves. In the literature on education and conflict, conflict typically is defined as any situation in which armed violence over government or territory emerges and disrupts the lives and livelihoods of citizens. The nature of such armed conflicts has changed since the end of the Cold War: Conflicts increasingly play out between competing groups within national boundaries, rather than as wars among states. Since 2000, there also has been a rise in external military intervention in internal conflicts—as in Afghanistan, Iraq, and Somalia. Contemporary conflicts are both more deadly to civilians and more destructive of civilian infrastructure (including schools) than traditional interstate warfare. They are particularly deadly for children. For example, UNICEF estimates that between 1998 and 2008, over 2 million children were killed in conflicts. Another 6 million were disabled, while 300,000 were recruited as child-soldiers. An estimated

20 million children had to flee their homes as refugees or internally displaced persons (UNICEF, 2010a).

The roots of conflict develop over many years, and the aftereffects of conflict can create an overhang of instability. For this reason, the literature on education and conflict tends to define as zones of conflict not only situations where there is active armed violence, but also those that have been affected by armed conflict in the past. For example, the UNESCO *Global Monitoring Report* includes in its list of conflict-affected states countries that have been affected by conflict over the past 10 years (see Box 1.1). The UNESCO definition of conflict-affected states is not, however, the only one in use. Save the Children includes 28 countries in its analysis of education in conflict zones, adding two countries that do not appear in the UNESCO list.[1] For example, Save the Children (2010) includes Haiti, which

---

Box 1.1. 35 Conflict-Affected Countries in 2009

Low Income: Afghanistan, Burundi, Central African Republic, Chad, Democratic Republic of Congo, Eritrea, Ethiopia, Guinea, Liberia, Myanmar, Nepal, Rwanda, Sierra Leone, Somalia, Uganda, Yemen

Lower Middle Income: Angola, Côte d'Ivoire, Georgia, India, Indonesia, Iraq, Nigeria, Pakistan, Palestinian Occupied Territories, Philippines, Sri Lanka, Sudan, Thailand, Timor-Leste

Upper Middle Income: Algeria, Colombia, Russian Federation, Serbia, Turkey.

Source: UNESCO, 2011

---

has had periods of weakly controlled violence against civilians by government-sanctioned militias. Other reports sometimes also describe as "conflict-affected" countries where the line between widespread criminal violence and armed conflict aimed at the state is blurred.

Efforts to describe conflict zones and their impacts on education frequently draw on the notion of "fragile states" as well (see contributions by Turrent, Kirk, and Davies, this volume). The concept of fragility has the advantage of including states where governance and institutional factors create a predisposition for future conflict. However, there is limited consensus on the key factors that predispose countries to armed conflict (and that therefore define fragility) (Brown, 2010). The World Bank, which in 2011 published a list of what it describes as 33 "fragile situations," includes low-income countries with ratings below 3.2 on its internal Country Policy and Institutional Assessment (CPIA), along with those that have had UN peace-keeping or peace-building missions in place during the past 3 years

(World Bank, 2011). The OECD defines fragility as simply those countries that are "failing to provide basic services to poor people because they are unwilling or unable to do so" (OECD, 2007a). Neither the OECD nor the World Bank claims that its definition of fragility is comprehensive or superior to others. Both organizations (along with the authors in this volume) recognize the inevitable need to change the list of conflict-affected/fragile countries when new conflicts erupt and older conflicts die down.

In this volume, we use the term *conflict-affected* to mean countries that are impacted by violent and armed conflict, resulting in weak governance and inequality in resource allocation that negatively affect the lives and livelihoods of children. Our use of the term *education in conflict zones*—as opposed to the more common *education in emergencies*—is intended to exclude natural disasters from our analysis and reflects the fact that contemporary conflicts are often protracted. Like other contributors to this volume, we recognize the conceptual advantages of using the term *fragility* in order to keep the root issues that lead to conflict more clearly in focus (Winthrop, 2010). However, as will be discussed in a subsequent section, readers also need to be aware that current understandings of the causes and dimensions of conflict are hotly debated. All lists of conflict-affected states— including those generated by UNESCO and Save the Children, and the OECD and World Bank fragility lists—need to be used with care by education researchers and practitioners. They are limited but important tools in any effort to monitor the scope of current and potential conflicts and their effects on children's education.

Definitional debates about conflict and fragility, along with the inherent challenges of collecting administrative and census data in situations of conflict, have made it very difficult to come up with exact numbers of children out-of-school in conflict zones. Nonetheless, using its list of conflict-affected states (and including only the regions of large countries affected by conflict), UNESCO estimates that there are currently 28 million children of primary school age out-of-school in low- and lower middle income conflict-affected states. This is 42% of the world's total out-of-school children (UNESCO, 2011, p. 132). Even in conflict-affected countries where considerable progress has been made in expanding access, primary school completion rates are very low. In Afghanistan, for example, of those children initially enrolled, 54% drop out during the first 4 years of school (Mansory, 2007, p. 28). The legacy of conflict is reflected in literacy levels: UNESCO calculations indicate that only 79% of youth and 69% of adults are literate in conflict-affected countries, as compared with 93% and 85% in other countries (UNESCO, 2011, p. 132). Furthermore, conflict contributes to disruptions in teacher training systems, destruction of physical infrastructure, and a culture of violence that impacts classroom pedagogy, resulting in poor-quality teaching and learning (Lewin, 2009; Save the Children, 2008; UNESCO, 2011).

Both UNESCO and Save the Children report that the majority of out-of-school children in conflict-affected situations are concentrated in a few countries.

In Nigeria, for example, Save the Children estimates that there are 8.2 million primary school-aged children who do not have access to school; in Pakistan, 6.8 million; in Democratic Republic of Congo, 5.2 million; in Ethiopia, 3.7 million; in Sudan, 2.8 million (Save the Children, 2010, p. 3). In addition, a substantial number of children in smaller, low-income, conflict-affected states are also out-of-school. A growing proportion of the world's children affected by conflict are displaced internally or have fled to neighboring countries with weak educational systems and limited capacity to provide education; many do not live in traditional refugee camp settings. Children affected by conflict today are thus particularly difficult to reach.

Recent research demonstrates that conflict disproportionately affects the school opportunities of the poorest and most marginalized groups, often because these children must contribute directly to household livelihoods or because their parents lack the funds to pay for schooling (Save the Children, 2010; UNESCO, 2011). Conflict also contributes to severely constrained opportunities for the education of girls, both because of family poverty and concerns for their security. As an example, in the conflict-affected region of North Kivu in Democratic Republic of Congo, adolescents and young adults are two times as likely to have received under 2 years of schooling as compared with populations in other parts of the country. Poor women are three times as likely to have had this little education (UNESCO, 2011, p. 134).

International human rights legislation and international protocols for child protection stipulate that each out-of-school child must be a priority for the international community. There is an urgent need for greater attention to the state of education in conflict settings in order to overcome the obstacles that conflict presents to meeting EFA targets of access to a quality education for all children.

UNDERSTANDING THE LINKAGES BETWEEN CONFLICT AND EDUCATION

Understanding the variety of social, cultural, economic, and political grievances and contests, as well as the economic and institutional factors that increase the likelihood of outright conflict, is one of the major challenges facing both researchers and practitioners involved in educational development today. In recent years, research has focused on "opportunity theories" of conflict, which emphasize the "pull" created by a weak state, the existence of "lootable" natural resources, and the availability of unemployed youth for armed combat (Brown, 2010; Collier & Hoeffler, 2004; Fearon & Laitin, 2003). A second school of thought emphasizes intergroup grievances as a motivating cause for violent conflict, suggesting that inequalities in the political, cultural, and socioeconomic spheres are fundamental risks, particularly when governments are believed to be treating one or another group inequitably (Stewart, 2008; see also Novelli, Chapter 4, this volume, for an overview of these debates).

In either explanation, education can be seen to play a central role. In the opportunities-based analysis, the provision of adequate education that is linked to employment is particularly important, since it lowers the attractiveness of joining in armed conflict. Grievance and inequality theories of conflict are more expansive about the role played by education. Structurally, such theories agree with the opportunities-based assessment that there is a link between education, employment opportunities, and conflict, but they emphasize in particular the fact that education can help to lower intergroup inequality in the labor market. However, if educational opportunities are unequally distributed (or if having an education is rewarded unequally for different ethnic or religious groups), this can become a major source of grievance (Brown, 2010). Furthermore, the content of schooling itself can feed socioeconomic grievances, exacerbating ethnic, religious, and language differences, and undermining intergroup trust (as seen, for example, in King's case study of Rwanda, this volume).

In this volume, Davies (Chapter 3) illustrates how what goes on in schools can quickly become a vector for grievances about political and social exclusion. Yet when carefully and equitably provided, schooling also can contribute to peace and stability, by assisting in the creation of shared identities and values (see Kirk, Chapter 2, this volume). Thus schooling has been described as having "two faces." One face increases the risk of conflict; the other mitigates against it (Bush & Saltarelli, 2000). In this volume, contributions by Davies (Chapter 3) and King (Chapter 9) provide nuanced accounts and examples of the often intersecting ways in which education both exacerbates and assuages conflict.

A PRAGMATIC TYPOLOGY OF EDUCATIONAL NEEDS IN DIFFERENT CONFLICT SITUATIONS

Beyond the conceptual debates about education's relationship to the push and pull factors that are at the root of violent conflict, this book addresses a much more pragmatic set of issues. How are educational opportunities affected by conflict and how can they be improved? In this section of our introduction, we offer a practical typology of different phases of conflict and their educational demands, as a starting point for answering such questions.

Traditionally, conflict-affected countries have been understood as going through several stages or phases of conflict: build up to conflict (latent stage); escalation of conflict; acute armed conflict; de-escalation and negotiation (often accompanied by a continued state of emergency for the population); and finally a phase of negotiated settlement, peace-building, and reconstruction. Of course, the history of each violent conflict is different, and these phases are idealized. Many conflicts are mediated before the acute crisis stage is reached; others are protracted, going through many cycles of escalation and de-escalation. These "stages" are only a heuristic for understanding some of the specific challenges and opportunities for education in conflict zones, useful for situating the chapters in this book.

In the *latent or build-up phases of conflict*, education can play an important role, either exacerbating grievances and creating (by omission) low opportunity costs for armed conflict, or assisting in the distribution of more equitable life chances and a shared sense of collective identity and values. The use of conflict analysis in planning and programming to monitor the roles played by education in contexts of fragility or latent conflict can be particularly useful, especially when paired with pedagogical training and curriculum development that support peace and a culture of "resilience" (see Davies and Bird et al., this volume). Efforts to ensure that children's fundamental human rights are protected in national legislation, including their right to equitable, high-quality basic education, also can be seen as making an important contribution to conflict prevention during this latent stage. At the international level, emergency watch systems that monitor changing levels of fragility and violence, as well efforts to monitor changes in the realization of children's rights, are essential.

Protection traditionally has been the main concern during periods of *conflict escalation and acute conflict*. Increasingly, education has come to be seen as providing an important dimension of this protection, especially for children, even though international humanitarian funding for education still appears to take a backseat to other "life-saving" measures (Save the Children, 2010; UNESCO, 2011, p. 255). New patterns of conflict have intensified the challenges of providing adequate and secure education to children affected by active conflicts—the fact that contemporary conflicts are more often protracted, and produce larger numbers of civilian casualties (including among educators and students) and long-term mass displacement of populations, makes children much more difficult to reach and protect. At the same time, awareness of the protracted effects of conflict on children has increased the emphasis on using education to ensure rights, human dignity, and long-term opportunities in crisis contexts (UNHCR, 2009a; Winthrop, 2010).

Many chapters in this volume argue that the provision of education during acute phases of conflict is essential because it provides more than protection: It feeds hope and future aspirations, and thus provides an essential bridge to future livelihoods and to the post-conflict stability of the wider society. During phases of direct conflict and displacement, the role of caring teachers and of a curriculum that links up to future opportunities for study or employment, is particularly important. As highlighted in the chapter by Dryden-Peterson, educational challenges can look quite different for children living in more traditional refugee camps (where educational entitlements are customary), as compared with the many who move into urban settings or settle locally in host communities. Furthermore, as

Kirk argues, attention also needs to be paid to gender-specific needs—particularly to ensure girls' safety and well-being. The importance of listening to children and to educators, when responding to educational needs in situations of protracted crisis, is a common theme for many of the authors in this book.

The *reconstruction phase* in conflict-affected countries presents a different set of educational challenges and opportunities. The early provision of education at the end of a conflict provides a tangible benefit for parents and communities and can enhance legitimacy and support for a new government. The phase of post-conflict reconstruction also is regarded as offering opportunities for innovation that are more difficult to achieve inside established educational systems, so long as adequate external finance and internal leadership are in place (Nicolai, 2009). At the same time, post-conflict governments face enormous challenges in terms of losses to physical infrastructure, shortages of teachers and educational administrators, the need for new, peace-promoting curricula and materials, and the urgent needs of returnees with interrupted education (including children who have been recruited into combat) (Buckland, 2005). Key questions about the sequencing of changes to contentious aspects of the curriculum are particularly difficult to address—as illustrated in King's case study of Rwanda (Chapter 9).

UNESCO (2011) argues that early interventions, such as withdrawal of user fees, scaling up and coordination of community education initiatives, rehabilitation of classrooms, and the provision of bridging or accelerated learning programs, can each provide a "peace dividend" in post-conflict situations. Utilizing the skills of returning teachers and students is especially important (see Shepler, Chapter 13; Buckland, 2005). Over the longer term (as the IIEP case study of its work in Afghanistan, presented in Chapter 12, suggests), strengthened educational planning capacity is needed, particularly in the areas of information and financial management, teacher recruitment and training, and building systems of participation and monitoring that ensure future equity and inclusivity within the educational system.

INTERNATIONAL PROGRAMS AND INTERVENTIONS
TO SUPPORT EDUCATION IN ZONES OF CONFLICT

The provision of education to children in zones of conflict relies heavily on the funds and interventions provided by international actors. For that reason, this book includes a group of chapters that focus on the international aid architecture (Buckland, Chapter 10); key international actors and their programs of support (Chapters 12, 13,15, and 16); and the overall trends in aid for education in conflict zones (Turrent, Chapter 11).

The focus on providing education for children affected by conflict has a long history—it has been shaped by the experience of major efforts to reconstruct school systems at the end of World War II, by the development of the International Convention on the Rights of the Child (with its focus on the right to education), and by the international Education for All agenda and the Millennium Development Goals, each of which set time-bound targets for the achievement of a universal right to education. As Buckland (Chapter 10) suggests, today many major international organizations are active in the provision of programs to support education in conflict zones, and their work increasingly is integrated around common protocols and standards for coordination. Key in the development of these common standards has been the Inter-Agency Network for Education in Emergencies (INEE), a network of intergovernmental and nongovernmental organizations and individuals formed in 2000. Its Minimum Standards for Education are now widely used by education providers (for a description, see Kirk, Chapter 5). INEE has been instrumental in the formation of a United Nations Humanitarian Response "Education Cluster," which further promotes coordination in fundraising and implementation among global actors. National- and regional-level Education Clusters are becoming increasingly common, existing in 34 countries in 2009 (UNICEF, 2010a).

Yet despite a growing system of conventions, standards, and coordinating mechanisms, each highlighting education as both a human right and an urgent need in situations of conflict, the international community has come relatively late to the issue of education and conflict. Aid flows to low-income, conflict-affected countries are weaker than to other low-income countries, and within the broader group of conflict-affected states, aid has tended to prioritize countries of special geopolitical interest to the Western world (see Turrent, Chapter 11). This has contributed to larger concerns that aid is being used for military purposes and is becoming increasingly militarized—an issue taken up in greater detail by Novelli in Chapter 4. Education also remains a neglected feature of humanitarian intervention: Less than 2% of all humanitarian aid is directed at education, and humanitarian appeals for education are consistently underfunded (UNESCO, 2011, p. 204). Adequate financing for the transition from humanitarian aid to reconstruction and development aid also is lacking, leading to reversals in the early gains to education brought about during the early recovery phase in countries like Liberia (Buckland, 2005; UNESCO, 2011, pp. 230–231). In contrast to the health sector, education has no "pooled fund" capable of addressing these gaps in financing for conflict zones; it relies on a variety of pooled appeals and on the weakly financed Fast Track Initiative, an organization that has had difficulty in providing fast and adequate support to conflict-affected states.

In addition to these major gaps in international support to education in conflict zones, recent reports have suggested a number of other areas where international interventions are inadequate. Key among these are the need for international efforts to monitor violence against children, including in and around educational settings; support for preventive forms of education-based peace-building (which could be bolstered by the combined efforts of the United Nations Peace-Building Fund, UNESCO, and UNICEF); and the need for better coordination between the UNHCR and UNICEF to address the needs of internally displaced populations and refugees (UNESCO, 2011, pp. 241, 253–258).

A FOREWORD TO THE VOLUME

Research in the nascent field of education in conflict has been centered in two traditions. The first examines the relationships, both positive and negative, between education and conflict, including the role of education in fragility, peace-building, reconstruction, and reconciliation. The second focuses on the empirical realities of education in conflict settings, specifically as related to the provision of education, and the quality and distribution of available opportunities. The synthesis of these traditions was a cornerstone of Jackie Kirk's work and personal commitment to education in conflict. Jackie's unique approach married, on the one hand, an emphasis on systemic challenges and the need for large-scale, programmatic intervention; and, on the other, the need for carefully tailored responses that listen carefully to the voices of children and educators.

Building on Jackie's approach, this volume is organized into four sections. The first part, "Definitions, Concepts, and Key Issues," addresses the interrelationships between education and conflict and outlines key issues that are central to this field of study. It begins with Jackie Kirk's seminal work, Education and Fragile States, in which she argues that education must be seen as much more than a basic social service and, indeed, as more than a mechanism for protection. The chapter explores in detail the ways in which education is "cause, effect, problem, and possible solution" to state fragility. Following Jackie's chapter, Chapter 3 by Lynn Davies draws on empirical data from Liberia, Afghanistan, Bosnia-Herzegovina, Cambodia, and Sri Lanka, to provide a more detailed framework for understanding the relationships between education and fragility, focusing in particular on education's role in building resilience among individual citizens and adaptability in the state. Chapter 4 shifts our gaze to the darker underbelly of support for education in conflict zones. Using historical and contemporary examples to examine how the policies and practices of Western donors influence the content of education in fragile states, Mario Novelli argues that there has been a dangerous merging of security interests with development priorities over the past decade, both in practice and in academic discourse. This is a highly poignant chapter as it reflects upon forms of militarization that may have contributed to Jackie's tragic death at the hands of Taliban militants in Afghanistan. This volume's first section closes with Jackie Kirk's overview of the importance of addressing gender disparities in education in situations of conflict, an issue for which she was a strong advocate. In addition to reviewing the many ways that gender vulnerabilities can be exacerbated or mitigated through education in conflict settings, this chapter provides an overview of the INEE minimum standards and their role in the promotion of gender equality.

The second part of this book is entitled "Listening to the Voices of Children and Teachers." Each chapter is informed by the experiences and perspectives of children and teachers in settings of conflict. In Chapter 6, Sarah Dryden-Peterson explores the multiple connections refugee children in Uganda make between their educational experiences and present and future livelihoods, relating their narratives to physical and economic security, integration in the local society, and aspirations for the future. In Learning for a Bright Future (Chapter 7), Rebecca Winthrop and Jackie Kirk examine the experiences of refugee children in Ethiopia, Afghanistan, and Sierra Leone and identify the centrality of schooling in their personal conceptualizations of well-being. Their study illustrates the importance of the combination of academic and social learning in refugee education, both for "coping" in the present and "hoping" for the future. In Chapter 8, Rebecca Winthrop builds upon this analysis, exploring in greater detail the technical, practical, and emancipatory forms of learning valued by refugee children. In Chapter 9, Elisabeth King provides an exploration of the interrelationships between education and conflict through different phases of the Rwandan civil war, using interview data from students and teachers as well as documentary evidence to provide a nuanced understanding of positive and negative "faces" of education in conflict settings.

The third part of this book, "Understanding International Educational Programs and Interventions," examines the role of international programs and interventions in addressing the challenge of educating children in conflict zones. In Chapter 10, Peter Buckland traces the development of institutional coordination in the field of education in conflict-affected areas, emphasizing its importance for bridging gaps between humanitarian assistance and the EFA agenda. Victoria Turrent (Chapter 11) compares the flows of aid to education in fragile states and other low-income countries, pointing out the need for increased and more predictable aid in conflict zones. Two national-level case studies conclude this section. In Chapter 12, Lyndsay Bird and a team from the International Institute for Educational Planning (IIEP) examine a capacity development program between the Ministry of Education in Afghanistan and the IIEP, which led to the development of a national education sector plan and enhanced administrative systems. They argue for the centrality of trust, participation, and national ownership in capacity development in post-conflict reconstruction. Susan Shepler (Chapter 13) examines the collateral effects of teachers returning home from Guinea after involvement in refugee education programs, showing how these teachers serve as agents of change in reconstruction processes, and yet are constrained by certification and ministry policies from contributing more fully to post-conflict reconstruction of an educational system.

The fourth, and final, part of this volume, "New Directions in Research on Education and Conflict," presents innovations in both qualitative and quantitative research on education in conflict-affected states. While other recent reports have explored gaps in the research literature on education in conflict (see INEE, 2010), this part of our volume is more concerned with the potential for alternative research methodologies. Employing participatory visual research methodologies, Claudia Mitchell (Chapter 14) documents the value and limits of giving voice to children, using research findings from Rwanda to explore what participation in research might mean. In Chapter 15, Stephanie Bengtsson and Lesley Bartlett provide an overview of efforts to use child-friendly, participatory research methodologies to study the impact of UNICEF's Child-Friendly Schools initiative. In the concluding chapter, Dana Burde (Chapter 16) argues for a very different and relatively novel methodology for the study of education in conflict: the use of randomized impact evaluations. Drawing on her study of community-based schooling in Afghanistan, Burde explores the feasibility, ethics, and ultimate importance of providing quantitative measures of outcomes for educational interventions in conflict zones.

NOTE

1. Save the Children has defined its list of "fragile and conflict-affected countries" as countries that experienced at least one armed conflict in the period between 1995 and 2004, or are classified as critical in the 2005 fragile states list by Project Ploughshares; or countries that were classified as "core" or "severe" in the World Bank's low-income countries under stress list. Using this definition, Cambodia and Haiti also are considered fragile/conflict-affected. UNESCO's definition is somewhat different: Developed by the Peace Research Institute Oslo (PRIO), the UNESCO criteria define conflict-affected states as those in which over the past 10 years there has been armed conflict involving "contested incompatibility" over government and/or territory where the use of armed force is involved, and where one of the parties to the conflict is the state. The selection criteria also include a threshold for battle-related deaths (UNESCO, 2011, p. 138).

Part I

DEFINITIONS, CONCEPTS, AND KEY ISSUES

CHAPTER 2

Education and Fragile States

JACKIE KIRK

In recent years the field of education in emergencies has developed as a specifically defined subfield, existing at the intersection of policy, programming, research, scholarship, and professional training in the areas of education in development, humanitarian aid, child rights, and child protection. Within this field there is a conceptual understanding of the linkages between education and conflict, supported by a number of significant texts (e.g., Bush & Saltarelli, 2000; Seitz, 2004; Smith & Vaux, 2003).

Education also is mentioned in most fragile states-related policy papers. Education usually is considered a critical social service for which delivery in fragile states is a particular challenge. However, as this chapter argues, education should have prominence in any discussion of fragile states as more than a basic service. As a number of recent studies indicate, education is in many states intricately connected with—if not a root cause of—conflict and instability. Education therefore should be part of the analysis of fragility, and in identification of priority stabilizing interventions. Conflict analysis in general, and the specific tools that are now being developed for analysis of and engagement with fragile states, all need to address education. Yet they need to go beyond a narrow concern with service delivery to look at systemic and structural elements of education provision that may contribute to or perpetuate state fragility—or mitigate against it.

Achieving gender equality is another significant international commitment articulated in the Millennium Development Goals. Gender equality in education is seen as both an aim in itself and a means toward (and indicator of) greater gender equality in general. As statistics highlight (e.g., UNESCO, 2004), conflict and emergencies have particular implications for girls and seriously compromise the possibilities for educational systems to meet the needs of girls and women. Fragile states are rarely in a position to provide gender-responsive education; curricula, untrained teachers, minimal resources, and lack of support and supervision for

This chapter is an abridged version of Kirk, J. (2007). Education and fragile states. *Globalisation, Societies and Education, 5*(2), 181–200. Used with permission.

teachers and head teachers are all contributing factors to gender inequalities in schooling. The complex challenges of promoting gender equality in and through education have not been adequately addressed in the context of fragile states policy. In fact, as Baranyi and Powell (2005b) highlight, none of the recent fragile states policies systematically incorporates gender considerations, even though the donor agencies have developed impressive policy and programming tools to promote gender equality in other domains.

Drawing on recent policy papers on fragile states, this chapter explores in more depth the connections between education and fragile states and makes recommendations for future policy, programming, and research. Government and donor agency development planners and policymakers need to include education in a gender-aware analysis of fragile states and to prioritize conflict-sensitive service delivery that is critically oriented toward peace-building and gender equality. Key recommendations for organizations and agencies working in education and emergencies are: firstly the need for critical engagement with the broad concept of fragility and its relationship with equitable access to education. Secondly, the efforts of different agencies, organizations, networks, and groups should be coordinated to ensure that concrete examples and evidence are generated and widely disseminated of how conflict and fragility-sensitive analysis, policy, and programming can be informed by attention to education.

After a first section that defines and briefly describes fragile states, the chapter continues with a discussion of the relationships among education, fragility, and stability. It highlights two dimensions of education as a force for fragility: education as omission and education as commission. It also discusses education's critical role as a force for peace-building and stability in which gender equality is an integrated factor. The chapter ends with some recommendations for moving ahead.

FRAGILE STATES: AN URGENT CONCERN IN A GLOBALIZED WORLD

Defining Fragile States

There is neither one definition of a fragile state nor one definitive list of fragile states. It is a contested term—and especially so by those whose own country has been labeled as fragile by the international community. At the same time, there is some consensus around the use of the World Bank Country Policy and Institutional Assessment (CPIA) scores to identify poorly performing, low-income countries. A working definition of a fragile state, used by the UK's Department for International Development (DfID), is a state where the government cannot or will not deliver core functions to the majority of its people, including the poor.

The most important functions of a state for poverty reduction are territorial control, safety and security, the capacity to manage public resources, the delivery of basic services, and the ability to protect and support the ways in which the poorest people sustain themselves (DfID, 2005c, p. 7). With this definition, DfID lists 46 countries considered as fragile states, in which 870 million people, or 14% of the world's population, live.

Within a broad definition of fragile states, which generally refers to failing, failed, and recovering states, USAID has made a further distinction between vulnerable states and crisis states. Vulnerable refers to states that are "unable or unwilling to adequately assure the provision of security and basic services to significant portions of their population and where the legitimacy of the Government is in question. This includes states that are failing or recovering from crisis." Crisis states are those where

> the central Government does not exert effective control over its own territory or is unable or unwilling to assure the provision of vital services to significant parts of its territory, where legitimacy of the Government is weak or nonexistent and where violent conflict is a reality or a great risk. (USAID, 2005b, p. 1)

The Canadian International Policy Statement (IPS) refers to "failed and fragile states" but does not give any specific definition of either, rather alluding to countries in or emerging from crisis—and elsewhere also to those that are at risk of crisis. However, the statement makes very clear the link between governance and fragile states and contrasts them with "good performers"—that is, states that have demonstrated that they can use aid effectively. Special funds were to be assigned to states that were "under stress from becoming failed states" and where the "need is great but the capacity to use aid effectively is weak" (GoC, 2005).

Fragile States in a Globalized World

From a globalization perspective, there are a number of key issues in relation to fragile states and to development agencies' interest in them. These include the stated concern that fragile states are a major obstacle to the achievement of the global development targets—the Millennium Development Goals. These are international commitments that are driving policy and programming interventions. Further linking fragile states discourses to the concept of globalization is the recognition within the policy statements that individual countries—and their development and/or defense programs—cannot alone address the complex realities of fragile states. Not only do the foreign policy and interventions overseas by defense, development, and diplomatic agencies of individual countries have to be more coherent and better coordinated, but there is also a need for better international collaboration. Multilateral agencies such as the UN, NATO, and the European Union have critical roles to play. As DfID (2005c, p. 17) suggests, the presence of too many donors can overload fragile states and an international mechanism is needed to decide who does what and where. This also should avoid the perpetuation of certain "donor orphan" countries that habitually are left aside by all donors.

However, it is the USAID (2005b) strategy that makes the strongest argument for addressing fragile states as a national security strategy.

> There is perhaps no more urgent matter facing USAID than fragile states, yet no set of problems is more difficult and intractable. Twenty-first century realities demonstrate that ignoring these states can pose great risks and increase the likelihood of terrorism taking root. At least a third of the world's population now lives in areas that are unstable or fragile. This poses not only a national security challenge but a development and humanitarian challenge. (p. 1)

The geopolitical motivations behind fragile states discourses cannot be ignored. The USAID policy made very explicit links between fragile states and terrorism and refers to a new level of urgency required to address instability. It quotes the conclusion of USAID's foreign aid in the national interest paper: "When development and governance fail in a country, the consequences engulf entire regions and leap around the world" (cited in USAID, 2005b, p. 1). Such statements perpetuate problematic notions of state fragility being an internal issue, constructed within a nation state paradigm without acknowledgment of external, international factors, including imperialism, that contribute to the success or failure of development and governance in different countries. These external, global forces and their interactions with national and local forces have to be brought into meaningful analysis of education's relationship with state fragility.

EDUCATION IN FRAGILE STATES POLICIES

Education is a development priority for the governments of Britain, the United States, Canada, and Australia, and, not surprisingly, education is mentioned in each of their fragile states policy papers. Education is referred to as a critical service that governments should provide for their populations, but in fragile states this is often not the case. Nine of the 46 DfID-listed fragile states have net primary enrollment figures of below 50% (and there are no figures provided for an additional 13 countries in which it can be presumed that enrollment is also very low). As already highlighted, fragile states policies are linked to the international imperative to achieve the Millennium Development Goals, one of which is to achieve universal primary school completion. In its assessment of MDG progress in fragile states compared with other low- and middle-income states, DfID points to an average of 70% primary school enrollment compared with 86% (MDG 2) and also to a lower enrollment ratio of girls to boys (0.84 compared with 0.92) (MDG 3). Within the DfID policy document, other references to education usually are made alongside health as one the critical services that in a fragile state may need to be provided through nongovernmental channels (DfID, 2005c).

The USAID (2005b) policy also considers education and health provision as areas of opportunity for strategic programming in fragile states, especially where "effectiveness deficits" are greatest (p. 6). Education is included as an area for social programming within a programmatic framework for vulnerable states and states in crisis with four specific domains: political, economic, social, and security. Assisting the government to ensure the provision of public health and basic education is suggested as an option for intervention (p. 7).

The DfID fragile states policy makes one passing reference to another dimension of the relationship between education and state fragility—that is, the impact of instability and insecurity on access to education for girls, who may be kept away from school if there is a fear of rape (p. 20). This reference contrasts with a recent policy paper on girls' education that articulates a more complex relationship and does highlight the fact that "conflict hurts girls most," stating:

> Girls are particularly vulnerable to abuse and unequal access to schooling in fragile states. States can be fragile for a range of reasons, including conflict, lack of resources and people, high levels of corruption, and political instability. What sets these countries apart is their failure to deliver on the core functions of government, including keeping people safe, managing the economy, and delivering basic services. Violence and disease, as well as illiteracy and economic weakness, are most intensively concentrated in these areas. Of the 104 million children not in primary school globally, an estimated 37 million of them live in fragile states. Many of these children are girls. (DfID, 2005b, p. 11)

The Canadian IPS makes the most explicit reference to education in emergencies and links education and progress toward stability.[1] This section of the statement does not refer explicitly to fragile states, but rather to emergency and, especially, conflict contexts. Education is identified as one of five areas for greater Canadian development aid attention, and "education for girls and boys in conflict, post-conflict and/or emergency situations" is one of the four areas of education focus. The statement asserts:

> In situations of crisis and conflict, it is now better understood that once immediate concerns are addressed—safety, security, nutrition—one of the best ways to introduce stability and protection in emergency settings, including addressing the problems of trauma for children, their parents and the entire community, is to get schools functioning and get pupils into them. Canadian assistance in post-conflict or post-disaster situations will take this into account. (GoC, 2005)

The IPS addresses gender equality as a separate but cross-cutting focus for all its development interventions—and most specifically within education; "removing the barriers that prevent closing the gender gap in education" is identified as another one of the four areas of education focus. Subsequent education-specific policy documents will need to ensure that gender equality priorities also are integrated into each of the three other areas of education focus, including education in emergencies.

EDUCATION AND STATE FRAGILITY

As highlighted in the attention given to donor support for the delivery of education in fragile states, the human and financial resources that once may have been dedicated to education often disappear in times of crisis. As Graca Machel (1996) points out, during conflict periods in Somalia and in Cambodia, public spending on education was virtually zero. Vickers and Sivard both point out that in times of conflict, governments can spend ten times more on each member of the armed forces than they spend on each child in education (cited in Karam, 2001). The incredible resilience of schooling to continue or to re-establish itself in the most difficult circumstances, usually by communities themselves for whom schooling is of strategic and symbolic importance, is recognized (World Bank, 2005). However, in fragile states education services often are disrupted or are of such low quality that they fail to remain relevant. This is especially true when survival and security concerns become priorities for communities and families. In Somalia, for example, formal schooling opportunities are available to very few children. At a 19.9% gross enrollment ratio (GER), Somalia has one of the lowest primary school enrollment rates in the world. Most existing schools are concentrated in and around urban areas and are supported mainly by parents and communities, with some external support (UNICEF Somalia, 2005).

The DfID policy acknowledges the impact of state fragility on school enrollment; however, the relationships between education and fragility are far more complex. As is explored in the following section, education is impacted by fragility, but education—or a lack of education—also can act as a contributing factor to fragility. In relation to fragility, education is at the same time cause, effect, problem, and possible solution.

Education as Omission: A Force for Fragility

Achieving Education for All, a longstanding international commitment, is a collective goal of UN agencies, national governments, international and national NGOs, as well as individual communities. The role of education in promoting individual, family, and community health, prosperity, and general empowerment is widely acknowledged. It also can have national repercussions, contributing to high levels of social cohesion, interpersonal and intergroup collaboration, and interdependence. Functioning educational systems accessible to all children are an important indicator of "normalcy" and a force for ongoing stability at all levels. In fact, it is argued that where educational opportunities are denied to the population—or to certain sections of the population—the risks of instability are high. Adolescents with no possibilities of attending secondary school or tertiary or vocational education, and therefore limited job opportunities, are a latent force for instability; in fact, the World Bank's Conflict Analysis Framework (CAF) lists "high youth unemployment" among its nine conflict risk indicators (cited in World Bank, 2005). As the USAID (2005a) *Education Strategy* highlights:

> Post-conflict settings and fragile states present problems, such as the presence of large numbers of illiterate and unskilled boys and young men—including ex-combatants—whose lack of economic prospects make them easy to recruit into rebel armies pursuing "lootable resources." (p. 15)

If there is little structure and pattern to adolescents' lives and they see no chances to improve their lives in other ways, then the temptation to join armed gangs and fighting forces may be high. Furthermore, when education and other services for youth, such as leisure and recreation activities and representative forums, are not provided or facilitated by the state, as has been the case in Nigeria and Pakistan, then the vacuum is filled by radical groups who can then create allegiances with poor, marginalized young people (USAID, 2005c).

As has been the case with many adolescent boys from southern Sudan who knew there were no prospects for furthering their education and otherwise would risk recruitment into the fighting (UNICEF, 2000), youth also may seek to leave their homes and take their chances as refugees outside the country. A vacuum is created where there is no development of the country's human resources, and those available to fill positions of authority and leadership have had no opportunity to develop the necessary skills to do so. A vicious circle is thus perpetuated. Not only is the intellectual capacity of a generation of young people left undeveloped, but a denial of education also can mean that the psychosocial effects of conflict and instability are not healed. It can inhibit learning processes for how to manage and resolve conflict peacefully and how to co-exist peacefully with other religions and ethnic groups, thus perpetuating conflictual intergroup relations (OECD & DAC, 1997). In socially and economically fragile situations, without schooling as a counterbalance, young people may experience difficulties in coping with stresses such as poverty, urbanization, migration, unemployment, and so on (USAID, 2005c).

Education as Commission: A Force for Fragility

Given the above arguments, the "natural" assumption that education is funda-mentally "good for children and youth," and the imperative to ensure Education for All, it is trickier to acknowledge the potential that the provision of education has for fueling or exacerbating conflict and perpetuating instability. A number of recent studies, however, point to the ways in which educational systems, structures, and processes impact negatively on ethnic relations, gender equity, and the distribution of resources and political and economic power. As Smith and Vaux (2003) assert, "Simply providing education does not ensure peace" (p. 10). According to a World Bank (2005) study, schools are almost always complicit in conflict (p. xv).

Corporal punishment, bullying, and sexual violence are examples of very di-rect forms of violence that are endemic in schools around the world. Even if not directly harmed themselves, children socialized in such environments are denied the opportunity to live in a peaceful environment free from fear. They also miss out on opportunities to develop skills and sensitivities to enable them to manage and resolve conflicts and to achieve their goals in peaceful ways. The impacts of such experiences have been explored in recent years by a number of academics and agencies, including Leach and colleagues (2003), Harber (2004), Government of North-West Frontier Province (NWFP), UNICEF, and Save the Children (2005), and UNICEF (2001); the recent report to the UN Secretary General on violence against children includes a chapter on violence in schools (Pinheiro, 2006).

More subtle, however, are the ways in which education is a conduit of indi-rect violence against children and their communities and a contributing factor in the ongoing instability of a country or region. "Social and ethnic relations" are prominent in the World Bank's conflict risk indicators (World Bank, 2005), and educational systems and institutions have a critical impact on social and ethnic relations. The mobilization of ethnicity through schooling is a relatively common phenomenon. In their paper, *The Two Faces of Education in Ethnic Conflict: To-wards a Peacebuilding Education for Children* (2000), Bush and Saltarelli identify seven distinct ways in which schooling has been used to mobilize ethnicity and to exacerbate ethnic divisions. These are: uneven distribution of education and educational opportunities; education as cultural repression; denial of education as a weapon of war; manipulation of history for political purposes; manipulation of textbooks; images of ethnic groups in ways which convey dominance; and ethni-cally segregated education.

Bush and Saltarelli provide numerous examples from around the world to illustrate their points, including the systematic repression of Kurdish culture and identity in Turkish schools and the processes of identification and separation of Tutsis and Hutus used in Rwandan schools. They also highlight the extent to which denial of education has served as a weapon of war in multiple contexts.

Other examples of the negative side of education have been identified in Afghanistan, where Spink (2005) reports:

The return to school in 2002 and 2003 was a double-edged sword. On the one hand millions of students were, in many cases, for the first time going to school and taking advantage of the BTS [Back to School] drive in Afghanistan. On the other hand, millions of children, who had never been to school, were for the first time learning the principals of intolerance, hatred and division. The whole education initiative in 2002 focused only on access of children to education, with very little consideration for the quality, or content, of tuition received in the classrooms. (pp. 203–204)

Spink (2005) explains in some detail how textbooks developed in the 1970s by the Mujahedin forces, with support from the University of Nebraska, were printed rapidly and distributed with only minor revisions.

All subject-based books were revised by a team of Afghans working for USAID to remove any direct reference to violence. References in all the books to the mistrust of the descendants of Ali were not removed. There was no representation for non-Sunni, non-Pashtun children of their own histories or culture in the books. The US Government stated that they would only support the printing of the non-religious textbooks, despite the fact that all books were full of religious references. As a result religious books, that instructed "true believers" to kill all non-Muslims, were not revised as a part of the USAID revisions. (p. 201)

This politically and historically charged example demonstrates the complex geopolitics that operate in relation to state fragility, stability, and instability, and illustrates how, as pointed out above, the concept of fragility as constructed exclusively within state boundaries is highly problematic. The current and past contributions of USAID interventions in education have to be integrated into critical analysis of education and fragility in Afghanistan. As highlighted in DfID's definition of fragile states, and in the listing of fragile states, ethnic conflict or tension is not always a major factor in state fragility, as it is in Afghanistan. Poverty and economic desperation are factors that can contribute to social uprising and to state fragility. Lack of resources; and government dysfunction, including corruption and low levels of management capacity, are also factors in state fragility—creating situations where there are no social services or safety nets to protect the populations (DfID, 2005b). Although there has been much less investigation into the linkages between education and economic and political instabilities, it is possible to surmise that ineffective and/or inappropriate educational systems also are both a result and a contributing factor.

Fragility, Gender Equality, and Education

As stated above, the linkages among gender, education, and state fragility are even less well explored. However, as highlighted in the USAID fragile states policy (2005b), state fragility does impact differently on men and women. Girls and boys, male and female children and youth, also will have different experiences of the state's inability or unwillingness to provide essential services such as education. Even though it may not be reflected in the policy papers of bilateral and multilateral agencies, gender inequality is certainly a feature of state fragility (Baranyi & Powell, 2005b). Evidence of the relationships between conflict and wide gender inequalities (e.g., World Bank, 2003) would suggest that there is also a strong relationship between gender inequality and state fragility. For example, the Canadian International Development Agency's (CIDA) five priority fragile states, Afghanistan, Iraq, Haiti, the Palestine Territories, and Sudan, all have high levels of gender inequality, and the countries listed by DfID tend to place low in the Gender-Related Development Index (GDI) (Human Development Report, 2005). Gender equality in education is also a feature of many fragile states. Of the 46 DfID-listed states, the gender parity index[2] for net primary school enrollment is available for 26.[3] Of these 26, 20 have an index of less than 1, and 10 have an index of less than 0.8. Access to education for girls in most fragile states is lower than that for boys.

When educational systems collapse and schools themselves are destroyed, boys and girls are affected, but the implications can be different for girls than for boys, especially as there tend to have been fewer schools or school places available for girls in the first place. In Somalia, for example, gender-related disparities are a major issue in school enrollment. Of a GER of less than 20%, only slightly over one third of lower primary school pupils are girls (UNICEF, 2005). The barriers to girls' education common around the world may be equally present in most fragile states; they may be exaggerated due to the state's inability or unwillingness to implement gender policies and targeted girls' education strategies. The specific issue of sexual violence, abuse, and exploitation, however, warrants further attention. Pervasive insecurity and the presence of fighting forces, militaries, paramilitaries, and other such groups are characteristic of many fragile states. Parents are especially unlikely to allow their daughters to attend school if they fear the girls will be victim to violence, and especially sexual violence, either in the school itself or en route to it. In such contexts, early marriage is a strategy parents adopt to protect their daughters, but one that usually results in premature school dropout. Another issue common to fragile states and of concern to agencies concerned with education and child protection, such as the International Rescue Committee (IRC), Save the Children, and the Women's Commission for Refugee Women and Children, is the impact of inadequate and irregular teacher salaries on students' well-being, and especially on the safety and security of girls in school (personal communications, 2006). Ongoing IRC-supported research in Liberia, for example, examines salary-related teacher demoralization, frustration, and apparent lack of motivation to rise to appropriate professional standards and conduct.

Such challenges can mean that even where it is widely accepted that women's contributions to the reconstruction efforts of the country are needed, the lack of education for many women and girls is a long-term obstacle. This is the case in southern Sudan.

> Many women are excluded from decision-making processes because of lack of education and their low status in society. Their voice is seldom heard in public forums, especially in war-affected communities. As one study succinctly put it: "neglect of both primary and secondary education puts the achievements of the rest of the aid operation in jeopardy." (*The Key to Peace*, 2002, p. 26)

Although various affirmative actions are being taken in Sudan, women are held back from positions as leaders, teachers, and community development and health workers, all of which are desperately needed throughout the country. It is not only literacy and numeracy that are critical for women to have in order to be able to play active roles in development, but also the knowledge and the confidence that they have a right to participate and to speak out. Furthermore, as has been shown in research in Afghanistan, where women are denied education, they are not considered by men in the family and community to be able to participate in decision-making processes (Wakefield, 2004a, 2004b). Access to school is therefore highly significant—symbolically as much as practically—in the efforts to ensure that women as well as men can contribute to positive change, to the strengthening of civil society, and to positive change away from state fragility.

At the same time, however, critical reflection on the ways in which educational systems typically construct gender identities, masculinities, and femininities is required in order to move beyond a problematic assumption that access to education is necessarily empowering to women and girls and necessarily a force to promote equal participation in peace-building and development processes. Numerous researchers have identified the overt and "hidden" ways in which schooling usually serves to maintain the status quo and to preserve dominant forms of masculinity and femininity that support the continued domination of men and boys in the public realm (Davies, 2004; Longwe, 1998; Mirembe & Davies, 2001) even when there is an official commitment to gender equality (Leach, 2000; Stromquist, 1996). Rubina Saigol (1995, 2000), for example, analyzes how the Pakistan national curriculum consistently promotes a male-dominated culture, glorifies war and culture, and confines the roles of women and girls to the preservation of the home and family honor. Davies (2004) discusses the relationships between different constructions of masculinity and femininity, and cultures of conflict, violence, militarism, and oppression. Education is integral to these identity constructions and may be a source of violence in and of itself; at the same time, as she highlights in eight specific recommendations, holistic, democratic, and equitable education can play a part in the mitigation of such violence (p. 72). Gender analysis has not been part of studies such as UNESCO's review of post-conflict curriculum development (International Bureau of Education, 2006), but, as this chapter argues, it should be an integral part of educational analysis, planning, and programming, especially in fragile state contexts where, as highlighted earlier, gender equality is a critical issue.

EDUCATION AS A STABILIZING FORCE

Despite the concerns raised with regard to the active involvement of education in fueling and prolonging fragility, and in perpetuating gender dichotomies and inequalities, education in general, and schooling in particular, are a source of hope for the future. If a lack of education can be a cause of instability, then there is a critical imperative to prioritize education in fragile states. There is increasing awareness of the particular need for relevant education programs for youth (e.g., USAID, 2005c). Yet this has to be done in ways that address the contradictions created when education is assumed to necessarily be a positive force for peace and stability. None of the authors who describe the extent of violence in schools, and especially the extent to which this impacts on girls, suggests that schooling be eliminated, but rather that the structures, processes, and content of education be revised and reworked, and considered from safety, protection, and peace-building perspectives. As the DfID (2005b) girls' education policy states:

> Our work in these environments [fragile states] is a reminder of the need to link education with attempts to build democracy, provide better health systems, offer social protection to the very poorest and develop multilingual and multicultural policies. (p. 11)

At the same time, as a recent paper for the German development agency GTZ (Deutsche Gesellschaft fur Technische Zusammenarbeit) concludes, despite increasing attention to conflict and crisis prevention, early warning systems, and so on, little emphasis is placed on the role to be attached to education in preventing conflict, promoting peace, and, by extension, promoting stability and transformation away from fragility (Seitz, 2004). As many educators and education advocates point out, there are multiple entry points that exist in both formal and informal educational settings for promoting peace through education. It is significant that Spink (2005), despite her concern with what has happened with the textbooks in Afghanistan, sees that education does have a critical role to play in peace-building and reconstruction. Bush and Saltarelli (2000) also conclude:

By looking at both faces of education, we develop a clearer understanding of the positive and negative impacts of education in areas prone to ethnic violence. There are very different operational and policy implications of this two-faceted optic. On the one hand, it suggests that by identifying which initiatives do harm we might be better able to "stop doing the wrong thing." In contrast, by developing a better understanding of positive impacts of educational initiatives, we can continue to nurture and "do the right thing." (p. 35)

A number of recent case studies have highlighted the importance of the re-establishment of education activities as quickly as possible after crises such as the genocide in Rwanda (e.g., Obura, 2003) and of the importance of such initiatives in stabilizing the situation and creating a much-needed sense of normalcy. The World Bank (2005) report on post-conflict education recommends prioritizing education as a critical post-conflict intervention for "reshaping the future" and identifies the need to focus on (re)establishing a functioning school system as a "peace dividend" that will foster confidence in the period of transformation to ward peace. An important concern for post-conflict reconstruction is to prevent a relapse into violence; certainly education should be planned in such a way as not to contribute to such a relapse. It also has a crucial, proactive role to play. According to the World Bank's CAF, there are four key characteristics of a society that is resilient to violent conflict: political and social institutions that are inclusive, equitable, and accountable; economic, social, and ethnic diversity rather than polarization and dominance; growth and development that provide equitable benefits across society; and a culture of dialogue rather than violence. Education has a relationship with all of these characteristics and arguably may constitute the most effective vehicle for promoting each of them; gender equality is also implicit in each. This being said, as has been articulated by authors mentioned above, the record of public schooling with regard to these characteristics is poor. Specific efforts, strategies, and approaches need to be developed in order to develop educational systems and processes that are truly a force for peace and stability.

Fragility-Sensitive Education Approaches

There is recognition of the need for conflict-sensitive education, particularly in post-conflict contexts. The World Bank (2005) report, for example, identifies the need for sensitivity to conflict and the concept of conflict prevention to be systematically integrated into World Bank instruments and analyses. The GTZ report (Seitz, 2004) also recommends the development and implementation of instruments and processes for conflict analysis and conflict impact analysis for the education sector. This chapter, however, suggests that conflict prevention and analysis are part of a broader sensitivity to fragility that is required for and of the education sector. This is recognized by a group of policymakers, technical advisers, and researchers from different organizations and agencies, who, with official closure of the Development Assistance Committee (DAC) sub-team on education, nonetheless are committed to further analysis and inquiry on education and fragility and are now establishing a specific Education and Fragility Working Group linked to the Inter-Agency Network for Education in Emergencies (INEE) structure and informing the new DAC workstream on state-building. This demands tools and processes that capture and unpack the interrelationships among social, economic, and political instabilities, and education, and guide the provision of education in ways that serve to strengthen the social, economic, and political fabric of society. An initial education and fragility assessment tool has been developed, initiated by USAID, that soon will be piloted in specific countries and then refined further over time. Research and practice discussed above would indicate that there are at least three dimensions of fragility-sensitive education provision: the equitable and effective delivery of education, the content of the education (i.e., the curriculum and materials used to convey that curricula), and the processes through which education takes place (i.e., the teaching methods employed and the management and administration systems and relationships).

The USAID Africa Bureau (2005) fragile states matrix highlights the importance of interventions to impact both the effectiveness and the legitimacy of state and community institutions and to contribute to improved governance at all levels and in all sectors. This has important implications for the education sector on two interconnected accounts. In terms of providing students with the knowledge, skills, and attitudes for good governance, education should be able to make a significant contribution (content and methods). At the same time, the imperative is there to ensure legitimacy through equitable service delivery and resource sharing *and* to promote good governance of the institutions of the educational system (program provision and process). As far as possible, schools and educational institutions should be models of democratic processes and structures in their communities. This imperative was taken up by the Sudan Basic Education Program, for example, where the peace education strategy identified financial management training for parent teacher association (PTA) and Board of Governor (BOG) members, as well as for the administrators of teacher training institutions, as critical steps toward the legitimization and the effective functioning of the governance structures in education and therefore as forces for the stabilization of the peace in southern Sudan (Kirk, Ogango & Pia, 2005).

Education, Gender Equality, and Stabilization

As highlighted through this chapter, gender matters greatly in education— and also should be an integral conceptual tool for analyzing state fragility and for designing strategies and programs aimed toward peace and greater stability; women, men, girls, and boys have much to contribute to transforming the dynamics of state fragility (Baranyi & Powell, 2005b). They can contribute to building alternatives at the community level, to challenging state fragility at the national level, and to linking with efforts in neighboring states. Attention to gender equality in and through education should be a priority for donor interventions in fragile states, and the tools and processes developed to support fragility-sensitive education necessarily should be gender responsive and attuned to the task of creating schooling systems and processes that promote new forms of masculinity and femininity—and that challenge rather than perpetuate dominant gender regimes. Such work is challenging, with a number of inherent tensions to overcome, not least of which is the tendency of schooling to reproduce gender inequalities and male-dominated cultures that promote physical, economic, and cultural dominance over women. Machel (1996) states that young people are key contributors in planning and implementing long-term solutions for peace, and youth engagement in peace-building is being promoted by various organizations. Such initiatives usually include girls, and may be sensitive to the general challenges of child and youth participation in "adult" activities, but as yet little work has been done to specifically and critically address youth participation from a gender perspective (Kirk & Garrow, 2003); this is even less so in fragile or conflict contexts. Protection *and* participation imperatives for girls and women provide another tension to be addressed in schools and more broadly within the educational system (Kirk & Winthrop, n.d.). Already highlighted are ways in which education exposes girls and women to increased risk of violence and exploitation; protection measures are needed to ensure safe access to school as well as in school itself, but measures that allow for rather than compromise opportunities for participation. It is significant that although UN Security Council Resolution 1325 recognizes the vulnerability of and the need to protect women and girls from sexual violence in conflict contexts, when it comes to participation in peace-building processes (the second part of the resolution), girls are noticeably absent (GPWG & WC, 2006). From a gender equality perspective, the potential of education to promote personal development and well-being for individual women also has to be leveraged, with its potential for collective empowerment through broad shifts in gender ideologies, patterns, and possibilities. This is a significant tension and/or potential to be strategically addressed at all levels in the system, especially in fragile states, where active participation for girls in education and in different school-based activities may be a starting point from which to foster the skills, knowledge, and attitudes to promote ongoing, active participation in civil society and to inspire and empower them for more positive and peaceful individual and collective futures. The stark reality, however, is that the educational systems in fragile states are hardly able to provide access to even the most basic schools and learning experiences for girls; in many of the most challenging contexts, EFA targets and MDGs for gender equality in education are unlikely to be met, even by 2015. Although there are examples of progress made, for example, in Rwanda, where gender equality has been seriously addressed in recent educational developments, enormous challenges remain.

CONCLUSIONS AND MOVING FORWARD

The above discussion highlights the need for the complex relationships among gender equality, education, and state fragility to be closely examined in specific contexts, especially in relation to bilateral and multilateral interventions to support educational development in fragile states. As Davies (2004) writes, the link between conflict and education is a "grossly-underanalysed area" (p. 7), and this is as true on a broad conceptual scale as at the more specific level of community, region, or nation. This is perhaps even more so in relation to the multiple dimensions of state fragility. The international community has a critical role to play in supporting educational interventions but also in ensuring that these are fragility sensitive and oriented toward stability and peace-building. Such approaches require addressing governance issues such as corruption and transparency, and safety and security, which are somewhat outside of the traditional parameters for education policy and planning; they therefore may require new partnerships.

This chapter ends with two broad recommendations. First, attention is required to the nature and quality of education service delivery in the challenging environments of different types of fragile states. Education should be part of any fragility analysis, and the findings from such analysis should be fed into the design and implementation model of any service delivery intervention. Second, progress is being made on bringing together the different complementary perspectives and agendas of service delivery of education in fragile states, financing mechanisms to support education in fragile states, education in emergencies, and gender equality in education. These should be further channeled to develop more concrete programs and case studies of fragility-sensitive education, to be shared among practitioners and policymakers.

Service delivery is important but has to be designed carefully and sensitively to contribute to stability, peace-building, and gender equality, for example, with attention to equitable access, careful choice of curricula, and teacher training that is grounded in principles of children's rights, nondiscrimination, of teachers' roles as agents of child protection. Complex situations require complex educational responses, and it is clear from the example of Afghanistan (Spink, 2005) that printing textbooks alone does not ensure that the potential of education to contribute fully to peace-building and stabilization processes will be fulfilled. Education interventions cannot remain neutral; they have to be designed in ways that challenge some of the driving forces of state fragility, such as discrimination, violence, misogyny, and the maintenance of elite privileges (Baranyi & Powell, 2005a). Education needs to be oriented toward challenging the current fragility factors and also toward building resilience to conflict and other crises.

As Machel (2000) states, "The principles of gender equality and inclusion are fundamental values on which every attempt at democracy and peace-building must be based." Education in fragile states has to protect and promote the rights of women and girls, and has to work to deconstruct harmful and limiting gender roles and stereotypes; education has the potential to promote a reworking of the gender status quo (Manchanda, 2001) that is apparently so critical to the transformation processes from state fragility toward stability. Efforts to mainstream critical issues such as peace-building and gender equality into education programming in emergency, chronic crisis and early reconstruction contexts are ongoing and are coordinated through the INEE (see www.ineesite.org). The recently developed Minimum Standards for Education in Emergencies, Chronic Crisis, and Early Reconstruction (see http://ineesite.org/post/know_updated_inee_minimum_standards_handbook/) are an important means to systematically enhance the quantity and quality of education, and to ensure that as far as possible it can help to reshape the future for crisis-affected young people, their families, and their communities. With attention given, for example, to community participation, sensitive choice of curriculum content, careful and transparent teacher selection processes, and ongoing teacher training and supervision, the minimum standards go far beyond guidelines for acute emergency situations and offer substantive guidance for education provision in fragile states and for ensuring that the service is delivered in as fragility-sensitive a way as possible. Gender equity strategies also are integrated into the minimum standards, not only in student enrollment but also for teachers, PTA members, and curriculum content. Future rollout and evaluation processes for the INEE minimum standards, and for any complementary tools being developed by the Education and Fragility Working Group, should provide more examples and more reliable evidence of how sensitive education planning and implementation can make positive impacts in fragile state contexts.

NOTES

1. The IPS was developed under the previous liberal government of Canada. IPS priorities are now taken up in a new CIDA policy document, *Sustainable Development Strategy 2007–2009*.

2. Gender parity index for net enrollment is a numerical measure of girls' enrollment expressed as a proportion of boys' enrollment. Any value of less than 1 is an indication of a disparity in enrollment to girls' disadvantage.

3. Statistics from 2001, in the 2005 UNESCO EFA *Global Monitoring Report*.

CHAPTER 3

Can Education Interrupt Fragility?

Toward the Resilient Citizen and the Adaptable State

Lynn Davies

In states affected by conflict and fragility, there is agreement that education has some part to play with regard to this fragility, whether for good or ill, and whether writ large or small. The issue is how to demonstrate this effect with any rigor, that is, how to isolate education from all the other features that impact the functioning of the state. It would seem undeniable that education is necessary but not sufficient for national advancement. Education for All appears to be a precondition for peace and stability, but not the whole answer. Conversely, if no direct connection can yet be made between an educational initiative, such as peace education, and beneficial changes in government policy, this does not mean we should not engage in it. Analysis is about weighing up opportunity costs of doing and not doing something in the educational realm. There will be no big breakthroughs, no grand narratives.

This chapter takes a very cautious view of educational impact, arguing that the first ambition simply may be that education does no harm. Yet this incurs the reminder, sadly, that merely removing the negative (e.g., biased textbooks) does not guarantee the positive (harmonious relations). The second aim, then, is to predict where education can actively interrupt patterns of fragility and conflict, and can make a small intervention that challenges those concepts of "normality" in a society that prevent progress. This echoes the notion of "teaching as a subversive activity" (Postman & Weingartner, 1967) and has that same sense of buzz or edge.

To see where education can positively subvert requires a complex analysis. This chapter tries to portray the intricate connections that emerge from considering the various types of fragility mapped against a spectrum of impacts that education may have on conflict. It is based partly on a recently completed synthesis report for INEE on education and conflict in Afghanistan, Bosnia-Herzegovina (BiH), Cambodia, and Liberia (Davies, 2010),[1] but also on experience in other conflict-affected states, particularly Sri Lanka. The concluding argument is that education can perhaps build individual citizens' resilience, but has a less direct impact on state functioning. Nonetheless, it can disrupt some unconstructive connections and help build adaptability. First it is instructive to isolate the various components of fragility to see where education is most influential.

DOMAINS OF FRAGILITY

There are numerous definitions and typologies of fragility, and it has become a contested concept and label (see Davies, 2009). Nonetheless, breaking down fragility into different domains does help to see where education is positioned. I use an adaptation of the categories used by the U.S. Agency for International Development (USAID, 2006) and others (e.g., in the FTI Progressive Framework, 2008), while admitting some overlaps and the arbitrary situating of features in this conceptualization of fragility. Five key domains or drivers of fragility can be identified: problems of governance, lack of security, weak economy, cultural barriers to change or cohesion, and environmental degradation.

Governance includes systems of governance, as well as the histories of power, invasion, or militarization that have created or conditioned particular ways of ruling a country. Governance also includes who or which group is in power, and therefore involves structures of inequality and the exclusion from power and resources. Fragile governance conventionally is defined as a lack of political will, as well as a lack of technical capacity and skills in areas such as policy, planning, implementation, monitoring, and budgeting. Corruption is often a key governance issue, although an expanded vocabulary is needed to cover a nuanced range of behavior and relations from patronage, nepotism, reciprocal favors, and bribery through large-scale siphoning of funds.

Security relates to problems of crime and lawlessness as well as to violent conflict deriving from ethnic or religious tension. The presence of militias and armed groups, whether opposing government or government-backed, is an indicator of security breakdowns. Violent struggles over land, resources, or the drug trade may be a feature. Gendered violence also can be placed under "security," although it could equally come under "culture." National security often is intricately linked to international security, for example, as with questions of extremism and terrorism, or invasions from other countries.

A *weak economy* implies economic stagnation or decline and relates also to the governance question in terms of who participates in the economy. Under this heading come demographic analyses of the "youth bulge," that is, the thesis that high levels of actual or potentially unemployed youth create a problem for stability. This is linked to the absorptive capacity of the labor market as well as the fit of skills to available employment.

The fourth domain I label *cultures of power*, although USAID and others use "social" as a descriptor. This domain involves all the traditions within a society that determine how individuals and groups act and relate to others. The particular concerns with regard to fragility are patronage, gender inequality, violence and fear, cultures of passivity, and lack of freedom of speech. My preference is for a cultural analysis because it tackles the deep questions of what is considered "normal" in a society and who has the defining power for this.

The final domain is the *environment*, with the problem for fragility being environmental degradation. Natural disasters can be compounded by manmade disasters and by existing inequalities of resources. Poorer people may not have the capacity to challenge environmental destruction or to claim compensation from industrial and other manmade disasters. Here, as elsewhere across the domains, it can be seen how the drivers of fragility intersect and reinforce one another.

SPECTRUM OF IMPACT

A second analytic framework is an expansion on the conventional "two faces" of the relation between education and conflict, into a spectrum of impact that considers a range of ways in which education may contribute to fragility or mitigate it. The "two faces" notion acknowledged that education could both contribute toward a peaceful society and reproduce or even worsen violent conflict (Buckland, 2005; Bush & Saltarelli; 2000; Davies, 2004; Seitz, 2004). Yet this is not a simple either/or effect with regard to fragility, and effects can happen simultaneously. Education can protect children through curricula on health, sanitation, or human rights. It can socialize them into citizenship roles and provide for greater gender, ethnic, or socioeconomic equity. However, while education pre- and post-conflict *can* contribute to peace-building, there is no guarantee that it *will* do so. Education also can contribute to a lack of, or breakdown in, social cohesion, owing to the provision of various sorts of divisive schooling. School culture and teaching styles also can be harmful: In the case of Rwanda, for example, there is evidence to suggest that the didactic methodologies of teaching, which smothered critical thinking and questioning, affected people's response to the genocide (Bird, 2003). Violence in schools, whether corporal punishment or gendered violence, also contributes to cultures of violence and the acceptance of violence as a solution to problems (Harber, 2004; Leach & Mitchell, 2006). How education actually is used—or manipulated—by government, religious groups, local politicians, or oppositional groups needs to be critically examined. To discuss this complexity more than a dualistic notion is needed. In Figure 3.1 I distinguish five types of possibility for education's role in fragility.

Figure 3.1. The Spectrum of Impact of Education on Fragility

Active reinforcement of fragility	Schools as reflection of normality	Thwarted or counter-productive policy attempts	Softening impact by building resilience	Making small inroads into fragility

Negative/contribution .... Positive/mitigation

In terms of *active reinforcement*, examples of the deliberate segregation of schooling, enhancing social and ethnic divisions, are found in countries such as Bosnia and Herzegovina, Liberia, and Sri Lanka (Lopes-Cardoso, 2008; Moran, 2006; Pašalic-Kreso, 2008). Biased or militarized textbooks and curriculum, as in Afghanistan (Barakat, Karpinska, & Paulson, n.d.) and BiH (Bartulovic, 2006), affect perceptions of "the other" as well as normalize military solutions to problems. At the same time, corporal punishment and other abuses of power promote violence and violent uses of authority. Schools may be used as sites of political contestation and manipulation, as in Nepal (Smith & Vaux, 2003) and, in the case of Afghanistan, of attack by the Taliban (Sigsgaard, 2009).

Less deliberate, but nonetheless still reinforcing, is the second category of *schools being a reflection of normality.* This includes access and outcomes of schooling reflecting or being unable to challenge the social fault lines of socioeconomic, gender, or ethnic stratification, so that these are reproduced over generations. The patterns of interaction between teachers and students, or among students in schools, can reflect the fact that outside the school violence is normal, corruption is normal and gender inequity is normal. Management styles and organizational cultures reinforce inefficient bureaucracy as the normal mode of operation. The link to fragility is the resulting lack of trust in the system and hence a lack of confidence in those that govern it.

A third category somewhere in between negative and positive relates to those initiatives that aim to be progressive or mitigate fragility but that are counterproductive, what I call *thwarted policy attempts.* The classic example is the Dayton agreement in BiH which aimed to negotiate peace but ended up cementing ethnonationalist divides, then played out in a divided educational system.[2] Other examples include artisan vocational education, which can be a very expensive way of creating frustrated youth when no jobs are available, as in Cambodia (U.S. Department of State, 2009) and Liberia (Walker, Millar Wood & Allemano, 2009); the Back to School campaign in Afghanistan, which pitted Sunni against Shi'a Muslims because of the textbooks used (Spink, 2005); human rights education in both Liberia and Afghanistan coming to be seen as a Western imposition (interview data from INEE field studies); and donor aid being delivered as projects in many countries, with such projectization leading to fragmentation and aid dependency (Eurotrends, 2010b).

Toward the more positive end are those education initiatives that *soften the impact of fragility* by building individual or group resilience. These do not directly impact state-level fragility, unless a sufficient number of people become resilient to economic or social shocks, but they enable people to survive within a context of volatility, uncertainty, or inequity. This would include everything from HIV/AIDS education and school-feeding programs to those life-skills programs that foster successful entrepreneurship. That education can give unemployed youth something to do falls into this category and may build hope for the future, however temporary. Much refugee education and post-conflict education comes under this category of building resilience, with education providing not just skills but aspirations and hopes (Winthrop & Kirk, 2008).

Finally, there are the interventions that could be said to make small inroads into state fragility itself, attempting to transform or at least interrupt politics or culture rather than merely enabling people to survive within them. I would place the successful initiatives that challenge gender-based violence in countries such as Liberia and Cambodia in this category, as this starts to reshape gender relations, which in turn also can impact the propensity for conflict more generally (Bernard et al., 2008). Striving to create and keep open girls' schools in Afghanistan can be viewed, for example, as part of eventual state-building. Common to Afghanistan, Cambodia, and Liberia is the success of community-based education that not only improves access and outcomes but is found to strengthen the community itself, as members build capacity and learn skills of making demands and negotiating for improvements (Eurotrends, 2010a; Richards et al., 2005; Sigsgaard, 2009). Community-led education has played this role in Afghanistan, where it has helped in some cases to produce a form of accommodation with the Taliban that allows for children to attend school, where this is seen as privately rather than state provided (Sullivan-Owomoyela & Brannelly, 2009). A very different type of interruption comes from BiH, where the push toward EU accession and therefore EU technical standards for education may have more impact on equity and coherence than direct drives for cultural integration of existing groups (Hromadžic, 2008).

CONNECTIONS: WHAT IS THE POWER OF EDUCATION OVER DIFFERENT DRIVERS OF FRAGILITY?

So far I have drawn five domains of fragility and five types of impact. Mapping these against one another makes a very complicated diagram, so for the purposes of analysis, I reduce the types of impact to three. The effects are summarized in the following matrix and then elaborated. It must be stressed that these analyses are derived from attempts to see what *evidence* there is: For example, we may hold assumptions that civic and human rights education will build the nation, but the actual long-term evidence is not there—or perhaps cannot ever be. The evidence about negatives is much clearer. I therefore have focused more on what is derived from the research than on aspirational conjectures about education's role. The intention is now to see which particular aspect of fragility is affected by education, and in what way. Sometimes negative and positive influences operate simultaneously, which further complicates the idea of "impact" (see Table 3.1).

Table 3.1. Impact of Education on the Drivers of Fragility and Grievance

Domains of Fragility	TYPES OF IMPACT		
	A. Education reinforcing or making no difference	B. Education building citizen resilience, protection, and survival *within* a fragile state	C. Education making small inroads into nation-building and state adaptability
Governance: Inequality in resource allocation; Lack of political will to foster inclusion and tackle marginalization; Lack of trust in government; Corruption; Problems of capacity	Unfair system; perceptions of lack of meritocracy; Urban/rural and rich/poor divides in education allocations; Bribes to teachers; Illicit fees; rent-seeking in allocation of jobs; Bureaucracy preventing efficiency; Donor projectization causing inefficiency and lack of government ownership	Increased access to education and abolition of school fees give opportunity; Resistance to political manipulation	Community self-reliance and confidence, civil engagement, parent teacher associations; Widening access helps feeling of national unity; Capacity development; National education planning EMIS, PETS, and accountability measures give greater transparency, enhancing trust in government; Technical reform, for EU accession; Voter education
Security: Crime, lawlessness, violent conflict linked to religion or ethnicity; Militias; Struggles over land and resources; International or regional drivers of conflict	Unresolved grievances; Manipulation of schools; schools used as sites of contestation; School segmentation and segregation; Politicization of identity; Militarized curriculum; Failed integration attempts	Resistance to recruitment into armed combat; Secular education for returnees and IDPs, avoiding local religious tensions	Building national identity or national pride; Fully integrated education; Public awareness campaigns/adult education helping against political manipulation

Table 3.1. *Continued*

Domains of Fragility	TYPES OF IMPACT		
	A. Education reinforcing or making no difference	B. Education building citizen resilience, protection, and survival *within* a fragile state	C. Education making small inroads into nation-building and state adaptability
Economy: Youth bulge, frustration; Unemployment; Static or declining national growth	Education unable to provide livelihoods because of job markets; Failed TVET projects creating false expectations; Perceived irrelevance of schooling; Limited access to schools, excluding people from economic opportunities	Relevant literacy for job acquisition or entrepreneurship; Skills for livelihoods in existing markets; Accelerated learning programs for potential employment	Mass literacy; Technological education to enable competition in international markets
Cultures of Power: Patronage, gender inequality, violence, and fear; Cultures of passivity; Lack of freedom of speech	Violence in schools; Corporal punishment; Biased curriculum; Gender divisions seen as normal; Human rights education seen as Western imposition; Caste systems	National code of conduct for teachers; Child-friendly schools teaching equity, self-esteem, and rights; Critical thinking and assertiveness; Working *within* patron–client cultures to reduce impact	Tackling gender-based and other cultures of violence; Political/civic education to learn advocacy and break cycles of acceptance; Youth parliaments and youth shuras
Environmental Degradation: Also affecting the poor disproportionately	Education failing to teach about environment and environmental dangers; Failure to provide the poor with skills to claim compensation from industrial or other disasters	Safe/sanitary schools; Health education; Disaster-preparedness; Giving land and seed to teachers to compensate for salary	

Governance

In this domain we can see education reinforcing power differentials and a declining trust in government if perceptions are of a lack of a fair meritocracy to handle the inherent selectiveness of an educational system. Conversely, fee abolition and widening access will help individual resilience or opportunity and at the same time help to restore trust that the government is on the side of the people, a symbol of national pride and confidence, as has been argued for Cambodia (Ratcliffe, Patch, & Quinn, 2009). If, as found from interview data in Liberia, education can help in resistance to political manipulation, then this can empower people to hold governments to account. A key element, as mentioned earlier, is the community self-reliance and confidence that come from participating in educational governance, which can enable a strengthening of civil society. It also may aid transparency: There has been some success with Save the Children Norway's Community Based Education Management Information Systems in Nepal, which tries to provide greater decentralization but also accountability. These community-based information systems have revealed the exclusion of low-caste and ethnic minority children from primary schools, and enabled the preparation of community-based school improvement plans that encourage out-of-school children to return and the disadvantaged to be aware of opportunities available to them. Using the community to collect data can tackle the partial and politicized allocation of school places and scholarships (Davies et al., 2008). However, in conflict-affected states, there is always a question mark over "strengthening community," as this can (as in BiH) cement ethnic or other divisions. Language claims and separatist religious claims from communities may polarize rather than unite. However, on balance, community empowerment is placed in the positive column, with the caveat that many of the features need to be seen in combination, that is, community power needs to be accompanied by accountability measures. Establishing the precise powers within community governance is also part of robust national education planning, which has been found crucial for Afghanistan in helping national unity and giving a sense of hope for the future.

Security

While there is limited concrete evidence that education can have a positive impact on security at a national level, education can have clear benefits to individual security and seems to play a protective role in limiting violence. To illustrate the first point, there are extensive programs of moral education in many countries, yet it has been difficult to demonstrate a direct linkage between education and a reduction of lawlessness and crime. Large-scale drug or other covert economics do not seem to be affected by what happens in schools, even if there is anti-drug education; and landmine-risk education does not stop people from laying landmines.

However, there are many instances in the case studies and beyond that suggest that if education were *not* there, conflict might have been worse. Schooling can help in children's resistance to being recruited into armed combat, by providing other sources of income or status. In Brčko in BiH, returnees and internally displaced persons (IDPs) were helped in reintegration by the provision of secular education that did not cement religious divides (data from INEE studies). Educational support for national security issues came primarily in the form of adult education and public awareness campaigns, which built resistance to the political manipulation of hostilities between groups. The Liberia case study that was prepared for the INEE report suggests that educational support for national unity (as in the "One Liberia" message) helps break down historical tensions and enables people to look to the future rather than carry old grievances. These findings are echoed in other recent research. Lucknow, for example, may have escaped violence in the 1993 Hindu–Muslim tensions because of the work of the City Montessori school, which brought together religious leaders and where students and parents took to the streets in loudspeaker vans to appeal to people to refrain from violence (Mathews, 2001); the Mindanao conflict between Christians, Muslims, and Lumads may have been slightly less costly in human lives because of the educational work that had gone on around dialogue (Tanada, 2001).

Nonetheless, it is important to remember that violent tensions arising from ethnic or religious divisions can be made worse or at best not improved if schools emphasize a separatist identity over a national one, through physically separated schools and/or through particular portrayals of "the other" in curriculum. Sometimes, the integration attempts themselves can be problematic, as can be seen in the case of the Mostar Gymnasium in BiH, which attempted "two schools under one roof" (Hromadžic, 2008). As in Sri Lanka, I would argue that this partial integration actually can act to emphasize differences, promoting the notion that these differences are so huge that students cannot be educated together.

The Economy

The relationship between education provision and economic growth is a much debated issue. In none of the four countries of the synthesis report was there evidence to support a direct causal or positive relationship. The phenomenon of the "youth bulge" was apparent, with the conclusion that youth frustration over lack of jobs is associated with conflict: in none of the four countries had this been resolved. In Liberia, programs such as the Accelerated Learning Programme had some success in creating a pool of skilled learners, but this was not matched sufficiently to needs in the labor market. Attempts at technical and vocational education were mostly counterproductive because graduates were unable to find employment. For this reason, Afghanistan decided to focus on basic education and also computer skills, but not on direct job preparation. Afghan youth wanted information technology and to connect to a globalized world, including mastery of English (Ghani & Lockhart, 2008). Cambodian youth also lived in a contradiction—seeing education as a route to a good job but being simultaneously aware of the lack of such jobs (ICA, 2009). The obvious point is reinforced that education cannot create jobs, and for Technical and Vocational Education and Training (TVET) to make any sense, it must be linked to the labor market. If the economy is primarily opium-based, as in Afghanistan, formal schooling would look almost irrelevant. While not covered in the case studies, there may be an argument to be made for higher education and advanced skills in reducing fragility (Ghani & Lockhart, 2008).

Cultures of Power

Under *culture* come issues such as gender relations, violence, and patronage linked to clan, tribe, or family. Admittedly, the latter could equally come under the category of corruption and therefore governance, but it is dealt with here because it is part of norms and values, and very difficult to shift. Cultural issues can be tackled through technical efforts around monitoring and transparency, but the INEE synthesis study also made the important point that culture cannot be "eradicated" (Davies, 2010). Thus, for example, donors and others had to work around patron–client relations in Cambodia (ICA, 2009)—as well as with the Taliban in Afghanistan (Sigsgaard, 2009). There was little evidence from these countries that education actually had changed cultures of power, although there were many attempts, such as civic education or human rights education, to make for a more equitable and transparent polity—in spite of resistance, as mentioned earlier.

More research is desperately needed to understand the long-term impact of curriculum that addresses cultural norms about power. Nonetheless, codes of conduct for teachers around issues such as corporal punishment were having an impact on violence within the school in several of the study countries, and this might be expected to impact student attitudes toward violence outside the school and their acceptance of violence as a solution when forms of social conflicts emerge. Many specific anti-corruption education initiatives, in places as far apart as Africa, Georgia, and Argentina, are promising (Davies, 2011.) Transparency International has a valuable *Corruption Fighters Toolkit* (2004).

Passivity, and a culture of fear, also can be problematic for fragility, as evidenced in the INEE study of Cambodia.[2] Decades of conflict and an authoritarian government have meant an older generation that is reluctant to criticize and willing to accept relative poverty and inequality as long as the country is stable in terms of physical security, and this seems to be reinforced by a tenor of fatalism in some aspects of Buddhism. At the same time, Cambodian youth were more likely to have high aspirations and make demands, and sometimes were viewed as posing a risk to stability. Positive notes sounded across a number of countries about youth parliaments, youth shuras, and other forms of youth engagement: These do appear to give confidence and voice, and challenge barriers to freedom of expression. Other researchers have found that participatory civic education provides a positive framework for collective civic identity in Iraq and Sudan (Levine & Bishai, 2010), while the Child-Friendly Schools (CFS) initiatives sponsored by UNICEF and other NGOs enable teachers to develop a capacity to promote emotional and physical safety for children and build their understanding of human rights in practical ways. In BiH, UNICEF is cited as a "key player" in models for socially inclusive, multicultural approaches to education through the CFS model and in the creation of a life-skills approach focusing on the prevention of risky behaviors. CFS approaches are part of the work of many NGOs—for example, Save the Children or PACE-A[3]—albeit sometimes under different names, such as the Healing Classroom Initiative (Brannelly, Ndurahutse, & Rigaud, 2009).

Environmental Degradation

The case studies suggested much less of a positive impact of education on environmental issues. This is mainly because of education's powerlessness to tackle the major harm done by big business or by government in activities such as logging, but also because environmental education was not high on the list of priorities during periods of post-conflict educational reconstruction. Individual survival within the environment is tackled through areas such as health and safety education, although it was argued that Cambodia needed to do more in terms of drugs education. Afghanistan had an interesting policy of giving teachers land and seed in lieu of a decent salary, which presumably would encourage awareness of environmental issues related to agriculture. Disaster risk education is now increasing, especially in countries affected by the Asian Tsunami of 2004. A study of education in emergencies in six countries of the South Asia region (Davies et al., 2008), however, drew attention to the lack of education about manmade disasters. This is reflected in international literature on emergencies, where there is virtually no mention of industrial disasters such as Union Carbide/Bhopal, nuclear industry/Chernobyl, large-scale mine disasters, and military pollution. The report surmised that this gap arose because governments are reluctant to promote an awareness of these forms of emergency, and that gap is "reproduced" in the literature of international organizations.

EMERGENT MODELS FOR THE ADAPTABLE STATE

This chapter now attempts to summarize the above by yet another model. The triangle of the impact and reinforcement of state fragility can be represented first

Figure 3.2. Mutually Reinforcing Relations of Fragility and Conflict

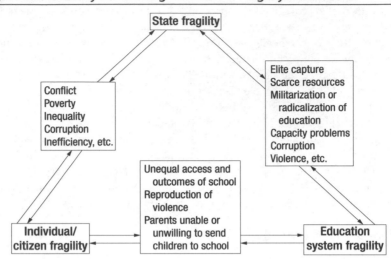

as shown in Figure 3.2. This (highly) simplified figure maps how state fragility impacts citizen fragility directly as well as indirectly through a fragile educational system. The decisions that parents make about sending children to school reflect their own fragility. All this then reinforces state fragility in the many ways described above. Conversely, the aim is a more virtuous triangle that can strengthen resilience, at least at the level of the individual citizen. For an individual, this means economic or livelihood resilience, health, absence of violence, physical security, and resistance to government or powerful manipulation.

It would be possible to use the term *resilience* for a state, but this could encompass many negative features; an authoritarian and oppressive state could well be resilient to change (as in Zimbabwe or North Korea) and may not seem fragile. In terms therefore of what is aimed for in state advancement and equity, I prefer to use the term *adaptable state*, because the opposite of fragility is not strength, but adaptability or flexibility and an ability to resist economic shocks, corruption, and the use of violence. Adaptability at the state level involves transparency and creativity and the basic elements of a democracy that enable citizens to hold their governments to account and to change them where necessary. The adaptable state is a dynamic one, able to take risks (of power-sharing, of devolution, of tax rises) and use feedback continuously to assess impact and shift course. An adaptable state is able to do deals and negotiate, whether with the Taliban or with the Chinese interests that are spreading across Africa. It recognizes that cultures of inequity, poverty, violence, and corruption may surround all apparently technical activities of planning or capacity development. Flexibility and pragmatism are called for in who is dealt with and how "corruption" is worked around.

The negative triangle is not fixed in stone. Various features in education can start to break detrimental connections. On the right of the triangle, the link between state fragility and educational system fragility can be interrupted by certain sorts of critical teacher training, capacity development, making national plans for education, and using transparency measures such as public expenditure tracking and educational system data (Education Management Information Systems [EMIS] or Public Expenditure Tracking Surveys [PETS]). On the other arm of the triangle, the link between state fragility and individual citizen fragility can be interrupted by universal access to schooling, the promotion of universal rights, and the development of adult education such as in public awareness campaigns or voter education. At the bottom, the link between educational system fragility and individual citizen fragility can be interrupted by interventions such as child-friendly schools and an education for livelihoods that takes account of the labor market. In time, the vicious triangle can be transformed into a virtuous triangle, with the arrows going in different directions, as shown in Figure 3.3.

Not all the connections can be shown here, but the examples are given to demonstrate that education's positive impact on fragility and building resilience is mostly indirect: A resilient or robust educational system will be able to build some citizen resilience through literacy, livelihood preparation, health, and cultural

Figure 3.3. The Virtuous Triangle for Resilience and Adaptability

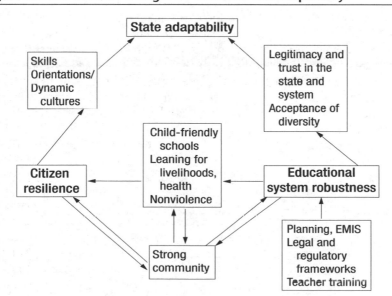

change in areas such as nonviolence and gender equity. In turn, if enough citizens are resilient (and there are livelihoods available), then their skills and orientations *may* have an impact on state fragility, as the structural causes of grievance and greed diminish. Directly, an educational system that is perceived as equitable in terms of access and outcomes will enhance the legitimacy of the state, so that people have greater trust in it. (And such trust will, of course, depend on legitimacy in other areas such as the law or police.) Figure 3.3 shows that the capacity development areas of planning, collection of education data (EMIS), monitoring, teacher training, and so on, are underpinnings of the resilience of the educational system, yet they are necessary but not sufficient for inroads into state fragility. It is necessary, for example, to acknowledge and tackle corruption inside the educational system, but this will not be sufficient to change corruption across society.

The "community" is shown separately in the diagram, as it can have a central role in strengthening educational system resilience through financial means such as cost-sharing (with parents willing to pay fees), and also political means such as participatory support for education. At the same time, community has a direct impact on citizen resilience. This is a two-way relationship, in that a resilient educational system can strengthen the way a community functions and the opportunities it gives for participation. However, the potential for negative impacts from separatist or patriarchal or violent communities must always be kept in mind.

CONCLUSION AND IMPLICATIONS

One of the key questions for donors and governments is how far to wade in with the conflict assessment tools and the extensive lists of questions in doing joint planning with stakeholders. The Eurotrends report for Liberia (2010b) states that one of the factors influencing education sector fragility is that fragility/resilience issues generally are not addressed as a risk in education program scoping or design processes. This would be true of many so-called fragile states, where such an overtly political stance would be threatening. Yet should everything be geared to fragility, in setting goals and in evaluating progress? In Afghanistan, for example, it was felt that the concept of fragility was viewed as a "development buzzword" that did not help education officials. They were more interested in learning very concrete planning techniques than in using international frameworks for conceptualizing fragility. Their undertaking was to learn to plan in a simple and effective way under challenging circumstances, aiming at sustainable technical self-reliance (Davies, 2010).

On the other hand, the two-way relationships between education, individual resilience, and state adaptability revealed in the INEE synthesis study and in many other recent studies suggest that some direct consideration of fragility is an important starting point for educational planning. Perhaps three simple-sounding queries can be the starting point for exploring how educational initiatives might interrupt fragility:

- Can this plan/policy/project/intervention do harm to citizen resilience or to state adaptability?
- What evidence do we have that this intervention will do good?
- What other dynamics of the system or the culture will intervene?

If nothing else, such questions might evoke two very important additional ones:

- How is the problem of conflict conceptualized, and therefore education's contribution?
- What sort of state is desired?

Critical and open thinking about these questions is very important. In Sri Lanka, for example, political economy analyses would portray the civil war as a political conflict, about grievance, land, and the sharing of power. However, educational strategies are predicated around its being an ethnic conflict, so the emphasis is on ethnic relations, intercultural understanding, and second language learning. In social science textbooks, learners are not exposed to causes of conflict in Sri Lanka or to questions of federalism. In Rwanda, genocide is not mentioned in the curriculum. In these situations, governments have adopted an educational strategy of suppressing ideas or issues that appear to threaten stability. One form of subversion I use is to argue that critical thinking about conflict and fragility is the best defense against extremism. Government money for education around preventing extremism should be geared to creating a generation of learners who can weigh alternatives and be critical of oppressive or violent elements in both religions and governments (Davies, 2008).

This links to a final question. So we can break down types of fragility and types of impact into ever smaller components, but does that help in policy decisions? The four-country synthesis report describes in more detail the choices and trade-offs that have to be made (such as quantity versus quality, public versus private, centralization versus decentralization, national identity versus cultural autonomy, and academic versus vocational curriculum). Mapping such trade-offs, I believe, can help in making these choices as they relate to specific country contexts. Such mapping also can help us to look for the greatest multiplier in education. For example, in the case studies, universal access to basic education appeared to be beneficial across more than one fragility or conflict dimension (breaking cycles of inequality in the governance dimension and building trust in government, as well as providing literacy and possibly life skills in the economic dimension). It is to be preferred to a politicization of education that fosters difference. Child-friendly schools also cut across both the culture dimension and the security dimension, challenging violence and fear and promoting rights. On the other hand, decentralization to community is not a universal panacea and was found to be highly dangerous for national unity in contexts such as BiH even if it was a way forward for improved governance and transparency in Afghanistan. The case studies also show that while TVET always seems an obvious choice for relevance and economic growth, failures in TVET can impact security as well as the economy. Most dramatically, the research suggests that the issue of national unity has to be tackled in the culture dimension, so that it is not about assimilation of minorities, but recognition that a nation is a dynamic collection of hybrid identities, not a pure form. Any calls for the purity of the nation should raise alarm bells for security.

The task in educational planning to interrupt fragility, I suggest, is to maximize the impact (and limit the harm) of any educational initiative in the key areas discussed in this chapter: governance, security, economy, environment, and cultures of power. This means, for example, looking at teacher training as not just increasing the numbers of teachers, but as an opportunity to promote awareness of peace/conflict, of rights, of nonviolence, and of participation in governance in the curriculum. Capacity development (as I have argued elsewhere) is not about the training and qualification of individual officers, but is about organizational change, designed around awareness of all the cultural and political factors that impinge on the workings of an educational system in a context that is fragile (Davies, 2009). Building citizen resilience to violence and challenging notions of violence as the normal response may be one of the most important things that education can do. The connections among education, fragility, and conflict may be tortuously complicated, but we should not stop trying to tease them out—and, like returnees, have some hope for the future.

NOTES

1. I acknowledge gratefully the draft reports prepared in 2009–2010 for the INEE Research Project *Field Based Situational Analyses of Education's Role in Fragile Contexts* by Morten Sigsgaard (Afghanistan), Clare Magill (Bosnia and Herzegovina), Mila Cerecina, Xixhi Liu, Nina Teng, and Chris Toomer (Cambodia), and James Williams (Liberia). Evidence about the four countries in my synthesis and in this chapter comes from these reports, and their secondary references are not reproduced; where evidence comes from other sources, the references are given as usual in the text and at the back of the book.

2. Dayton created two entities, the Federation of Bosnia and Herzegovina (FBiH) (predominantly Bosniak and Croat) and Republica Srpska (RS) (predominantly Orthodox Serb). FBiH was then divided into ten cantons each with its own responsibility for education policy, while RS remained centralized. Both state-building and education reform have been severely compromised by this complex and fragmented structure.

3. PACE-A (Partnership for Advancing Community Education in Afghanistan) is a consortium of four international NGOs: CARE, the International Rescue Committee (IRC), Catholic Relief Services (CRS), and the Aga Khan Foundation.

CHAPTER 4

Are We All Soldiers Now?

The Dangers of the Securitization of Education and Conflict

MARIO NOVELLI

> As I speak, just as surely as our diplomats and military, American NGOs are out there serving and sacrificing on the front lines of freedom. . . . I am serious about making sure we have the best relationship with the NGOs who are such a force multiplier for us, such an important part of our combat team. [We are] all committed to the same, singular purpose to help every man and woman in the world who is in need, who is hungry, who is without hope, to help every one of them fill a belly, get a roof over their heads, educate their children, have hope.
>
> —Powell, 2001

Since the 1990s, the relationship among education, conflict, and international development has risen up the policy agenda of the major international organizations, nongovernmental organizations (NGOs), and bilateral agencies. Initially this was driven by concerns over the right to education, linked to the international Education for All (EFA) objectives. However, since 9/11 both development assistance and education therein have been focused increasingly on the security concerns of the major Western donors. The quote above from ex-U.S. Secretary of State Colin Powell, while dramatic, reflects an ongoing process that extends well beyond U.S. policymakers and practitioners. This process sees international development assistance from the United States, United Kingdom, Australia, and Canada, among others—and educational assistance therein—becoming reconceptualized as a tool for fighting the war on terror. International development institutions and their practitioners become framed as allies, foot soldiers, and force multipliers in deeply problematic ways.

The argument that I will develop in this chapter is that the post-Cold War/post-9/11 security agenda is having a profound effect on development policy and practice, that education is emerging as a central component of this, and that it is producing a range of challenges and dilemmas for development agencies, NGOs, and practitioners and academics working in the field, which we need to open up to critical debate. In order to do this I will develop the argument in four parts. First, I will begin by exploring the rise of the security agenda in international development since the end of the Cold War and link this to the education sector. Second, I will look at the way the relationship between development and security is conceptualized by key authors and the policy influence and implications that arise from this relationship. Third, I will explore the dangers of the merging of security, development, and education by initially looking at an example from the Cold War and then exploring some contemporary issues in the post-9/11 era. Finally, I will conclude by raising some issues on the challenges and choices that lie ahead for those of us working in the field of education and conflict, as practitioners, policymakers, and academics.

EXPLORING THE RISE OF THE SECURITY AGENDA IN INTERNATIONAL DEVELOPMENT AND EDUCATION

Since the beginning of the 1990s there has been a rising interest from development actors about the relationship between international development and conflict (Bagoyoko & Gibert, 2009; Collier, 2009; Duffield, 2001a, 2007, 2010). This renewed concern over the relationship between development and conflict can be traced back to post-Cold War concerns with the emergence of "new wars," particularly in Africa, and their international effects in the 1990s (Duffield, 2001a; Kaldor, 1999). These concerns were accelerated after the 9/11 attacks, with the realization that development failures in low-income countries could have direct security repercussions in highly industrialized countries. More recently, and particularly related to Afghanistan and Iraq, there has been a resurgence of interest in the role of international development in potentially "winning hearts and minds" as part of a changing U.S.-led counterinsurgency war (Duffield, 2008; English, 2010; Gregory, 2008; Hayden, 2009; Hoffman, 2009; Lopez, 2010; Mezran, 2009; Miller & Mills, 2010; Zambernardi, 2010).

Linked to these post-Cold War developments, we have witnessed an increased capacity and interest by Western nations, generally under the leadership of the United States, to engage and intervene in a wide range of high-profile conflicts from the Balkans to Rwanda, Somalia, Sudan, Iraq, and Afghanistan. Importantly, these interventions also were framed discursively as "humanitarian interventions" (Fearon, 2008, p. 52), drawing on issues of human rights, democracy, and freedom for their justification, paralleling the intentions and objectives and discourses of many of the international humanitarian and development organizations. On occasion they also were preceded by calls from some humanitarian organizations themselves for armed intervention (Roberts, 2000). This newfound willingness to directly intervene into sovereign states reflected a real shift in the post-Cold War balance of power. During the Cold War the threat of superpower retaliation or UN Security Council veto would have blocked this type of direct intervention by either side across the Cold War divide.

This new "humanitarian interventionism" was accompanied by a massive increase in the number of humanitarian and development actors operating in conflict situations. By 1995, humanitarian agencies were responding to a total of 28 complex emergencies around the world, increasing from just 5 in 1985 (Bradbury, 1995; Slim, 1996). By the mid-1990s, emergency spending had increased by over 600% from its mid-1980s point to over 3.5 billion USD and has continued to rise (Fearon, 2008). According to the 2008 Reality of Aid Report, "Aid allocations to the most severely conflict-affected countries. . . . increased from 9.3% of total ODA (Official Development Assistance) in 2000 (for 12 countries) to 20.4% (for 10 countries) in 2006" (p. 8). Coupled with the general increase in ODA during the same period, aid to conflict-affected countries nearly tripled in real terms between 2000 and 2006. In 2007, according to a recent Organisation for Economic Co-operation and Development-Development Assistance Committee (OECD-DAC) report, 38.4% of total OECD country ODA (37.2 billion USD) went to conflict and fragile states (2008, p. 8).

In a similar manner, military peace-keeping, which is not counted under OECD-DAC rules as official development assistance, has increased exponentially over the past 2 decades. In 1994, total UN peace-keeping expenditure was estimated to be in the region of 3.2 billion USD a year (Duffield, 1997, p. 539). The OECD-DAC (2008, p. 11) reported that United Nations peace-keeping expenditures had reached an historic high, with 20 ongoing missions. It also noted that personnel had increased by over 700% since 1999 to 110,000 personnel with a budget of 7 billion USD.

What is also clear from the literature is that the distribution of official development aid among severely conflict-affected countries was, and remains, highly unequal. In 2006, Iraq and Afghanistan accounted for over 60% of all aid to conflict-affected countries. Another eight countries shared the remaining 36.7% (Reality of Aid, 2008, p. 217). In 2007, of the 38.4% of total ODA (37.2 billion USD) that went to conflict and fragile states, over half was directed to just five countries: Iraq (23%), Afghanistan (9.9%), and Ethiopia, Pakistan, and Sudan (sharing 17% of the total) (OECD-DAC, 2008, p. 8). Most strikingly, the almost 50 billion USD of new resources for Iraq, Afghanistan, and Pakistan since 2000 "represent[s] the largest ever donor country commitments for aid" (Reality of Aid, 2008, p. 207). Figure 4.1 demonstrates these disparities.

From the evidence presented in the figure, we can clearly see how international development policy has become increasingly intertwined with security concerns. As part of this trend, the lines between military, humanitarian, and development interventions are increasingly blurred. Since the mid-2000s, many of the major international development agencies (DfID, USAID, the Dutch Ministry of Foreign Affairs, CIDA, AusAID) have developed a new policy related to international development assistance known as the "3D" approach (Diplomacy, Defense, and Development), which seeks to integrate and embed development assistance within national diplomatic and security priorities. This "3D" approach appears to be institutionalizing the previously ad-hoc merging of security and development within Western governments' aid policy, which is likely to have an effect well beyond the current conflict epicenters of Iraq and Afghanistan (Keenan, 2008).

WHERE DOES EDUCATION FIT IN?

Similar to trends in the broader field of international development, the rise in interest about education and conflict appears to have been prompted initially by a human rights-driven agenda. The late 1990s saw a mounting realization that reaching the international targets of Education for All would be impossible without addressing conflict-affected states, where it was estimated more than 50% of the world's out-of-school children reside (Save the Children, 2010). As intervention expanded, in the variety of forms outlined above, there emerged a growing recognition of the importance of education delivery in conflict and post-conflict zones. Education, like food and shelter, slowly became seen as part of the core building blocks of human development and a necessary and vital part of humanitarian response in conflict situations in particular (Save the Children, 2007, 2010). As described in more detail by Peter Buckland in this volume (see Chapter 10), since 2008, there has been a Global Education Cluster, headed by UNICEF and the International Save the Children Alliance, that coordinates the educational response in emergency situations as part of the Inter-Agency Standing Committee (IASC), which assumes overall coordination and develops policy involving UN and non-UN humanitarian partners operating in conflict zones.

Central to the rise in prominence of education within conflict situations have been the actions of the Inter-Agency Network for Education in Emergencies (INEE), which emerged out of the World Education Forum in Dakar and is a network created to improve inter-agency communication and collaboration within the context of education in emergencies. The INEE has proved to be an effective lobbying, advocacy, and policy coordination institution. As with the more

Figure 4.1. Fifty Percent of Net ODA Has Benefited Just 5 of 48 Fragile and Conflict-Affected Countries

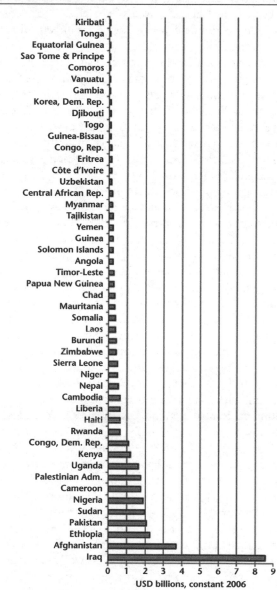

USD billions, constant 2006

Source: OECD-DAC, 2008, p. 9

general increases in development aid to conflict-affected zones, increases in aid to education in conflict-affected countries are due at least partly to the capacity of organizations like Save the Children, INEE, and UNICEF to successfully lobby for an expansion of their own mandates and activities in education—by justifying why education service delivery should be at the heart of humanitarian and development responses to conflict and post-conflict situations. As Lynn Davies in this volume suggests, an important part of the justification comes from the notion that education can play a potentially catalytic and preventive role in situations of conflict (Bush & Saltarelli, 2000; Smith & Vaux, 2003). Furthermore, over the years practitioners and the agencies they represent have developed a variety of approaches to address the particular needs of children in conflict and post-conflict situations that can deal with the often deep and long-lasting psychological effects of war and conflict (Aguilar & Retamal, 2009).

Further impetus for attention to education and conflict emerged after the events of 9/11, when Northern governments became increasingly concerned with the relationship between zones of conflict in low-income countries and their own citizens' (in)security (Duffield, 2010). Prompted by concern over radical madrasas operating as terrorist training camps, out-of-school youth being recruited into insurgent groups, and educational systems failing millions of poor people around the world, there was a merging of concern and interest by international development agencies and national security institutions focusing on the importance of education's role in conflict-affected states. More recently, and linked to the failure of the U.S.-led military strategy in Iraq and Afghanistan, there has been an appreciation of the role of international development, and particularly education therein, as forms of "soft power" to "win hearts and minds" in broader U.S.-led counterinsurgency strategies (Gregory, 2008; Hayden, 2009). School-building initiatives in Afghanistan, education-based deradicalization programs, and education for reintegrating ex-combatants into society have become key tools in the global war on terror.

In its recent *Learning for All: DfID's Education Strategy 2010–2015*, the UK government's Department for International Development (DfID) committed itself to spending around 50% of all international assistance in conflict-affected states, including 50% of the UK's overall aid, to education. Other bilateral development agencies appear to be following a similar path (see Lopes-Cardozo & Novelli, 2010). As a result, concerns have been raised as to whether there is a move away from a focus on the poorest countries and regions in the world, and whether the increased presence of development workers in conflict-affected states, and their closer proximity to partisan military forces (both national and international), has placed development workers under increased danger of attack. There is also concern that NGOs' relationships with the populations they serve in conflict affected-states are being transformed, and in many cases weakened and undermined (Stoddard, Harmer, et al., 2006, 2009).

In summing up, we can say that post-Cold War Western interventionism has led to a massive increase in both peace-keeping and development assistance directed to conflict and post-conflict countries, resulting in an expansion of humanitarian and development personnel and a broadening of the nature of the activities that these organizations engage in. Furthermore, rather than the steady flows of funds toward key allies during the Cold War, resources appear now to both flow and shift swiftly toward countries where key conjunctural conflicts or potential conflicts are considered of strategic importance to Western governments. A form of "geopolitical fire fighting" might be an apt metaphor for this process, which is a sign perhaps that development aid, and perhaps development itself, is now concerned increasingly with containing, managing, and engaging with conflicts rather than acting as a catalyst for sustainable growth (Duffield, 2007).

UNDERSTANDING THE SECURITY AND DEVELOPMENT NEXUS

Before elaborating on the effects that this new approach to education in conflict is having, this section briefly explores the way the relationship between security and development is conceptualized in academic and policy circles. Within the social sciences, different views have emerged about the underlying causes of security problems and conflict, and what type of interventions therefore might be appropriate (Duffield, 2001b; Jung, 2003; Münkler, 2005). Picciotto (2005) lays out three broad theoretical approaches to the relationship between development and conflict, which, while not comprehensive, offer important insights for our research. The first draws on the modernization theorist Samuel Huntington (1993, 1996) and his thesis surrounding a "clash of civilizations." The second draws on the work of Mark Duffield (2001a, 2001b) and explores the relationship between structural inequalities within the global economy and polity, and the ongoing generation of violence. The third draws on the work of the academic and World Bank adviser Paul Collier (1999) and explores intrastate conflict from a neo-liberal rational choice perspective, where violent acts are regarded as generated by individual motives of "greed." Each of these underlying theories is likely to lead to very different developmental and educational policy interventions in the field.

Clash of Civilizations

Huntington's post-Cold War work (1993, 1996) argued that while previous conflicts engaged "princes," "nation states," and then "ideologies" (Cold War), today's conflicts are located around civilizations. He suggests that cultural differences have become the key driver of global insecurity both within and between states, with the key conflict being between Islam and Christianity. While Huntington's work has been widely criticized (Said, 2001; Sen, 2006), it was nevertheless influential in Washington policy circles, particularly under the Bush administration.

Within this worldview, one can see how educational policy interventions would likely be targeted at addressing the cultural obstacles and differences that divide "civilizational" groups. This can help us to understand why, in the present period, one of the central thrusts of USAID's educational aid thinking is directed particularly, although not exclusively, toward altering negative perceptions of the West within Islamic societies. According to one prominent USAID administrator, James Kunder (2005), the American "education approach responds to the overall goal of moderating radical intolerance and anti-Western ideologies" (p. 10).

Structural Inequalities and (In)security

Duffield (2001b) argues that increased violence is a product of the highly exclusionary contemporary "informational economy and polity" where large geographic parts of the world are marginalized. He suggests that the neo-liberal global economy and its related governance mechanisms lock many groups out of the benefits of "globalization" and increase the likelihood of entry into illicit activities, such as crime and violence. Intervention, drawing on this way of thinking, is likely to try to address forms of "human security" and "insecurity" that produce violence. Here the traditional literature on development meets security studies, and the interventions seek to address issues of social exclusion, marginalization, and inequality. Elements of this kind of conceptualization are evident in many of the major agencies' policies and programs. DfID (2005a), for instance, notes that

> UK development assistance helps build global peace and stability for the longer term, by reducing inequality and exclusion, supporting the development of capable, responsible states and reducing conflict. Money spent on reducing poverty is money spent for a more secure world. (p. 23)

The United Nations Development Programme (UNDP) (2005) also acknowledges this link.

> Development in poor countries is the front line in the battle for global peace and collective security. The problem with the current battle plan is an over-developed military strategy and an under-developed strategy for human security. . . . While there is no automatic link between poverty and civil conflict, violent outcomes are more likely in societies marked by deep polarization, weak institutions and chronic poverty. The threats posed by terrorism demand a global response. So do the threats posed by human insecurity in the broader sense. Indeed, the "war against terror" will never be won unless human security is extended and strengthened. (pp. 12, 152)

This type of thinking about education and conflict tends toward a focus on the underlying structural reasons for the emergence of conflict. Poverty reduction and policies addressing the poor and marginalized that seek to give them a greater stake in society are favored interventions. This link between poverty and conflict, however, may divert resources away from addressing the poorest and most marginalized population groups in nonconflict zones. It also suggests shifting aid away from those countries whose conflicts are least likely to affect "Western" security interests, with aid shifting to countries that pose a greater direct threat to Western interests. The data presented on both Iraq and Afghanistan (see Figure 4.1) demonstrate how uneven development funding has become.

Homo-Economicus and Rational Choice Theories of War and Conflict

The third and final major approach reflects mainstream (neo)-liberal ideas (Collier, 1999). Drawing on rational choice theories of human action, Collier suggests that wars are driven less by justified "grievances" and far more by personal and collective "greed." In this approach, humans are viewed as engaged in conflict as "economic agents" seeking out profit. As a result, the route to peace and security is not through addressing inequality and structural exclusion, or by "winning hearts and minds," but through cutting off access to the resources of "violent actors."

This approach has gained a privileged position in the United States and the World Bank over the past decade. In practical terms this results in attempts to cut off financial networks and illicit activities that lead to the purchase of weapons. This framework treats security issues as crimes and seeks to increase the "opportunity costs" of engagement by cutting off funds and addressing "enemy" groups through military force. While this strategy appears to have less substantive education content, it does place increased emphasis on "good governance," involving, for example, training civil servants to prevent corruption.

In summary, each of these theories sheds some light on aspects of the security issue, while obscuring other important aspects. Both Huntington and Collier avoid issues of poverty and inequality, while both Collier and Duffield avoid issues of cultural conflict. Being able to identify these different theories of conflict enables us to understand why most development actors agree on the importance of the relationship between development and conflict, but for very different rationales. Furthermore, it helps us to understand the underlying rationales for educational interventions and their implications.

EDUCATION AND THE MERGING OF SECURITY AND DEVELOPMENT

Having laid out some tentative thoughts on the broader literature on conflict and security studies, I now turn to an analysis of the ways in which education gets caught up in these agendas. In many ways development aid has always been political, and perhaps the merging of security and development interests should come as no surprise. During the post-World War II period, aid appears to have been allotted largely on the basis of where a country stood in the great Cold War confrontation (Lundborg, 1998; Christian Aid, 2004; T. Y. Wang, 1999). Crucially, the geography of aid was based less on perceived humanitarian need and more on political alliances, and donors often turned a blind eye to human rights violations and repression in "friendly" states.

What is less well known is the way education aid was implicated in these processes. In this section I will explore the case of Afghanistan during the Cold War, as an extreme example of the way education, development institutions, and education practitioners can become caught up in the bigger geopolitical conflicts of our time. My intention is to demonstrate how "education and development" activities can be captured and subverted by security and military agencies, which then in the name of "development" carry out activities that seek to contribute to the war effort and undermine long-term and sustainable education and development practices and processes.

USAID and Cold War Education in Pakistan/Afghanistan

After the Soviet Union invaded Afghanistan in 1979, the United States and its Cold War allies sought to undermine the occupation through a variety of means. One central plank of the strategy was to assist the various "mujahideen" resistance fighters in their guerrilla war. Much of the resources for this process were channeled via Pakistan, and many of the fighters were recruited from youth living in the Afghan refugee camps that developed along Pakistan's northern border and from Pakistani youth studying in religious madrasas. Education appears to have played a key part in this recruitment process. In 1984, a USAID-funded project was begun. The project was led by the Center for Afghanistan Studies at the University of Nebraska–Omaha, to develop textbooks for use in the camps. As the International Crisis Group (2002) notes:

> Written by American Afghanistan experts and anti-Soviet Afghan educators, they aimed at promoting jihadi values and militant training among Afghans. USAID paid the University of Nebraska 51 million dollars from 1984 to 1994 to develop and design these textbooks, which were mostly printed in Pakistan. Over 13 million were distributed at Afghan refugee camps and Pakistani madrasas where students learnt basic math by counting dead Russians and Kalashnikov rifles. (p. 13)

Craig (2000), in research on primary education in Afghanistan, provides evidence of the nature of these texts from a 4th-grade math textbook that raises the following question:

The speed of a Kalashnikov bullet is 800 meters per second. If a Russian is at a distance of 3,200 meters from a mujahid, and that mujahid aims at the Russian's head, calculate how many seconds it will take for the bullet to strike the Russian in the forehead. (pp. 92–93)

When the Taliban eventually took power in the wake of the Soviet withdrawal and the defeat the Afghan government, the curriculum was implemented across the country. Perhaps even more shocking is the fact that, according to Stephens and Ottaway (2002), even in the wake of the defeat of the Taliban after the U.S.-led invasion in 2002, the text continued to be used. They state that UNICEF, in a campaign in 2002 to get all children in Afghanistan, and especially girls, back to school, reprinted the texts for widespread distribution. UNICEF eventually recognized the error and destroyed the texts, and this "wartime curriculum" was changed into a "peacetime curriculum."

Meanwhile, in Pakistan, many madrasas continued to use the textbooks. It is these same madrasas that were to become the focus of U.S. concern as alleged promoters of Islamic violence, militancy, and anti-U.S. feeling. Restructuring the curriculum in these schools has now become a top priority for USAID, yet critical self-reflection on USAID's role in producing the "hate" curriculum is conspicuously absent.

From Post-Cold War De-Politicization to Post-9/11 Securitization

After the end of the Cold War, many development policymakers and stakeholders hoped that the type of activities recounted above would become things of the past, and that a new era of development cooperation would be born, free of the damaging politicization of aid of the Cold War years. There is evidence that this was beginning to happen. While initially there was a drop in overall development aid, this was followed by both an increase in aid and a shift of focus in development policy and education policy toward the least developed countries and poorest population groups. This shift led to an increasing focus on Sub-Saharan Africa and increased efforts to improve the coordination of international development policy among major donors. These efforts culminated in the Millennium Development Goals—and the Education for All objectives therein—sector-wide approaches to education, the Paris Declaration, and so on (K. King, 2007; Mundy, 2002, 2006). While these efforts were not without critiques, there was a sense that at least the rhetoric of development policy was heading in the right direction, even if the financing was not always forthcoming (Global Campaign for Education, 2009).

However, in the post-9/11 environment, the role and rationale of international development assistance and its geographical distribution began to be revised away from human development objectives and toward military and security objectives. The opening quote of this chapter from Colin Powell marks this shift in stark terms, and it and other similar comments fueled the concern of many within the development community that the United States and other Western powers were prioritizing "terrorism" over development. During the Bush administration, development and humanitarian organizations often were treated simplistically as "force multipliers," and while the language has softened under the Obama administration, the central thrust of linking development aid to national security objectives has remained intact. In June 2008, USAID released its new "civil military cooperation policy," explaining that: "Development is also recognized as a key element of any successful whole-of-government counterterrorism and counterinsurgency effort" (p. 1).

While the United States, in the wake of 9/11, was the most active in initially promoting this merging of security interest and development, the European Union (2003) quickly followed suit:

> European assistance programmes, military and civilian capabilities from Member States and other instruments such as the European Development Fund. All of these can have an impact on our security and on that of third countries. Security is the first condition for development. (p. 13)

For both the United States and Europe, then, national security and international development have become increasingly intertwined, and this has been extended to the policy documents of DfID and other major bilateral and multilateral institutions, reflected in the fact that they now talk of the "3D" approach as a natural and normalized strategy.

In September 2009 then-UK Prime Minister Gordon Brown, in a speech on Afghanistan, made clear the links between the need to be in Afghanistan and UK homeland security:

> The Director-General of our security service has said that three quarters of the most serious plots against the UK have had links that reach back into these mountains. At present the threat comes mainly from the Pakistan side, but if the insurgency succeeds in Afghanistan, Al Qaeda and other terrorist groups will once again be able to use it as a sanctuary to train, plan and launch attacks on Britain and the rest of the world.

He also stressed that "development" and, within that, "education" were central planks in the UK strategy of both "winning hearts and minds" in Afghanistan and protecting the UK from attack:

> When the Taleban ran the country, only a million children were in school, all boys. Today there are 6.6 million—with more than 2 million girls. With the help of British development funding, 10,000 new teachers were recruited from 2007

to 2008, with more expected in 2009. This is an investment in the future of Afghanistan, in its stability and its resilience against extremism—and therefore in our security. (Brown, 2009)

While the renewed commitment of Western governments to the importance of development might be welcomed, this "joined up" whole-of-government approach brings with it dangers for the development and humanitarian community of being taken over by the generally more powerful security wing of national governments, precisely as happened in the case of Afghanistan, discussed earlier. As the failure of both the Iraq and Afghanistan occupations is becoming increasingly evident, so it appears that there is an increased emphasis on the "hearts and minds" strategies (read: development) alongside the military activities. This raises questions as to how those organizations working in conflict and post-conflict zones separate the "military" and "security" interest and their "development" and "humanitarian" activities (Woods, 2005). What might be the cost for these organizations of being seen as too close to certain belligerent forces? Will long-term goals of development be subordinated to the short-term objectives of winning the hearts and minds of target population groups? Among humanitarian organizations this has provoked heated debate, with some announcing the end of humanitarianism. One researcher from Médecins Sans Frontières raised the difficult problem of carrying out humanitarian and development activities under the overarching rule of an occupying power, arguing that whether they directly engage with the occupying forces or not,

> over time, the resentment that often builds up within a population against foreign rule can lead to an equally violent rejection of all changes brought about by outside actors, their claimed neutrality notwithstanding. (Crombe, 2006)

The merging of security and development thus appears as a process of reinterpreting both the purposes and the practices of development—seeing activities as having potential "security benefits." An illustration of this is the prevalence of references to the role of education in the U.S. counterterrorism strategies elaborated in the *Patterns of Global Terrorism Annual Reports* (since 2004 renamed *Country Reports on Terrorism*). As an example, the 2007 report, in Chapter 5, Terrorist Safe Havens, subsection 7, focuses on Basic Education in Muslim Countries. In this section it notes that

> The Department of State, USAID, and other U.S. agencies continued to support an increased focus on education in predominantly Muslim countries and those with significant Muslim populations. The United States' approach stresses mobilizing public and private resources as partners to improve access, quality, and the relevance of education, with a specific emphasis on developing civic-mindedness

in young people. In many Muslim-majority countries, such as Afghanistan and Yemen, the challenge was to increase country capacity to provide universal access to primary education and literacy. (U.S. State Department 2008, p. 243)

Similarly, as part of the U.S. military's counterinsurgency strategy in places such as Iraq and Afghanistan, "humanitarian and civic assistance" can include such nonemergency services as constructing schools, performing dental procedures, and even vaccinating the livestock of farmers (Brigety, 2008, p. 5). Crucially, it appears that educational provision (particularly for girls) has become a key discursive justification for the military intervention in Afghanistan, and educational progress a means of demonstrating the success of the occupation. As a result, attacking education seems to be a key strategy of the Taliban, with attacks on education in Afghanistan both widespread and increasing. According to Human Rights Watch, educational systems and personnel are attacked for three overlapping reasons:

> first, opposition to the government and its international supporters by Taliban or other armed groups . . . ; second, ideological opposition to education other than that offered in madrassas (Islamic schools), and in particular opposition to girls' education; and third, opposition to the authority of the central government and the rule of law by criminal groups. (Human Rights Watch, 2006, p. 33)

Clearly in the case of Afghanistan, education has become a central battleground in the war and emphasizes the increasing dangers that all education personnel and students face there. This also appears to be occurring in Somalia (United Nations, 2008) and Iraq (Bonham Carter, 2007; O'Malley, 2007). Most problematically, both sides in these polarized contexts increasingly are interpreting education provision as a battle between Western secular education and Islamic madrasa education (McClure, 2009).

The dilemma for education aid workers is that the counterinsurgency and counter-terrorism strategies of the Western powers become the perceived major rationale for educational interventions. While activities may remain largely the same, their discursive representation means that they can be interpreted as part of the "war effort": civilian modes of counterinsurgency, aimed at winning hearts and minds and producing certain types of subjectivities. In doing so they increase the danger for all involved.

In situations such as Iraq and Afghanistan, it appears that humanitarian and development organizations have become overwhelmed by the counterinsurgency agenda, making it almost impossible to distance themselves from the occupying forces and present a picture of neutrality. As Torrente (2004) notes:

> The U.S. government failed to preserve space for the politically independent and principled role of humanitarian organizations. Instead, the United States sought

to bring humanitarian aid efforts under its control and claimed that all assistance supports its cause. . . . The U.S. efforts to associate assistance with its political objectives have jeopardized the ability of humanitarian organizations to distinguish themselves from all parties and to provide aid based solely on need during times of crisis. (p. 3)

This situation has worsened with the establishment by the Western occupying countries in both Iraq and Afghanistan of Provisional Reconstruction Teams that under the control of the military also carry out development-like activities such as the construction of schools. In 2009, an alliance of NGOs operating in Afghanistan produced a strong report condemning the behavior of the Western occupying forces. They alleged that the military (particularly the U.S. and French) were continuing to use "unmarked, white vehicles . . . conventionally used by the UN and aid agencies" and were carrying out infrastructure work traditionally done by development organizations as part of their counterinsurgency "hearts and minds" strategies (Waldman, 2009, p. 5). All this, they argued, was producing the "blurring of the civil–military distinction . . . [and] contributed to a diminution in the perceived independence of NGOs, increased the risk for aid workers, and reduced the areas in which NGOs can safely operate" (p. 9).

They alleged that these activities were contributing to the causes of

a marked increase in violence against aid workers globally, which has a range of causes, however one important factor is military engagement in assistance activities. In Afghanistan, such engagement is extensive and wide-ranging, and has blurred the line between military and humanitarian actors. This has adversely affected NGO security, endangered the lives of NGO workers, and restricted their ability to operate. NGOs are being increasingly subject to direct threats and attacks, and in 2008, 31 NGO workers were killed, twice as many as in 2007. This is significantly decreasing humanitarian operating space: currently, large parts of the country are inaccessible to humanitarian actors, leaving many communities deprived of humanitarian assistance. NGOs regularly receive warnings that any perceived association with military forces will make them a target. In many areas, NGO offices and staff have been searched for links to the military, and threatened with severe consequences if such links are established. Likewise, NGO projects have been forced to close after visits from PRTs or foreign donor agencies in heavily armed escorts. In the aftermath of such visits, communities have informed NGOs that they can no longer guarantee the safety of project staff. (Waldman, 2009, p. 16)

In a further report, Stoddard, Harmer, and colleagues (2009) noted that in Afghanistan locals were no longer making a distinction between those organizations working with the military and those that were not. They suggested that for Afghan locals, "all Western-based international humanitarian organizations are judged as partisan" (Stoddard, Harmer, et al., 2009, p. 6). This breakdown in trust in humanitarian and development organizations can only increase the dangers that aid workers face.

While the cases of Iraq and Afghanistan are indeed extreme, it does appear that there is a growing tendency for humanitarian and development organizations, because of their largely "Western" nature, home location, and political orientation, to be targeted in locations where the "West" is seen, at least by a substantial section of the population, as the enemy. That is, aid workers are being targeted not just because they somehow are collaborating with the occupying forces, but more because they are seen as an integral part of that force. While attacks on aid workers, and all civilians, are war crimes and can never be justified, what seems clear is that the increasing blurring of the lines between Western military objectives and the practices of humanitarian and development organizations seems to be increasing the danger for these organizations.

> When governments drape their military and political actions in the cloak of humanitarian concerns, they undermine humanitarian action's essential purpose: the unconditional provision of assistance to those in need. When all aid efforts are presented and perceived as being at the service of political and military objectives, it is more difficult and dangerous for independent humanitarian organizations to carry out their work. (Torrente, 2004, p. 29)

Furthermore, the relationship between education and this new geopolitics of the war on terror does not stop in the direct theatre of operations. Increasingly, aid is being targeted at strategic locations in the post-Cold War world, and education is seen as a vital mechanism in the battle of hearts and minds across the Muslim world (Indonesia, Yemen, Phillipines). Investment in low-income educational systems also can serve as a sweetener for cooperation in other domains. The increases in aid flows to Kyrgstan in Central Asia, and Djibouti in Africa, represent examples of flows of aid to education post-9/11 that are occurring in parallel with the development of U.S. military bases used as launching pads for military activities in Afghanistan and Somalia, respectively.

CONCLUSION

On August 13, 2008, my friend and colleague Jackie Kirk was murdered by Taliban militants in Afghanistan along with three other aid workers from the International Rescue Committee (a U.S.-based NGO working on issues of refugees and internally displaced peoples). They were attacked while traveling on the road to Kabul in a clearly marked "IRC" car. Jackie was a brilliant Canadian gender, education, and conflict specialist. The Taliban argued that Jackie and her colleagues were part of the "illegal occupation forces." She saw herself as neither "force multiplier" nor "enemy combatant," and her tragic death, and that of many other humanitarian workers who died in Afghanistan and elsewhere, reflect the much deeper and ongoing problem of this increased blurring of the lines between military and humanitarian operations in contexts of war and conflict that I have outlined above.

Our field of research and practice is now becoming caught up in powerful political agendas and strategies based on short-term military and political advantage, with potentially long-term and catastrophic effects for our credibility, effectiveness, and security, and to the detriment of the people we serve. As education and development academics, practitioners, and policymakers, it is time for us to think through our own relationships and alliances, what we agree with and what we oppose, and to put forward alternative strategies and proposals that resist the ongoing militarization of our field.

CHAPTER 5

Addressing Gender Disparities in Education in Contexts of Crisis, Post-Crisis, and State Fragility

Jackie Kirk

Of the 43 million children living in crisis-affected countries who are not in school, well over half are girls (International Save the Children Alliance, 2006). Crisis situations create challenges for girls to gain access to education. But crises also can create some windows of opportunity for improving educational access and quality for girls and women, as well as for education to contribute to enhanced gender equality. There are no simple relationships among crisis, gender, and education. Nevertheless, as girls are disproportionately marginalized from education in such contexts, addressing the interconnected gender- and crisis-related barriers to quality, relevant education is an important rights issue.

It is important to acknowledge that women and girls experience crises differently from men and boys. Crises affect girls' education opportunities in particular ways. School-going girls often are forced to drop out, and those excluded in pre-crisis times may have even less chance of access. In times of conflict and crisis, when resources are scarce and families are intent on survival, education discrimination in favor of boys can be even stronger. Girls who are further marginalized by factors such as disability, ethnicity, and location are even more likely to miss out on education. For women and girls, sexual and gender-based violence (GBV) is a particular risk. As discussed in the following sections, this risk affects both access to and quality of education, with particular repercussions for adolescent girls.

This chapter is an abridged version of Kirk, J. (2008a). Addressing gender disparities in education in contexts of crisis, postcrisis and state fragility. In M. Tembon & L. Fort (Eds.), *Girls' education in the 21st century: Gender equality, empowerment, and economic growth* (pp. 153–180). Washington, DC: The World Bank. Used with permission.

At the same time, as mentioned above, new and improved learning opportunities for girls may be created in a crisis or post-crisis situation. The involvement of new education actors (e.g., nongovernmental organizations [NGOs] and community-based organizations), additional funding, as well as shifts in gender roles and relations create opportunities. These issues have serious implications for the ways in which education in emergencies is designed and implemented. Education interventions should be both preventive and responsive, and also build on any new opportunities that are created for gender equality.

This chapter presents some of the prevailing gender inequalities in education programming during emergencies. The chapter discusses some of the concrete global policy developments that may support increased attention to gender equality and GBV. These developments include the Minimum Standards for Education in Emergencies, Chronic Crises, and Early Reconstruction developed by the Inter-Agency Network for Education in Emergencies (INEE), and the Education Cluster within the UN humanitarian reform processes.

CHALLENGES AND OPPORTUNITIES: GENDER ISSUES IN EDUCATION IN EMERGENCIES AND FRAGILE STATES

Access to Education for Girls

In contexts of crisis, post-crisis, and state fragility, gender issues in education may look similar to issues in development contexts. Access to education for girls is limited by factors such as accessibility of schools, girls' workloads, sibling care, early marriage, and motherhood. Yet there are other specific issues and aspects of these limitations for girls that are of particular concern in unstable contexts. These include, for example, safety and security issues, which can be of great concern to parents. The journey to and from school may place girls at considerable risk of attack and sexual violence, especially in areas in which fighting forces are present. Early marriage and motherhood tend to mean the end of schooling opportunities for girls, and the rates of early marriage and teen pregnancy tend to be particularly high in insecure environments. This may be the result of high levels of GBV, as well as parents' desire to secure early marriage for their daughters for both their protection and economic survival. Feelings of insecurity and uncertainty, frustration with the current situation, lack of access to education and other opportunities, and a sense of futility among youth also may fuel risk-taking behaviors such as early sexual activity, as well as aggressive and violent attitudes toward women and girls by men and boys (UNESCO & UNHCR, 2007).

Although conflict can bring with it some positive changes in gender roles and expectations, conflict both exacerbates inequities in education for women and girls and increases vulnerabilities (World Vision International, 2001).

Gender roles and stereotypes often are reinforced by the need to protect women and girls and by the additional time and energy spent in traditional roles such as collecting water. In southern Sudan, the work of women and girls has doubled or tripled, and yet the situation has left boys with no new or heavier work. There is very little time or energy left for girls to attend school, yet schooling for boys is planned to give them something to do (Obura, 2001). Conflict and its aftermath also can be a time when gender roles have to change. The practical and economic imperatives of survival and reconstruction take priority over education, especially for girls and women, who may be forced into new roles such as petty trading to generate income.

Other issues for girls in crisis include limited access to school places (when schools are destroyed or just fail to operate as usual). Education for all children suffers. But because of their different social positions—possibilities for movement outside of the home or community and income-generation activities to pay school fees and other costs—boys often are more able than girls to seek out opportunities for learning. Protection risks also may inhibit women teachers' mobility and access to school and professional development opportunities. In some contexts, the lack of women teachers also creates a barrier to girls' access to education, particularly older girls in upper primary and secondary classes (Kirk, 2006a).

Quality in Education for Girls

There are many issues related to the quality of education for girls and young women that, although similar to issues in other development contexts, may have particular dimensions in contexts of crisis, post-crisis, and state fragility. These include safety and security, the relevance of the curriculum and learning content, and the quality of instruction.

Recent research indicates the sad reality that, in many contexts, GBV is inextricably linked with education. Girls may be at risk of sexual attack, harassment, and abuse on the way to and from school. Teachers or male students may perpetrate violence within the school buildings and grounds. Furthermore, girls who have no other way to raise the necessary money for school fees, books, uniforms, and other "hidden costs" may agree to transactional sex. In conflict contexts, there are additional layers of complexity to examine. The vulnerability of girls to sexual violence may be increased because of the presence of high numbers of security and fighting forces in a location and forced or "voluntary" recruitment into the fighting forces. In addition, security and survival imperatives may pressure families to ensure protection through early marriage. Furthermore, sexual violence—rape in particular—has become a weapon of war widely used as part of the struggle for power and domination of one ethnic or religious group over another. Through all these scenarios runs a common theme of aggressive masculinities, the socialization of men and boys to assert their masculinity through physical and sexual domination of women and girls. In such contexts, violent and asymmetrical power relations between men and women and between young boys and girls are normalized. Men and boys may learn to constitute their identities as fighters and defenders of the family honor—but as teachers and male students, also through the sexual abuse and exploitation of women and girls (Enloe, 1989, 2000; Kirk, 2008c; Whitworth, 2004).

The relevance and appropriateness of curricula is also an important issue. It is common for curricula to be more focused on the experiences of boys, not to reflect the specific experiences of girls and women, and not to explicitly challenge gender stereotypes or to promote gender equality. International Rescue Committee (IRC) reviews of sample learning materials used in refugee camp programs in Ethiopia and Sierra Leone revealed startling disparities between the portrayal of women and men and of boys and girls. There was very little presence of women and girls—and then only in roles of servitude, assistance, and vulnerability (Kirk, 2004a, 2004b). Various possible factors contribute to crisis-affected contexts, including the lack of a coherent, unified curriculum and the fact that curriculum is often itself a factor in conflict. For example, this has been the case in southern Sudan for many years and even since the signing of the Comprehensive Peace Agreements. In the absence of a full southern Sudanese curriculum, schools make do with a combination of materials from neighboring countries. With such scarcity of resources, gender responsiveness is not a priority. Especially in the case of ethnic or religious conflicts, the importance of curriculum may be reflected in the peace agreement texts. However, even in conflict contexts in which the rights of women and girls have been violated, gender issues in curriculum are not necessarily discussed. Curriculum may be used to reinforce traditional notions of family honor dependent on women's and girls' behavior (Saigol, 1995, 2000).

An additional, important point relating to the relevance and responsiveness of girls' education is the quality of instruction provided in schools and learning spaces. In many crisis-affected contexts, communities rely on inexperienced and underqualified teachers. Although NGOs and other partners may support communities with rapid teacher training and ongoing supervision, the teachers may be struggling with basic teaching methods. Gender equality in the classroom is not prioritized. Training tends to focus on basic teaching and classroom management skills. Gender training may be considered only later in the teachers' careers.

Furthermore, factors such as few female school graduates, safety and security concerns, and increased household chores and income-generation responsibilities mean that in many situations the teaching profession is dominated by men. Although this may not necessarily create a specific barrier for girls, the lack of female role models and confidantes in the school creates learning environments in which girls may not feel particularly supported, encouraged, or represented. It also means that the activities in the school inevitably reflect the experiences of the boys and men who dominate.

Opportunities in Education for Girls

Graça Machel (2001a) stresses the importance of education for all children in times of conflict: "Education gives shape and structure to children's lives. When everything around is chaos, schools can be a haven of security that is vital to the well-being of war-affected children and their communities" (p. 31). However, she also points out that this is especially important for girls: "Education, especially literacy and numeracy, is precisely what girls need during and after armed conflict. Education can help prepare adolescent girls for the new roles and responsibilities that they are often obliged to take on in conflict situations" (p. 32). Machel's statement adds extra weight to the EFA and MDG imperatives and should encourage different actors at international, national, and local levels to increase efforts to ensure quality and relevant education for girls affected by conflict.

While highlighting many of the education challenges for girls and young women affected by crises, it is also important to highlight how, in certain circumstances, crises can create new opportunities for girls to access education. Crises sometimes can create windows of opportunity for education and particularly for improvements in access and quality. One example of this is in the earthquake-affected areas of Pakistan, where access to education for girls in the remote, mountainous, and conservative communities was very limited. After the earthquake, however, girls who moved with their families to IDP camps in the valleys were able to attend school for the first time. Factors that allowed this included the accessibility of NGO-supported schools with women teachers within a safe, walking distance from the students' homes, the reduction in household chores and other tasks for girls in the IDP camps, and the increased parental confidence in the quality of education assured by NGOs (Kirk, 2008c). Although in general the conflict in Nepal has had a devastating impact on education, there is also some evidence of a positive impact on girls' education opportunities. For example, in a region affected by Maoist insurgency, parents have sent their sons away to school in Katmandu to avoid the politicization of schools and campuses, but girls have stayed and entered the local schools (Manchanda, 2001). Afghan refugee girls and women teachers in Pakistan also have been able to access education opportunities that were denied to girls and women inside Afghanistan. Programs such as the IRC's Female Education Program, running since 1992, continue to contribute to human resource development for Afghanistan (Qahir, 2008). Although there are no specific tracer data available, individual stories provide evidence that graduates of the refugee schools are now filling important jobs in NGOs and government departments in Afghanistan.

Becoming a teacher also may be a transformative experience for women affected by crises (Kirk, 2004c, 2004d). It can be a way for women to provide important income or supplies for themselves and their families. This is a critical issue in conflict contexts. There are often high percentages of female-headed households because of the large numbers of men killed or displaced. Even in the absence of government salaries, small incentives paid by agencies and NGOs can have a significant impact on the well-being of teachers and their families. In addition to meeting the practical gender needs of women, becoming a teacher may start to address women's strategic interests.[1] The personal and professional development that women can experience through being a teacher can be empowering in different ways. Being able to support one's family can have an important impact on the psychosocial well-being of women who have been affected by conflict. Teachers in Afghanistan, for example, have indicated that—instead of being alone, surrounded by their own problems, and constantly reliving the trauma and loss of the conflict—the opportunity to teach gives them something else to think about. Especially if there are no other opportunities for them to continue their own education, teaching often is considered a good way to extend their knowledge.

Teaching also benefits women psychosocially because they feel a sense of contributing to their community, knowing that they are doing their best, and contributing positively to the future. In some contexts it is harder for women to be active in the public realm than for men, but teaching can be a culturally acceptable way to do so and a means to gaining status and respect in a community. In Afghanistan, women teachers returned from Pakistan to find that the girls in their villages had no opportunities to go to school at all. Being able to do something for these girls, and for their community, is clearly important to these women, even though they have no formal training as teachers (Kirk, 2004c). In a refugee camp in Ethiopia, Kunama women teachers, who had fled with their community from Eritrea in 2001, were nominated by the community to teach. Although they had not yet completed secondary education, there were no more-educated women in the camp. Still somewhat tentative in their professional identities as teachers, these women felt that it was important to share with the students what they had learned in Eritrea before they had to flee. Six years later, women who have continued to teach and to develop their skills are now interested in formal teacher certification (Kirk & Winthrop, 2007).

PROMISING POLICY DEVELOPMENTS AT THE GLOBAL LEVEL

Women, Girls, Peace, and Security

Unlike in previous eras, war and conflict of the late 20th century occurred largely within, rather than between, nations. Fighting happens within communities and involves ordinary civilians, spilling into homes, workplaces, and even schools. Although more men and boys are killed in conflict, ethnic hatred, oppression, and intolerance are played out on the bodies of women and girls. Fighting forces commonly use sexual violence as a weapon of war. Rape is now recognized as a specific war crime in the statutes of the International Criminal Court (art. 8). This recognition at the highest international policy levels is significant, but it may create little improvement in the lives of the many women and girls who experience such horrors (Kirk & Taylor, 2007). It is also well documented that GBV does not necessarily abate with the signing of peace agreements. Many women and girls face a high risk of GBV during the early reconstruction period and beyond. Rape and sexual attacks continue and other forms of GBV occur, including harmful traditional practices such as female genital mutilation, forced early marriage, honor killings, and domestic violence (IASC, 2005).

At the same time, there is an increased recognition of the extent of sexual violence and exploitation of women and girls in conflict and a number of positive developments addressing the protection and participation needs of women and girls. The landmark UN Security Council Resolution on Women, Peace, and Security (UNSCR 1325) (United Nations Security Council, 2000) recognizes the need to protect women and girls from sexual violence. This inclusive language (i.e., *women and girls*) has been translated into policy documents of different agencies and organizations. However, as discussed by Kirk and Taylor (2004), there is less specific attention paid to the age-differentiated dimensions of sexual violence and to the particular experiences of girls and young women. To adapt a phrase from Susan McKay (Karam, 2001), a *womenandgirls* approach tends to dominate, and there is less attention given to the particular experiences of sexual violence against young women and adolescent girls. Sexual violence in and around schools and related to education, for example, particularly affects girls rather than women.

Although not explicitly addressed in the UNSCR 1325 text, education clearly plays an important role in supporting the active and meaningful participation of women in peace-building. Furthermore, education for girls promotes their participation as active agents in peace-building and ensures a future generation of women who are able to participate in the highest levels of peace negotiations and of state reconstruction. With specific attention to the particular protection and participation of girls, UNSCR 1325 can provide a very useful policy framework with which to link gender equality in education in emergencies and fragile states to activists and interventions working in the area of women, peace, and security.

INEE Minimum Standards for Education in Emergencies, Chronic Crises, and Early Reconstruction

The Minimum Standards for Education in Emergencies, Chronic Crises, and Early Reconstruction, developed by the INEE, represent a comprehensive picture of current practice and future priority directions. The standards were developed in a participatory way, drawing on existing good practice and field-based experience with realistic targets (Kirk, 2006b). Grounded in the rights of the child as well as in other relevant rights-based instruments, the standards were developed through a highly consultative process as a tool to guide policy and programming. They also are intended to ensure that the commitments made in human rights instruments, such as the Convention on the Rights of the Child and the EFA and MDG targets, are implemented in these challenging circumstances.

Gender equality does not have a separate category in the Minimum Standards, but it is a cross-cutting theme integrated across all categories of standards. This is considered essential to ensure that not only do girls have equal access to the benefits of education, but also that the content and processes of education in such circumstances meet the needs and priorities of girls as well as boys. Gender-specific rights instruments such as the Convention on the Elimination of All Forms of Discrimination against Women and the Beijing Platform for Action are not explicitly mentioned in the standards, but the standards reflect their priorities in terms of access to relevant and gender-responsive education.

The field of education in emergencies is premised on the recognition that children in contexts of emergency, chronic crisis, and early reconstruction have particular protection needs, some of which may be met through schooling, at least to a certain extent. Protection in this context encompasses both physical and psychosocial protection, and Standard 2 (Access and Learning Environment) insists that education providers ensure that "learning environments are secure, promote the protection and mental and emotional well-being of learners." Gender equality priorities relate to the need for ensuring equal access for girls to the protection benefits of education. At the same time, girls' vulnerabilities to sexual violence may even be heightened precisely because they come to school. Guidance Note 4, Standard 2 (Protection and Well-Being, Access and Learning Environment) provides:

> Students, especially minorities and girls, often become targets for abuse, violence, recruitment or abduction when going to and from school. In these cases students' security can be improved by a combination of community information campaigns and by having adults from the community escort them. . . . In addition, education programmes should include monitoring of the level of harassment experienced by girls and women. (INEE, 2004)

The standards provide a holistic framework for the integration of gender equality and protection concerns through all aspects of education in emergencies, chronic crises, and early reconstruction. For example, the Assessment Standard in the category Teaching and Learning pays particular attention to fair and non-exploitative assessment processes. A code of conduct for all teachers and other education personnel should address protection for students from sexual and other forms of exploitation and abuse. Such a code should include the teachers' responsibility to promote, among other things, a positive learning environment and the well-being of learners (Standard 2, Teachers and Other Education Personnel).

Although not specifically gendered, the standards recognize the need for education content appropriate to the particular circumstances of children affected by conflict and, in particular, education content and key messages that are life enhancing or even life saving. Standard 1 on Curricula in the category Teaching and Learning asserts, "Culturally, socially and linguistically relevant curricula are used to provide formal and non-formal education, appropriate to the particular emergency situation." Within this standard, we also are encouraged to consider relevant learning content related to peace-building, conflict resolution, and other similar skills. While the vulnerability of girls to sexual violence and exploitation is more widely acknowledged, it is important for educators to work with young people and their communities to identify and respond through curriculum content and other means to the gendered risks and protection needs of girls *and* boys. It may be, for example, that boys have heightened risks of abduction and conscription into fighting forces than girls. Although less documented and discussed, the vulnerability of boys to sexual abuse and exploitation is also a reality to be addressed in certain crisis-affected contexts.

Access to education, learning content, processes, and the interactions between teachers and students are important areas for attention to gender equality. The standards framework also highlights the complementarity of efforts in the areas of community participation, analysis, and education policy and coordination. Community participation, for example, should involve women as well as men (Community Participation, Standard 1, Guidance Note 1). Women in the community can play a special role in the schools (Community Participation, Standard 2, Guidance Note 2). From the needs assessment stage through monitoring and evaluation, analysis should be as comprehensive and in-depth as possible (including gender-desegregated data) (Analysis, Standard 1). At the same time, strong and relevant education policy is needed to protect the rights of vulnerable groups (Education Policy and Coordination, Standard 1). Good coordination and information sharing among different education stakeholders (Education Policy and Coordination, Standard 2) can help to ensure that girls and other vulnerable groups do not fall through the cracks and that there are accessible and appropriate learning opportunities available for all.

INEE Gender Task Team

The above section highlights the potential of the INEE Minimum Standards as a framework for gender-responsive education in emergencies, chronic crises, and early reconstruction contexts. After the second INEE Global Consultations in Cape Town in December 2004, the IRC initiated the INEE Gender Task Team (GTT) to create additional attention, tools, and resources to ensure gender-responsive implementation and the fullest realization of the potential of the standards. The GTT consists of education specialists with an interest in and commitment to gender, who have identified technical gaps and prioritized group tasks.

Regular contact and communication between the GTT and the INEE Secretariat, as well as regular reports to the INEE Steering Committee and the INEE Working Group on Minimum Standards, facilitate enhanced attention to the integration of gender perspectives. For example, as the training materials for the Minimum Standards Training of Trainers and the INEE Minimum Standards Toolkit have been developed, piloted, and reviewed, the GTT has provided additional gender content and materials.

Gender Mainstreaming in the Education Cluster

The UN Secretary General's report, *Strengthening the Coordination of Emergency Humanitarian Assistance of the United Nations* (United Nations, 2001), and the *Humanitarian Response Review* (United Nations, 2005) highlighted serious gaps in the capacity of the humanitarian community to respond effectively to crises and made recommendations for addressing these gaps. The IASC subsequently established clusters for nine sectors and issues in which particular gaps had been identified: logistics; telecommunications; shelter; health; nutrition; water, sanitation, and hygiene; early recovery; camp coordination and camp management; and protection. Different UN agencies were nominated as the cluster leads for each. Although initially the IASC did not establish an Education Cluster, subsequent advocacy from education actors resulted in the formal endorsement of the cluster approach in education in November 2006.

According to IASC, the cluster approach aims to improve the predictability, timeliness, and effectiveness of humanitarian response and pave the way for recovery. The cluster approach should strengthen the collaborative response by enhancing partnerships and complementarity among the UN, the Red Cross Movement, and NGOs (IASC, 2007). The cluster approach operates on two levels: global and field. Global-level cluster activities, for which funding was requested through a cluster appeal to donors in April 2007, include up-to-date assessments and reviews of the overall needs for human, financial, and institutional capacity, as well as actions to improve rosters, stockpiles, training, and systems development. There are links with other clusters, including preparedness and long-term planning, standards, best practice, advocacy, and resource mobilization (UN OCHA, 2007). At the field level, the cluster approach is oriented toward addressing the specific needs in a particular response effort, particularly through the mobilization and coordination of different humanitarian agencies.

The UN's Global Education Cluster aims to improve the coverage and quality of the response to a need for education in an emergency. Planned cluster activities include the preparation of tools and resource materials, needs assessment protocols, and rosters of experienced staff. These activities intend to address gaps in capacity, especially surge capacity, to ensure predictable, quality, and comprehensive education interventions that reach all children in an emergency situation.

A preliminary gaps analysis was conducted, and priority projects were developed by the Education Cluster for inclusion in the cluster appeal document. Gender is identified by the Education Cluster as a key gap to be addressed through the cluster approach. The gap relates to human resource capacities, limited mechanisms for preparedness, response and coordination, the variety of approaches, lack of standardization, and specific technical gaps such as gender analysis. The Education Cluster is committed to increased attention to equity issues involving age, gender, and vulnerable groups, and has referred explicitly to gender in three of its four cluster projects.

The IASC Sub-Working Group (SWG) on Gender in Humanitarian Assistance existed prior to the establishment of the clusters. The SWG is committed to integrating gender equality into the humanitarian response system, particularly through the rollout of the *IASC Gender Handbook* (to which the INEE GTT contributed an education chapter) and the *IASC GBV Guidelines.* The SWG also developed three projects to include in the cluster appeal to donors in April 2007: sex-disaggregated data collection and management, the integration of gender equality into all policy and program work of the clusters/sectors, and building capacity of field actors to understand and use the *IASC Gender Handbook* and *IASC GBV Guidelines* in all sector/cluster work.

Through the GTT Convener, INEE is represented on the IASC Gender SWG, as well as on other relevant "sub-sub-working groups." In these settings, INEE works to ensure that education is represented among the different sectors, that lessons from other sectors about gender mainstreaming in humanitarian action can be applied to education, and that the strategies and lessons learned from education work can inform other sectors.

As the operating structures and processes of the Education Cluster are being defined and the specific projects further worked out, efforts are now being made to ensure a strong and integrated focus on gender equality. The role of the INEE GTT therefore will expand. With a new recruitment process, the team's mandate has expanded to support gender mainstreaming within both the INEE and the Education Cluster, thereby leveraging the links already made and the interest and capacities of the individuals and agencies already involved.

IMPLICATIONS: LEARNING FOR PEACE AND EQUALITY

The above discussion has highlighted the need and the possibilities for systematic mainstreaming of gender equality concerns throughout education in emergencies and fragile states. It has presented the INEE Minimum Standards as a framework that highlights gender equality concerns across all aspects of education planning, content, methodology, and policy development and coordination. Drawing on this discussion, the following section presents three broad areas for particular programming attention: ensuring strategic protection; taking holistic perspectives on protection, water and sanitation, hygiene, and reproductive health; and building the capacity of women teachers and education leaders.

Ensure Strategic Protection for Girls in and Through Education

The attention given to the protection of women and girls affected by crisis and to the imperative for girls to attend school is encouraging. From a critical gender and empowerment perspective, however, an exclusive focus on protection is somewhat problematic. There is a tendency to focus on solely the girls as somewhat problematically in need of attention and protection; thus the potential for protection strategies becomes limiting and restrictive. Furthermore, interventions developed to mitigate against sexual violence and reproductive health issues focus on the immediate and practical needs of either girls or women. Little attention is given to the strategic and long-term collective gender needs of both. In general, there has been limited discussion of the ways in which women and girls can work together to promote gender equality and to change school and community cultures. More attention is required to learn how to successfully shift school cultures from ones in which girls require protection to ones in which girls and boys and male and female teachers are able to enjoy stimulating teaching and learning experiences. Girls can be active developers of strategies to increase their own and others' security and well-being.

Drawing on fieldwork in Guinea and Sierra Leone and assessments of a classroom assistant program initiated to protect girls from abuse and exploitation by teachers, Kirk and Winthrop (n.d) promote the concept of strategic protection. Strategic protection engages girls and boys as "knowers" of their own worlds and experiences. Girls and boys are key agents in identifying their protection needs and in proposing and evaluating solutions. It also involves attention to the collective empowerment needs of girls and women while acknowledging that women recruited to protect girls may have a somewhat different personal gender empowerment agenda. Strategic protection is also responsive to the changing gender identities of men, women, boys, and girls in the contexts in which they live, and to the dominant forms of masculinity and femininity that prevail. In this way it responds to the work of scholars of gender and conflict and of masculinities and conflict (Enloe, 1989, 2000; Whitworth, 2004). Strategic protection is attentive to questions such as the following: How do teachers who exploit girl students understand their own personal and professional roles? What are the pressures on these men to assert certain forms of masculinity? Such approaches contrast with the research and practice related to GBV in schools, which have focused on the girls and their vulnerabilities. Even where there are female teachers, classroom assistants, or other women able to provide sex and reproductive health education for young students, strategic protection contrasts with perspectives that focus exclusively on protection, with no space for a positive discussion of healthy and safe sexuality as a dimension of gender identity. Certainly accurate information about their own bodies is of critical importance to adolescents and is understood as a strategic protection need, especially for girls. But strategic protection allows young people to discuss and understand the pleasures and the risks of sexuality in their own particular contexts, and to work together to develop strategies to protect themselves and one another. Such discussions also would engage boys and men in exploring sexuality, masculinity, gender identity, and their roles in eliminating sexual violence. Finally, strategic protection, as suggested above, involves girls as active and knowledgeable participants in the design, implementation, and evaluation of activities and strategies to protect and empower themselves.

The notion of strategic protection enhances attention to education for peace and equality. The protection mandate remains imperative, but through alternative program approaches, participation and empowerment imperatives are also integrated. Teacher training is an obvious starting point, especially as this is one of the most common program activities in education in emergency contexts. Specific gender training should go beyond questions of increasing girls' access to school. It needs to allow male and female teachers to openly discuss (in separate groups if necessary) issues such as what it means to be a man, woman, boy, or girl of different ages in the camp or community; whether or how this has changed over time; what sort of pressures there are to conform to certain ideals of masculinity and femininity; what the negative results of this might be; and how to create some positive changes. Increased attention to teacher codes of conduct (as recommended in the INEE Minimum Standards, for example) does reflect progress on these issues. But codes of conduct are inadequate to bring about the changes in the culture of schools, of teaching, and of "being a male teacher" that are necessary to really create protective environments for teachers and students. Activities have to go beyond training teachers on a given code of conduct to complement gender training. Activities need to allow for discussion of sexual and gender identities and power dynamics: how they are both challenged and reinforced in emergency contexts and how teachers may act as agents of change and support their students to do likewise.

Take Holistic Approaches to Protection, Well-Being, Hygiene, and (Reproductive) Health

Lack of access to water and sanitation facilities in schools particularly affects girls' education. Adolescence and puberty can be difficult times for all young people. For girls, however, in emergencies, chronic crises, and early reconstruction contexts, puberty—and especially the onset of menstruation—pose particular challenges, not least of which is lack of adequate rest rooms and water at school to comfortably change sanitary pads or other materials and wash themselves in private. Refugees, IDPs, and girls otherwise affected by crises may not be able to afford commercially produced sanitary pads and may not have access to rags or other materials for homemade solutions. The situation may be even more difficult for girls whose clothing is either too small and tight or just torn and worn and who do not have underwear. Both of these factors are known to affect the participation in education of girls in southern Sudan, for example. Menstruating girls may miss classes each month during their period (Kirk & Sommers, 2005). Even if they are able to attend school, they may be very uncomfortable with limited and makeshift sanitary materials and unable to fully participate in class. The same may be the case for women teachers who either fail to attend school during menstruation or who attend but are restricted in their activities. Girls who have to use rest rooms that are far away from the main school compound, and possibly out of sight of the school authorities, may then risk sexual violence.

In many social contexts, these issues are not openly discussed, and there is embarrassment surrounding personal hygiene, health, and menstruation. Particularly where education levels are low, pubescent girls and boys may have very little understanding of what is happening to them and their bodies. Crisis-affected parents may lack the time and energy to talk with their children about puberty and adolescence. Furthermore, school curricula typically do not cover topics such as puberty and menstruation in a very sensitive way and so do not help girls or boys to understand the changes in their maturing bodies. In emergency situations, schools tend to be dominated by male teachers because of difficulties recruiting women. These male teachers may be undertrained with little understanding of or sensitivity to the challenges faced by post-pubescent girls in regularly attending school. Where there are women teachers, they often are fully occupied in the lowest grades, and so older girls have no confidante with whom to share questions and concerns.

There is increasing recognition that providing separate, private, and safe rest rooms for girls has the potential to improve school access, attendance, and retention, especially for adolescent girls. Safe, adequate facilities, however, are only part of the solution. Girls and boys should be engaged in planning and implementing new sanitation projects. They should have information to understand and cope with puberty. Links should be made between the infrastructure improvements in the school and the nature and quality of teaching and learning for girls and boys.

Build Capacity of Women Teachers and Education Leaders

The above perspectives on strategic protection need to be linked to discussions and policy development on gender-responsive recruitment and deployment and support for male and female teachers. Men and women should have equal status in schools. Both should be able to act as positive role models for girls and boys. The teachers' different opportunities for positive interaction with parents and community members also should be exploited. In training and professional support of women and men, possible priority differences also should be assessed and incorporated into training plans. It may be, for example, that women teachers need additional support to develop leadership and management skills in education to support promotion and career development. In locations where women have fewer opportunities to interact in English, French, or another lingua franca, language skills may be prioritized. Teacher support, development content, and the processes for professional development warrant gendered consideration. Teacher networks and learning groups may provide very supportive development opportunities for women, which can be adapted to fit with other family responsibilities. Other recommendations include ensuring links between women teachers and community-based women's organizations, providing mentoring opportunities to partner a young and new woman teacher with an older and more experienced educator, as well as recruiting and deploying women teachers in pairs (INEE GTT, n.d.).

CONCLUSIONS

This chapter has presented some of the prevailing gender inequities in education in contexts of crisis, post-crisis, and state fragility. It has highlighted some of the concrete global policy developments that may support increased attention to gender equality and education. These developments include the INEE Minimum Standards for Education in Emergencies, Chronic Crises, and Early Reconstruction and the Education Cluster within the UN humanitarian reform processes. Concrete programming strategies to promote gender equality in education in contexts of crisis, post-crisis, and state fragility described in the final section of this chapter provide strategic directions for policy and program development. The strategic directions exist within an overarching framework of the INEE Minimum Standards, through which the principles and practices of gender mainstreaming in humanitarian action are interwoven.

NOTE

1. Molyneux's (1985) differentiation between women's practical gender interests and women's strategic gender interests has been particularly influential in the framing of gender and development theory. It draws attention to the differences between responses to the concrete, practical, and more immediate needs of women, and responses that are more strategic interventions, aimed at longer term, more transformatory goals, such as women's emancipation. Moser (1989) takes up the differentiation and applies it to policy planning, but also suggests the need for more-considered policy interventions that, even if aimed at meeting practical gender needs, are aware of longer term needs and larger, strategic possibilities.

Part II

LISTENING TO THE VOICES OF CHILDREN AND TEACHERS

Refugee Children Aspiring Toward the Future
Linking Education and Livelihoods

Sarah Dryden-Peterson

Education often plays a role in creating stability in the daily lives of refugee children. Once overlooked in favor of "life-saving" interventions related to food, shelter, and health, education recently has become the fourth pillar of humanitarian assistance for precisely this reason: It is protective in meeting cognitive and psychosocial needs, providing space for conveying survival messages, and developing skills for conflict resolution and peace-building. At the same time, refugee children often see education as the principal way of building a better future, economically, socially, and psychologically. Educational programming and policies for refugee children are usually shortsighted, focusing on children's present situation in isolation from their futures. Yet refugee children connect the present and the future, often through the lens of education.

This chapter examines the ways in which current educational realities shape refugee children's constructions of their future livelihoods. In the first section, I outline a conceptual approach to refugee livelihoods and examine the possible relationships between education and livelihoods for refugee children. The second section includes an overview of the methodology used in this study, a unique design that allows for a longitudinal view of children's experiences as well as a comparative examination of emergency, protracted, and urban settings of exile. The third section presents portraits of refugee children who live in each of these three settings in Uganda, with a focus on their understandings of the role of education in their own future livelihoods. The final section discusses the connections between refugee children's educational experiences and their aspirational constructions of future livelihoods, and it outlines the implications for program planning and policymaking in the field of refugee education.

REFUGEE CHILDREN'S LIVELIHOODS AND EDUCATION

Defining Refugee Livelihoods

The term *livelihoods* has been conceptualized in recent research as the resources and strategies people use to maintain and sustain their lives and their living (Chambers & Conway, 1991, p. 5; Jacobsen, 2002, p. 98; Kaag, 2004, p. 49, in Horst, 2006a). A livelihoods approach to poverty reduction, which focuses on the agency and strengths of individuals and communities, is common in the development field. Over the past decade, a livelihoods approach also has gained popularity in the humanitarian field (De Vriese, 2006, pp. 5–6).

Two shifts in understanding of the refugee experience have contributed to the rise of a livelihoods approach within academic thought and field-based practice. First is a growing awareness of the personal agency of refugees and documentation of the ways in which refugees actively seek self-reliance. The dominant model of handout-based assistance is rooted in conceptions of refugees that emphasize their dependencies and is ineffective in providing the conditions in which refugees can develop the means of sustainable livelihoods (Crisp, 2003; Horst, 2006b; Jacobsen, 2005). A livelihoods approach promotes alternative models of programming and policy, centered on refugee agency. Second, the protracted nature of most contemporary refugee situations means that many refugees are in a "long-lasting and intractable state of limbo" (UNHCR, 2006, p. 106) and spend, on average, 17 years in exile (p. 109). Given the length of displacement and resource constraints, the United Nations High Commissioner for Refugees (UNHCR), donor and host governments, and NGOs have needed to find ways of incorporating refugee participation into development planning (Betts, 2005). Attempts to bridge the gaps between relief and development with the creation of livelihood opportunities also have grown more frequent (Women's Refugee Commission, 2009).

As a result of their diverse trajectories of migration, refugees experience discontinuity and disruption in their livelihoods, such as loss of land or lack of recognition of educational credentials. Horst (2006a) underlines that, even more than for most other people, refugee livelihoods are dynamic and constantly changing over time (p. 9). In many host countries, refugees also face structural barriers to the realization of livelihoods, such as when freedom of movement is restricted or legal employment not permitted. Jacobsen (2002) argues that, given these unique characteristics of a refugee's situation, understanding of refugee livelihoods needs to be adapted to emphasize how people access and mobilize resources and strategies to reduce the vulnerabilities created and exacerbated by displacement and conflict (p. 99). UNHCR (2009b) estimates that 44% of displaced people globally are children under the age of 18 (p. 9). And yet the idea of "livelihoods," now so central to academic work and practice in the field of forced migration, is understudied vis-à-vis refugee children.[1]

Refugee Children's Livelihoods

Development discourse and practices, including in the humanitarian field, increasingly portray children as having agency distinct from their parents or family (Cheney, 2007, pp. 42–72; see also Bengtsson & Bartlett, Chapter 15, this volume). This advancement of children from objects to social actors echoes shifts in conceptualizations of adult refugees. It is, however, accompanied by continued emphasis on the vulnerabilities of children. UNHCR publications and policies, for example, typically describe children as a "vulnerable group," implying passivity and dependency on others (Clark-Kazak, 2009a). Children are vulnerable to exploitation, particularly at the intersections of age and other characteristics such as refugee status, gender, ethnicity, and disability (Dryden-Peterson, 2010; Lewis & Lockheed, 2007). They are also resilient, constructing their own pathways to livelihoods even in difficult circumstances (see, e.g., R. A. Hart, 1992; Wessells, 2006).

What shapes the ways in which refugee children construct their livelihoods? Several factors make the pursuit of livelihoods by children different from that by adults. First, economics, often conceived of as central to the pursuit of livelihoods for adults, can be less instrumental for children. Refugee children are both objects of parental/familial obligations as well as parts of webs of family relationships of interdependencies. These relationships may shape their decisions and the ways in which they access and mobilize resources and strategies related to maintaining and sustaining their lives. Refugee children often contribute to the economic base of their families, through subsistence or wage labor (Fredriksen, 2009; King & van de Walle, 2007; Lewis & Lockheed, 2006); while they may feel as if their labor is central to the family's collective livelihood strategy, they usually are not primarily responsible for ensuring the family's economic livelihood, which is an important psychological difference.[2]

Second, the developmental phase of children places them in a future-oriented position (Elder, 1998; Erikson, 1950). The situation of refugees is unique in that they confront uncertainty related to the duration and location of their exile in addition to structural constraints imposed by host governments that circumscribe how they imagine and plan for the future. Programming and planning for refugees, both adults and children, typically respond to these realities by focusing on the present. Yet recent research has identified ways in which refugee children maintain hope for the future, despite the limitations of their present situation (Winthrop & Kirk, 2008). The forward-looking position of refugee children's developmental phase may translate into a dual focus on the present and the future as they pursue their livelihoods.

Finally, refugee children have been socialized to believe that their livelihoods are inextricably linked to formal schooling. It is at once "something to do" in the present, a way to "absorb their energies," and, at the same time, a way to "lessen their frustrations and anxiety about the future" (International Institute for Educational Planning, 2006a, p. 2). Despite the value placed on schooling, refugee children remain out-of-school in large numbers. Approximately one third of primary-school-aged refugee children are not enrolled in primary school and, at secondary levels, over two thirds are not enrolled (UNHCR, 2009a). Refugee children who are enrolled in school consistently describe the "better future" enabled through their pursuit of education, whereas children who do not have access describe having no pathway to a future livelihood (Clark-Kazak, 2011; Winthrop & Kirk, 2008). Education may play several roles in the ways in which refugee children construct their livelihoods. It may be a resource for security, related to both present physical security and future economic security. It may be a strategy for integration to the host society on the way to self-reliance outside of humanitarian aid structures. And it may be both a resource and a strategy for refugee children as they aspire toward the future. These connections between education and livelihoods for refugee children are the subject of this chapter.

THE STUDY

The analysis presented in this chapter draws on data from a 3-year longitudinal study of the educational experiences of refugee and national children in refugee-hosting areas of Uganda. Uganda is at the center of the Great Lakes region of Africa and hosts refugees from Sudan, Rwanda, Democratic Republic of Congo (DRC), Somalia, and Burundi. At the outset of this study, in 2002, Uganda was host to a refugee population officially registered at 217,302 (UNHCR, 2002, p. 494) and, at the conclusion of this study, in 2005, the number had risen to 257,256 (UNHCR, 2005, p. 79). The number of self-settled refugees living amid local populations in urban and rural areas was likely greater than the number of those officially registered during the period of the study (Hovil, 2007).

The broader study uses an ethnographic case study approach, in which analysis of the experiences of children, parents, and community members are embedded within three geographically bounded case study sites (Yin, 2003). In this chapter, I draw on the larger dataset[3] to inform an in-depth analysis of three refugee children from DRC who participated in the longitudinal study. Reflecting my use of elements of portraiture (Lawrence-Lightfoot & Davis, 1997), I present data and embedded analysis in the form of narrative portraits, with the goal of conveying a holistic, in-depth understanding of the educational experiences of Annette, Julie, and Amaziah[4] as they pertain to livelihoods.

While each of these children is unique in many respects, their stories highlight themes I found to be common across the larger dataset, particularly as related to the connections between current educational realities and constructions of future livelihoods. Of particular relevance are the sites in which they access education, which are the types of displacement situations most common in Uganda and globally. Annette lives in an *emergency* setting, or acute crisis situation, in which there has been massive population change in a short period of time; Julie lives in a *protracted* setting in which refugees have been in exile for 5 or more years without any prospect of returning home, being resettled, or integrating into the host society; and Amaziah lives in an *urban* setting in which refugees settle, without legal status, in a city rather than in settlements/camps. While the data presented in this chapter are unique to these three individual children, the findings and theoretical propositions reflect the broader dataset from the larger study of which this analysis forms part.

FINDINGS: THE CONSTRUCTION OF
FUTURE LIVELIHOODS THROUGH EDUCATION

Annette

"Kyaka is a good place," Annette says. She has lived in Kyaka II refugee settlement in western Uganda for 2 years, after fleeing what she calls the "killing" in eastern Democratic Republic of Congo. Her family has felt comfortable setting down early roots in this refugee settlement. Family members express, on the one hand, a knowledge that they will be a long time in exile and, on the other hand, a sense that they could become integrated into this part of rural Uganda. The family quickly moved from a shelter made of UNHCR tarps and straw to one constructed of mud and sticks, and they planted bananas, a long-to-mature crop, around the compound. The Camp Commandant at Kyaka II calls bananas "the sign of establishment."

For Annette, however, Kyaka is a "good place" primarily because of education. "I feel safe here," she says, "as schooling and books are free," unlike in DRC. Annette has every reason to resent the kind of education she has received in Kyaka. In DRC, she had been in the first year of secondary school. When she arrived in Kyaka, she was told she would be eligible only to enroll in Primary Three, the third year of primary school. The reason: She did not speak English and would need to learn the language with the young children. Undaunted, Annette maintained her dreams of becoming a nurse, certain that "my studies will lead me there." She clearly links what she learns in school to concrete skills that she believes will assist her in building the kind of future she hopes for. She says: "Math will help me to deal with big amounts of money and do calculations. Science will help me in administering first aid in case someone falls sick. English will help me in communicating with foreigners."

One year later, Annette seems to have lost her indomitable spirit and optimism. She has nothing good to say about life in Uganda. She describes how she eats the same food every day, and she reminisces about how good life in DRC had been before the war, where her house was even roofed with iron sheets. This was a year without rain in which the crops burned in the ground. Annette's father explains that "enjoying life here depends on how the season is. During a dry season, the harvest is poor and therefore food is scarce." This particularly dry season, Annette was also sick often and did not have proper access to medical care. In addition, the refugee settlement was experiencing dramatic changes, with the population almost quintupling due to new arrivals from eastern DRC (Dryden-Peterson, 2006). Annette's description of herself at this time was: "I am a refugee, I am poor."

When asked to draw her school, Annette looks at me blankly. I had observed her in classes in Kyaka for 2 years, and she had told me about the secondary school she used to attend in DRC. I was curious as to what Annette considered *her* school and how she would describe it. She breaks the silence, but her blank look does not dissipate: "I study under the trees," she says in a monotone. The emergency situation in the settlement resulted in a tripling of the school population without any new construction. That she was studying under the trees was to Annette a symbol of how unimportant her education was to others, to her teachers and to those in power. Indeed, weeks of observation in her classes convinced me that Annette was not exaggerating to say that she was learning "very little" at school. At this time, Annette parroted what she heard from her parents in terms of a rationale for continuing her studies: "Studying is important because it will help me find a job and make money." But she had lost her daily desire to attend school and to learn, and her dream of the fulfilling work she hoped to do as a nurse had disappeared.

As the population of the refugee settlement began to stabilize, so did Annette's feelings of security. Another year later, she again described detailed hopes for the future. She would like to be a nurse in Uganda and to have "the capacity of helping my family." Her father used to have a fishing business in Congo that was very successful, but in Kyaka he can only farm, and he is "fed up with this work." On the other hand, he says, "I would also like to stay in a place free from suffering. It is a natural need to have a good life." For him, the sense of physical security for his family in Kyaka overrides his lack of ability to fulfill his economic potential. Indeed, Annette's family struggles with poverty. She is the only child in her class not to have a uniform. She does, however, have shoes for the first time. In these shoes, poised, and appearing quite grown-up, Annette is on the cusp of completing primary school in Uganda, in English. She is confident that this kind of integration in Uganda that she has gained through education will allow her to fulfill her dreams for the future, in terms of both becoming a nurse and helping her family. "When I look around at the people who were educated," she says, "who have been to school, I see that their lives are good."

Julie

The first description Julie uses for herself is "sick." She has eye problems, she often gets headaches, and, she says, "I only feel like staying home to sweep." She is usually quiet and, when asked a question, speaks as few words as possible. She has a sadness about her, and a fear. When asked about her hopes for the future, she says: "I hope God will let me live." This fatalism relates only in part to Julie's physical health. "I don't [feel safe in Nakivale refugee settlement]," she says, "because I fear they may kill us, saying that we go out of their country." One of Julie's classmates describes how the tent where he lives is encircled at night with people chanting, "We do not want you here, we do not want you here." He can't sleep, fearing what might happen.

Julie is one step removed from this kind of concrete threat to her physical security. She does not live in Nakivale refugee settlement, in southwest Uganda. Her parents came to Uganda from Rwanda as refugees in 1959 and form part of the population known in Nakivale as the "old refugees." Julie's family is ambivalent about whether they are refugees. "*We are not refugees*," her mother says firmly, "because . . . we pay tax, I have tax tickets." This paying of taxes leads Julie's uncle to declare that they are "citizens." Living outside the refugee settlement allows Julie's family access to more land on which to grow beans, sorghum, and maize on a subsistence basis; they also are able to graze their cattle, which is not permitted in the settlement. From the cows, Julie's family also has access to money, unlike most refugee families. Julie's mother describes how she "shake[s] the milk cream I get from my four cows. I keep the cream daily and get ghee and sell it." Julie's compound is made up of several round huts, which are made of dried mud, have been whitewashed, and are topped with thatch; they are of much sturdier construction than refugee homes in the settlement. On the other hand, Julie's sister explains, "*We are refugees*," benefiting from the services provided for refugees, as they are "helped by friends that side [in the refugee settlement]" to get food rations from UNHCR. Being both refugee and national, pursuing both integration and continued exile, is a livelihood strategy that Julie's family uses to meet its needs.

Julie herself lives a similarly dual life that feeds the fear she feels for her safety and security. She vacillates between passing as a refugee and as a national, and she is constantly afraid of the consequences of being caught. She was born in Uganda and has never been to Rwanda. For a year, before she became comfortable telling me her real story because of fear of jeopardizing her family's UNHCR rations, she claimed that she was born in Rwanda and came to Uganda when she was 6 years old. She talks of going "home" to Rwanda, but at the same time explains that in the future, "I hope to be this way [in Uganda] because my parents are not interested in going back to our country."

Further, every day, Julie leaves the relative safety of the national area where her family feels integrated for an hour and 10-minute walk (each way) to the largest primary school in Nakivale refugee settlement. Julie describes both negative and positive consequences of her family's decision for her to attend this far-away, refugee school. On the negative side, Julie perceives the walk to and from school as a threat to her physical security. She and her sister choose a different route each day, afraid that "[the refugees] may even kill us because they think we have money." A national member of the School Management Committee (SMC) confirms that there have been many confrontations between nationals and refugees in the area of the settlement: "[The refugees] attack us, they steal our things and sometimes they kill." The children at school exhibit the same tendencies, with "cases of fighting, injuring each other. . . . They are not getting along." These tensions affect the way Julie experiences school. "Refugees don't like Ugandans," she says. "Some of them fight." According to Julie, this "hatred" makes concentrating in school and learning difficult.

On the positive side, education is free in the refugee settlement. Julie's family is not asked to make any contribution for school fees, unlike at the national school outside the settlement that is closer to their home. Julie describes not feeling safe at home because even her parents cannot help her when she is sick: "There is no money." If school were not free, Julie insists, she would not be able to attend. It is the liberal implementation of government of Uganda policy by one particular District Inspector of Schools that facilitates this free access to school. He sees how the schools in Nakivale struggle to teach children from seven countries, most of whom have fled violent conflict. He sees how the school struggles to attract teachers to its remote location and low standard of living. He also sees how many of the refugee children at this school grow up to remain in Uganda. And he believes that if these children are going to remain in Uganda and contribute to the country, then the government of Uganda should support them. So, rather than restrict government contributions to the school to the number of national children in attendance, this Inspector reports the total number of children, refugee and national, thereby effectively doubling the funds available to this school through government and UNHCR sources combined.

As Julie and her mother state, another positive element of the refugee school is that English is the language of instruction, unlike at national schools where the local mother tongue is used. Julie's mother explains that "at that school they teach in English so each child gets an opportunity to learn and know English. The reason is that pupils there speak very many languages. So English unifies them." She links knowing English to a more prosperous future livelihood for her daughter, especially given that she expects the family to remain in Uganda. Finally, Julie describes how she is happy at school. Despite her fears and her sickness, Julie says that school is the one place she feels good: "When I am at school, I play, and I don't feel headaches." Unlike at home, where she worries about whether there will be food for the next meal or money when she next falls sick, being at school allows her to think about the future, she says. Her mother attended school only through the end of the first year of primary school, and she is not able to read. Having completed Primary Six, Julie feels as if she can build a better life than her mother. Particularly, she says, education will help her to be "self-supportive" in a way that her parents are not, still reliant on UNHCR for assistance after more than 40 years.

Amaziah

Amaziah's family is well-off by urban refugee standards. The family lives in a house with concrete walls and floors and a high, tin roof. Their sofa and chairs have new, soft cushions. In the main room, one of two rooms in the house, there is a small black wheeling cart holding four videotapes and a paraffin lamp, a sign of at least some leisure and nights filled not only with sleeping. Mosquito nets hang from the rafters, indicating that while by day the main room is a comfortable sitting area, by night it is where all six children sleep.

Amaziah and his family are refugees from DRC. They obtained their refugee status, and are registered, in Kyangwali refugee settlement, in western Uganda. But they have decided to make their life in exile in Kampala, Uganda's capital city. Amaziah's father is an artist. He wears blue jeans and a khaki button-down shirt with orange trim around the pockets. On his wrist is a gold watch, and his feet sport desert boots. He is self-assured and poised in appearance, but he bears the scars of an inexplicable war. The scars are physical and emotional. He pulls up his pants to reveal a bullet wound on the inside of his right thigh. His face creased with sadness, he describes how he is deeply regretful of what the war in Congo has done to his livelihood and to the livelihood prospects of his family.

Amaziah had been in the fourth year of primary school in Congo before his family was forced to flee their home. He says, "In Congo, we learn and then war comes. We are cut short and then we begin again. They come again and it is cut short. Like that. That is the reason why I don't like learning there." Amaziah does not fear for his life in Uganda, but he does not feel secure. The problems are many, he explains, including his family not being able to pay rent and himself being chased from school for failure to pay school fees or for lack of a uniform or exercise books. School fees are high in Kampala, and there is no assistance for almost all of the refugees in the city. The urban environment is also inhospitable for refugees like Amaziah, who experience discrimination and xenophobia in their attempts to pursue education and who, without legal status in the city, have little recourse (Dryden-Peterson, 2003). Amaziah has been refused entry to school both for lack of money to pay fees and after being told that he "does not belong here." Amaziah's education is cut short and begins again, cyclically, in Uganda just as it did in Congo.

There is a further downside, for Amaziah and his family, of life as urban refugees. While their present lives are in Kampala, the family plans for a future in Canada, Australia, or the United States. They have applied for resettlement to these countries through UNHCR. The problem, however, is that in order to be eligible for resettlement, the family must live in a refugee settlement; almost no refugees are resettled from the city. Yet Amaziah's parents are not willing to give up their present livelihood and the children's education in Kampala for the long-shot opportunity of resettlement. Accessing education in the city is difficult, but Amaziah believes that the quality of education available in Kampala is far superior to that he would receive in the refugee camp. He sees a direct connection between studying, "aquir[ing] skills," "get[ting] a job" in the future, and "mak[ing] his own life." His father also believes that Kampala is the only place in Uganda where he can practice his profession, selling his art informally to support his family.

Amaziah's future aspirations are connected both to current pursuit of education and to prospects of resettlement. Yet the policies of UNHCR and the Ugandan government regarding refugee residence in an urban area and resettlement, place the paths to these futures in conflict. Amaziah's family thus pursues dual livelihood strategies, playing the odds by living in both the city and the refugee settlement. When they get word that UNHCR is conducting a population census in Kyangwali, they quickly board up and lock their house in Kampala and travel back to the settlement to take up residence there. As soon as the family has been counted and included on the register, Amaziah's father returns to Kampala alone in order to make enough money doing odd jobs to send back to Kyangwali to pay for the rest of the family's transport back to Kampala.

The conscious livelihood decision of ongoing migration, even in a country of exile, has continued for Amaziah's family over 8 years. This decision has not borne fruit for the family's current economic livelihood. "I am a person who likes work," says Amaziah's father, "but I don't have a stable work to support my family." Amaziah explains that his lack of feeling physically secure in Kampala is wrapped up in these issues of money and his sense that even his parents are not able to care for him. The back and forth movement between Kampala and Kyangwali also has not yielded any developments for the family in terms of prospects of resettlement, with no word of any forward movement of their dossier. Amaziah is progressing in school, having obtained his Ugandan primary leaving certificate and begun his Ordinary Levels (O-Levels) at a well-regarded secondary school in Kampala. His hopes for how this education will contribute to his future are bifurcated. If he is resettled, like his best friend was, he hopes the educational foundation he has from Uganda will allow him to continue studying, to be an "important person." If he is to stay in Uganda, he believes that as a refugee the most he can hope for, even with a secondary education, is to be a mechanic. In seeking to keep alive the possibility of resettlement, however, Amaziah's education suffers. The timing of the population census in Kyangwali during his second year of O-Levels (Senior 2) meant that he could not be in Kampala for his final exams. He missed them and, as a result, repeated Senior 2 the following year.

DISCUSSION: SECURITY, INTEGRATION, AND FUTURE ASPIRATIONS AS CONNECTIONS BETWEEN EDUCATION AND LIVELIHOODS

The experiences of Annette, Julie, and Amaziah point to three particular mechanisms through which current educational realities shape the constructions of future livelihoods for refugee children: security, integration, and future aspirations. These mechanisms play out differently in the three settings. In particular, refugee children's construction of the connections between education and future livelihoods depends on the balance between their roles as dependents and agents; their interrelationships with family members and the impacts on their roles as social, economic, and political actors; and their reconciliation of present reality and future prospects. Below, I discuss the three mechanisms across the settings and experiences of the three children.

Security

In all three settings, refugee children describe the foundation of maintaining and sustaining their lives—their livelihood—as a sense of physical security. In order to build a new life, Annette seeks feelings of safety and freedom from the "killing" she witnessed in DRC and abatement of the continued sense of chaos that accompanies massive influxes of refugees to the settlement where she lives. Julie wishes for an end to the fear of xenophobic threats on her life and the development of a sense of belonging in the country where her family has lived in a protracted situation for more than 40 years and where she was born. And Amaziah equates his feelings of physical insecurity in an urban area where he does not have legal status to his family's lack of economic security, worried that even his parents are not able to care for his needs.

Annette, Julie, and Amaziah do not feel as if they have the agency to control situations related to their security, exacerbating their vulnerability. In particular, the refugee children's security is inextricably linked to the economic livelihood possibilities of their families and the structural and social constraints on their reception in the host country. Annette and Julie find that the one space of security for them is school. While physical and sexual abuse have been well documented in refugee schools (Kirk, 2005a; Kirk & Winthrop, 2006), these girls describe the overwhelming feelings of security and happiness that being at school engenders on a daily basis. And they join Amaziah in valuing the way in which pursuing education is linked to their ability to imagine secure future livelihoods based on employment.

The longitudinal nature of this study, however, also sheds light on the transient experiences of refugee children in education. At various times, Annette, Julie, and Amaziah all feel as if they are not in control of their continued daily attendance at school or their educational pathway and the future livelihoods they connect to it. This is most obvious in Amaziah's case. He has experienced a cycle of continuous disruptions to his education, first due to war in DRC and then due to his family's decision to live in Kampala while simultaneously pursuing resettlement options from a geographically distant refugee settlement. He ascribes to persistence in school the ability to change his life course and to build economic and psychological stability for his future, whether in Uganda or elsewhere. Yet his experience, embedded within the relationships of his family and the resettlement policy structure of UNHCR, leaves him feeling helpless—and insecure—to prevent disruptions of his life and the educational pathway he is trying to pursue to his future.

Integration

The concept of integration, of building a life embedded in the society of exile, emerges as a second central link between refugee children's educational experiences and their construction of future livelihoods. Annette, for example, is willing to be demoted from secondary school to primary school in order to learn English and acquire a Ugandan primary school leaving certificate, a skill and an educational qualification that she believes will facilitate employment in the host society. And yet the experiences of Annette, Julie, and Amaziah also demonstrate ambivalence about integration into the host society; at times, they act in active pursuit of integration and, at others, in active rejection of it. Depending on the conditions in the settlement, Annette either is optimistic about how her education can lead to a fulfilling future in Uganda or actively rejects what she sees as the inescapable poverty wrought by the life of a refugee. Julie lives a dual life, benefiting, for example, from access to land for grazing of cattle that residential integration with nationals brings, while at the same time seeking additional food security through UNHCR rations and free schooling in the refugee settlement. And Amaziah seeks integration to a high-quality education within the national system, while at the same time pursuing options for resettlement outside of Uganda.

In all three situations, there are tensions between agency and dependency as refugee children seek various educational experiences to construct their future livelihoods. Amaziah's personal agency to pursue dual strategies of integration into Ugandan society, through education in Kampala, and resettlement abroad through the distant refugee settlement, is hamstrung by dependency on UNHCR policy, forcing him to miss his year-end exams and repeat a year of school. Julie feels the limits to her integration into Uganda, and to her own agency over decision-making, as she must walk an hour and 10 minutes each way to school in order to avoid school fees that her family cannot afford. Indeed, the way in which she pursues education is wrapped up in the current livelihoods of her family members and their economic conditions. At the same time, she expresses the hope that through education, her future will include economic integration into Ugandan society and will allow her to be less dependent on UNHCR assistance than her parents are after 40 years in the country. In this hope is embodied the connection refugee children see between education and the stability of integration, which allows them to construct and pursue a future livelihood that places them in control of their own futures, even in a situation of exile that is indeterminate.

Future Aspirations

For refugee children, abiding uncertainty about the future clashes with the forward-looking position of their developmental phase. This research shows education to be a critical link for refugee children between the present and the future. Analysis across the experiences of the three refugee children demonstrates that the content of future aspirations is inextricably connected to the type of current educational experience a child has and the meaning the child ascribes to it. Annette persists in school even after being demoted from secondary school to primary school because she believes that education will lead her to a secure social and economic position as a nurse. For Julie, school is the one place she feels good in the present, on a daily basis. The experience of being there allows her to think about the future, rather than only the disappointment and hardships of the present, and to imagine a prosperous future in terms of less dependency on assistance from UNHCR.

Given the uncertainty of his future and the multiple livelihood strategies his family pursues, Amaziah's aspirational construction of his future livelihood is at times in conflict with his current reality, as seen through his educational experiences. His interrelationships with his family and their priority of resettlement leave him with little agency or decision-making power to act on the current pathway he has constructed toward his future livelihood. His trip to Kyangwali refugee settlement forfeits his existing educational opportunities for the slight possibility of a future livelihood secured through resettlement. Annette's experience reveals a further connection between a child's aspirational construction of future livelihoods and current educational reality. Her position studying under the trees convinces her of the lack of value her education holds for those with oversight of refugee education. As has been documented elsewhere (Winthrop & Kirk, Chapter 7, this volume), it is the learning that happens in school, and not just the act of attending school, that connects the pursuit of education with the ability to hope for a better future. Annette finds both security and integration through her educational experiences, but she watches the potential of education to shape the future livelihood she has constructed in her mind dissipate in the context of lack of investment in quality (see Winthrop, Chapter 8, this volume).

CONCLUSION

This research points to three central connections between education and the construction of future livelihoods by refugee children. First, education can promote current physical security and the promise of future economic security. Second, it can create the conditions for children to imagine future stability through integration into a social, economic, and political system, whether in a current country of exile or elsewhere. And third, it provides a critical link between the present and the future through aspirations. While a livelihoods approach is common in the humanitarian field, program planning and policymaking for children have not benefited from the alternatives suggested by this approach. Adopting a livelihoods framework for the education of refugee children could provide a much-needed catalyst for addressing gaps in the current education strategy, as guided by UN-HCR. The strategy, at present, is based on technical interventions related to increasing access, promoting quality, and ensuring protection, with a defined focus on immediate needs. With an integrated education and livelihoods approach, educational programming and policymaking could reflect the connections that refugee children make between education and future livelihoods, synthesizing their educational needs in the present and their aspirations for the future.

NOTES

Thank you to the children, families, and teachers in Uganda who participated in this research, to Jacques Bwira and Kyohairwe Sylvia for research assistance, and to Christina Clark-Kazak, Cindy Horst, and Karen Mundy for helpful comments.

1. For the purposes of this study, the chronological age definition of children is used, as put forth in the Convention on the Rights of the Child (United Nations, 1989) and as employed by UNHCR (2009a): "A child means every human being below the age of eighteen years." There is nevertheless a growing body of literature that critiques the chronological age definition of children (see, e.g., Clark-Kazak, 2009b; Rogers, 2003).

2. Most refugee children are not heads of household, with just 4% of asylum claims made by children who arrive in a country of exile without parents or family members (UN-HCR, 2010, p. 19). Many of these children who have been orphaned or separated during flight are fostered by other families (Duerr, Posner, & Gilbert, 2003; Gale, 2006). Some do

become heads of household at a very young age; however, the situations of these refugee children have not been analyzed as part of this study.

3. Data were collected using a variety of methods, including semistructured interviews with refugee and national children (year 1: n = 60; year 2: n = 55; year 3: n = 53); semi-structured interviews with participating children's families in years 2 and 3 (n = 53 in each year); frequent informal conversations with participating children and their families in the intervening periods; a household survey of the participating families (n = 52); sustained participant observation in three case study schools (6 weeks in each year); semistructured interviews with teachers and school leaders (n = 45); and semistructured interviews with key informants (n = 30).

4. All names have been changed.

CHAPTER 7

Learning for a Bright Future
Schooling, Armed Conflict, and Children's Well-Being

REBECCA WINTHROP

JACKIE KIRK

During and after armed conflicts, policymakers and practitioners often advocate education to support the physical, psychological, and social well-being of children. In such advocacy they reference education's role in promoting children's welfare, although there is evidence that schooling in particular can jeopardize children's well-being. For example, schools can be sites of political contestation where armed groups deliberately attack students and teachers and where teachers promote—through formal and hidden curricula—intolerance and exclusion of certain social or cultural groups (Bush & Saltarelli, 2000; Davies, 2004). In addition, the argument that education promotes children's well-being very often is made without reference to children's lived experiences of education during and after conflict. There is a dearth of information about the best ways to ensure in practice that education does support children's well-being, if indeed it does at all.

In this chapter we argue that, under certain conditions and with certain approaches, schooling can support children's well-being. This subject has been given little attention in existing literature and practice. Using data collected on primary school students living in refugee and post-conflict contexts through the International Rescue Committee's Healing Classrooms Initiative, we examine the diverse ways in which Eritrean refugee students in Ethiopia, Afghan students in Afghanistan, and Liberian refugee students in Sierra Leone conceptualize their

This chapter originally published as Winthrop, R., & Kirk, J. (2008). Learning for a bright future: Schooling, armed conflict, and children's well-being. *Comparative Education Review, 52*(4), 639–661. Used with permission.

own well-being in relation to their school experience. We then draw out the implications for policy and practice of these children's experiences and perceptions.

CONCEPTS OF CHILDREN'S WELL-BEING AND SCHOOLING

Within the broad field of education in emergencies, despite evidence to the contrary, there exists a general assumption that schooling supports children's well-being. There has been very little research, however, to explore this relation in more depth. Studies that do address this relation typically originate from one of two perspectives: the *educationalist* approach, the primary concern of which is educational systems and which rarely incorporates children's own perspectives, and the *child protection* approach, the primary focus of which is children's experiences of conflict and which thus does incorporate children's voices, although rarely in relation to schooling. There are notable exceptions to this dichotomy, including Anna Obura's (2003) case study, for UNESCO's International Institute for Educational Planning (IIEP), on educational reconstruction in post-genocide Rwanda, which includes students' perspectives, and Roberta Apfel and Bennett Simon's (2000) psychoanalytic study of Palestinian children, which includes an examination of their school experience. Collectively, however, educationalists' and child protection advocates' arguments about the ways in which schooling can shape children's well-being generally can be classified into four categories: a return to *normalcy*, a mechanism for *socialization*, the provision of a *nurturing environment*, and as an instrument for *coping and hoping*. What is striking is that learning is rarely a central concern. Indeed, many of the benefits cited in the literature can apply to children's participation in a range of social institutions.

The first argument, which is one of the most common, for schooling in conflict situations is that education restores a sense of normalcy and gives children a much-needed routine in an otherwise unpredictable and often chaotic environment (Apfel & Simon, 2000; Bragin, 2004; Bruce, 2001; Buckland, 2005; Kos, 2005; Machel, 1996; Nicolai & Triplehorn, 2003; Pigozzi, 1996; Sinclair, 2001). While schooling certainly may offer students a sense of stability, this argument is concerned only with the act of going to school. It makes limited reference to what actually happens to children when they attend school. Attendance, not learning, is important. It is possible that the same benefit could come from the restoration of other normal activities in children's lives, such as daily religious routines.

The second argument, schooling as socialization, focuses on children's interactions with peers and adults when in school. These encounters allow students to develop appropriate social behaviors, to form positive relationships, and to cope more effectively with difficult circumstances (Apfel & Simon, 2000; Arafat & Boothby, 2003; De Berry, 2003; Kos, 2005; Loughry & Eyber, 2003; Machel, 1996). In this perspective, schooling is seen as a convenient venue for positive socialization, but the learning of specific skills, attitudes, and ideas related to positive social interaction and social cohesion is not central. One weakness of this argument is that it assumes that children always have positive relationships in school, when during and after armed conflict there are actually serious risks of abuse and exploitation of students by teachers or by their peers (De Berry, 2003; Leach & Mitchell, 2006). In addition, as with the normalcy argument, it is possible that participating regularly in another social institution, such as a place of worship or community center, could provide children with similar benefits to their well-being.

The third argument focuses on schooling as creating safe, protective, and nurturing environments for children. While the quality of social interactions at school is important to this argument, the focus is on how schooling itself, and teaching and learning processes in particular, can be adapted to support children's well-being. Schools can be modified to provide additional social services; the standard curriculum may be enriched with either critical information on topics such as health and safety or increased opportunities for students to express their feelings and process their experiences (see, e.g., Bragin, 2004; Machel, 1996; Nicolai, 2004; Nicolai & Triplehorn, 2003; Pigozzi, 1996; Sinclair, 2001). Creating a child-friendly school means ensuring that teaching methods and school management consider children's perspectives, address children's particular needs and concerns, and allow children's participation (see, e.g., Bird, 2003; Bragin, 2004; Kos, 2005). In this approach, the effects of different elements of the learning environment and learning processes are central to the promotion of students' well-being.

The fourth argument is far less common in the education in emergencies literature, but we include it here because it reflects an important theme that emerged in discussions with students in our study. It addresses how schools can assist children to "cope and hope," or deal with the difficulties in their lives and find reasons to believe in a better future. In humanitarian settings, children often confront harsh living conditions and limited ways to improve their present lives. Schooling in these contexts can provide children with goals for their lives and tangible ways in which their actions can, they believe, improve their future. By adopting ways to hope for a better future, children are able to cope with and transcend the negative effects of conflict and disaster (see, e.g., Apfel & Simon, 2000; Delap, 2005; Kos, 2005; Nicolai & Triplehorn, 2003).

As mentioned previously, learning plays a limited role within most of these arguments. Throughout this study, we employ a broad definition of learning to recognize its varying forms. Gaining basic literacy and numeracy skills, as well as knowledge and skills in subjects such as science and history, is clearly of central importance. In addition to academic learning, we also recognize the significance of what we term *social learning*. While acknowledging general research in the field of social emotional learning (e.g., Greenberg et al., 2003), we ground our understanding of social learning in a more general framework developed specifically for conflict contexts by Susan Nicolai and Carl Triplehorn (2003). In their discussion of what they term *cognitive protection*, they identify, beyond academic subjects, a range of knowledge, attitudes, and skills that children can learn in school that will help them live better and safer lives. These abilities include, for example, citizenship skills, health and security knowledge, and evaluation skills to help them process and respond to diverse sources of information, including propaganda. We take the examples articulated by Nicolai and Triplehorn, as well as students' descriptions of diverse learning opportunities in school that fall outside of traditional subject areas, to define social learning.

THE INTERNATIONAL RESCUE COMMITTEE
AND ITS HEALING CLASSROOMS INITIATIVE

Founded in 1933, the International Rescue Committee (IRC) is a humanitarian aid organization working with populations victimized by oppression or violent conflict. The IRC works with communities from the outset of an emergency, through protracted crises or refugee contexts, to post-conflict reconstruction and development. At work in 25 countries and serving a population of over 15 million people, the IRC seeks to help communities save lives, strengthen institutions, and promote social cohesion. The IRC employs multisector interventions; education, health, and governance and rights programs are three of its core programming areas.

Globally, the IRC's education strategy is to support displaced and war-affected children's, youths', and adults' access to relevant, high-quality education. The IRC gives special attention to flexible and innovative approaches to program design and implementation, which allows full respect for contextual and cultural factors, the cross-cutting issues of gender and child and youth protection and well-being, and ongoing organizational learning, including evaluation of program effectiveness.

In 2003, the IRC launched its Healing Classrooms Initiative (HCI) in response to an internal evaluation of its education programs. This assessment highlighted teaching quality, especially around understanding and supporting children's well-being, as one of the major barriers to achieving success in the IRC's programs. The HCI is a global organizational learning endeavor that has as its goals gaining insights into the lived experiences of teachers and students in conflict and post-conflict contexts, and using such insights to develop and pilot better approaches to teacher development and student well-being.

METHODOLOGY

This chapter presents data from the HCI's initial in-depth studies in three of the four pilot countries. The goal of these initial studies was to develop a deep and contextualized understanding of teachers' and students' perceptions of (1) students' well-being in relation to their school experience and (2) the actions of teachers and students that could influence students' well-being. These initial studies served to develop conceptual frameworks upon which programming approaches were later built. As such, the purpose of the initial studies was not to evaluate the IRC's programs per se but to identify the range of factors and experiences—both positive and negative—that shaped student well-being in these diverse contexts. In this work, we use a broad conceptualization of student well-being and seek students' own perspectives on their schooling experiences, regardless of whether these experiences relate to physical, emotional, psychological, cognitive, social, or cultural aspects of life.

At the time of this writing, the authors were part of the IRC's education team. While we aim to present the findings from the in-depth studies as objectively as possible, we clearly do so from positions of invested practitioners.

The data presented here come from month-long studies conducted in 2004 with Liberian refugee primary school students and teachers in Sierra Leone, Eritrean refugee primary school students and teachers in Ethiopia, and Afghan primary school students and teachers in rural communities in Afghanistan. As displacement and conflict often cause children to miss years of schooling, the primary school students participating in these studies ranged widely in age (ages 8–16 in Ethiopia, ages 8–12 in Afghanistan, and ages 7–19 in Sierra Leone).

In each country, the lead researcher was an Anglophone Canadian, while the research assistants were hired in country to ensure that their cultural and linguistic expertise corresponded to the communities in which the studies took place. Principles of informed consent, confidentiality, and child protection were observed throughout the studies. Research assistants were prepared for revelations of abuse, exploitation, and rights violations from the children they would interview, and they were instructed in procedures for follow-up should such disclosures occur.

Research tools were drafted in English, and in each country they were translated, piloted, and adapted prior to use. Research was conducted in the most appropriate language for the setting (often the local language) and then, if required, translated back into English for analysis. To minimize translation error, ongoing careful translation and back-translation were employed throughout the research process, and this was complemented by discussions with the research assistants about word choices and translation possibilities. The potential loss of nuance and possible confusions of meaning are, however, recognized limitations of this study.

While the same research questions were used in all three countries, a mix of qualitative and quantitative methods was employed, depending on the context. These methods included in-depth interviews, focus group discussions, questionnaires, classroom observations, school mapping, video and photo documentation, and textbook analysis. The data were then coded and analyzed for major themes, and the most salient findings are presented here. Table 7.1 provides a summary of the data used in this chapter, which focuses primarily on student data but also incorporates teacher, classroom observation, and parent data to contextualize and deepen understanding of the findings.

Table 7.1. Summary of Research Methods and Participant Numbers

Research Method	Ethiopia	Afghanistan	Sierra Leone	Total numbers
*Student data**				
Student questionnaire	64	...	...	64
Student focus group discussions based on questionnaire		4 groups (with average of 12 students per discussion)	22 groups (with average of 12 students per discussion)	26 groups (with total of 312 students participating)
Student interviews	48	15 group interviews with total of 40 students	38	101 interviews (with total of 126 students participating)
Teacher, parent, and classroom observation data†				
Teacher interviews	25	20	21	66
Teacher questionnaire	23	19	25	67
Classroom observation	33	36	30	99
Parent interviews	...	6	...	6

*Primary focus of this chapter
†Secondary focus of this chapter

COUNTRY CONTEXTS

The three countries examined here are important case studies because the conditions in each of them are representative of circumstances with which children and families in conflict zones must regularly contend. As a result of armed conflicts, there have been significant challenges for every aspect of human development. In the cases of Ethiopia and Afghanistan, drought has compounded these problems. At the time of the study, Ethiopia and Sierra Leone were in the bottom 20 of the UNDP's Human Development Index, while Afghanistan was not included (UNDP, 2004).

In Ethiopia, the study was conducted in a refugee camp in isolated, harsh, and rocky terrain along the Eritrean border. The participating students were Eritrean refugees of Kunama and Tigrigna ethnicities who were displaced because of political oppression and persecution within Eritrea. At the time of the research in Spring 2004, the IRC's education programs in this camp included both formal and nonformal education for children and youth, including a primary school with 22 classrooms in a semipermanent structure. Teachers were chosen by the refugee community, and although the men and women who were selected were among the most educated in the population, very few had completed their own education.

As in Ethiopia, teachers in Afghanistan were volunteers supported by the community. A number of the teachers were *mullahs*, or Muslim religious leaders. In contrast to the Eritrean refugee study, however, the research in Afghanistan centered on IRC-supported, home-based schooling for girls and boys in 15 rural communities without access to government schools. The IRC-supported classes were held in a range of environments, including under trees, in small rooms, and in partitioned gateways in teachers' own compounds and in the main prayer rooms of mosques. These schools followed the formal Ministry of Education curriculum and school policies.

The IRC program in Sierra Leone supported formal and nonformal education for refugee children and youth, with students attending formal primary schools in eight refugee camps or urban settlement areas in the eastern region of the country. The refugee schools were open to Sierra Leonean host communities' children and youth. Particular focus in this study was on girls and women, for whom the refugee experience has been especially traumatic.

Girls and young women were, and continue to be, vulnerable to exploitation from men in the community, especially men with financial power. A small number of male teachers had taken advantage of their authority over girls by sexually exploiting female students (UNHCR & Save the Children, 2002).

FINDINGS

Students in all three countries consistently described learning and gaining knowledge as the parts of their schooling experience that they most enjoyed and valued. Indeed, all the children interviewed shared this view, as did children participating in the focus group discussions and the survey.[1] When asked open-ended questions on what they liked most about school, all students spoke about learning, although they described learning differently. Some students talked abstractly about gaining knowledge and wisdom and "learning all things found in books," while other students spoke very specifically about learning particular skills such as reading, writing, and speaking English, and adding and subtracting. In addition to learning, students discussed other elements of school that they enjoyed and valued.

Most notably, 24% of the students discussed making and spending time with friends, with students in Afghanistan particularly emphasizing the importance of friendship.[2]

The focus of this chapter is on unpacking what students meant by learning and why they felt that learning was important. The rationale for this focus is that, in general, students placed heavy emphasis on learning as a benefit of schooling, and, more specifically, in discussing their experiences with friends at school, they described the ways in which their friends did or did not help them to learn. First we will review the ways in which students discussed learning in school as a positive influence on their well-being, and then we will address the elements of their school experience that they indicated negatively affected their well-being.

School as the Path to a Bright Future

In all three countries, students talked about how learning in school suggested to them that they had a bright future. This finding corresponds to the coping and hoping category in the education in emergencies literature discussed above. The students in our studies, however, explicitly connected learning well with the ability to hope for a better future. While nuances emerged across the three countries, the data show that students consistently believed that being in school put them on a path to a better future. In response to open-ended questions, students in all three countries used similar phrases to describe this belief. The imagery of darkness and light, echoing for us Plato's description of the learning process in his "Allegory of the Cave" (Bloom, 1991), was used by students, who talked about learning as moving them from "darkness to light," allowing them to "be free from the blindness and darkness of illiteracy," and helping them to have "a bright future." An Afghan girl reported: "They [children who do not go to school] will have a dark future, but they [those in school] will have a bright future." Achieving future goals, being a good person, and becoming a professional, such as a teacher or a doctor, were other ways in which students in all three countries recognized that their participation in school, and specifically their learning in school, would put them on the right path.

In these examples, neither the learning process nor the course content was important. Instead, schooling, and specifically learning at school, gave students the sense of being on the correct path. It is not surprising that they believed that attending and learning at school could give them a bright future. In addition to receiving from their family members and teachers clear messages about the importance of school, they also saw educated members of their communities occupying respected and lucrative positions, such as teachers, doctors, and nongovernmental organization (NGO) and United Nations (UN) workers. Students described how parents, siblings, and extended family encouraged them to attend school regularly, to study hard, and not to "spend your time in vain." For example, one 14-year-old girl in class 4 in Sierra Leone noted: "My mother is encouraging me that education is the key to life and to learn to become somebody important in the society tomorrow."

Students explained how their teachers encouraged them to attend school regularly and to study hard, and also how these teachers connected this behavior with positive personal attributes and good futures. According to students, the teachers told them stories that illustrated that children who attended school had good future prospects while children out-of-school did not. Students also reported that teachers pointed to examples of leaders and "wise men" in the community, suggesting that students could attain these positions if they studied hard and stayed in school. In Ethiopia, one 12-year-old girl remarked: "He [the teacher] gives us the idea to join the wise men of the community." Teachers in all three countries spoke of the importance of education for the development of their communities today and for the future. In Afghanistan and Ethiopia especially, teachers discussed the community leaders' messages that education is of the utmost importance and should be valued and prized. Many of the teachers in these countries reported that they were nominated by their community leaders to be teachers and are happy to, in the words of one teacher in Ethiopia, "share what little I know with the children" to improve their futures.

Our finding that students (and the adults with whom they interacted) valued schooling is consistent with scholars' arguments that, in the developing world, the school has taken on increasing symbolic power. With the proliferation of Western-style schooling and the globalization of information, images, and cultural forms, participation in school is, some argue, more and more seen as the key to becoming "modern" and connected with "the educated" (Appadurai, 1996; Fuller, 1991).

These perceived benefits of learning in school are tied closely to the social and symbolic value of the school in society. Therefore, would children associate the same benefits with less formal types of learning? The issue of official recognition and certification of students' learning is important in the education in emergencies field, especially when schooling is delivered by NGOs in situations in which governments are unwilling or unable to do so (Nicolai & Triplehorn, 2003). For example, students learning in NGO-supported schools in refugee camps wanted to make sure that their learning would be recognized by the government of their home country, if and when they returned, or by the host government, if they integrated locally.[3] In this study, all three education programs addressed this issue through close negotiations with home and host country governments, as well as by following government policies and curricula. The Ministry of Education authorities in each country recognized the students' learning, and in the cases of Sierra Leone and Afghanistan, the students were able to transition seamlessly from IRC-supported schools to government schools when the opportunity arose.

In Afghanistan, students and teachers were asked how they would compare their home-based schools to government schools. The vast majority of students indicated that their home-based schools were real schools. Teachers reinforced this notion, confirming that the schools were perceived as such by parents and the wider community. One female teacher described how she reminded her female students that she would be with them until grade 6, at which point she would make sure that they had documentation to attend secondary school. Such continuity may not, however, be the case for all schools. One Afghan boy said that he would prefer to be in a government school because "they are forever," perhaps alluding to the precarious nature of home-based schools, which depend on the volunteerism of the teachers. Indeed, teachers also expressed worry about what would happen to their schools if they were not able to continue teaching, especially given their lack of salary and their personal life demands (Kirk & Winthrop, 2005).

Perhaps the key is not the means by which learning is delivered (e.g., physical structure, location, salaried or trained teachers) but rather whether what students are learning is recognized by the broader community. Typically, this recognition comes from the government. Research on displaced Chechen youth who participated in a nonformal emergency education program provides some insight on this question. The research showed that the youth were particularly upset because of the nonformal nature of the program, which did not include subject learning. The informality, students said, reinforced the feelings of estrangement and alienation that had arisen from their displacement. What they desired was to attend a formal school, which they argued they needed for their future (Betancourt, Winthrop, Smith, & Dunn, 2002). In this case, the notion of education supporting student well-being does not apply because the students did not perceive the learning in which they were participating as putting them on the path to a bright future.

Academic and Social Learning in School

Students' recognition of "learning well" as a primary way in which schooling supports their well-being is not limited to the internalization of messages that education leads to a bright future. When asked to talk broadly about teachers, school peers, and daily routines, students in all three studies consistently returned to the concept of learning. Examining the data by location provides a rich picture of what students mean when they say that learning—in both academic and social forms—is the element of school that they value and enjoy the most. While there are interesting differences between the individual studies, there also exist common themes.

Ethiopia

As Eritrean refugee students in Ethiopia looked to the future, they expressed great enthusiasm for learning specific skills, especially if such skills would help their families and communities. Among the skills that boys and girls identified as fundamental were literacy and communication skills, including reading and writing, speaking English, and for the Kunama students, learning their own native language. A Kunama boy in grade 4 said that school helped him "to solve my problems by myself. If I get a letter from any foreign country, to be able to read myself." He added that his ultimate goal for coming to school was "to get knowledge and abolish illiteracy." Many students—girls and boys and Tigrigna and Kunama—echoed this boy's priorities, and several children envisioned themselves sharing this knowledge with others, particularly their siblings, the "next generation," and their tribe.

Students' interest in giving back to their community and their understanding that they are learning not just for themselves but on behalf of their families and tribes are illuminated in relation to the conditions of il/literacy among the refugees, particularly the Kunama refugees. At the time of the study, a majority of the Kunama refugees in the camp were illiterate. While a small percentage of the camp population had accessed schooling in Eritrea, many members had not had the opportunity to go to school. Children in the camp had had especially limited access to education previously because of the ongoing conflict in the region.

From almost the moment the Kunama refugees arrived in the camp, their leaders identified as a priority teaching their children to read and write. Community members who had had some schooling and who were literate were selected to be teachers. Only 40% of the teachers in the school at the time of the study had reached grade 12, and 28% had been trained as teachers previously. Many of them, while never previously considering themselves to be teachers, agreed to help as a service to the community. The notion that any education is valuable and can be shared was reflected in many of the teachers' perspectives on their own teaching and emerged in students' expressed desire to share their school learning with siblings and others.

Some students also described their appreciation of what can be described as social learning. A Kunama boy in grade 5 explained why he liked school: "My desire is to know and to identify what is good and bad in my daily life and how I might prevent if something happens in my life. Because of this I have more interest and desire in education." Several students also discussed how they learned at school to keep themselves clean, healthy, and "free from danger." A Kunama girl in grade 1a described a particularly useful lesson: "We learned in health education to bathe our body [2 times] within 1 week and to wash our hands after using latrine and before taking our meal. When we learned about this point a teacher drew a picture of a latrine and a man washing his hand before meal and after using latrine so we understand."

The realities of camp life necessitate a particular focus on health and hygiene, since people must live in such close proximity to one another. These arrangements are very different from the large territory in Eritrea from which the Kunama refugees came. Basic acts, such as going to the bathroom, take on new meanings in refugee life and require new social patterns, information, and habits. These students appreciated the health and safety messages that they received in school, and it appears that these programs supported their confidence in navigating safely through their new environment. In this way, the health and hygiene learning represents the nurturing environments category in the emergency education literature.

What is of particular interest in the above student's description of health class is her articulation of the teaching strategy—the picture—that the teacher used. Although she was a young student, she was aware nonetheless of when and how she was learning. Indeed, many students spent a great deal of time talking about the specific pedagogical techniques that they found most useful, which is especially surprising in a context in which teachers had limited formal training. Students cited teachers' use of teaching aids, illustrative stories, small-group discussions, and field trips as teaching tools that they especially liked. "The teacher uses a lot of teaching methods to be clear to the students," said one girl in class 1a. "For example, the teacher shows us the pictures of animals from textbook or by drawing on the blackboard." Several students talked about how teachers helped them by giving them breaks when they saw that the students were getting bored and tired. Students also appreciated teachers listening to their questions and explaining things repeatedly and in detail until they understood. Such teacher efforts were especially valued because they helped the students to master academic content.

Friends also played a significant role in the students' learning process. Perhaps unsurprisingly, students reported that friendships in school were important to them. Students' emphasis on the relation between friendship and learning merits specific attention, however. Students talked animatedly about how much they valued their friends' help in, and encouragement of, their own learning. School friends were often a source of support, especially on difficult homework assignments and when family members were not able to help. One Tigrigna boy in grade 3 commented: "I have a classmate and a friend. I study with them in order to have good results and to be a good student too. My family wants to help me. . . . They are interested but they are illiterate and the only thing they can do is advise me and encourage me to be a good student." Students also reported that they appreciated and enjoyed their friends when they helped one another with in-class assignments and tasks.

Afghanistan

While some Afghan students mentioned that they especially enjoyed academic subjects such as math, language, and Islamic studies, in most interviews, students emphasized how social learning, including lessons on proper manners, would help them to have a bright future. "I like everything," said one girl, "reading, being able to write, doing prayer, learning manners." For these students, learning manners went beyond learning social norms, which they could learn in other contexts such as the home, and they associated these skills with their attendance in school and their identity as students.

Good moral character is very important in Afghan culture, and teachers and community members expect education and schooling to instill this trait. In Afghan culture, the concept of *tarbia* is the key to understanding community and student focus on manners:

> Children who have tarbia are polite, obedient, respectful, sociable and peaceful. They know how to eat, sit, dress, and pray properly. They do not fight unnecessarily, and they do as their parents suggest. In contrast, children without tarbia (what in Dari is called "be tarbia") are rude, antisocial, and argumentative. (Save the Children, 2003, p. 8)

The intimate setting of the home-based schools, along with the trust that parents placed in teachers to educate and develop their children, shaped these students' school experience. Teachers talked about the responsibility that the community had given to them to guide and support the children's social as well as intellectual development. Teachers viewed teaching *tarbia* as an important responsibility to the community. In interviews, several parents reinforced the expectation that schooling had an important role in the social development of their children.

Displaying behaviors associated with *tarbia* is important to children, perhaps because of the link with their student identity. Students in this study were especially concerned that community members recognize them as school students. They strongly identified with being schoolgirls and schoolboys instead of being children who spend time on the street. They equated going to school and being a student with being good, and they listed a range of distinguishing characteristics that illustrated this association. For example, they described schoolchildren as being clean, treating elders with respect, and behaving well in public. When two schoolboys were asked whether they spent time outside of school shooting sparrows (a common diversion for young boys), they responded: "We are schoolboys and not street boys. We don't do those sorts of things. Schoolboys are very polite and say *salaam* to others. They help people, for example, blind people, to cross the road. Street boys tease, make fun, and say bad things."

Although schoolboys and schoolgirls are expected to observe Afghan traditions, they also take pride in distinguishing themselves in the community. When asked about daily routines, several students—boys and girls—discussed the special clothes that they wore to school, even though none of the schools had uniforms. Teachers might recommend clothes for school, but they do not mandate them. In an interview in which three girls were wearing the same type of clothes—black *shalwar kameez* (traditional outfit of loose fitting pants and long tunic) and white *chador* (large headscarf)—the girls remarked that they liked to wear these clothes "because we feel like school students." One girl said: "When I come to school people recognize that I'm going to school because of my uniform and my clean white *chador.*" In addition, students noted that they kept their school clothes clean, taking them off and putting them in a safe place after school so that they could wear them the next day.

Having a student identity and being recognized as a student by the community are important to Afghan students because they understand that education will assist them in being good people today and in the future. Students link being on the path toward a bright future with being a student, and they feel rewarded when they follow proper social codes, wear particular clothes, and behave as good schoolgirls and schoolboys.

Sierra Leone

Liberian refugee children in Sierra Leone also reported enjoying the recognition that being students inspired, but like the Eritrean students in Ethiopia, they also placed a high value on academic skills such as reading, writing, and speaking English because these skills would allow them to assist their families and community. While the official language of instruction in both Sierra Leone and Liberia is English and many of the UN documents refugees must read are in English, it is not the refugees' mother tongue. So children who learn English can provide great assistance within their community. A boy in grade 5 described how he likes school "because I am learning new ideas every day. I know how to read and write, unlike my mother and father, who are . . . illiterate." Similarly, a girl in grade 5 remarked: "I feel proud [of my school] because I am learning an international language. I am important in the community. I can read and write in English."

Being literate and being important in the community are sources of pride for many students because they connect a bright future with personal attributes and with others' recognition of those attributes. Students talked about the importance of learning in school as helping them, as one boy put it, to "be somebody important in the society." Students' focus on external recognition may be related to what some scholars have described as the heavily hierarchical nature of Liberian society, with wealth and power concentrated in a social elite. The resultant inequity has been cited as contributing to the Liberian civil war, but more recently it has been identified as an ongoing challenge that marginalizes many people and groups (Richards et al., 2005).

Liberian refugees in Sierra Leone referred repeatedly to "big men." There are various paths to achieving this status, including family lineage, financial prosperity, and, as the students in this study seemed to appreciate, being educated. Students associated education with respect and importance, which, in turn, would lead to their getting a good job, earning money, and supporting their families. The Liberian refugee students differed from their counterparts in Ethiopia and

Afghanistan because of their explicit focus on jobs and money, which a student in grade 4a clearly articulated: "It is important for children to come to school because education pays more. When you are educated you make good money and also people respect you in the community or everywhere else."

In addition to academic skills, Liberian students also valued the social learning that they acquired in school. Several students emphasized the importance of learning what is "good and bad" so that they could protect themselves. Students indicated that social learning would help them to develop personal attributes with which they could navigate the world safely and, most important, not be tricked. One 15-year-old girl in grade 5 said that what she liked most about school was "to learn, acquire knowledge so that nobody can fool me in the future." A grade 6 student's remark encapsulated other students' concern about avoiding manipulation and exploitation: "I want to make good use of the world in that nobody can fool me and my family."

Students' concern about being fooled or tricked indicates an awareness of the sexual and labor exploitation that exists in the camp and surrounding area. Girls especially often are promised payment of school fees in return for sex, only to have the deal broken. Such abuse has followed the refugees from Liberia, where some armed groups successfully manipulated the poor and rural classes in part because of their low literacy levels. It is clear that, for some students, learning empowers them to protect their own interests. In the words of one 17-year-old girl in grade 5: "What I most like about coming to school is that I like to be a responsible person or woman in the future. [This] will help my family and friends ... [and enable me] not to be under somebody."

When asked to discuss her teachers, this fifth-grade girl returned to the theme of learning. She echoed the perspectives of many of her peers when she emphasized how much she valued her teachers' assistance in both academic and social learning: "My teachers in school help me in many ways.... My teacher can help me to read my note that I did not understand. He can also help me to explain my note well. He can also help me find solution to some of my personal problems at home by giving me suggestions. ... He can also help me to respect elderly ones and also make peace between me and the next person in class."

Not Learning Well: Student Distress in School

While students in all three studies were able to articulate positive influences on their learning in school, they also described aspects of their school experiences that undermined their well-being. These impediments greatly distressed them, especially when they originated with peers and teachers. Among the three groups, the extent and severity of negative school experiences differed dramatically, with students in Sierra Leone reporting that they were subjected to extreme abuse and exploitation, and students in Ethiopia and Afghanistan describing milder challenges.

In Ethiopia and Afghanistan, classroom observations confirmed student reports of generally positive and supportive school environments, although some
teacher and peer behavior disrupted learning and distressed students. Most students in Ethiopia had difficulty identifying aspects of school that they did not
like. Students claimed that, when their teachers punished them, they deserved it
because they were disrupting class or misbehaving. Several students also remarked
that the teachers did not hit hard. One teacher, however, was known to be harsh
and mean, hitting students hard and punishing them excessively. In Sierra Leone,
classroom observations also confirmed children's reports of severe corporal punishment and harsh treatment by teachers.

While students in Ethiopia generally were pleased with their teachers, 15 of
the 48 student interviewees talked about being annoyed and upset by peers disrupting class, "running over desks," fighting, laughing and teasing, and stealing
pencils and books. Although the majority of girls and boys reported that they
felt like brothers and sisters, girls mentioned that boys were more disruptive in
school and were known for fighting and stealing. One girl in class 1a explained:
"It is better to sit with girls than boys. Boys, sometimes they may steal our pens,
pencils, exercise books and they will fight with us, but the girls could not steal,
fight and disturb." Boys also criticized girls, generally for being overly "chatty"
in class.

Afghan students did not talk much about negative teacher behavior, focusing instead on disruptions by their peers. As in Ethiopia, Afghan girls and boys
described their relationships as "brother and sister." There were conflicts, however.
Several girls expressed discomfort with attending school with boys. One girl said
that she felt shy in front of boys in class and that it would be better if boys and
girls were separated. Another girl also explained that separate classes for boys and
girls were better, because it would save embarrassment when they did not know or
understand course content. Students in close to half the interviews also cited fighting between peers as something that they did not like about school. They reported
that fighting happened in class, during play time, and when walking to and from
school. According to one boy: "The girls are fighting right from the house door to
the school. They don't hit each other, they just argue. But the boys hit. It is over
things like losing a pencil or sometimes one will make a face at another."

In Sierra Leone, Liberian refugee students described more severe behavior
among both teachers and peers. Many students talked about teachers' practices of
physical beating, harsh yelling and making insults, bribery, corruption, and ejec-
tion of students from class. Students seemed to find the last strategy particularly
unfair and hurtful, because it forced them to miss entirely the important learning
that they had come to school to obtain. The practice of teachers exploiting and
bribing students—trading grades for money or in some cases sex—is well documented in Liberian refugee camps in Sierra Leone and elsewhere in West Africa
(UNHCR & Save the Children, 2002). This abusive behavior is extremely upsetting

to students, particularly in terms of the impact it has on their ability to progress through school. One 16-year-old boy in grade 5 reported: "The things that a teacher does that I hate are: beating me roughly like a criminal; depriving me of my right, for example, when I take a test and pass and he reduces my grade and fails me; provoking me to anger by saying, 'You are too big to be in this class, you are too stupid'; requesting a bribe, for example, when I fail the test, the teacher requests for money for me to pass me."

Two girls, aged 16 and 17 and in grade 5, identified teachers approaching them "for love" after school hours as a source of discomfort at school. Students did not discuss this issue in depth, although they listed it among other negative aspects of school and teachers' behavior. In the words of the 17-year-old girl: "What I like least about coming to school is hitting, shouting at me, a teacher abusing me, and also a teacher approaching me or telling me he wants me for love at home."

Perhaps surprisingly, while refugee students in Sierra Leone were extremely upset by these harsh forms of treatment by their teachers, they described their overall school experience as positive. Students' favorable perception of education was due in large part to the great value they placed on learning for their future. The 17-year-old girl who was upset by sexual harassment from her teacher also described how happy she was to come to school because she had learned to read and write, unlike some of her peers. She also articulated high hopes for her future and her ability to help to develop her country. "I am proud of my school because I am getting good learning, and also I'm improving in terms of speech among my friends," she said.

Students in Sierra Leone also reported struggles and distress from peer behaviors, such as teasing, bullying, fighting, disrupting class, and stealing books. Although many students noted that the recent arrival of female classroom assistants reduced incidents of stealing and fighting in class, challenges remained. As an 18-year-old girl in grade 6 stated: "I also hate my classmates to tell me that 'I love you.' I also don't want to sit down among the boys in the class." Sexual advances by male students are common, and sexual relations between students result in a large number of pregnancies each year. Cumulatively, these negative peer relations, like abuse from teachers, have adverse effects on students' well-being.

Students Actively Shape Their School Experience

As students in these studies spoke about learning, they presented themselves as active participants in the process, making choices about their school experience. Social trauma scholar Veena Das and colleagues (2001) describe the power of individuals to establish an active role within their daily life as the "retrieval of voice in the face of recalcitrance of tragedy" and argue that, in political violence contexts, such engagement can be healing. Students' descriptions of how they actively created their school experience indicate both pride and agency.

In all three studies, students discussed making time between their many home or external work responsibilities to study hard and do their homework. They also emphasized paying close attention in class and listening to their teachers as key to ensuring that they learned well. If they did not understand a lesson, students explained, they asked questions and sometimes consulted their classmates. One grade 1 boy in Ethiopia stated that when he does not understand something, "I will never keep silent but I will raise my hand and ask the teacher [about what] is not clear to me and sometimes I will ask my classmates if they understand clearly." Similarly, in Sierra Leone, one boy in grade 5 explained his strategy for getting help: "When I find something that I don't understand, I can go to my teacher for explanation or my friends if my teacher is not around. And if it is at home, I can ask my parents for their views about my problems. And if they too are not around, I can go to my brother for an answer or my sister for an answer, but I cannot keep it to myself!"

Another strategy that students in all three cases reported that they employ is showing respect to their teachers by obeying their instructions, helping to clean classrooms, being punctual, and having good attendance. Students in Sierra Leone also talked about not cheating on exams as a form of respect, a strategy not emphasized by students in other countries but likely connected to corruption in their particular circumstances. Afghanistan provided another context-specific illustration. Given that schooling there occurred in teachers' homes, students also considered their teachers' personal needs. For example, a group of Afghan students explained that their teacher had a baby, and if she were called from class to attend to family matters, they would study on their own and not make noise.

Afghan students also described strategies that they employed to help their teachers with the teaching and learning process. Two girls in one interview described how they often helped their teacher with her household chores so that she could be available to teach them sooner. One of these girls explained that "sometimes when the teacher doesn't notice a mistake, then we tell her." In another class, students said that they would bring water for the teacher whenever she was thirsty, presumably so that she could continue with the lesson. Students also talked about what they did to help other students learn. When their peers missed class, the students lent them notes to copy so that they would not fall behind. The multigrade environment in Afghan classes also provided opportunities for older or more advanced students to help their classmates.

CONCLUSION

The preceding discussion illustrates how children in conflict areas emphasize different ways in which schooling does and does not support their well-being. Most significantly, students in Sierra Leone, Afghanistan, and Ethiopia related that concerns about their learning experiences and their well-being in school should not be treated as separate issues. Education programs that support students' well-being by restoring normalcy through regular school attendance, social opportunities with peers, and nurturing environments with access to counselors are all likely to have a positive influence on children. The literature analyzing such programs, however, tends not to emphasize a central element of the school experience that contributes to their well-being: learning. As the children in these studies explained, the combination of academic and social learning is what gives them hope for the future.

Students' perspectives on the importance of learning well show us that one of the most important ways to support children's well-being is through education programs that prioritize the quality and relevance of students' learning. This emphasis resonates well with recent international studies that demonstrate that the number of years that girls spend in school is not an adequate measure of the expected outcomes that school has for girls. Instead, the level of skill acquisition, regardless of years in school, is a much better measure of positive long-term schooling outcomes for girls (Schleicher 2007). Indeed, children in this study showed that they were keenly aware of when they were learning and when they were not learning. Attending school was not enough. They were focused on understanding their lessons, passing their classes, behaving properly, taking on a student identity, and using the knowledge and skills they acquired in school to help themselves and their friends, families, and communities.

Establishing learning as central to educational programming may seem to be an obvious approach to ensuring students' well-being, but the everyday realities of program development and implementation often result in the assumption that these core components are happening, rather than specific focus on these issues. Scholars of children's well-being in armed conflict contexts argue that humanitarian programming for children often can disregard children's own perspectives, resources, and agency. The conceptions of childhood that underlie international humanitarian work are, they argue, built on notions that children are innocent, vulnerable, helpless, and "in formation" (Boyden, 2000; J. Hart, 2006; Marshall, 1999).

That children do articulate alternative perspectives compels us to ensure not only that policies and programs can and do respond to these priority needs but also that we institute regular opportunities for children to speak about their learning, their educational priorities, and the extent to which they feel that their needs are being met. The students' voices in this study remind us that children can be agents of their own lives. They understand themselves not as helpless objects that are acted upon but as subjects who actively construct their school experience.

Rights-based educational programming implies not only fulfillment of the right of children to education through the provision of schooling but also that the processes and approaches used in such education support the children in the fulfillment of other rights, such as the right to participate in decisions that affect them. We heard from the students in this study that they actively pursued learning and sought additional explanations of what they did not comprehend, making use of the people around them as resources for their learning. We learned from these students that learning is both cause and effect of remarkable agency on the part of children who are incredibly motivated to learn. What is especially notable is that these children persevered despite the challenging conditions in which they lived and the generally poor quality of the education offered to them. In these contexts, successful learning required children to use their own creativity, resourcefulness, and imagination. At the same time, the confidence and senses of purpose and possibility that constitute this agency were reinforced by students' awareness of present and future learning outcomes.

Children affected by conflict deserve the best possible opportunities and resources for learning, but schooling also should act as a forum to exercise the children's own agency. In this environment, students can play key roles and contribute to their families, schools, and communities. Engaging children in monitoring and evaluating teacher development, school improvement projects, and community education activities, for example, is a possible way to instill in children their own sense of agency. Such practice also would result in more child-centered family, school, and community development.

This study has provided significant insights into the learning lives of children affected by conflict. It also has exposed numerous areas for further research. As educators, we intentionally use the term *well-being* broadly and in a nonclinical way, but we recognize that there is much more to learn about how to identify, articulate, and respond to the variety of well-being needs of the diverse groups with whom our programs work. From a programming perspective, we would suggest using action research approaches (Hart & Tryer, 2006) to discern whether the recommended strategies have the desired effects on students' academic and social learning.

In addition, we want to know more about productive ways to work with teachers to encourage them to understand and support their students as active constructors of a meaningful and productive schooling experience. We also wonder, given the symbolic importance of schooling and school learning, about the implications that this study will have for understanding how to support the well-being of out-of-school children. Clearly, fellow academics, policymakers, and program implementers have numerous opportunities to expand the evolving and challenging research agenda around education during and after armed conflict.

NOTES

1. In Ethiopia, 86% of the students surveyed specifically identified learning as the aspect of schooling they valued most, as did students in 95% of the focus group discussions in Sierra Leone.

2. Learning and making and spending time with friends were the two most important themes to emerge from the data. A handful of other students mentioned such benefits as receiving pens and copy books.

3. At the time of these studies, return (repatriation), local integration, and third-country resettlement (the three main options proposed by the UNHCR as durable solutions for refugees) had not been implemented on a large scale for the refugee populations in Ethiopia and Sierra Leone.

CHAPTER 8

Understanding the Diverse Forms of Learning Valued by Children in Conflict Contexts

REBECCA WINTHROP

A caricature of the education quality debate in conflict contexts would place on one side the reading enthusiasts—those that are narrowly focused on ensuring children learn fundamental reading skills—and on the other the well-being enthusiasts—those that are focused on the range of psychosocial and other benefits of schooling for young people. While exaggerated, this scenario is not far from the discourse in policy circles. In a meeting with policymakers on education and conflict, I once witnessed a very similar discussion play out between a representative of a multilateral donor and a representative of a bilateral donor. One argued that in the early post-conflict period the focus should be on rapid restoration of learning of formal, core subjects (e.g., language, history, and math), and the other argued that a focus on learning outcomes was not important; instead, schools should focus on expressive activities and other forms of psychosocial support.

This chapter argues the need for a more nuanced understanding of education quality in conflict contexts, one that connects the multiple dimensions of quality by drawing on the insights of children themselves as to the values they place on learning. As Jackie Kirk and I have argued previously, literacy and numeracy skills greatly augment children's and young people's survival and life skills (see Chapter 7). For example, being able to read medicine labels, signs, newspapers, and registration or identification cards is an important and useful skill for navigating a new and shifting environment. The perception of learning well, even if in fact children are learning very little, also supports their psychosocial well-being. The belief that they are on the path to a brighter and better future, through the knowledge they are gaining at school, especially at the primary level, is a powerful force in helping children cope with difficult environments.

This chapter deepens the exploration of primary students' own perspectives on learning in the three conflict settings (in Afghanistan, Eritrean refugee students in Ethiopia, and Liberian refugee students in Sierra Leone) presented in Chapter 7 of this volume. To understand and conceptualize the different ways that children express the importance of learning, the study draws on a framework informed by Habermas's theory of knowledge (Habermas, 1971; Winthrop, 2008). Methodologically, the chapter draws on data collected in 2004 for a study of the International Rescue Committee's Healing Classrooms Initiative (see Winthrop & Kirk, 2008, and Winthrop, 2008, for a complete review of the study methodology).

A FRAMEWORK FOR UNDERSTANDING MULTIPLE FORMS OF LEARNING

How to conceptualize and understand learning has been much debated in educational philosophy and theory. In this study Habermas's delineation of technical, practical, and emancipatory learning is adapted to help clarify how learning is understood by students participating in schooling in contexts affected by armed conflict. Habermas's theory of knowledge constitutive interests is used here as a heuristic, and the intent is not to reflect upon or critique the theory itself.

In *Knowledge and Human Interests*, Habermas (1971) elaborated three distinct forms of knowledge: (1) the *technical*, which relates to knowledge directly used in shaping or mastering one's environment, (2) the *practical*, which corresponds to knowledge supporting one's expanding understanding of self in relation to others, and (3) the *emancipatory*, in which knowledge fosters critical consciousness aimed at overcoming social dogma and domination. His theory of tripartite human interest was quickly taken up by a range of theorists and educators to further concepts of ways of knowing and learning. Most notably, Jack Mezirow (1981), often referred to as the father of transformational learning theory, uses Habermas's three interests to develop a theory of adult learning focused on the development of critical consciousness. Mezirow's theory of adult learning, along with Habermas's theory of human interests, has been taken up by scholars, such as Cranton, who seek to translate the theory into practical guidance for educators working with adults (Cranton, 2006; see also Furth, 1996, for an example of how Habermas's theory of tripartite human interests has been used to explore issues concerning the social development of young children). In this study, the concepts of technical, practical, and emancipatory learning provide a useful tool for analyzing the place of learning in the debate over schooling and well-being. This tripartite model has been critiqued for drawing clear distinctions among three forms of learning, when in practice they manifest more as multiple, overlapping dimensions (Castagno, 2006). I recognize that, in practice, learning is complex and that an individual at any given time may be multitasking in terms of more than one interest. Nonetheless, as a heuristic, the model allows for an analysis across a range of learning forms, which will help clarify the ways in which conflict-affected children view school-based learning.

Inspired by work in using these three modes of knowledge to analyze teachers' learning (Castagno, 2006), this study understands these three forms of learning in the following way. *Technical* learning is an instrumental process in which the knowledge acquired holds value because it enables the learner to directly manipulate or control elements in his or her life or environment. For example, learning proper hygiene practices is valued because it can be applied to learners' daily routines for health improvement. *Practical* learning is a social process in which the learner acquires knowledge and understanding related to social norms and expectations and reflects on his or her role within them. For example, learning acceptable patterns of behavior with important members of a social network, such as elders, is valued because it gives learners the confidence and capacity to engage appropriately. *Emancipatory* learning is a critical process in which knowledge acquired is valued for its ability to demystify or transform social conditions, as in students developing literacy skills in order to teach and empower other, illiterate members of their community. Here the form of emancipatory learning is adapted to include the development of social consciousness, such as the understanding that an individual can contribute to and shape society, not just be shaped by society. This adaptation allows for the inclusion of socially conscious perspectives on learning that children in crisis may exhibit.

With this explanation of the framework, I now turn to its application. The following section describes the findings from analyzing student interviews, focus groups, and surveys in relation to these different forms of learning.

DIVERSE FORMS OF LEARNING VALUED BY CHILDREN

What do students mean by learning and how do they envision learning leading them toward a bright future? For students in this study, learning is conceived as sets of skills, knowledge, or social conventions that go beyond the school subjects in the curriculum. When they refer to learning helping them to have a bright future, they often describe how they believe that the knowledge, skills, or social conventions they learn, help them to be, to have, or to do something good or useful today or in the future. The most frequently cited knowledge and/or skills that students deem especially important are literacy (e.g., reading, writing, and speaking properly) and social norms (e.g., proper behavior with elders). In Ethiopia, 33% (16/48) of students interviewed specifically cited literacy as important, while 50% (19/38) in Sierra Leone and 40% (6/15) in Afghanistan did as well. Learning a range of social norms was identified by 21% (10/48) of students interviewed in Ethiopia, 50% (19/38) in Sierra Leone, and 73% (11/15) in Afghanistan.

Students, especially in Ethiopia and Sierra Leone, emphasize the importance of technical learning. Focusing on literacy, numeracy, and other skills acquired in school, they describe the ways in which they can use learning in their current and future lives for a range of purposes. They are not focused on engaging with others in their world but rather on their individual abilities, capacities, and actions. They describe technical learning on two levels. First, they discuss the way in which learning enables them to take *instrumental action* to benefit themselves, now or in the future, such as using numeracy skills to count money. Second, they describe how learning can help their *personal development* by cultivating desired personal characteristics, such as being clever or wise.

Practical learning is also very important, especially to students in Afghanistan. They describe the ways in which learning enables them to enter into and play a role in the social world. They appreciate how their learning helps to identify and understand important social norms and to fulfill social expectations. They discuss practical learning on three levels. On the *normative* level, they emphasize the importance of learning social norms that help them behave appropriately with others, such as treating their elders with respect and deference. Students are also interested in learning because it helps them achieve an important *status* in their communities by, for example, being respected for knowing how to read and write. Focusing on *altruistic* aims, they discuss how learning can help them help others, such as enabling them to take care of their parents after they graduate.

Table 8.1. Technical, Practical, and Emancipatory Forms of Learning

Forms of Learning	Levels	Examples
Technical	Instrumental Action	Communicate in daily life (literacy)
		Count in daily life (numeracy)
		Use healthy personal practices in daily life (health education)
		Become a professional in the future (e.g., teacher, doctor)
		Earn money in the future
	Personal Development	Develop wanted personal characteristics (e.g., clever, wise, not easily tricked)
Practical	Normative	Behave properly with others (e.g., respect elders, do not fight with peers, wear clean clothes)
	Status	Become important in society (e.g., respected)
	Altruistic	Help family, relatives
Emancipatory	Social Consciousness	Contribute to social change in community, tribe, country

Less prevalent is students' focus on emancipatory learning. Students in all locations, but especially in Ethiopia, do discuss learning as a means of transforming the social context in which they find themselves. Here they focus on *socially conscious* aspirations such as using the literacy skills they learn in school to educate illiterate members of their community and contribute to the "liberation" of their tribe.

Table 8.1 summarizes the different levels within the three forms of technical, practical, and emancipatory learning.

TECHNICAL LEARNING

Instrumental Action

Students articulated a range of ways in which the learning they do in school can be useful in bringing them present and future benefits. They described applying their learning in daily communication, counting money, or hygiene practices; in the future they believe it will enable them to get a good job and earn money. This focus on learning for instrumental action related to personal improvement is technical learning at the most basic level. In the three study locations, students emphasized different aspects of learning for instrumental action, although in all locations they emphasized becoming a professional in the future. This desire, especially becoming a teacher or a doctor, is heavily emphasized across all students, reinforcing the focus on learning for a bright future.

In Ethiopia, 4 out of 48 children interviewed spoke specifically about how they like learning math because it helps them in their daily lives. For example, one 14-year-old boy in grade 4 said, "Maths helps me in my daily life," while a 13-year-old boy in grade 3b expanded on this, saying his favorite subject is math, "because I get it easy to understand and in addition the reason why I chose maths is because maths can help you count money." Numeracy skills learned in school are seen to be easily applied to improve students' activities outside of school.

While many students identified learning to read and write as especially important, only one student mentioned how he used the literacy skills he learned in school to help him personally. A Kunama boy in grade 4 said that school helped him "to solve my problems by myself. If I get a letter from any foreign country, to be able to read myself." Interestingly, students in Ethiopia focus mainly on how literacy skills enable them to fulfill social expectations (practical learning) or transform their community (emancipatory learning).

In Ethiopia, 6 out of 64 of the children also expressed appreciation for school because it helped them learn how to keep themselves clean, healthy, and "free from danger." Clearly the knowledge and skills learned in health education can be easily applied to improve daily routines. Given the constrained environment in which the Eritrean refugees are living, basic life processes such as using latrines can be totally new experiences for children and their parents.

By far the most dominant way in which students in Ethiopia envision using their learning is by becoming a professional in the future. In the survey, more than half (37/64) of students said that becoming a teacher or a doctor is one of the most important reasons they come to school. Undoubtedly teachers and doctors are people who are admired in their community and whom students themselves admire. For example, in an interview in Ethiopia one 13-year-old boy in grade 4 said that what he most values about school is "to learn—to get knowledge, because I want to be either a doctor or a teacher. Other things are less important to me." In the refugee camp, teachers and doctors are visible members of the community, working at the school and clinic to provide important social services. Children have few role models of other jobs or professions to which they may aspire.

Students in Sierra Leone talk about how much they value learning to read, write, and speak English. In interviews, almost one third of the students (11/38) specifically explained how they use the literacy skills they are learning in school to benefit themselves in their daily lives. For example, one 17-year-old girl in class 5 stated, "I am proud of my school because I am getting good learning and also I'm improving in terms of speech among my friends." In addition to the value of verbal communication skills, written skills are valued by students. A 16-year-old boy in grade 6 explained that he really likes school because "I can read by myself a note written to somebody, comic and novel, and other history concordance without asking anybody to show me or teach me. I am out of illiteracy level my mother and father are in." This boy especially emphasizes the importance of his literacy level given the illiteracy of his immediate family. In Sierra Leone, students make virtually no mention of health education or numeracy as useful learning in their lives, with only two boys mentioning learning math as something they enjoy generally about school.

As in Ethiopia, students heavily emphasize their desire to become a professional and have a job, such as a teacher, doctor, nurse, government worker, or news broadcaster. In more than two-thirds (15/21) of the focus group discussions in Sierra Leone, students assert that they value school because they want to get a job and become a professional, which they claim will help them in their lives. At times students connect their desire to become a professional with earning money. For example, a 5th-grade boy says, "I will like to be a teacher because teacher can get much pay."

This focus on using learning to earn money in the future appears only in Sierra Leone. Students there spoke specifically about the importance of earning money in close to one-third of the focus group discussions (6/21). For example, a boy in a class 6 focus group discussion said that he likes coming to school so he can "get a good job and get plenty of money." One of his fellow students in a class 4a focus group further explained by saying, "It is important for children to come to school because education pay more. When you are educated you make good money." It is not only students who link the benefits of schooling to earning a living. Teachers interviewed frequently mentioned concerns over their rates of pay, with many expressing the desire to get advanced training so they one day could be certified teachers with job security and, it is assumed, higher levels of compensation.

In Afghanistan, students expressed limited interest in technical forms of learning. Fewer than one third (4/15) of the students interviewed focused on instrumental aspects of their school learning, often talking about their desire to be a teacher or doctor. For example, in one interview, a girl said, "In the future I should be something like a doctor or a teacher," when she described the reasons she most enjoys school. Here too students likely have limited exposure to a range of professionals and are most familiar with teachers and doctors. While appreciative of learning a range of knowledge and skills, such as literacy, math, and religion, students did not articulate how they envisioned applying this learning in their daily lives.

Personal Development

Students in Ethiopia and Sierra Leone articulated their appreciation of another level of technical learning. The learning they do in school helps them develop positive personal characteristics, such as being clever, wise, and not easily tricked. While still focused on ways in which they can use learning to build personal capacities, students' discussions implicitly engage their relations with others. For example, building your capacity to not be fooled by others recognizes the possibility that people whom you encounter may by trying to trick you. In this sense, this level of technical learning is nearing the border of practical learning.

Students in Ethiopia described their aspirations to develop laudable personal characteristics through learning in school. Of students surveyed, 14 out of 64 talked about enjoying their school especially because they hope it will make them clever, great, or wise. For example, in an interview a 12-year-old girl in class 3b said, "I like to come to school to grasp knowledge and to be a great person," and another student, an 11-year-old boy in grade 4, said he comes to school "to be a wise man and have knowledge." This focus on valued personal traits is future-oriented. Students perceive their schooling as helping them over time to develop personally so they can be or become great or wise.

Similar to students in Ethiopia, children in Sierra Leone also described how they perceived that school helps them become wise, civilized, and a good person. In interviews, 8 out of 38 students described how they believed their school learning helped them take on such laudable personal characteristics. For example, a 16-year-old boy in class 5 said, "School can make me to be civilized . . . can make me to think correctly and make wise decisions." For some students this is something they hope to gain in the future; for example, a 14-year-old girl in class 4b stated, "I like to come to school and learn to be a good person in the future." Here students focus on learning for personal development that helps them today as well as in the future. Being able to think correctly and make wise decisions certainly can help students better navigate their daily as well as their future lives.

In Sierra Leone, students in 5 of 21 focus group discussions emphasized the importance of learning what is "good and bad" in life so they could protect themselves and, most important, not be fooled or tricked. For example, one 15-year-old girl in class 5 said that what she likes most about school is "to learn, acquire knowledge so that nobody can fool me in the future." This imperative to avoid manipulation and exploitation is echoed in the words of a grade 6 student who explains why she finds school important: "I want to make good use of the world in that nobody can fool me and my family."

This notion of being fooled or tricked likely pertains to the types of sexual and labor exploitation that exist in the Sierra Leonean camp and its surroundings. Girls, especially, often are promised payment for school fees in return for sex, only to have the deal broken later. For students who are concerned about this, learning empowers them to protect their own interests. In the words of one 17-year-old girl in grade 5: "What I most like about coming to school is that I like to be a responsible person or woman in the future . . . [and] not to be under somebody." Students in Sierra Leone have very immediate concerns, which they believe their school learning can help them address. By developing confidence, critical thinking, and literacy skills, children and youth in Sierra Leone hope to better navigate the difficulties that lie ahead both today and in the future.

PRACTICAL LEARNING

Normative

Students describe a range of ways in which the learning they do in school helps them understand social norms and behave appropriately with others. They discuss learning proper ways to interact with others, such as elders and peers, and to behave as students, including how to dress appropriately. This focus on learning social norms is practical learning at the most basic level, and students focus heavily on it across study sites, particularly in Afghanistan. Students emphasize different aspects of learning social norms.

In Ethiopia, 10 out of 48 students interviewed appreciate the social norms they learn at school. They focus on advice they get from their teachers on how to interact with friends in a "peaceful" way. For example, one boy in grade 1a says his teacher often counsels his class that "we should never fight with our friends." Students cite teachers' advice and admonishment on getting along with friends, especially during recreation and sports activities. Students also talk about a range of other behaviors that they are encouraged to display. For example, a 13-year-old boy in class 3b says about his teachers, "They don't allow us to spend our time in bad places that are found in town, but they allow us to play at school as we wish." Encouraging students to come to school regularly, to spend time studying with friends, and not waste time also are cited by students as good behaviors they are encouraged by teachers to take on. Students appear to appreciate this counsel because it gives them confidence that they understand what is expected of them and they are then able to engage with others accordingly.

In Sierra Leone, students also value learning good, proper behavior and ways to interact with others. In interviews, half of the students (19/38) discussed a range of social norms that they appreciate learning. They described teachers' guidance on respecting elders, interacting peacefully with peers, dressing properly, and not having sex. For example, a 13-year-old girl in class 5 says her teacher "directs me how to behave in public—out of school there is no other help." Here she implies that she is not receiving this type of guidance or orientation to social norms from other sources besides her teacher. A 15-year-old girl in class 6 is more specific about the advice her teacher gives about public behavior, saying, "My teacher help . . . encourage me not to move with bad company like going to night dance." Students also talked about learning how to interact with peers and elders. For example, a 10-year-old boy in class 3a said his teacher "help me to learn good behaviors, like when I make a quarrel with my friend, she can encourage me to know what is good or bad," and a 17-year-old girl in class 5 said, "My teachers . . . help me to respect elderly ones." Like students in Ethiopia, students in Sierra Leone appreciate learning that enables them to understand social norms and hence have greater confidence in interacting with others and fulfilling social expectations.

In Afghanistan, this level of practical learning is the most heavily emphasized by students out of the range of different learning forms. Students are much more detailed in their discussions of learning social norms than in the other two study locations. Students in more than two-thirds (11/15) of our interviews discuss the importance of learning social norms in school. Many of these students cited learning manners as one of the aspects of school they enjoyed the most. For these students, learning manners goes beyond acquiring a set of social norms, which one would expect they could learn in other places such as the home, and is directly connected to their attendance in school and hence identity as a student. Good manners are a way of displaying good moral character, which is very important in Afghan culture, and are reflected in teacher and community expectations of education and schooling. The concept of *tarbia* is essential to understanding students' focus on manners. There are four especially important aspects of good *tarbia*: good and clean language, respect for elders and parents, bodily cleanliness, and hospitality.

The intimate setting of the home-based schools, along with the trust that parents place in teachers to be able to educate and develop their children, certainly shape students' school experience. In this environment and cultural setting, learning good manners is a highly valued part of school. Teachers interviewed talked about the responsibility that the community had given to them to guide and support the children's intellectual as well as social development. Teaching *tarbia* is seen by teachers as an important aspect of their position in the community. In interviews with several parents, this expectation of schooling—that it has an important role in the social development of their children, especially by learning *tarbia*—was reinforced.

Displaying the range of behaviors associated with *tarbia* is important to children; however, *tarbia* from their perspective would seem also to be closely linked to their student identity. As discussed in Chapter 7, students in the study are especially concerned with being identified as school students by community members. They discuss how the way children behave in public and interact with others can be a signal indicating whether or not they are schoolchildren.

Teachers, students say, also encourage schoolchildren to be good people and respect their elders. They tell students how to behave with others when they are in public; for example, if they run into elders, they must show respect, say *salaam*, and not fight in front of them. One girl who is learning in a mixed boys and girls class says her teacher tells his students that they should not hug each other when they are outside in public. Learning these social norms is an important aspect of *tarbia* and gives students confidence that they know how to act with others, especially in public spaces.

Wearing special school clothes and being clean are other behaviors that students describe as distinguishing themselves in the community as schoolgirls and schoolboys. When asked about their daily routines, students in several interviews spontaneously started talking about the clothes that are only for school.

Status

In addition to learning social norms, students in Sierra Leone value learning in school because of the status it gives them in their communities. Almost a third (11/38) of students interviewed described learning as one of the most important aspects of school because it helps them, now or in the future, to become important and respected members of society. For example, a 13-year-old girl in class 5 says:

> I feel proud because I am learning international languages, I am important in the community, I can read and write in English. I know as a girl, when I learn well and finish well, I shall be important among my friends.

This girl specifically identified her peers as a social group from which she seeks to gain respect. Other students simply articulated their vision more generally, as a 13-year-old boy in grade 5 did when he explained that one of the reasons he values school is because "I know I will become somebody in the society tomorrow." This idea that learning can bring respect, importance, and status to students recognizes the importance of schooling for children's relatives, peers, and community members. Children likely see others who are educated, such as doctors and UN workers, being treated as "somebody" and important in their community.

Altruism

For students in both Ethiopia and Sierra Leone, learning in school is greatly valued because it enables them to help their families and relatives. While in this level of practical learning the focus is still very much on how learning helps students fulfill social expectations, students' desire to help and support others implies a level of awareness of others' needs that brings it near the border of emancipatory learning.

In Ethiopia, 17 out of 48 students interviewed describe enjoying school because they perceive it enables them to help others. This altruistic motivation appears to fulfill social and family expectations: Students describe wanting to help their parents, siblings, and relatives. For example, a 12-year-old girl in class 3b explains that one of the things she likes best about school is "to get knowledge and to be clever student, to improve my ability after that to help my parents." A 16-year-old boy in class 4 focuses on his desire to help his siblings, saying that what he most enjoys about school is "to get knowledge, to help my little brother and sister, to lead them." Clearly, for students, school learning is connected with being a support for their families. Learning well in school makes students feel more confident that they will be able to take on this important responsibility.

In Sierra Leone, students also recognize being able to help their families as an important responsibility that schooling can help them fulfill. Almost a third (11/38) of students interviewed discussed this as one of the reasons they most value and enjoy school. Students talk about their parents, their siblings, and their friends as especially important people in their lives whom they hope to support and help. For example, "School helps me to assist my parents in times of need," says one 12-year-old boy in grade 4. Another student, a 16-year-old boy in grade 5, explained in more detail how learning enables him to help his parents, saying, "School can . . . help me to help my parents. That is, I sometimes get the challenge of writing letters for my parents, and I can do so." Being able to contribute to and assist their families today and in the future gives students a sense of pride and purpose underlying their focus on learning.

EMANCIPATORY LEARNING

Social Consciousness

Students in Ethiopia, out of all the study locations, were the most focused on how the learning they are doing in school could enable them to change the social context of their community. Of the students interviewed, 11 out of 48 girls and boys, both Tigrigna and Kunama, envisioned themselves sharing the literacy skills they learned in school with others, particularly the younger or next generation and their tribe. Many students talked of school helping them to fulfill personal goals to eradicate illiteracy in their communities, demonstrating an underlying conception that they are learning not just for themselves but on behalf of their families and tribes. For example, a 14-year-old boy in class 5 said the reason he most likes coming to school is "to get knowledge and to complete my education without interrupting. And to teach my little brother as I was learning and to make illiteracy disappear from my tribe and my country."

The idea that any amount of education is valuable and can be shared, which is reflected in many of the teachers' perspectives toward their own teaching, comes through in students' expressed desire to share their school learning with others. In this context, students literally are learning on behalf of others and in all likelihood will be a crucial link to the modern world for their family, community, and tribe. This can help explain students' discussion of the "darkness of illiteracy" or, in one Kunama boy's words, why "having no education is like being blind."

Students in Sierra Leone and Afghanistan focus much less on this type of emancipatory learning. In Sierra Leone, 4 out of 38 students interviewed mentioned wanting to help their country or the next generation learn as they did, while only 1 out of 15 students interviewed did so in Afghanistan. In these two countries there is not the same focus on eradicating illiteracy as there is in Ethiopia. Instead, students talk generally about their desire to help develop their country. For example, in Sierra Leone a 17-year-old girl in class 5 said that one of the most important reasons she comes to school is because "I want to help my country."

RE-ENVISIONING QUALITY
EDUCATION IN CONFLICT CONTEXTS

The children in this study clearly articulated a vision of learning that provides much-needed nuance into the debate on quality education in conflict and post-conflict contexts. In essence, students in these contexts told us that neither of the policymakers described at the outset of this chapter had it right. For them, learning is not only essential, but it takes on multiple forms. It is important, but not sufficient, to ensure that core subjects are taught well. Many other forms of learning, such as learning important skills to help navigate daily life as well as social norms, are seen as equally important by the students.

A major implication of this study's findings for education in conflict contexts is the importance of learning for students' well-being. Children's perspectives show that concerns about their well-being in school and their learning experiences in school should not be seen as separate issues, but rather as one and the same. Education programs that aim to support students' well-being by ensuring that they restore normalcy—by providing for children to regularly attend school, socialize with peers, and have access to psychosocial support or safe spaces in which to share their feelings—are all likely to be positive and to help children, yet may fail to emphasize a central element of their school experience that contributes to their well-being, namely, learning. At the same time, any program that takes a narrow view of quality learning, such as literacy or numeracy only, will be missing an important emphasis on the diverse forms of learning that students find valuable.

This careful balance of ensuring that students are supported across multiple forms of learning has particular implications for teacher support and practice in these contexts. In addition to school providing a forum for children to spend time with peers and interact with caring adults, students appreciate peer and teacher relationships that facilitate and support their learning, and become frustrated at those that limit or block it. Children discuss how much they appreciate their peers' support in doing homework, understanding class notes, and studying. Students are appreciative of what they perceive as teachers' support of their learning through useful pedagogical techniques such as storytelling and illustration, willingness to repeat explanations, and take questions after class.

Equally, students describe how they appreciate teachers who help them learn culturally appropriate social codes. Students discuss how much they appreciate learning how to do such things as dress appropriately, greet elders, treat peers in public spaces versus in school or in the home, be a good student, and identify and avoid harmful activities. As discussed, this type of mastery of appropriate behavior is classified as the normative level of practical learning.

Students also value other levels of practical learning, particularly as these relate to opportunities for altruism. Here, students especially appreciate what they learn in school because it will help them fulfill social expectations or personal desires to help their families and relatives. Being able to better understand, navigate, and enter into the social world is seen as a valuable outcome of school learning by students. This learning usually comes from teachers' guidance and advice and is seen by students as equally important to the subject lessons on which teachers also focus.

In practice, education programs in conflict and especially post-conflict contexts can place heavy emphasis on school construction and establishing safe learning environments, both of which are important. But perhaps the most important element is ensuring that good teachers, who know the community and cultural context of the children, are regularly in place and supporting children's multiple forms of learning. This is undoubtedly difficult given that trained teachers are frequently lacking and teachers rarely are compensated regularly for their work. Rapid teacher preparation courses should be sure to incorporate an awareness of the different forms of learning children value in these contexts. Ultimately, children in this study show that they are keenly aware of when they are learning and when they are not, and they have strong opinions about what they find most helpful in their lives. Education practitioners in these contexts would do well to listen to them.

CHAPTER 9

The Multiple Relationships Between Education and Conflict

Reflections of Rwandan Teachers and Students

Elisabeth King

Conversations with Rwandan teachers and students illustrate multiple and complex relationships between education and conflict. In the research described in this chapter, one Rwandan teacher explained: "Sometimes you had to go to school with grenades. You had to go to school with something that could save you,"[1] reflecting on how schools became sites of violence during the civil war and genocide. A student commented, "During that period of war, we had to stop going to school." Students and teachers also raised the role of education in fomenting conflict. As one high school student put it: "I think what caused the genocide was bad education. It is both bad education, and a lack of education for some." In contrast, a teenaged boy talked about how schooling helped normalize his life after the violence ended: "At school, it was really good. There was no segregation there. We are schoolchildren. . . . We have to study our subjects, not go into political things." Others discussed the important role of education in promoting future peace: "We teach about reconciliation. We teach to never again take the same actions as in the past and to find ways to bring everyone together, to foster friendship, and to not dream of killing others."

As the foregoing quotations from interviews suggest, this chapter provides case-based empirical evidence of both the "negative" and "positive" faces of education and conflict that have come to be recognized in the literature (Bush

& Saltarelli, 2000). It also nuances these faces. This chapter argues that at least six different relationships between violent conflict and education have manifest themselves in Rwanda in the lead-up to and aftermath of the Rwandan civil war and genocide.[2] It further argues that there is an often-overlooked complexity to these relationships. In a number of cases, education is the independent variable, with conflict as the dependent variable. In these cases, education has an impact on conflict. In other cases, conflict is the independent variable, with education as the dependent variable. Here, conflict affects education. Moreover, many inter-relationships exist simultaneously. The multiple relationships between education and conflict, as well as the tensions among them, have important implications for both scholars and practitioners and should encourage reflection on the design and impact of education initiatives.

To begin, this chapter introduces the case of Rwanda and reviews my research methods. Then, it discusses six possible relationships between education and conflict and how they transpired in Rwanda. First, schooling can contribute to underlying conflict. Second, conflict can disrupt the provision of education. Third, schools themselves can be sites of violence. Fourth, conflict can provide an opportunity for educational change. Fifth, in the aftermath of conflict, schools can provide a nurturing environment and help students "cope and hope" for the future. Finally, schools can help build peace and prevent future conflict. These relationships suggest both opportunities and limits for education in contemporary Rwanda.

THE SETTING: EDUCATION IN RWANDA

Rwanda has a population of approximately 10 million people, roughly 84% Hutu, 15% Tutsi, and 1% Twa, according to conventional wisdom. It is among the poorest states in the world. Rwanda ranks only 167th out of 182 countries on the Human Development Index, and nearly 60% of the population live below the poverty line of just 0.44 USD per day (UNDP, 2007, 2009).

Rwanda also has the unfortunate distinction of being best known internationally for the 1994 genocide that followed a civil war from 1990–1993. During the genocide, approximately 800,000 people were killed, including at least 500,000 Tutsi, but a large number of "moderate" Hutu as well (Des Forges, 1999). The United Nations Special Rapporteur on Rwanda estimated that between 250,000 and 500,000 Rwandan women and girls were raped (Brouwer, 2005). While the genocide was led by Hutu hardliners, a significant proportion of the population participated in the killing.

The Tutsi-led Rwandan Patriotic Front (RPF) brought the genocide to an end through military victory and remains the government of Rwanda today. Although the government often is praised for its efforts in bringing about stability and its ostensible ethnic blindness, it also is criticized as authoritarian, where freedom of speech and diversity are harshly repressed, where justice has been one-sided, and where genuine reconciliation is limited (Buckley-Zistel, 2006; Gourevitch, 2009; Nyamwasa, Karegeya, Rudasingwa, & Gahima, 2010; Reyntjens, 2004).

Despite this history of poverty and violence, Rwanda often has been considered a model developing country and has made important advances in many areas, including education, both before and after the genocide. For instance, Rwanda significantly expanded primary school enrollments and achieved gender parity in primary schools by 1990 (RoR, n.d., p. 9). In the post-genocide period, Rwanda often has been praised for its developmental model. The United Nations Development Program (UNDP) specifically commends the education sector as "an example of what well-planned, coordinated and targeted investments can achieve in terms of human and economic development" (UNDP, 2007, p. 22). Rwanda's most recent figures suggest that the primary Net Enrollment Ratio (NER) may be as high as 97%, although provincial disparities are significant and Rwandan secondary enrollment is very low, even in comparison to its peers (Kanyarukiga, van der Meer, Paalman, Poate, & Schrader, 2006; Muramila, 2007). At the same time, education has long been a contentious issue in Rwanda. In a country often characterized by competition for access to the state and resources along ethnic, regional, and class lines, schools have been one of the key sites of this competition.

METHODS

This chapter is based primarily on 35 interviews conducted in Rwanda in 2006 and is part of a larger project on education, conflict, and peace-building (King, 2008, 2010a). Respondents, introduced to me through a "snowballing" methodology, had been students and/or teachers in Rwanda's primary school system sometime between the mid-1970s and 2006. Since trust is so tenuous in this post-conflict context, interviews were one-on-one, as Scott (1990) puts it, "the most protected format of spoken communication" (p. 162). I tried to vary ethnicity, gender, rural/ urban setting, socioeconomic background, and region in which primary school was attended, knowing that these factors could reveal important differences. By foregoing a translator and conducting the interviews in French and English, second languages for most Rwandans, I sacrificed the knowledge that Kinyarwanda-only speakers would have added, and worked with a participant pool that was biased toward those with more-than-average education. Overall, though, this chapter focuses on a good range of Rwandan students and teachers and recounts their views in their own words (for more details, see King, 2009).

This chapter uses the terms *schooling* and *education* interchangeably and examines what might be called "ordinary" education—that is, the government-run national school system at the primary and secondary levels. *Conflict* refers to societal-level violent conflict such as civil war and genocide.

FINDINGS

Findings are reported below as six principal relationships between education and conflict. Across these relationships, education and conflict are both independent and dependent variables and play positive and negative roles in society. Some of the roles are clearly intended, whereas others are not. While an order had to be imposed upon the six relationships below, the order of presentation should not be taken to suggest necessary progression or linearity. Education and conflict can play multiple roles simultaneously, sometimes supporting each other, other times working at cross-purposes.

Education Can Contribute to Conflict

There is increasing awareness that certain kinds of education can contribute to violent conflict (Bush & Saltarelli, 2000; Davies, 2004; Smith & Vaux, 2003; Tawil & Harley, 2004). In this vein, Williams (2004) calls for empirical work asking at least five questions of educational systems. "Who gets schooling?" and "How is schooling provided?" get at questions of structural exclusion; "What is taught?" and "Who are we? [in curriculum or the national story]" invoke questions of curricular content and pedagogy; and, "How are decisions made?" focuses on educational management (pp. 474–475, 479–480). In the case of Rwanda's schools, the answers to these questions suggest a history of inequalities between Hutu and Tutsi and collectivization and stigmatization of these groups—processes that are recognized to underlie conflict (King, 2010a).

In brief, access to schooling has long been unequal in Rwanda, reinforcing and entrenching inequalities between ethnic groups. During the colonial period, the Belgians who administered Rwanda favored Tutsi for positions in school and the state. Under the two Rwandan Republics (1962–1994), the Hutu governments generally favored Hutu. Secondary entrance exams were graded in light of ethnic identity, and ethnic equilibrium policies were partial to Hutu, especially those of certain regions. As one interviewee noted, "To get accepted to secondary school, they would say that you need perhaps 80% [on the exam], but for Tutsi it was 90%, so as to diminish the number of Tutsi that could enter secondary school." One teacher recalls that when the list of those accepted into secondary school was posted in her community, she asked herself, "What? I am not on the list? That is not possible. And then I saw all of the [Hutu] students that were always [ranked] behind me in class had succeeded [in getting a place at secondary school]. . . . I cried for almost a week." The merits of quotas can be debated, and may in some instances contribute to improving relations between groups. Respondents in Rwanda, however, suggested that differential access to schooling promoted several processes recognized to underlie conflict: horizontal inequalities and group collectivization and ranking.

From independence to the genocide, during two Hutu governments, classroom practices also were ethnically based and collectivized students into two distinct groups. For example, most interviewees remembered having to stand up according to ethnic identity in class. As one teacher recalled, "I myself did it, I did it to students. I asked, 'Hutu go there, Tutsi go there.'" Some Tutsi explained that this experience made them fearful, humiliated them, and opened them to teasing or harassment by other students. Several recalled it being paired with an exercise wherein the teacher explained the physical traits of Hutu, Tutsi, and Twa. As one interviewee recalled, "Especially the problem came when we did the 'census' [and had to stand up by ethnic group to be counted] at the beginning of the year. During that period, there were misunderstandings. . . . People didn't have confidence in others. We came to understand that we are different and that we cannot trust the other." Mere categories need not contribute to conflict—many societies are peacefully multiethnic and, as I discuss in the conclusion, repressing differences sometimes can hinder peace-building—but in Rwanda, different values also were assigned to the groups. As the interviewee continued, people might think, "Maybe I deserve these privileges because I belong to [a particular] group."

Sometimes, history curriculum also differentiated, collectivized, and stigmatized Rwanda's groups. As one interviewee reflected of history teaching, "[The students] took it personally, not as a history. You know? The way the teacher taught history, was not really a history [but the present]." He explained that teachers taught that "the [pre-colonial and colonial] kingdom belongs to Tutsi and . . . the Hutu, they were slaves to the Tutsi," as if the students in the class at that time played these roles. "And it [was] so embarrassing and so frightening."

This first relationship between education and conflict—that education arguably contributed to underlying conflict in Rwanda—is among the most difficult for scholars and practitioners of education. Since often those working in education in emergencies are fighting for funding and support, they may be reluctant to discuss schooling's weaknesses. Nonetheless, today's post-genocide government explicitly blames the quantity, quality, content, and management of past education for having "failed the nation" (RoR, 1995).

Conflict Can Disrupt Education

Second, conflict can significantly disrupt education (Machel, 2001b). It is anticipated that conflict will hinder the achievement of universal primary education targets and, in fact, more than half (42%) of the 67 million children around the world who are not attending school live in conflict-affected and fragile states (UNESCO, 2011, p. 132). In Rwanda, the civil war and genocide severely impacted the school system, and, in many ways, the legacy of violence continues to affect education to this day.

Conflict directly interrupted education in Rwanda. The last normal year of schooling was 1990 and schools and the Ministry of Education closed completely during the 1994 genocide. The experience of Rwandan students and teachers varied significantly. Since more than 2 million Rwandans fled the country before, during, and after the genocide, many children were educated in refugee camps in Democratic Republic of Congo (DRC), Tanzania, and elsewhere, where they often had to repeat classes (Bird, 2003). The majority of primary-level students who stayed in Rwanda lost several months of schooling before primary schools reopened in mid-September 1994. Students at higher levels of education lost approximately 1 year; public secondary schools and the National University of Rwanda reopened in April 1995, a year after the genocide began. Unlike in other places, pre-war national education rates were soon reached and surpassed in post-genocide Rwanda, although at least one study finds that school-aged children exposed to the consequences of the 1994 genocide have lower educational attainment than similar individuals in the pre-genocide period (Akresh & de Walque, 2010).

When schools reopened, the experience and consequences of conflict continued to disrupt education in multiple ways. For example, much of the educational infrastructure was destroyed and the teaching cadre was decimated. As one teenaged girl explained: "Education in Rwanda is very difficult after the genocide. There are many unqualified teachers. There is a lack of material. . . . There is the destruction of laboratories, roads, everything." In fact, about 65% of schools were damaged and the Ministry of Education was shelled (Bridgeland, Wulsin, & McNaught, 2009). About 75% of teachers were killed, fled the country, or were imprisoned on charges of genocide (RoR, 1997, p. 13). The National University lost more than 80% of its staff (Bridgeland et al., 2009). This left a heavy burden on those who remained. As one long-time teacher recalled, "The principal was killed in '94, so I became immediately responsible [in his position] already as of September '94." While many teachers are very committed, some expressed concern that teachers also had been victims and that this continues to affect them and their teaching.

There were also multiple challenges for the children who returned to schools. One teenaged girl explained: "It was terrible at public schools. There were lots of sick children. There were others who had lost their parents—who didn't know where their parents had gone. And there was a lot of famine and problems with school fees, so there was really no stability. And we were still scared that war was going to return to the country." Unsurprisingly, many psychologists and medical practitioners assessed Rwandan children as a deeply traumatized and vulnerable population. Eighty percent of children interviewed by UNICEF, for example, experienced a death in their family, 91% thought they would die, 36% saw other children participating in violence, and 16% had, at some point, hidden under dead bodies (reported in Obura, 2003, p. 50).

Orphanhood is another serious consequence of conflict that has plagued Rwanda's educational system. More than 1.2 million children were left orphaned after the war and genocide, representing 16% of the entire population, or nearly one third of all children, and 100,000 children were left in child-headed households (Geltman & Stover, 1997; Obura, 2005, pp. ix, 19). As one teacher told me: "When you receive a child head of household, who leaves the house without eating, with no clothes, you'll really find a very sad child." He continued to explain that in class, "there are children who were thinking of their mothers or their fathers from whom they were separated. So, even listening to the lesson was very difficult." Some teachers complained of misbehavior due to orphanhood: "The children behave badly because they don't have parents to give them basic education." One orphaned girl explained from her perspective:

> I started having a lot, a lot, of problems after [my parents were killed]. I failed one year of school. But for me, I was capable of restarting my studies, but I still had a lot of problems. My neighbors, now my father and mother, were not able to get me the material to start my studies. But I got some help for my problem and now I am better. But these families are not able to erase everything that is in my heart. But, little by little, little by little, I leave things behind. For now, I've started with school, but for others, the problems of having no mothers, no fathers, no brothers, no sisters, remain.

In her study of orphans and other vulnerable children, Obura (2005) found that orphans are "more likely than any other group to be at risk for school exclusion" (p. x). More than a decade after the genocide, Rwanda remains one of the countries with the highest proportion of child-headed households in the world (UNICEF, 2006).

The war and genocide also left a strong legacy of fear in classrooms. Children survivors of genocide were scared to be in classrooms alongside the children of those accused of killing or with teachers from the opposite ethnic group. Teachers too were afraid. As one female teacher explained: "The children were really not at ease. Not the children, nor the teachers. There were even children that did not stay in class because when it was a Tutsi child, and when his scars were everywhere, and there was a Hutu teacher in front of him, he left class."

The disruption of conflict also proved a challenge for classroom logistics and learning. In the years after the genocide, many children discovered Rwanda for the first time after growing up in exile. Others came back from a few years in refugee camps. As one Rwandan student told me: "It was very serious. We were mixed because we had people that came from other countries. From Tanzania, from Burundi, from Congo. Some spoke Swahili, others English, others French. All in one classroom!"

A number of interviewees talked about how political events associated with conflict and genocide continue to filter into schools to this day. As one student recounted: "1995 was really hard, then times were okay, but with *gacacas* [local courts for genocide crimes] now, things are again difficult. When someone hears in detail how their family members were killed with machetes, there is trauma and anger and some want revenge." In summary, conflict and genocide disrupted education in multiple ways, and the legacy of conflict continues to disrupt Rwandan classrooms more than 16 years after the genocide.

Schools Can Be Sites of Violence

Third, schools themselves sometimes become sites of violence. Schools have been places of intimidation and violence throughout Africa and around the world, for instance, as sites of armed recruitment and gender-based violence (Harber, 1996, 2004). This is a trend also evidenced by interviews in Rwanda. Before Rwandan schools closed, some students experienced harassment, violence, and intimidation. For example, one former student shared stories of dorm room pranks and attacks by Hutu students on Tutsi students, such as wetting down Tutsi mattresses or throwing them in the trash to try to scare the students or drive them away. A student told me how other students would say of him, "That's a Tutsi!" and how "the students started to harass me during recess and in my classes. You know how children bother others. When we were in class they'd pull my ears and they'd flick and hit me." While no one spoke to me about gender-based violence, there are widespread reports of girls being sexually harassed and abused by teachers in Rwandan schools to this day (Mukarugomwa, 2007). During the genocide, as one interviewee told me: "teachers [were also] killers. Sometimes they killed some students. . . . Other times, they helped [killers to] identify Hutu and Tutsi children." Another teacher told me how he left the profession after his former students tried to kill him.

Recent reports note widespread attacks and threats against students, teachers, and schools around the world (O'Malley, 2010; UNESCO, 2010). During the Rwandan genocide, people gathered in churches and schools and were massacred. Over 40,000 people were killed from April 19 to 22, 1994, at the *École Technique Officielle* at Murambi, still under construction at the time (National Museum of Rwanda, n.d.). At least two schools were sites of violence in post-genocide Rwanda, with incursions from remaining *génocidaires* in the DRC (Gourevitch, 1998, p. 352). Several interviewees told me about "the schoolchildren from Inyange [in Gisenyi, Northern Rwanda] who were massacred" in their school in 1996 and who are now celebrated as national heroes. "There were some children who were killed [in their school] because the *interahamwe* came, the people who were committing genocide. They [the *interahamwe*] told them to separate Hutu and Tutsi, and the people refused. They remained one. And they killed them, all of them." Because schools had become sites of violence, and because some teachers committed genocide, many parents were reluctant to send their children back to school once peace had been declared.

Conflict Can Provide an Opportunity for Educational Change

Fourth, conflict sometimes provides an opportunity for change. In the aftermath of conflict, some countries endeavor not just to reconstruct their schools and educational systems, but to improve them. While the above sections attest to the extent of educational damage wrought by conflict in Rwanda, as Bridgeland and colleagues (2009) note, "the experience also galvanized the country around reform, leading to major changes and new investments in the education sector" (p. 7). For example, in 1996, the Rwandan government established the National Curriculum Development Centre and a new National Examination Council, since exam processes, discussed above, had been a major grievance in pre-genocide Rwanda. In 2003–2004, they introduced no-fee primary schooling and made school uniforms optional. A World Bank report notes that "despite the disruption to the education system caused by the 1994 genocide, Rwanda's labor force had a better educational profile in 2000 than in 1991" (quoted in Bridgeland et al., 2009, p. 9).

Many interviewees spoke of improved access to education for all Rwandans in the aftermath of conflict. One teacher highlighted the strides Rwanda has made toward meritocracy in education: "Now, if a parent comes and begs a Minister to allow his child to go to school, now it's no longer the case [that this works]. We mark exams, and it is the national council [that] sends you to the schools you are supposed to go to. . . . The Minister does not have the right now to allocate schools like before." Another teacher noted of these changes in Rwanda: "It is really positive, because the person is appreciated by merit, not only her origin. Although there is [still] the problem of rich and poor [that impacts educational distribution], but [educational access is] mostly based on success. And that is really encouraging for all sides."

A number of interviewees mentioned the commitment that the post-genocide government has made to all levels of girls' education and to improving the position of women in the country more generally.[3] As one female student explained, "Today, it is the law that all of the population must send their children to school. But before, it was just the boys. . . . Girls, when they arrived in the 6th grade, it was finished for them." A male student explained, "The mentality has started to change because before, they would say that girls shouldn't continue their studies. That they have to go find husbands. That they had duties. . . . But today, there are not those problems." One female teacher explained that in general "African women are really unhappy" but went on to say that "we are in the midst of a [better] era where women go to primary school and secondary school, and even university." Indeed, in most of the country, about the same number of boys and girls enroll in primary schools, but fewer girls than boys complete primary school and enroll in secondary school (UNDP, 2007, pp. 24–25).

A number of Rwandans also mentioned that there are more post-conflict tertiary opportunities than there were in the past. Rwanda welcomed the creation of 17 new institutions of higher education within a few years after the genocide. Nonetheless, remarks on increasing tertiary opportunities are a comment of the elite since even secondary school, with NER around 10%, is beyond the reach of the vast majority. The tertiary gross enrollment rate in Rwanda is 3.2% (2003), on the low side of the Sub-Saharan African average of 5% (RoR, 2007, pp. 23–25).

While Rwandan students and teachers noted certain improvements in the educational system, highlighting the potential for conflict to result in some positive changes, they also remarked on many further challenges. Interviewees explained that classrooms are too full; that the quality of rural schools lags far behind that of those in urban areas; that students are too poor to pay even basic ancillary fees; that teachers need to be better trained and better paid; that schools require more material and better infrastructure; that the quality of language training is very low; and that more girls should be encouraged to pursue nontraditional subjects, such as sciences. Moreover, while education can provide an opportunity for change, these changes may have a negative impact, as I discuss in the conclusion.

Education Can Promote Well-Being after Conflict

Fifth, as Winthrop and Kirk argue in Chapter 7 in this volume, it is widely recognized that certain types of schooling can support children's well-being in the aftermath of conflict. This relationship lies in contrast to the three first relationships presented above—education contributing to conflict, conflict disrupting education, and schools as sites of violence—but can co-exist with these other relationships, precede them, or follow them.

In reviewing the literature, Winthrop and Kirk discuss four key mechanisms by which education can promote well-being after conflict, all of which emerged to some extent in interviews in Rwanda. First, education can provide "children a much needed routine amidst an otherwise unpredictable and often chaotic environment" (Winthrop & Kirk, 2008, p. 640). As one boy said, in response to a question about the difficulty of going back to school after the war and genocide, "No, [it wasn't hard]. They welcomed us. Very warmly too. . . . They knew us well there and wanted things to be more normal. That's why they welcomed us so well."

Second, Winthrop and Kirk (2008) note that schooling can help socialize students to interact with their peers and teachers and to build positive relationships. Much like Allport's contact hypothesis, respondents highlighted the role of classrooms in bringing together different parties to conflict and changing their views of one another through interaction (Allport, 1958; Pettigrew, 1998). One student talked about interaction between the children of victims and those of accused killers: "I have a lot of friends who no longer have parents. When they arrive at school they have problems. When they study, they don't study in peace, because they have a lot of thoughts, of memories. So, it pushes them to be extreme, eh? To not communicate with others because they think they are like the killers. So, [at school] we try to calm them, to tell them that it was their parents [that were killers], but that it doesn't mean that their children did that."

Third, schooling can create a "safe, protective, and nurturing environment" for students (Winthrop & Kirk, 2008, p. 641). Several interviewees talked about the nurturing role of schools in addressing the trauma of violence. One student talked about her teacher's efforts in this regard:

> Mostly, when the children are traumatized [and are at] their schools,
> they feel they have no peace. They feel they are abandoned by everyone.
> Everything they have kept in their heads, it comes out. They start crying.
> They run mad. They're traumatized. Our teacher, he told us that the best
> thing to do to them when we hear them crying, is to encourage them. . . . You
> just keep quiet and they go on telling you [about their experiences]. When
> they cry, you just encourage them to cry.

In an effort to make her classroom a nurturing environment, one teacher tells all of her students that "you are all my children, my beloved. There are no 'these ones' and 'those ones,' you are all Rwandan."

Another teacher talked about how schools have tried to become safer places by providing students with the knowledge to protect themselves from abuse and disease. "Before [the war]," she recounted, "we were scared to talk about AIDS. But for the moment, everyone, even the youngest children, knows what AIDS is and how you can catch it." New social studies textbooks have sections on "children's rights," "avoiding AIDS and STDs," "avoiding malaria," and "avoiding alcoholism" (Bamusanire, Byiringiro, Munyakazi, & Ntagaramba, 2006a, 2006b, 2006c).

Fourth, and least common, note Winthrop and Kirk (2008), education can help students to "cope and hope," that is, to "deal with the difficulties in their lives and find reasons to believe in a better future" (p. 641). Rwandan schooling is seen to make a major contribution in this regard, both for individual students and for the country as a whole. At the individual level, a number of students were confident that schooling could help them improve their lives. Some children talked about their dreams of becoming doctors, pharmacists, and accountants, and of the important role of schooling in reaching their goals. As one representative from a nongovernmental organization in the education sector explained, "Kids know that the possibility is there," and even the street children with whom she works "feel excluded if they don't go to school." At least some students felt assured that schools were helping them learn the skills that they would need to succeed, including information technology, which has been a key goal in post-genocide Rwanda.

At the national level, there is also much hope vested in education. Many believe that education can help Rwanda attain a better future. The government presents education as "the only factor that is likely to support the sustained modernization and diversification of modes of cultivations and systems of production"

(RoR, 1997, p. ii). Schooling is considered a crucial step for achieving Vision 2020, Rwanda's comprehensive framework for economic development based on the UN Millennium Development Goals, and the goal of Rwanda becoming a knowledge-based economy (MINECOFIN, 2000, p. 13). As one teacher explained,

> We have seen that the richness of those who have studied, who have intelligence, is that they can make discoveries. This is the reason for which we have now given everyone the liberty to study. We have a vision in Rwanda, Vision 2020. It says that everyone must study. So, the objective for the year 2020 is that all Rwandans will have at least studied at primary school.

Rwanda's Poverty Reduction Strategy also includes the important role of education in "economic growth and poverty reduction" (RoR, 2002). Many Rwandans are very optimistic about the educational strategy. "You see," explained one high school student, "we have Vision 2020 that will enable us to develop our country. . . . Why not arrive at the status of Norway or Sweden?"

While schools help some cope, and especially hope, there are also important limitations to education's impact in this regard. The low quality of schools remains a common concern in Rwanda and many feel that educational quality has declined in the post-genocide period as quantity has risen. "We give diplomas, but to those that don't deserve it. . . . They have nothing in their heads. . . . It wasn't like that in the past." A number of high school graduates also talked about failed aspirations: "Now we're unemployed." There are multiple ways that schooling can contribute to students' well-being in the aftermath of conflict but these benefits are not guaranteed.

Education Can Contribute to Peace-Building and Conflict Prevention

Finally, the sixth possible relationship between conflict and education relates to the role of schooling in peace-building and conflict prevention. The United Nations Education for All documentation presents education as one of the best means of averting conflict (UNESCO, 2004). There is also an entire field of "peace education" dedicated to developing the values, knowledge, attitudes, behaviors, and skills for conflict prevention and building sustainable peace (see Salomon, 2002).

Peace-building education may include addressing history and the legacy of conflict (Cole, 2007a, 2007b; Minow, 1998). Scholars suggest that narratives can contribute to sustainable peace when they encourage learning about each side's framings; create alternative narratives, including points of convergence; foster mutual affinity between groups; highlight stories of past cooperation; frame narratives in more nuanced ways; and promote common views of the future. These strategies will likely have a more positive effect on reconciliation than on imposing a common, supposedly "neutral" frame (Al-Haj, 2005; Ross, 2002). Opening opportunities for students to engage with and to influence social and political conflict, developing critical thinking and analytical skills, and encouraging agency also are widely believed to contribute to peace-building (Avery, Johnson, Johnson, & Mitchell, 1999; Johnson & Johnson, 1994; Wahrman, 2003).

In Rwanda, schooling today is assigned a key role in promoting unity and reconciliation. According to the government, schooling in post-genocide Rwanda is aimed at "training citizens free of any type of discrimination, exclusion and favoritism and thus contributing to the promotion of peace, Rwandese and universal values of justice, solidarity, tolerance and respect for the rights and duties of human beings" (RoR, 1997, p. 23). It is charged with the "detoxification" of youth and with the re-creation of "recently eroded Rwandan values" (RoR, 1995, p. 12). Education also is considered a "structure to neutralize the ideology of genocide" (RoR, 2006, p. 219).

Peace education is an important part of the curriculum in post-genocide Rwanda. New social studies textbooks include sections on "things everyone can do to maintain peace in the district," "factors of harmony and disharmony in the district," and "equality among people" (Bamusanire et al., 2006a), and "the genocide," "unity," and "co-operation" (Bamusanire et al., 2006c). As one former student noted: "We have to continue to educate students in the sense of teaching them to love and to know that we all have the same rights to the country, that we are all Rwandan, and that no one has more rights than another." One long-time teacher similarly explained that "the principal thing to get into heads is that we must not harm others. If you are Hutu or Tutsi, one must not harm. That's all." There are also, however, major limits to peace-building education in Rwanda today, discussed below.

CONCLUSION

This chapter provides evidence of at least six different relationships between conflict and education, all of which were raised by students and teachers in post-genocide Rwanda. These relationships are diverse, complex, and interacting. Education and conflict take turns as both dependent and independent variables. The relationship between conflict and education can be positive or negative for society. In addition, the relationships are not mutually exclusive: They co-exist and interact.

Two further examples from contemporary Rwanda illustrate the complex conflict–education nexus and the challenges for moving forward. First, the government seized on this post-conflict moment of change to make English the language of instruction. Although French was the primary European language of instruction since the colonial period, the new plan aims to fully integrate English as the medium of instruction at all levels of both public and private schools by this year (2011). English-language teaching is said to be for improved international commerce and trade, especially as Rwanda has joined the English-speaking East African community. From one perspective, this is an example of conflict having created the possibility of re-examining the educational system and making changes.

But, as this chapter has demonstrated, multiple relationships between education and conflict co-exist. Simultaneously, the inclusion of English reflects the importance of Rwandan English speakers, who were exiles in Uganda and form the core of the government, and the move toward English in schools helps legitimate this dominant form of linguistic capital. In this way, language policies are producing new inequalities that intersect with background. Tutsi with English-language backgrounds of exile, as well as upper class Rwandans who can access private schools, are likely to learn more quickly and thus have better access to general education, as well as English, the language of opportunity. Language has become a very sensitive political issue at risk of dividing the society into Anglophone and Francophone Rwandans, or of replicating "historical language divides related to power and ethnicity" (Kanyarukiga et al., 2006, p. 4). From this perspective, educational change may contribute to future conflict.

Second, as noted above, education in post-genocide Rwanda in some ways is supporting peace-building and conflict resolution through teaching about peace education. At the same time, schooling may be working at cross-purposes to peace through teaching a selective history curriculum and repressing critical thinking. In brief, the Rwandan government is presenting a simple, one-sided, homogenizing narrative from which a number of students and teachers, especially Hutu, feel excluded. As one Hutu student remarked: "Some people say that my father committed genocide or that my grandfather committed genocide. But there were also a lot of people killed because of the RPF [Tutsi] soldiers that passed. Yes, they came by and killed a lot of Hutu. But the state will not accept that we say that." Moreover, Tutsi are being collectivized into an all-encompassing "survivor" group, while Hutu often are grouped as "perpetrators" (King, 2009, 2010b).

The process through which the history curriculum is being generated lacks genuine dialogue and consensus, critical thinking is repressed, and Rwandans experience censorship and self-censorship. Teachers work in an increasingly repressive context at odds with openness to talking about the past (Freedman, Weinstein, Murphy, & Longman, 2008; King, 2008, 2009). According to at least some, "Even if people are quiet, that does not mean that they are calm." In the end, the complexity of the relationships between conflict and education suggests that scholars and practitioners would do well to locate educational strategies within a broader understanding of the multiple interrelationships.

NOTES

Thanks to the many Rwandans who made this research possible, to Aliénor Westphalen-Lematre for research assistance, and to Dana Burde and the editors for helpful comments.

1. All quotations are from interviews conducted between January and April 2006. Most are my translation from French. A few are direct quotes in English.

2. Elsewhere, I also consider the relationship between education and conflict during the colonial period and early independence (King, 2008, 2010a).

3. Rwanda now holds the world record for women parliamentarians at 56% in the lower house. The global average is 19% (Inter-Parliamentary Union, 2011). There are still many challenges for women in Rwanda (Baines, Brown, & Thomson, 2008).

Part III

UNDERSTANDING INTERNATIONAL PROGRAMS AND INTERVENTIONS

Alphabet Soup

Making Sense of the Emerging Global Architecture of Aid to Education in Fragile and Conflict-Affected Situations

PETER BUCKLAND

In the Universal Declaration of Human Rights (United Nations, 1948) the international community expressed a global commitment to the right to education. Article 26 (out of 30 Articles) affirmed the universal right to education that is free and compulsory, "at least in the elementary and fundamental stages." But it was not really until the 1990 Jomtien World Conference on Education for All (EFA) that the international education community[1] found its voice with a global commitment and established an "Agenda for Action" to ensure all children access to basic education within a decade. That commitment had profound implications for donors and development agencies on the one hand, and developing country governments on the other.

The role of the international community in "humanitarian assistance" also expanded substantially during the period leading up to and following Jomtien, so that by the mid-1990s international involvement in education had become very complicated. A range of international agencies, donors, and international non-government organizations (NGOs) were engaged in committing (and sometimes competing over) resources and support for education reconstruction and education reform in a wide range of countries, especially those made vulnerable by conflict, natural disaster, or "complex emergencies."

Since 1990, donors, development agencies, and international NGOs have led a series of initiatives to achieve more effective and coordinated support to education, and to encourage governments to deliver on their obligations to basic education. While these efforts at improved coordination and more effective use of aid take place largely in the rarefied air of international forums and are articulated in international agreements and documents, they can have a significant impact on the way international attention, and therefore resources, are directed to countries. This chapter traces the development of that process from 1990 to the present, with a particular focus on how it impacted upon countries affected by conflict and crisis.

FROM EDUCATION FOR ALL TO
EDUCATION AND CONFLICT (1990–2000)

At the Jomtien conference, in a world not yet feeling the full impact of the disintegration of the Soviet Union, the focus of the international community was on ensuring access for all children to "basic education," a target rather ambitiously set for 2000. There was only one mention of the word *conflict* in the entire declaration, and two mentions of the word *war*, both of which were seen simply as factors that make access to schooling more challenging. By 1995, when the international community gathered together again in Amman, Jordan, to review progress, the world was still reeling from the violent civil conflicts in Bosnia and Herzegovina, and the horrors of the Rwanda genocide. The 1995 EFA "Amman Affirmation," while recognizing that some progress had been made toward the goal of basic education for all by 2000, also noted the role that education had played in fomenting the conflicts, and the hope that it could help to heal the wounds and prevent further conflict (UNESCO, 1996).

During the 1990s considerable progress was made in the wider international community to improve communication and coordination in both development aid in general, and humanitarian assistance in particular. The UN Development Group was established, and a system of Resident Coordinators put in place to facilitate better coordination of UN operations in development. In the humanitarian assistance world, the Office for the Coordination of Humanitarian Affairs (OCHA) made significant gains in establishing policies and procedures designed to improve coordination of humanitarian assistance. Part of this move was to establish an Inter-Agency Standing Committee for Humanitarian Assistance (IASC), which meets regularly in Geneva and includes representation from two global federations of International Nongovernment Organizations working in humanitarian assistance (INGOs). A new mechanism for coordinating appeals for humanitarian assistance to UN agencies was introduced in the form of the Consolidated Appeals Process (CAP), and a new emergency financing mechanism in the Consolidated Emergency Relief Fund. During the same period the uneven progress made in implementing the Jomtien EFA Declaration led to the emergence of more robust arrangements for coordinating and monitoring progress toward EFA targets, including the UNESCO *Education for All Global Monitoring Report,* first published in 2002 (UNESCO, 1990).

At the first Inter-Agency Network on Education in Emergencies (INEE) Global Consultation held in Geneva in November 2000, this emerging process was summarized in a diagrammatic depiction of the complex web of institutional arrangements that framed international aid to education in emergencies. The diagram, which consisted of a series of boxes linked by lines, each box labeled with an acronym or abbreviation, induced howls of amusement, and subsequently was referred to as the "Education in Emergencies Alphabet Soup." A slightly less cryptic version (with more abbreviations decoded) subsequently was included in the World Bank publication *Reshaping the Future* (2005) and is represented in Figure 10.1. The figure reveals a complex maze of institutions, committees, and programs all reflecting attempts to improve coordination at the global or country level. The development of these institutional arrangements was driven by three trends that have their roots in efforts to improve international support to education during the 1990s. First, there was a growing recognition of the need for incorporating education into humanitarian response, and therefore accommodating it to the emerging coordination arrangements for humanitarian assistance. Up to this time, education had not been considered a core need for populations affected by conflict.

At the same time, the global EFA movement that took root in 1990 at Jomtien helped precipitate the emergence of new governance arrangements for that global agenda. These finally were given some firmer institutional form after the World Education Forum in Dakar in April 2000, with the establishment of an EFA Secretariat based in UNESCO in Paris, and the establishment of the UNESCO *Education for All Global Monitoring Report.* A series of "flagship initiatives" emerged at UNESCO, one of which was entitled Education in Emergencies. A third trend was the growing move, starting in the early 1990s, to better coordinate the multiplicity of UN agencies involved in development work under the UN Development Group umbrella (UNDG), with the establishment of formal coordination arrangements at global and country levels.

At the highest levels there were some connections as the topmost bodies in each stream—the Executive Committee for Humanitarian Assistance the UN Development Group Executive Committee (UNDG EXCO), and the EFA High-Level Group—included, in many cases, the heads of the same UN agencies. Yet there were differences. UNESCO initially was not part of the UNDG EXCO and had virtually no access to the OCHA structures. The United Nations High Commissioner for Refugees (UNHCR) had little or no access to the EFA mechanisms and little influence on deliberations in the UNDG. The World Bank, the largest single provider of external finance for educational development, was not part of this cast

Figure 10.1. Coordination of Education in Emergencies in 2000

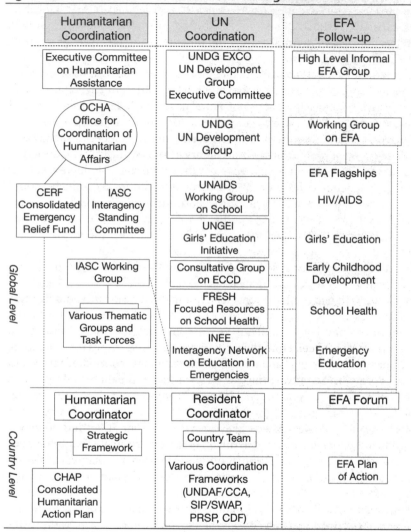

Source: World Bank, 2005, p. 65

of actors, as it is precluded by its articles of agreement from engaging in humanitarian assistance. While there was evidence in these early years of improved coordination vertically within each of the columns depicted in Figure 10.1, there were few examples of lateral coordination between them. This lack of coordination was particularly apparent between the humanitarian assistance structures and those of the UNDG and EFA.

Efforts subsequently were made to establish linkages between the EFA initiatives and the programs that were driven under the aegis of the UNDG—especially in girls' education, HIV/AIDS, school health, and early childhood development. The linkages of these initiatives to the humanitarian actors, however, were more tenuous.

It was in this context that the Inter-Agency Network for Education in Emergencies (INEE) was established in November 2000, with the specific purpose of facilitating better coordination in the area of education in emergencies. It was established not as a coordinating committee, since coordinating mechanisms already existed, but as a network for knowledge sharing and information exchange, building on the existing coordination mechanisms and seeking to facilitate better collaboration among them. Overall, however, the complex list of global and local institutions, structures, and committees that are indicated on the "alphabet soup" chart signaled a largely uncoordinated set of "coordination" mechanisms at the turn of the century.

THE AGE OF AID ARCHITECTURE: FROM 2000 TO 2010

While "alphabet soup" provided a wry metaphor to describe the bewildering array of institutional arrangements, each referred to by insiders by a three- or four-letter abbreviation, the dominant metaphor to emerge during the first decade of this century was more concrete. From the early 2000s there were growing references to "aid architecture" and "global architecture," reflecting a strong demand, especially within the donor community and among recipient governments, for a simpler and more coherently designed institutional framework for humanitarian and development aid.

The metaphor of "global aid architecture" is somewhat misleading, however, as it implies the existence of a single architect or guiding influence that has shaped the design and construction of the institutional arrangements that serve to coordinate international support for education in emergencies. Rather than a well-conceptualized and planned superstructure, what emerged was an enormously complex, rambling series of institutions and networks that is more akin to an informal settlement that has grown up on the edges of a boom town, without the benefit of a town planner or any coherent building regulations. Various groups of institutions, each driven by their own logic and needs, converged on the field to create a confusing multitude of organizations with that bewildering array of acronyms.

At the global level the drive for simpler and more transparent design was shaped by six compacts in the first decade of this century that reflect significant commitments on the part of donors and international humanitarian and development agencies and NGOs to improve performance and reduce the transaction costs to donors and governments alike through better coordination and adherence to shared principles.

The first of these was the Dakar Framework for Action hammered out in deliberations at the World Education Forum in Senegal in April 2000 (UNESCO, 2000). Most significant for this discussion is what became known as the "Dakar EFA promise," which read, "We affirm that no countries seriously committed to education for all will be thwarted in their achievement of this goal by lack of resources." While this declaration included the kind of wriggle room ("seriously committed") that is typical of such global accords, it did serve to place considerable pressure on international donors to do their share of resource mobilization to meet this commitment, while the obligation on governments was to prepare a "credible plan." The momentum here was driven by the international agencies that sponsored the meeting and the member governments that participated. The major donor governments attending the forum were more guarded in their enthusiasm and articulated a concern that there was a need for greater clarity on what obligations such declarations made on recipient governments.

Shortly after the Dakar EFA promise, the world community committed itself to another set of development goals, which also reflected mounting international concern with establishing a global, time-bound compact among richer and poorer countries to achieve specific goals. The Millennium Development Goals (MDGs) were agreed to by 192 UN member states and more than 2 dozen international organizations at the 2000 United Nations Millennium Summit. The MDGs set targets for development in the areas of poverty, hunger, gender equality, child mortality, maternal health, other diseases, and the environment. Goal 8 addresses the need for a more comprehensive and coordinated approach to global poverty. Education figures prominently in two of the MDGs.

By 2002, the concern for more clarity about what obligations should be placed on recipient governments in return for aid was articulated in another global accord: the Monterrey Consensus on Financing for Development (United Nations, 2003). The consensus used a wider frame of reference than either the Dakar Framework or the Millennium Development Goals, and started with an emphasis on the role of national governments in ensuring good governance in order to create an "enabling environment" for development. The agreement took the form of a compact among donors, development agencies, and developing countries, placing responsibilities and obligations on each of the partners. Interestingly, official development assistance came only fourth in a list of key mechanisms for financing development, after domestic resources, foreign direct investment and other private flows, and international trade.

In the education sector, the Monterrey Consensus laid some of the groundwork for the development of the EFA Fast Track Initiative (EFA-FTI), which began after early 2002 to make the case for a compact with national governments on accelerating progress toward the EFA and MDG education goals. The

EFA-FTI was an initiative led initially by the World Bank to provide a more effective mechanism for "EFA follow-up" than that provided by the EFA Secretariat based in UNESCO. This Secretariat had driven an initiative based on the Dakar Framework for Action to help every country to develop an "EFA Action Plan" by 2002; by 2003, the initiative had stimulated the development of 120 national EFA plans, many of which were extremely ambitious and offered very little clarity about how these ambitious plans would be financed (UNESCO, 2005, p. 205). The World Bank-led EFA-FTI partnership included a compact that required national authorities to provide evidence of both political will and commitment of domestic resources (financial and institutional) to the sector, in what became known as the "FTI Indicative Framework." Countries that prepared an education sector plan that incorporated the benchmarks of the Indicative Framework and a set of assessment guidelines prepared by the FTI Secretariat could seek "endorsement" from the Local Education Group, which consisted of the government and key development partners, including donors and representation of civil society. Such endorsement was intended to mobilize donor resources at the country level; where a "funding gap" persisted, application could be made to the FTI Catalytic Fund for additional resources to supplement national, bilateral donor, and multilateral financing mobilized at the country level. For those countries that lacked the capacity to prepare a "credible plan" that would meet the demanding FTI standards, the FTI Education Program Development Fund was established to support capacity-building and technical assistance. Both funds were administered by the World Bank and financed from contributions to the fund from the major bilateral donors.

By 2005, the focus of international attention had shifted back to the donors and the issue of aid effectiveness, which finally was articulated in the Paris Declaration on Aid Effectiveness (OECD, 2008). This gathering of donors, "partner governments,"[2] and development agencies outlined a series of principles emphasizing the importance of national ownership of development initiatives, supported by clearer alignment and harmonization of development assistance, and a renewed focus on results and accountability. The declaration was backed by a strong commitment on the part of donors and development agencies to monitor and report on progress on implementation of the principles, a commitment that was reviewed 3 years later in Accra.

Gradually, the rhetoric of international development began to incorporate the language of "fragile states" and "fragile situations," with a growing awareness that unless some specific steps were taken to address the particular needs of countries that lacked either the political will or the institutional capacity to deliver services to their people, the world would fall far short of the MDGs. The OECD-DAC *Policy Commitments and Principles for Good International Engagement in Fragile States and Situations,* cited in the 2005 Paris Declaration as "draft," were endorsed in an international meeting and published in April

2007 (see OECD, 2007b; c). The ten principles, none by itself particularly original or new, together constituted the most comprehensive and coherent set of guidelines for work in fragile contexts to date. They were based on a systematic analysis of experience over the previous decades and emphasized using the local context as starting point, "doing no harm," and making state-building the central objective of initiatives in fragile situations. They also emphasized prioritizing prevention; recognizing the links among political, security, and development objectives; ensuring nondiscrimination and use of practical coordination mechanisms between international actors; balancing quick response with sustained engagement; and avoiding "pockets of exclusion."

In 2008 the Paris Declaration's commitment to review progress against the Paris principles was realized in Accra, where both the Paris Declaration and the OECD-DAC principles of engagement in fragile states were placed under scrutiny, leading to the Accra Agenda for Action.[3] This declaration, among other things, emphasized the importance of ensuring predictability in financing, using country systems wherever possible, and included a specific section on the importance of adapting approaches for fragile situations.

In the education sector there was a corresponding acceleration in attention to fragile and conflict-affected contexts over the decade between 2000 and 2010. This was reflected, among other initiatives, in the growing work of the INEE, and in the EFA-FTI establishing a Fragile States Task Team. This task team built on the work of the OECD-DAC workstream on fragile states and reviewed some aspects of the FTI approach, producing, among other outputs, the FTI Progressive Framework for Fragile States (FTI-PF) (EFA-FTI, 2008). The FTI-PF was a tool for dialogue to help countries that were unable to meet the benchmarks contained in the FTI Indicative Framework to identify a set of priority activities in order to elicit interim donor support and financing for both ongoing service delivery and capacity-building until a more comprehensive sector plan could be prepared, reviewed, and endorsed. Since 2007, the FTI-PF has been used in a number of fragile and conflict-affected countries as an input to deliberations among partners and has now been accepted by the EFA-FTI Board as a tool for use in any fragile or conflict-affected context (EFA-FTI, 2010). The tool is intended to be illustrative and to provide a basis for country-level dialogue. Its purpose is to ensure that the discussions about strategy take into account the current situation in the country with regard to four key variables:

- Sector assessment, planning, and coordination
- Resource mobilization and financial management
- Service delivery (teachers, learning spaces, learning process)
- Monitoring system improvement

Integrated into the framework is consideration of the kind of factors that are common in conflict-affected fragile states, such as peace- and state-building, war-affected youth, and so on. The full framework can be found at http://www.educationfasttrack.org/media/library/pfguidelines.pdf. Table 10.1 provides an illustrative extract from the section on sector assessment, planning, and coordination.

Table 10.1. Extract from Sector Assessment, Planning and Coordination

INTERIM STATUS		DEVELOPMENT TARGET
Sector Assessment, Planning, and Coordination		
Local/ad hoc Education Working Group established with education authorities for assessment and strategic planning with IASC Education Clusters coordination where appropriate	Agency and government joint task force established to assess, plan, and provide oversight to education sector program	Government/country-led coordinating mechanism for aid management, delivery, and results endorsed for FTI
Assessment of fragility; strategies and priorities developed for support to targeted regions and sub-sectors; reaching underserved groups, including NFE programs for youth Ad hoc humanitarian assistance provided which is largely uncoordinated	Mid-term education strategy (at national, sub-national levels, inclusive of formal, and NFE; Coordinated aid management (with some pooled funding, MDTF, etc.)	*National education sector plan embedded within PRS (or equivalent) and MTEF*
Community authorities participating in education planning and provision Establishment of representative school-community boards (gender, ethnicity, etc.)	Coordinated planning mechanisms for representative community and local government, inclusive of underserved groups	Civil society involvement in system planning, and community participation in school improvement and management

Source: EFA-FTI, 2008, p. 7

THE CURRENT AID ARCHITECTURE FOR AID TO
EDUCATION IN CONFLICT-AFFECTED CONTEXTS

Concern among donors, partner governments, and international development agencies over improving their performance in delivering assistance to children and youth in zones of conflict has grown considerably over the past decade. Not surprisingly, this concern has had a significant impact on the institutional arrangements through which aid is mediated, and talk has turned again and again to the "architecture" of international aid. The challenge was not a simple question of design, but the much more taxing and demanding task of trying to induce better collaboration, coordination, communication, and resource sharing that a new town planner might confront in seeking to impose some order on a collection of informal settlements and institutions that had been established by different communities driven by different agendas.

Figure 10.2 presents an updated version of the original organizational chart of aid relationships for education in conflict-affected situations. For the sake of brevity, acronyms are used for those structures that survived from the earlier chart (see Figure 10.1), while new institutional arrangements are shown in bold. While many of the old structures persist, there are several new and more streamlined structures that have an impact particularly on education in fragile states and situations.

There are two sets of institutional arrangements in particular that have been shaped by the drive for better, more coordinated and sustainable education service delivery and system development support in fragile contexts. The first of these is the remodeled FTI initiative, which emerged from an intensive review in 2009 to present a more streamlined and more consistent framework for operations. The previous FTI Steering Committee has been replaced by a formally constituted Board. This steering committee is more representative of both developing countries and nongovernmental actors, including teachers' organizations, NGOs, and the private sector.

Following considerable deliberation and an unsuccessful initiative to establish a dedicated international FTI fund for education in fragile states to be managed by UNICEF, the EFA-FTI reached an agreement in 2009 that FTI resources would be organized into one fund. This fund is now available to countries that prepare an Interim Plan that uses the Progressive Framework as a starting point toward reaching the benchmarks established in the FTI's Indicative Framework. This development effectively brings together under the FTI umbrella all countries "seriously committed" to achieving the EFA goals, and removes the unclear and confusing distinction between countries considered "fragile" and those that are not. Perhaps the most significant contribution of this innovation has been to provide new energy, stimulated in many cases by additional funds, to coordinated planning at the country level led by each "local education group" (a generic term that describes local institutional arrangements that include all key stakeholders under leadership, or co-leadership, of the national authorities). While such processes were envisioned in previous decades under various versions of the "sector-wide approach," the FTI has helped give this solid institutional form in many countries.

The other significant development indicated in Figure 10.2 is the emergence of sector "clusters" under the auspices of the IASC. Initially envisioned as a mechanism to bring together the various UN initiatives at the country level, these quickly evolved into local-level stakeholder coordination bodies, bringing together all humanitarian actors working in the sector to help ensure more coordinated responses and to involve, as far as possible, the authorities in decision making and information sharing. As a result of committed lobbying by the education sector, led in many cases by the INEE, a decision was made in the OCHA and its Inter-Agency Standing Committee Working Group in 2008 to establish Education

Figure 10.2. Coordination of Education in Emergencies 2010

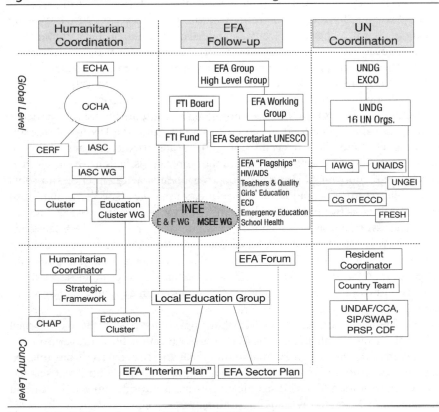

Source: Adapted by author from World Bank, 2005, p. 65

Clusters at the country level and to endorse the establishment of an Education Cluster Working Group based in Geneva.

As noted by Kirk earlier in this volume (see Chapter 2), the establishment of the Education Cluster Working Group signaled an important breakthrough in support to education in fragile and conflict-affected environments in two ways. First, it was an official and formally constituted institutional arrangement specifically for the education sector within the framework of humanitarian assistance. For decades there had been strong resistance to acknowledging a role for education in humanitarian assistance, since it was regarded by many as a "development" matter. Despite individual commitments of organizations to making education a "fourth pillar" of humanitarian response in the early 2000s, specific institutional arrangements of the kind signaled by the Education Clusters had been relatively rare and often ineffectual. Now the establishment of an Education Cluster is relatively routine whenever an international humanitarian response is initiated. By 2010 at least 38 countries had established Education Clusters.

The Education Cluster Working Group also established a stronger institutional role for INGOs. In a bold innovation, the Education Cluster Working Group has been co-chaired by UNICEF and Save the Children. This arrangement for co-chairing with a nongovernmental organization of a major coordinating body helped to cement into place new forms of partnership that provide the flexibility and responsiveness that fragile contexts demand. In the Education Clusters, this spirit of partnership usually is replicated at the country level.

The expansion of the INEE, the development of a more inclusive governance structure for the FTI partnership, and the establishment of a UN-led cluster approach in education have opened the way for greater partnership and improved information sharing at both the local and the global levels. This has been complemented by the growing inclusion of nongovernmental actors in efforts to coordinate international education assistance in conflict zones. The World Bank also has become an active partner in the drive for a more effective linkage between humanitarian response and "reconstruction and development," which falls fully within its mandate. It has had observer status on the IASC since the mid-1990s and representation on the INEE Steering Group since 2003. It recently has established a State and Peacebuilding Fund as a mechanism to channel resources to assist countries caught in the gap between humanitarian assistance and development aid.

While these arrangements are not yet strongly reflected in most of the formal institutional arrangements, the fact that in the education sector these processes often involve the same individuals at both global and country levels has resulted in better and more effective information sharing and collaboration. The INEE has played and continues to play a significant role as an information warehouse and locus for knowledge exchange to support this process.

CONCLUSION

As with town planning and other attempts to retrofit order on institutional arrangements that have grown out of disorder, the process is far from perfect. The new marriage between UN agencies and NGOs, which proceeded relatively smoothly in the INEE, has encountered its own challenges at global and local levels when the task involves not simply collaboration but coordination and control. The FTI is still working through the implications of its reorientation to support countries in their struggle to make progress toward the EFA goals from any stage of development, including those that are "seriously off-track." Donors, development agencies, and partner countries alike often view the new attempts to widen participation as too complex and too prone to delays.

Financing instruments such as the new EFA-FTI fund and the United Nation's humanitarian appeals (CAP), still operate largely independently of one another and often fail to mobilize the kind of resources suggested in needs assessments and sector plans. Authorities in fragile states are confronted with a bewildering array of different financing "modalities" to which are attached a complex string of acronyms and their own regulations and procedures, which leave national authorities at a distinct disadvantage when financing and implementation modalities for aid are discussed. Much remains to be done in moving from improved institutional arrangements to actual change on the ground, which is still uneven due to the role of local context and national and organizational politics.

Efforts to link up initial humanitarian aid programs to more sustained financing for educational development are still in their infancy. Yet there has been distinct progress both in establishing more flexible and appropriate institutional arrangements, and in imbuing them with a spirit of collaboration and commitment to a common purpose. Today there is broad recognition that linking up different aid modalities and partners is necessary to ensure that children in zones of conflict receive uninterrupted opportunities to learn. These are changes for which Jackie Kirk, to whom this book is dedicated, strove tirelessly at both the global and country level.

NOTES

1. At Jomtien this consisted of representatives of 155 countries, 20 intergovernmental bodies, and 150 nongovernment organizations.

2. The shift in language from "recipient governments" and "developing country governments" to "partner governments" was not insignificant.

3. http://siteresources.worldbank.org/ACCRAEXT/Resources/4700790-1217425866038/AAA-4-SEPTEMBER-FINAL-16h00.pdf

CHAPTER 11

Aid and Education in Fragile States

Victoria Turrent

The flow of aid to education in fragile states has become an important and pervasive theme in development discourse, reflecting concerns in the international community about the implications for global stability resulting from state fragility, and the role that key public services play in demonstrating good governance. In many fragile states progress toward universal primary education has been stagnant, with estimations of up to half of all out-of-school, primary-aged children living in fragile contexts such as Afghanistan, Central African Republic, Democratic Republic of Congo, and Zimbabwe.[1] Fragile states have difficulty mobilizing domestic resources to finance national education strategies and consequently rely heavily on other sources of educational investment. Significant amounts of education financing for these countries need to come in the form of humanitarian and development aid.

Drawing on, and updating, research by Turrent and Oketch (2009), this chapter starts by exploring definitions of state fragility. It then examines aid allocation trends over the past ten years for which data are available (1999–2008) in the context of achieving universal primary education, exploring differences in the flow of official development assistance to the education sector in 19 low-income countries that are widely considered "fragile" (see Table 11.1), as compared with 21 other low-income countries. Consideration also is given to the challenges of delivering aid in these contexts—focusing on issues of aid effectiveness, absorptive capacity, and the predictability of aid flows. The chapter concludes that fragile states continue to be sidelined due to the complexities of "doing business" in difficult development contexts, and argues that donors urgently need to find ways of creating more reliable mechanisms for releasing education resources when the underlying partnership basis for doing so is largely absent.

DEFINING STATE FRAGILITY

In recent years, concern has grown over the effect that weak or ineffective states have on global stability, heightening academic and foreign policy interest in conceptualizing the notion of "fragile" states. The proliferation of labels—ranging from "crisis states" to "countries at risk of instability" and "countries under stress"—reflects the range of ways in which the core problem of state fragility has been conceived (Moreno Torres & Anderson, 2004). While there is no single agreed-upon definition of fragile states, the international community has been converging on an approach that recognizes common characteristics of weak governance and vulnerability to conflict, together with fragile situations of prolonged crisis; post-conflict or political transition; and deteriorating governance (Moreno Torres & Anderson, 2004; OECD, 2007c; World Bank, 2006). Although these countries are highly heterogeneous, they face a common set of challenges, including high security risks and threats to development (Leader & Colenso, 2005).

The discussion in this chapter utilizes the World Bank's "fragile situations" definition, as this provides measurable criteria (Menocal & Othieno, 2008). The World Bank's Country Policy and Institutional Assessment (CPIA) defines a country as a fragile situation if it is a low-income country and has either a harmonized CPIA score of less than 3.2 (an average taken from CPIA ratings of the World Bank, the African Development Bank, and the Asian Development Bank), or the presence of a United Nations and/or regional peace-keeping or peace-building mission during the past 3 years. Not all fragile situations are low-income economies; therefore, in order to compare like-with-like, the definition of fragility employed here focuses on those fragile situations that are characterized as low income: Afghanistan, Burundi, Central African Republic, Chad, Comoros, Democratic Republic of Congo, Eritrea, Guinea, Guinea-Bissau, Haiti, Liberia, Myanmar, Nepal, Sierra Leone, Solomon Islands, Somalia, Tajikistan, Togo, and Zimbabwe.[2]

Table 11.1. Fragile and Other Low-Income Countries (Based on World Bank Definition of Fragile Situations)

Fragile low-income states	Other low-income countries
Afghanistan, Burundi, Central African Republic, Chad, Comoros, Democratic Republic of Congo, Eritrea, Guinea, Guinea-Bissau, Haiti, Liberia, Myanmar, Nepal, Sierra Leone, Solomon Islands, Somalia, Tajikistan, Togo, Zimbabwe.	Bangladesh, Benin, Burkina Faso, Cambodia, Ethiopia, Gambia, Ghana, Kenya, Korea, Kygryz Republic, Lao PDR, Madagascar, Malawi, Mali, Mauritania, Mozambique, Niger, Rwanda, Tanzania, Uganda, Zambia.

METHODOLOGY

The following sections explore the provision of aid—both development and humanitarian—to the education sector in fragile states. They draw on data on both development and humanitarian aid flows collected from donor countries, published by the Organisation for Economic Co-operation and Development Development Assistance Committee (OECD-DAC) and the Office for the Coordination of Humanitarian Affairs (OCHA FTS) respectively.

As noted above, in order to examine the flow of official development assistance (ODA) specifically to the education sector in fragile states, this chapter draws on a comparative analysis between two mutually exclusive groups of low-income countries: 19 fragile states (as defined by the World Bank) and 21 other low-income countries (see Table 11.1). There are a number of precedents for comparing aid flows to different groups of countries using OECD-DAC data (see, e.g., Levin & Dollar, 2005; Save the Children, 2009; Turrent & Oketch, 2009). The chapter updates the research carried out by Turrent and Oketch (2009), which used the World Bank's discontinued definition of fragility, the "low income countries under stress" (LICUS) definition of fragility.

Data on ODA commitments and disbursements are compiled by the OECD-DAC, the principal body through which the OECD deals with issues related to financial cooperation with developing countries.[3] The Creditor Reporting System (CRS) is internationally recognized as a source of data on the geographical and sectoral breakdown of development aid granted by bilateral and multilateral institutions. It gives detailed information on individual aid activities and includes information from DAC countries, the World Bank, the regional development banks, and some UN agencies, providing readily available data that enable analysis on where aid goes, the purpose it serves, and what policies it aims to implement. CRS data are required to examine the sub-sectoral breakdown of ODA (e.g., basic education as a share of aid to education) and to add a geographical dimension to the analysis.

To obtain an accurate profile of ODA flows supporting the education sector, the analysis accounts for both reported education ODA and 20% of general budget support. Basic education here accounts for reported basic education ODA, 10% of general budget support, and 50% of the category "education—level unspecified." Commitment data are referred to—as opposed to data on disbursements—as these have been more fully reported by the DAC and are complete for the education sector since 1999. As commitments are likely to fluctuate from year to year, a 3-year average is taken between 2006 and 2008 (the most recent year for which data are available) to smooth out any variability. All statistics are adjusted for inflation and reported in 2008 U.S. dollars.

Humanitarian funding also forms a significant portion of aid to fragile states. The OCHA FTS provides a sectoral breakdown of this emergency-oriented aid.

The FTS is a global, real-time database that records all reported international humanitarian aid, including that for NGOs and the Red Cross/Red Crescent movement, bilateral aid, in-kind aid, and donations. FTS features a special focus on consolidated and flash appeals, because these cover the major humanitarian crises and because their funding requirements are well defined—which allows FTS to indicate to what extent populations in crisis receive humanitarian aid in proportion to their needs. This data source is particularly useful as it allows for an examination of humanitarian aid at the education sector level, an examination that cannot be made using the OECD CRS database. Humanitarian aid to education figures are cited here in current U.S. dollars.

EDUCATION AID FLOWS TO FRAGILE STATES

Most developing countries depend heavily on aid as a means of increasing their gross national income. A crude measure of this dependence is the net flow of approximately 150 billion USD per year in aid from developed to less developed countries.[4] Given the low tax base in many fragile states, coupled with limited foreign direct investment and trade, ODA is an important additional source of revenue for the government. That need is heightened and revenue more limited in these contexts does not mean, however, that additional aid is forthcoming.

ODA flows to education in developing countries have shown an upward trend, rising from 4.4 billion USD in 1999 to 11.6 billion USD in 2008. On average between 2006 and 2008, 29% of total education ODA commitments were directed to 40 low-income countries in which the gross national income per capita was less than 995 USD—evidence that the majority of education aid remains focused on middle-income economies. Although since 2001 there has been a significant increase in the amount of aid for education directed to low-income economies as the result of intensified political effort to meet the Millennium Development Goal (MDG) of universal primary school completion by 2015, this has been focused largely on those "good-performing" countries able to demonstrate intensified political and financial commitment for education (see Figure 11.1). Donors are understandably concerned by the potential for the misuse of funds and/or the proposition of inadequate returns on their investments in fragile states, but such thinking has meant that these countries are in receipt of consistently low levels of education aid—between 2006 and 2008, just 37% of education ODA committed to low-income economies was allocated to fragile states.

This finding is consistent with the trend in the international aid architecture for donors to link aid allocation to assessments of the quality of recipient country policies and institutions, in the belief that aid works better in countries that do better in terms of these assessments. But this paradigm has drawbacks, especially for those countries that are poor and in great need of assistance. These countries

Figure 11.1. Education ODA Flows to Low-Income Countries

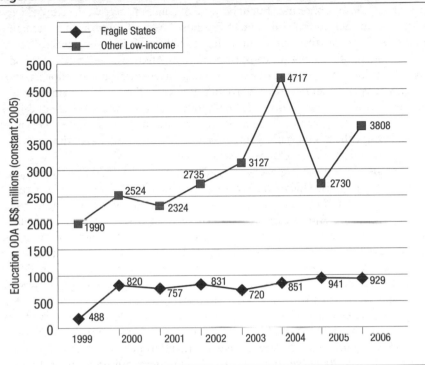

Source: Turrent & Oketch, 2009, p. 360

are penalized with less aid in a purely "selective" aid regime that is based on policy performance (Turrent & Oketch, 2009). However, it is clear that institutional and policy performance is not the only factor donors consider when allocating aid. DAC-commissioned research shows that total aid to fragile states could be increased by 43% without affecting the performance basis of aid committed in these contexts (Levin & Dollar, 2005, p. 13). This suggests that there are other factors—including, quite probably, the perceived risk of engaging in fragile states—influencing donor decisions on where to apportion their aid for education. Fragile states are unable to mitigate concerns of corruption and ensure the fiduciary requirements that are demanded by donors of their development partners.

Overall, increases in education aid are in line with general aid increases in recent years and reflect greater recognition among donors of the importance of funding the education sector. However, the share of ODA committed to education remains low, particularly in fragile states. On average between 2006 and 2008, 7% of total aid in fragile states was committed to education compared with 9% in other low-income countries. This may be due, in part, to the fact that education in fragile states is not a priority sector for donor investment because of concerns over weak state capacity and/or will. In such scenarios donors have tended to focus support on governance and civil society initiatives (Save the Children, 2009). While ODA flows to fragile states can be significant in some countries—notably Afghanistan—much of this aid may be spent on issues related to governance, stability, security, and elections, rather than education. Rose and Greeley (2006) posit that while the establishment of strong state structures will be a priority for many fragile states, the part that education can play—both in terms of its role in development and as one of the most visible state services, with an important symbolic value in establishing the legitimacy of the state—needs to be more systematically acknowledged.

Analysis of the education needs of fragile states in line with the goal of achieving universal primary education suggests that basic education in fragile states is underfunded by donors when this funding is compared with that of other low-income countries. Despite being home to a smaller out-of-school primary population than fragile states (13 million versus 20 million), other low-income countries are allocated 75% of aid to basic education committed to low-income countries, while fragile states are allocated just 25%. If the amount of basic education aid allocated to each group of countries is broken down on a needs basis (according to the number of out-of school children in each group), this equates to just 24 USD per child in fragile states compared with 111 USD in other low-income countries. Given the additional cost implicit in reaching the most marginalized children (who are overrepresented in fragile states, and the hardest to reach), it appears that more aid will need to be funneled in support of demobilization, the reduction of child labor, and addressing household poverty in these contexts.

Both low-income countries and low-income countries affected by fragility appear to be benefiting from a greater share of education aid allocated to basic education. ODA flows to basic education in low-income countries between 1999 and 2008 showed a broadly similar trend to those of total education. A sharp increase in basic education commitments to other low-income countries starting in 2002 may be attributable to an increased focus on the education MDG commitments and related to the introduction of the Education for All—Fast Track Initiative (EFA-FTI) established the same year. This trend has continued since 2006, suggestive of a renewed donor focus on primary education in the countdown to the MDG deadline.

However, fragile states continue to receive lower shares of education aid allocated to the basic education level. Turrent and Oketch (2009) found that, between 2004 and 2006, 50% of education aid in LICUS (the World Bank's former categorization for fragile states) was allocated for basic education compared with 57% in other low-income countries. The focus on basic education has since risen to 61% of total education aid in other low-income countries, but is still lower, at 56%, in fragile states.

Education for All—Fast Track Initiative

The EFA-FTI was established as a global partnership between donors and developing countries following the international consensus reached at Monterrey on financing for development. It was the first global initiative to operationalize the Monterrey Consensus as a partnership between developing countries and the donor community at both the international and country levels. Over the past 6 years, the partnership has aimed to accelerate progress toward universal primary school completion by explicitly linking increased donor support for primary education to recipient countries' policy performance and accountability for results, regardless of a country's specific social or political status. The EFA-FTI framework encourages donor actions to provide predictable resources to developing countries in a manner that minimizes the transaction costs for recipient countries. It also promotes improved coordination and harmonization in donor financing to support country-owned education sector strategies (EFA-FTI Secretariat, 2004).

EFA-FTI endorsement of an education sector plan is intended to signal to the international community that the plan is sound and sustainable, and therefore a good investment. Ideally, sustainable resources are made available directly to the country by bilateral and multilateral partners. For most fragile states, the typical absence of education sector plans and the low credibility of institutions at the sectoral and financial management levels, in addition to weak systems and low capacity, make fragile states a high-risk proposition for bilateral donor investment. One of the major challenges, therefore, has been to find a suitable financing and management channel for education aid. The EFA-FTI has sought to increase aid commitments to fragile states by establishing a task team to explore options for the establishment of a mechanism for delivering education aid to those states.

Research suggests that until recently the new international aid architecture, as embodied by the EFA-FTI, was not able to address the most pressing needs of fragile states, with few of these countries qualifying for EFA-FTI funding (Turrent, 2009). EFA-FTI support to fragile states had been limited, with just a handful of countries—Central African Republic, Guinea, Haiti, Liberia, Nepal, Sierra Leone, Tajikistan, and Togo—allocated funding (EFA-FTI, 2010). Moreover, the EFA-FTI demonstrated severe disbursement issues in relation to its allocation of monies to fragile states—Sierra Leone's grant, for example, was in process for over 2 years. This is worrying as fragile states tend to have large financing gaps and, as "donor orphans," little ability to attract donor assistance or mobilize domestic financing via government structures (Levin & Dollar, 2005). Until recently, the EFA-FTI arrangement reflected a prevailing orthodoxy for rewarding good performance, emphasizing a strong policy and institutional environment as a basis for allocating aid.

As noted by Buckland (Chapter 10, this volume), the FTI has now agreed to a reform agenda that includes steps to better meet the needs of fragile states. The reformed FTI merges the Catalytic and Education Program Development Funds into one streamlined process. The result is a single new Education for All Fund that purports to allow all countries—regardless of whether they have already developed an education sector plan or not—to approach the EFA-FTI for funding and technical support. Additionally, a Results Framework based on the Progressive Framework" (see Buckland, Chapter 10, this volume) replaces the old Indicative Framework, emphasizing evidence as the primary basis for policy dialogue. This goes a long way to addressing concerns that while the EFA-FTI could be seen to provide longer term aspirational targets, its benchmarks and data requirements were often too ambitious for fragile states (Turrent, 2009). What remains to be seen is the degree to which additional funds can be leveraged for the fund when the risk of donor engagement in fragile states has not been fully allayed.

Humanitarian Aid

Humanitarian aid is a major form of support in both acute and protracted crises, playing a much greater role in fragile states than in other developing countries due to the greater propensity for conflict and states of emergency. Turrent and Oketch (2009, p. 362) show that 15% of total aid is allocated to humanitarian activities in LICUS countries, compared with just 1% in other low-income countries. As a substantial contribution to external assistance, understanding how humanitarian aid supports the education sector in emergency and crisis situations is of fundamental importance.

Turrent and Oketch (2009) note that one of the longstanding issues with humanitarian aid is a general lack of resources, with contributions to the Consolidated Appeals Process (CAP)—the humanitarian sector's main tool for coordination, strategic planning, and programming—covering only two-thirds of the total humanitarian appeal. Low levels of contribution create a difficult dilemma around how to prioritize CAP funding. The OCHA FTS shows that in 2009, just 1.5% of humanitarian aid was apportioned to education, making it the sector in receipt of the least aid. Thus, while all humanitarian needs are underfunded, this holds particularly true for the education sector. In the same year, less than a third—32%—of the funding requirements were met for education, compared with 71% coverage for all sectors. Again, the education sector was in receipt of the least coverage for the needs identified.

Underfunding of education is an important issue for humanitarian funding, and organizations such as the Inter-Agency Network for Education in Emergencies (INEE) and Save the Children have been fighting to move it up the humanitarian agenda. The basis of their argument rests on the belief that education has positive long-term effects that contribute to the rebuilding of state systems in the wake of an emergency or crisis. Education is seen to provide protection for children and to promote justice and respect for human rights, thereby enhancing peace and stability (Aguilar & Retamal, 2009).

A further issue for the humanitarian funding of education—indeed for humanitarian aid in all sectors—is the transition from humanitarian to development aid. The notion of a "relief–development continuum" originally was conceptualized with the aim of identifying complementary objectives and strategies in humanitarian and development aid in order to bridge the operational gap that typically arises between the end of emergency aid and the start of development programming. However, conceptualization of this as a chronological issue has been largely rejected as overly simplistic. Attempts to fill the conceptual gap between humanitarian/emergency situations and development have re-emerged with the concept of "early recovery," which argues for the integration of development work into relief efforts. It is increasingly believed that development work should begin as early as possible—in the case of conflict, often before the peace process is complete (GSRDC, 2010). However, the humanitarian–development gap remains largely unaddressed, and there is often a failure of transition financing once acute emergencies have passed. This poses severe problems for the continuity of education services and rebuilding of educational systems in many fragile states.

LESSONS AND TRENDS FROM OTHER RESEARCH ON AID EFFECTIVENESS AND FRAGILE STATES

The benefits of aid have been under scrutiny for decades. Several observers argue that a large portion of aid flowing from developed to fragile states is wasted and only increases unproductive public consumption (Easterley, 2006). On the one hand, poor institutional development, inefficiencies, and bureaucratic failures in these countries often are cited as reasons for these results. On the other hand, there remain staunch advocates of aid insistent that aid is essential to spurring on pro-poor growth and development (Sachs, 2005).

Chauvet and Collier (2007) propose that dysfunctional governance and policies, as well as civil war and its aftermath, have an important consequence for development aid: Recipient governments are liable to lack either the capacity or the volition to use aid effectively. Hence, the very conditions that make fragile states a priority for donors limit the scope for remedy. The case for scaling up development assistance in fragile states, then, ultimately rests on demonstrating that more aid can improve access to schools as well as equity and quality in education. Understanding aid effectiveness; the capacity of the state to absorb additional financing; and the way in which donor aid ebbs and flows, is vital to justifying any call for increased resources for education in fragile development contexts.

Aid Effectiveness

Research on the impact of aid flows shows that aid increases growth and contributes to poverty reduction (Hansen & Tarp, 2000). A more controversial finding, however, is that this impact on growth is dependent upon the quality of the recipient country's institutions and policies (Burnside & Dollar, 2000). These findings have clear implications for aid allocation, suggesting that if global poverty reduction is to be maximized effectively, aid should be allocated primarily to countries in which it would have the greatest impact. Indeed, this is common practice in aid allocation, with institution and policy performance being the fundamental principles upon which the World Bank's aid allocation model is built. It also has been the means for determining eligibility for EFA-FTI financing.

However, the Collier and Dollar (2002) selectivity model upon which aid effectiveness has been assessed, and which is used to determine where aid should be allocated, would channel aid to many more poor countries than donors support in practice. The model gives a higher weighting to aid in populous poor countries than those that score highly in policy and institutional assessments. Critics have raised serious questions about the link between aid effectiveness and policy at the bottom end of the policy scale (Hansen & Tarp, 2000; McGillivray, 2006). Further research on the link between aid effectiveness and policy in countries that do poorly in terms of indices like the CPIA is certainly warranted.

Absorptive Capacity

Absorptive capacity is a term frequently adopted by development practitioners in education as a reason for cautiousness in the scaling up of aid to the sector (Rose, 2009). It is argued that aid, like other investments, has diminishing returns, with a saturation point of anywhere between 15 and 45% of GDP, beyond which the marginal benefits of additional aid flows become negative (Overseas Development Institute (ODI), 2005, p. 1). The notion of an aid saturation point has been interpreted as indicating limited absorptive capacity, with recipient governments being limited in the amounts of aid that they can use effectively (Clemens & Radelet, 2003). This finding poses important questions about the provision of significant additional education aid to fragile states, many of which are already defined by their limited institutional capacities.

The transparency and efficiency of public expenditure and accountability systems to hold governments responsible are just two examples of institutional and policy factors that can determine a country's performance in generating positive development outcomes. It is thought that in some fragile states such systems may not be adequate to absorb large increases in available resources without increasing wastage or fueling corruption. However, Rose (2009) finds that—specifically in the education sector—absorptive capacity should not be seen as a reason for not increasing aid and that, rather, effort should be directed to ensure that bottlenecks in the aid delivery system are readily identified and addressed. An understanding of capacity constraints may make it possible to identify alternative strategies that donors and national governments can use to increase the amount of aid that reaches schools and improves educational outcomes.

Predictability of Aid Flows

By definition, fragile states suffer from very low or weak capacity and are generally much further than other countries from achieving the MDGs. Thus, in order to build stronger and more sustainable institutions to enable these countries to make progress toward the MDGs, the duration of aid flows needs to be longer term than may be the case in many higher capacity developing countries. The result of selectivity in aid allocation and concerns regarding reduced absorptive capacity have meant that aid volatility in fragile states is more acute than in more stable countries. In addition, donors operating in fragile states are more likely to use technical assistance and off-budget assistance that is channeled via nongovernmental or UN organizations. This is intended to help avoid corruption. However, it can mean that donors are bypassing the opportunity to build the capacity and transparency of government systems (Turrent & Oketch, 2009).

Levin and Dollar (2005) undertook a study on aid volatility in fragile states between 1992 and 2002 and found that aid volatility is twice as high in fragile states as it is in low-income countries. They also found that aid to fragile states comes in spurts, with a particular country receiving substantial aid flows in one year, with donors moving on to another country the following year. This is particularly damaging to growth and prospects for poverty reduction. Furthermore, high aid volatility makes budgetary policy more difficult and can increase exchange rate variability, thus offsetting any positive impacts of aid (Bulír & Hamann, 2003; Edwards & Van Wijnberg, 1989). Levin and Dollar (2005) also demonstrate that the results take longer to materialize in these environments, making volatility particularly damaging. For low-income countries and fragile states, they found that donors disbursed a total of 86% and 80% of committed funds, respectively, whereas in middle-income countries it was around 100% (Levin & Dollar, 2005, p. 38).

Even where strong international commitment is present in a country suffering from state fragility, issues of weak financial management systems and capacity may mean that donors are unable to disburse funds quickly. The usual response of donors to persistently poor performance by their country portfolios has been to curb lending, precipitating a vicious circle: weak governance and low disbursement rates resulting in reduced financial support and worsening performance (Fayolle, 2006).

CONCLUSION

The dominant paradigm that has evolved on how aid should be allocated to developing countries, based on the widely accepted premise that not only is aid effective in promoting growth, but it is more effective in countries with better policies and institutional settings, appears to have had negative repercussions for aid flows to fragile states, where institutional capacity and political will are deemed to be weaker than in better performing countries. Emphasis on the MDGs, performance-based allocation systems, and aid modalities, while suitable in many environments, do not seem well tailored to help the world's most vulnerable countries. It is clear that meeting education goals in fragile states has been hampered by a lack of resources, as they are seen as high-risk environments for aid delivery (Collier, 2007).

That education is accorded less of a development priority in fragile states than in other low-income countries, and that it is not a priority sector for humanitarian assistance, does not alone provide a case for allocating aid to these difficult development environments. However, given the potential costs of nonintervention, it may be argued that there is a compelling case for finding ways of making aid work in these countries (Turrent & Oketch, 2009). More needs to be learned about the effectiveness of education aid in both fragile states and developing countries in general, with further research into the relationship between aid allocation and access to education required. Aid flows to the education sector in fragile states are less than might be expected given the distance many of these countries are from achieving Education for All, and this is clearly the result of donor allocation politics and processes. Development assistance is a scarce resource, and it is vital for donors and aid recipients—guided by issues of efficiency and aid effectiveness—to work together to maximize the benefits it generates.

While the limits of education aid in fragile states must be recognized, so must the potential for it to help remove the barriers to accessing schooling created by poverty, conflict, weak governance, and other sources of marginalization. There is increasing commitment among donors to work effectively in fragile states; however, improved ways of disbursing funds that address donor concerns over institutional capacity and corruption will need to be found before these donors begin to scale up aid activities in these countries. The challenge faced by donors is the uncertainty over how education resources can be released when the underlying partnership basis for doing so is largely absent. This suggests the need to drop good governance as an absolute precondition for development aid, because being too dogmatic about good governance has led to a great reluctance to help fragile states. As the international community comes to terms with the corollaries of failing to meet the MDGs, and specifically the consequences of nonintervention—terrorism, spill-over effects on the global economy, drug trafficking—new strategies and policies for effectively supporting education in these countries will need to be established. There are no blueprints for fragile states—every case is different and will require its own approach. How donors meet the challenges posed by fragile states will determine whether universal primary education will be achieved.

NOTES

1. Estimations of the number of out-of-school children living in fragile states tend to differ significantly due to insufficient data for many countries experiencing weak governance and/or conflict, and a lack of consensus over a definitive list of fragile states. Save the Children (2009, p. 1) estimates there are 40 million out-of-school children living in "conflict-affected fragile states," while UNESCO (2010, p. 240) approximates the number living in "conflict-affected countries" at closer to one-third of the global out-of-school population.

2. According to the Atlas Method by which the World Bank classifies economies. Data accessed October 5, 2010, from the World Bank Web site: http://data.worldbank.org/about/country-classifications/country-and-lending-groups. As the definition of fragile states applied to the present research refers only to low-income countries, those countries identified by the World Bank as being fragile situations but that are categorized as being lower middle or upper middle income—Angola, Bosnia and Herzegovina, Cote d'Ivoire, Georgia, Iraq, Kosovo, Democratic Republic of Congo, Sao Tome and Principe, Sudan, Timor-Leste, and Yemen—are not included.

3. The core definition of ODA, agreed to by the DAC, states: "ODA consists of flows to developing countries and multilateral institutions provided by official agencies, including state and local governments, or by their executive agencies, each transaction of which meets the following two criteria: (1) it is administered with the promotion of the economic development and welfare of developing countries as the main objective, and (2) it is concessional in character and contains a grant element of at least 25 percent" (cited in Fuhrer, 1994, p. 24). It is important to note that the ODA definition of aid accounts only for aid committed and disbursed by DAC member countries and does not account for other financial flows—some of which may be directed to education—captured in other, broader definitions of development aid, for example, South-South cooperation, financing proffered from private foundations, and remittances from the Diaspora.

4. In 2008, 155 billion USD in ODA was committed to developing countries by the OECD-DAC (OECD-DAC, 2010).

CHAPTER 12

On the Road to Resilience

Capacity Development for Educational Planning in Afghanistan

LYNDSAY BIRD, DORIAN GAY,
MORTEN SIGSGAARD, AND CHARLOTTE WILSON

The World Bank (2009) estimates that around 600 million people live in countries affected by fragility and conflict, and 40% of post-conflict countries relapse into conflict within 10 years. While international agencies often are unable to operate effectively in these countries, the cost of not doing so is greater, with an "annual global cost of conflict . . . estimated to be around [US] \$100 billion" (World Bank, 2009). Conflict and disasters are perhaps the most persistent barriers to achievement of the Millennium Development Goals (MDGs), and therefore contributions toward conflict prevention are "central to poverty reduction and sustainable development" (OECD-DAC, 2001, p. 17). As the Organisation for Economic Co-operation and Development (OECD) suggests, "Development agencies now accept the need to work in and on conflicts rather than around them, and make peacebuilding the main focus when dealing with conflict situations" (p. 17).

Despite increasing global emphasis on preventing disaster and conflict, many chapters in this book have argued that too little attention is paid to education as part of the solution. Priority rarely is given to protecting and preserving educational systems, despite the role that education may play in mitigating potential drivers of conflict in multiethnic societies (see Davies, Chapter 3, and King, Chapter 9, this volume). Particularly ignored are the functions of ministries of education. For example, by utilizing conflict-sensitive education sector diagnoses, a core component of the education planning process, it is possible to identify the risks and vulnerabilities that affect an educational system and that may contribute toward greater tension or conflict. Such analysis can lead to specific strategies to prevent tensions from escalating into full-scale violence. It is critical to ensure that ministries have the capacity (1) to develop an education sector plan that is realistic and implementable, and (2) to conduct a comprehensive risk or "fragility" analysis, if conflict prevention efforts are to be embedded within educational systems.

The reality remains, however, that ministries of education in conflict and emergency situations often require great support in order to adopt this leading role. While many organizations undertake capacity development work in education, the International Institute for Educational Planning (IIEP) has a particular mandate in relation to capacity development for educational planning. IIEP works in many conflict-affected countries, including Angola, Afghanistan, Cambodia, Chad, Côte d'Ivoire, Democratic Republic of Congo, Ethiopia, and Iraq, among others, and its approach to capacity development, particularly in such countries, focuses on a set of core principles that strengthen individual and organizational ownership and capacities:

- Goals should be owned by countries or organizations, and change comes from within
- It is important to recognize and build on existing capacities
- Capacity development is an incremental process
- Strategies that are relevant are planned within a specific context
- Capacity development is an ongoing process and a long-term commitment
- Capacity development leads to sustainable change
- Sufficient resources and effective monitoring and evaluation are necessary to support the process. (De Grauwe, 2009, p. 17)

These principles can become part of an integrated methodology for vulnerability management that builds on existing planning processes. This approach is more sustainable than creating parallel emergency education structures. By using educational planning to increase understanding of potential drivers and tensions within the education system, more effective interventions can be developed to reduce or prevent future conflict (MacEwen, Choudhuri, & Bird, 2010).

The focus in this chapter is on Afghanistan as an illustration of how capacity development in educational planning can be a means to analyze the risks within the educational system. The longstanding technical partnership that IIEP initiated with the Ministry of Education (MoE) in Afghanistan began in 2002 and is deeply rooted in mutual trust and respect. It is well known that Afghanistan has gone through decades of armed conflict, leading to destruction and the near disintegration of the educational system, meaning that schools have needed to be rebuilt, teachers trained, and textbooks produced (as described in Sigsgaard, 2009). The scarcity of qualified educational planners and managers was a major obstacle to ensuring that Afghanistan's MoE took the leadership in educational development. In order to support the MoE to take on this role, IIEP adopted a long-term approach to capacity development that has been crucial to the formulation of Afghanistan's National Education Strategic Plans (NESP-I and the draft NESP-II Interim Plan).

This chapter reviews the necessity of such long-term engagement, where attention to process matters at least as much as attention to product. Drawing from the successes and challenges of IIEP's collaboration with the MoE in Afghanistan, we make a case for a model of capacity development that is sustainable and relies on key principles such as participation and national ownership, and focuses on both individual and institutional capacities. The principles of taking context as the starting point in planning, coaching, mentoring, and working alongside the MoE staff are applicable in most countries. However, they are particularly important in contexts such as Afghanistan, where national pride and dignity need to be nurtured as part of a sustainable reconstruction process.

THE CONTEXT OF EDUCATION IN AFGHANISTAN

Education is considered by both national and foreign state-builders as a "critical force in the process of reconstruction and peace-building in Afghanistan" (Kirk & Winthrop, 2009, p. 104). This commitment is reflected in one of the founding statements in then-Education Minister Hanif Atmar's foreword to NESP-I:

> One of the top priorities of the government is to rebuild an education system that will act as a fundamental cornerstone in shaping the future of the country through peace and stability, democracy and good governance, poverty reduction and economic growth. The centrality of education to the development growth and thereby stability of Afghanistan cannot be overstressed. (Ministry of Education, 2007, p. 9)

Despite the decades of civil war and ongoing instability, there have been remarkable achievements for education in Afghanistan. Between 2002 and 2009, the school population in basic education almost tripled from 2.3 to 6.5 million, and the number of schools and teachers doubled from 6,039 to 11,460 schools and from 80,000 to 156,000 teachers (MoE, 2011, pp. 14–15). At the same time, "high repetition and drop-out rates, together with very low time-on-task rates (schools operating in multiple shifts or constrained by weather and security factors) result in a very internally inefficient system" (MoE, 2011, p. 2). The achievements made to date are a significant and dramatic demonstration of the Afghan government's commitment to education, despite ranking sixth from the bottom in the Failed States Index 2010 (Fund for Peace, 2010).

One of the ways that the increase in enrollment has been achieved is through a system of community-supported schools. In many conflict-affected states such as Afghanistan, where the central government often is unable to provide basic services for security reasons, communities need to rely largely on their own resources. Approximately 20,000 community-based schools are operating in Afghanistan and about 3% of all students in Afghanistan have attended some form of community-based school (MoE, 2007, p. 9). The increase in community-based schooling has helped to expand girls' enrollment, as girls are more likely to be allowed to study within the community rather than walk long distances to the formal school (Burde & Linden, 2009; see also Burde, Chapter 16, this volume). In addition to filling a resource gap, community-based schools help to mitigate against severe security risks, including direct attacks on schools, particularly where attacks on education have a gender dimension (Glad, 2009, p. 45). Attacks were much less likely to occur if negotiations had been held with local religious leaders and community elders. In contrast, where schools were built without community support, or rebuilt by international actors, there was more likelihood of attack (pp. 42–50).

However, to ensure consistency and quality of educational interventions, local efforts need to be structured within an overall government framework. An example of such a joint initiative is demonstrated by the Partnership for Advancing Community Education in Afghanistan (PACE-A),[1] an international nongovernmental organization (INGO) consortium that, alongside other organizations such as UNICEF and Save the Children, worked to support the MoE to "adopt" the community-supported schools and to bring them within an overall policy framework for community-based education. As the former PACE-A project directors Anastacio and Stannard (2011) suggest, "The goal was to see the MoE's policy enacted in such a way that community-based schools would fall under the ownership of the government so that they would be recognized and supported in years to come."

The education sector development plan has been central to the legitimacy of the Ministry of Education in its coordination of the disparate education efforts by a multitude of actors. In 2007 the NESP-I (2006–2010) was widely recognized as the most comprehensive national education sector plan developed in Afghanistan's recent history and was adopted by all partners as the reference document to guide their programs. Not only was the plan perceived as a symbol of national hope and resilience, but it also served to demonstrate the MoE's capacity to support rebuilding the nation and to restore the population's trust by gradually delivering highly demanded education services. It was also a demonstration to donors that the government was en route toward a sector-wide approach that they would be willing to fund through national systems. As seen in other countries affected by conflict, investing in a "development process and sector plan implementation, through general or sector budget support, in preference to project funding," can lead to faster and greater recovery (Obura & Bird, 2009, p. 21). For example, a "feature of the Rwandan post-conflict recovery was the early use of a Sector Wide Approach (SWAp), particularly by the Department for International Development (DfID). This gave confidence to other donors to do the same" (p. 21).

The positivity surrounding the development of the national education sector plan has also provided a demonstration of national pride, resilience and capability for both men and women working in the education sector. It was an important milestone in the history of the sector. Confidence also comes from transparency, and from a realistic diagnosis of the core issues affecting education in a given context. Like in many conflict-affected countries, the first planning process that led to the NESP-I circumvented systematic analysis of the relationship between education and the ongoing conflict. In contrast, the National Education Sector Plan-II (NESP-II) Interim Plan (MoE, 2011) included a risk analysis section covering key issues affecting education that relate to security, governance, economy, and chronic poverty (MoE, 2011, pp. 36–43). The NESP-II Interim Plan was generated from within the MoE and led by the Planning Department, and served to demonstrate the increased maturity of the MoE in accepting and dealing with weaknesses in the system. By using better tools for planning, such as the 2007 School Survey, the Education Management Information System (EMIS), the Teacher Registration System, and recent school maps, the data highlighted the limitations of education provision in the 17 "Insecure Provinces" when compared to the 17 "Secure Provinces" (MoE, 2011, pp. 37, 128).

The NESP-II plan recommends community-based education as the preferred strategy in these insecure provinces (MoE, 2011, pp. 69–72). The plan also recognizes the risks created by lack of education for girls, which is perceived as a barrier for future national development: "Due to the lack of education, particularly post-elementary education, women lack the skills and experience required for many occupations, a hindrance further compounded by their restricted mobility" (MoE, 2011, p. 47). There is a commitment in the plan to redress these imbalances. For example, the plan says that by 2014 the government will aim to increase the number of female teachers by 50%; increase female enrolment to 60%; improve female literacy rates from 15% in 2010 to 43% in 2014; and 75% of schools will have facilities for girls' education (MoE, 2011, p. 48). These targets, while ambitious, signal a positive intention, and their inclusion in the NESP-II Interim Plan also provides a mechanism for civil society groups to hold the government to account on its commitments.

Risk and vulnerability analysis must be an integral component of an education sector plan in order to demonstrate awareness of contextual issues and to present strategies to address them. In Afghanistan, there is increased recognition that, ". . . the security situation makes long-term planning more difficult, flexibility and pragmatism are needed, both in donors' funding mechanisms and within agencies" (MoE, 2011, p. 42). These issues are explored in more depth in the following section, which examines how a strategic national education plan was developed and discusses how capacity development has become a key tool for nationally owned long- and short-term reconstruction of the education system in Afghanistan.

CAPACITY DEVELOPMENT FOR EDUCATIONAL PLANNING IN AFGHANISTAN

> When I first came to the Ministry of Education (MoE) and joined Department of Planning and Evaluation (DoPE) in 2002, there were only two broken desktop computers. The DoPE staff used old instruments for their daily work such as pens and paper in an absolutely traditional and out of date manner. Now, in 2010 almost everybody in the department has access to a computer and internet. They have developed several systems such as Planning System, EMIS, new processes and procedures. The Ministry has developed National Education Strategic Plans which was led and coordinated by DoPE staff. (MoE Human Resource Department staff member interview, March 2010, cited in Arefee, 2011, p. 89)

During the period 2002–2010, IIEP developed a strong technical partnership with Afghanistan's MoE, particularly the Department of Planning and Evaluation. IIEP's approach gives as much attention to the complex processes that lead to the formulation, and eventually the implementation, of a sector development plan as to the products of the planning process.[2] Founded on principles of participation and national ownership, IIEP's engagement in Afghanistan focuses on both individual and institutional capacities and will culminate over the next 3 years in prioritizing national capacity development programs. Capacity development in this way is seen as a holistic process at different individual, organizational, and institutional levels (De Grauwe, 2009, pp. 43–45). It is a pragmatic approach, where capacity development agencies do not impose, but remain in a mentoring and technical backstopping position to focus on solutions that work in spite of obstacles and contradictions. Service delivery, however, is not the only outcome of this approach. Other important capacity development outcomes include inspiring hope and confidence, and increased ministerial capacity to take leadership of a fragmented education sector.

To achieve these outcomes, a number of processes have been developed over time, such as strengthening capacity for planning and implementation, enhancing human resources, and building trust and mutual respect. The approach requires flexibility, diagnostic analyses, and long-term engagement, and aims to ensure that "decision-makers and experts [are able] to conceive a clear vision of their priorities and how to achieve them" (De Grauwe & Gay, 2010, p. 2).

DEVELOPING CAPACITY FOR PLANNING AND IMPLEMENTATION

During the 3 years that followed the fall of the Taliban regime (2002–2005), IIEP was a permanent technical partner of the MoE through the provision of training workshops, but also a provider of technical advice. In 2003, IIEP responded to a request from the Ministry of Higher Education (MoHE) (2004) to develop a strategic sector plan. At this time, Afghanistan was still in the so-called "early recovery" phase. The MoHE had only recently started functioning and was in effect operating in a vacuum without policy or legal frameworks to guide its work. IIEP's support was called upon in a context characterized by severe time constraints and the lack of qualified or experienced MoHE personnel capable of developing a strategic document.

The fertile period of relationship building during this time enabled the MoE and IIEP to scale up its technical partnership in early 2006, through the Strategic Planning and Capacity Development Project, which arose from the collaboration among three key actors: the MoE, which was willing to develop an education sector plan; the Norwegian Ministry of Foreign Affairs, which provided financial support for the program; and IIEP, which had technical expertise in educational planning and recognized long-term engagement with Afghanistan as an institutional priority. The project aimed to improve the capacity of the MoE in planning and managing the education sub-sector, as well as in leading efforts directed toward education and human resource development. It focused on assisting the MoE in the formulation of its first strategic national education sector plan (NESP-I) through the development of national capacities in plan preparation, implementation, and monitoring both at central and decentralized levels of the educational system.

The move toward a more ambitious long-term technical partnership was not without certain tensions. The interests and priorities of IIEP and those of the Ministry were not always identical. For example, IIEP's support for the development of a 5-year strategic plan came under pressure from the MoE (itself under pressure from the Afghan government) to produce a medium-term education strategy within 3 months. This situation stemmed primarily from the favorable impression the MoE created within the government and donor community, where it was believed that recovery and reconstruction would be demonstrated by a credible sector plan. This confidence was due in part to the then-Minister of Education's excellent prior record as Minister of Rural Rehabilitation and Development and his former work in the NGO sector.

Consequently, the MoE decided to embark on the formulation of its first national strategic plan of the post-Taliban era, even though most of its staff were not experienced in education sector planning. As Arefee (2011) suggests, the decades of insecurity and consequent low levels of literacy and education had left

the Ministry unable to identify and recruit competent employees and consequently . . . unable to plan, manage and implement successfully its education
projects and capacity development activities. This is a vicious circle: Since the capacity of MoE is low, it is not able to spend the allocated budget; and conversely,
because of low budget, it is not able to improve its capacity (p. 89).

Initially, the MoE had conceived of the plan as an already finished "product"
that would bring direct benefits to the MoE in terms of visibility and as a major
fundraising tool—both defendable and necessary positions for a Ministry of Education in need of such support. However, this view lacked the critical dimension
of long-term participatory planning, the bedrock of IIEP's approach. The trust between the two institutions that had been developed over previous years was essential in order to effect a change in methodology. Instead of a quick product turned
around in 3 months, IIEP spent 16 months coaching and working alongside the
MoE staff in a process that developed longer term capacity for the MoE staff and a
sense of ownership of the process as well as the product.

NESP-I was launched in 2007 and released publicly by the President of the
Islamic Republic of Afghanistan, Hamid Karzai, and then-Minister of Education,
Hanif Atmar, at the Education Development Forum (EDF) in February 2008. The
EDF was the first joint NESP implementation review meeting that gathered to-
gether the MoE and all development partners to the education sector, including
the Ministry of Higher Education.[3]

Under Minister Atmar's leadership, the MoE had made a long-term strategic
choice, despite external pressures to produce a plan quickly (Shah, 2010, p. 10). As
a consequence, the process became as important as the product. For the MoE staff,
some of the most important processes included the following:

- setting up organizational arrangements to ensure Ministry-wide
  participation in the plan preparation process: forming working groups,
  defining their respective functions, assigning tasks, and elaborating work
  schedules;
- data collection and analysis, especially for the situation analysis of the
  educational system contained in the plan;
- consulting with national and sub-national MoE representatives and with
  donors;
- adjusting staffing and Terms of References (ToRs), based on the ongoing
  Tashkeel[4] and the organizational needs emerging from the NESP
  formulation process;
- drafting the plan's chapters and specifically the action programs,[5] which
  meant balancing policy and political aims with technical constraints; and
  making hard choices in the process; and
- costing the priority programs and facilitating collaboration between the
  planning and budgeting processes and personnel.

The development and finalization of NESP-I gave the MoE an opportunity to take its rightful place as the leader of the many agencies in the education sector. In particular, NESP-I went a long way in fostering donor alignment on nationally defined priorities and on the underlying premises of a SWAp. What was missing was a structure that would make this policy dialogue more regular. On its missions to Kabul, IIEP therefore convened informal meetings of "like-minded" education donors. These meetings in 2007–2008 helped to increase trust, mutual knowledge, and coordination, and were a precursor to what later became the Education Development Board (EDB), now the Human Resource Development Board (HRDB), and the start of an increasingly more effective coordination mechanism for the education sector.

ENHANCING HUMAN RESOURCES

For capacity to become sustainable, it is necessary for a ministry of education to develop the human resources and skills to plan, implement, and monitor over time and without the full-time support of technical partners. In 2008, the MoE in Afghanistan began the process of revising NESP-I to better align it to the Afghan National Development Strategy. It was soon apparent that the revision of NESP-I in fact should become the formulation of a new sector plan: NESP-II.

The reformulation process was conducted in Dari, and the fact that the planners could draft in their own language was a strong sign that the MoE essentially owned and drove the process. This was a significant development from NESP-I, and indicated a much greater technical autonomy on the part of MoE. A detailed study by the Afghanistan Research and Evaluation Unit (AREU) describes how

> The department also successfully gained the confidence and support of the minister by convincing him that it had the capability to undertake and lead the revision process. . . . The director of the Planning Department said in an interview: "We had technical people in the ministry and decided to revise the NESP with the involvement of nationals in the Dari language first and then translate it into English and consult with IIEP only if we needed." (Shah, 2010, p. 22)

The MoE also made good use of its recent technical breakthroughs, such as the 2007 EMIS, the Teacher Registration System, and school maps. For the first time, the Ministry was using its human and technical resources to plan using real data instead of estimates.

As part of IIEP's support during both the development of NESP-I and the reformulation process for NESP-II, issues of gender were mainstreamed throughout the ongoing work with educational planners. IIEP also conducted workshops on gender policy in education to support the technical capacity of the MoE during its attempts to adopt a more gender-sensitive approach to policymaking and planning.

These workshops gave staff from various ministries an opportunity to exchange ideas and find support on gender-related issues, and offered the prospect of introducing new thinking. The workshops were conducted in collaboration with the Ministry of Education, Ministry of Higher Education, and Ministry of Women's Affairs. The second of these workshops in 2005 was facilitated by Jackie Kirk in Kabul. In addition to her two publications with IIEP (Kirk, 2008c, 2009a), Jackie was actively involved with IIEP's team working on capacity development in fragile contexts. She was especially committed to promoting the right to quality education for women and girls in conflict and disaster settings, and to increasing the understanding of the gender dynamics of education. Through this type of work, Jackie demonstrated her gifts as a trainer, researcher, and scholar with a deep grounding in field operational realities in the most difficult of environments.[6] The aim of the workshop was to discuss gender policy in education and to draft a document to guide policy development for gender equality in—and through—education in Afghanistan (Kirk, 2005b).

At this workshop, participants, who had been identified as key liaison people in each ministry, were chosen according to their positions of responsibility in departments where gender in education would be particularly relevant. The workshop revealed that only limited interaction had taken place between the different ministries prior to the workshop and that many of the participants were meeting one another for the first time. Many of the issues discussed, such as women's empowerment or a higher level of participation of women in senior decision making, were new to the majority of the participants, as were the frameworks for gender analysis in education. Afghan traditions and culture often were perceived as clashing with international frameworks, particularly following the country's "isolation" during its 25 years of conflict. Attempts to promote gender equality were particularly challenging. Yet participants demonstrated a commitment to taking forward the outcomes of the workshop within their own departments as well as sharing the new knowledge among friends and family (Kirk, 2005a).

Therefore, as part of the Strategic Planning and Capacity Development Project, IIEP attempted to prioritize women staff in the capacity development activities organized by the project. The purpose was to try to redress imbalance between men and women staff at all levels within the MoE (IIEP, 2006b). To this end, IIEP requested that at least half of the national Monitoring and Reporting Officers recruited for the project should be women. Eventually, three women were recruited out of eight officers. IIEP consistently supported gender promotion in a number of ways: (1) affirmative action in hiring technical assistants to support the DoPE, and advocacy for more women participants in training activities; (2) creating special incentives for female technical assistants, such as free car transportation for protection and comfort; (3) organizing gender-focused training; and (4) supporting the MoE to integrate a more gendered focus in the sector plans.

It is difficult to claim that IIEP has succeeded significantly in promoting gender-sensitive human resource development, as there remains poor representation of women at MoE when compared to men. However, the revision of the NESP-II includes greater emphasis on gender issues. For example, it is stated in the Interim Plan that:

> The MoE [...] will put in place an accountability mechanism for gender assess-
> ment and reporting on gender equality in education, with particular emphasis
> on gender-related MDGs and targets. A gender cell will be established. More fe-
> male staff will be recruited including in the decision making positions [...] and
> school shura training will include topics on the gender dimension of education
> [...]. Special attention will be paid to developing and utilizing tools that facili-
> tate gender mainstreaming in the MoE, such as gender-responsive budgeting,
> gender analysis of the policies and strategies, gender-responsive planning with
> setting gender equality objectives and indicators, and integrating goals that pro-
> mote gender equality in staff performance (especially at management levels).
> The MoE will actively engage the HRDB [Human Resource Development Board]
> taskforce on Gender Mainstreaming and Afghanistan Girls Education Initiative
> (AGEI) [...]. (MoE, 2011, pp. 48–49)

These are commendable commitments to support enhanced human resources where women are able to take up leadership positions, and where equality of opportunity and human rights are at the forefront of national reconstruction efforts. The fact that the NESP clearly states such commitments also provides the opportunity for civil society and gender activists to hold the government to account where pledges are not met.

DEVELOPING TRUST AND MUTUAL RESPECT

The long-term cooperation program of IIEP with the MoHE and then the MoE, starting in 2002, followed three basic principles: to be pragmatic, to avoid setting overambitious targets, and to collaborate closely in a relationship of mutual trust and respect. Learning the basics of planning was at the center of the initial capacity development process, where topics ranged from management and financing of higher education to basic educational statistics, educational indicators, budgeting, and gender in education. Over 100 MoE staff from central-level departments and some provinces benefitted from training in educational planning and management strategies.[7]

Because the MoE had four Ministers of Education between 2002 and 2005 and priorities were constantly shifting, it is hard to evaluate the long-term impact of this initial phase. High staff turnover in ministries implied constant readjustment to a fast-changing environment, and much of the human capacity that was developed, was lost. Nevertheless, dozens of ministry staff were trained, some of whom still are MoE and MoHE civil servants today. This long-term training process enabled a relationship built on trust and mutual respect to be established with officials from both Ministries, and proved to be of strategic importance during later stages of IIEP's engagement in Afghanistan.

The imperative to develop MoE planning and management skills for future plan implementation and subsequent reformulation of the NESP required taking a long route to capacity development, focusing on process more than product. The trust and mutual respect built in the early stages was a critical component to ensure that the advantages of a participatory capacity development approach were recognized. It was a process of which the INGOs working in Afghanistan also were only too well aware. For example, the PACE-A coalition's 28 years of experience and commitment to education in Afghanistan resulted in a degree of trust and mutual respect that enabled the coalition to ensure that community-based education initiatives could be maintained and sustained through government structures (Anastacio & Stannard, 2011).

Through the long-term process of developing capacity, the MoE's technical capacity was enhanced. The MoE also gained much greater confidence in leading donor coordination mechanisms. One of the most significant results of the Education Development Forum was the establishment of the EDB in February 2008. This was the first official coordination mechanism created in the education sector, co-chaired by the MoE and a representative of the development partners on a rotating basis. After 2 years of operation, the EDB efficiently met its coordination objectives, and in April 2010, it evolved into the Human Resource Development Board (HRDB), a forum with a broader mandate and larger representation. Apart from the MoE and its partners (NGOs included), other ministries involved in education and skills development[8] now sit on the HRDB Steering Committee. This long-term strategic approach taken during the development of the two sector plans has been critical to the sense of ownership and increased capacity, dignity, and self-esteem of the MoE officials.

While of course such elements are critical to the education sector as Afghanistan moves forward in its reconstruction efforts, ultimately the future of education depends on its political will as much as its increased capacity, confidence, and national pride. Afghanistan is at two stages of development: state formation and state development against a background of a heavy foreign military presence. The challenges are huge but there are clear signs that the will is as great.

CONCLUSIONS

True strength comes from recognition of one's vulnerabilities. For Afghanistan, as with other countries affected by conflict, the education sector planning process offers an opportunity to identify those vulnerabilities and to plan strategies to overcome them.

Over a relatively short period of less than 8 years and despite considerable adversity and ongoing insecurity, the MoE has managed to make considerable headway in the diagnosis of risks to the educational system, and to identify strategies for development of the sector. The development of the second National Education Sector Plan (NESP-II), even if overambitious, is a symbol of hope and of a genuine desire by the Afghan authorities to deliver much-demanded education services. The planning process not only has enhanced capacity and self-reliance within the ministry; it also has resulted in a product that hopefully will engender greater confidence in donors to invest in education through national structures and systems.

The lessons learned from Afghanistan, as outlined below,[9] offer insights that also might be applicable in other contexts.

Building Trusting Partnerships Takes Time and Is Required for High-Level Political Backing

Decade-long engagements in Afghanistan allowed agencies to gain credibility and develop trusting partnerships with the MoE. The agencies needed this base of trust and credibility in order to capitalize on windows of opportunity. Political backing also was ensured through advocacy and through collaborative work.

People Come and Go But Systems Remain

Service delivery and enactment of the MoE's many positive policies hinge on effective systems. They enable planning based on facts, can reduce corruption, and reduce reliance on individuals. Investing in systems is a long-term commitment.

Donor Flexibility, Long-Term Commitment, and Coordination Mechanisms Are Essential

A number of donors in Afghanistan adhered to the Paris principles by engaging over several years, showing flexibility, and taking "responsible risks." Permitting sudden changes in project design and accepting bottom-up participatory program design were examples of good donor support.

Coordination mechanisms such as the HRDB in Afghanistan can be instrumental in a number of ways, for example, in solving a major human resource challenge: the salary disparity between civil servants and technical assistants. This could reduce tension and improve aid effectiveness.

Start with Pragmatic and Basic Solutions

In extreme situations, there are sometimes very basic solutions that need to be instituted, before longer term measures take over. For example, the partnership between IIEP and the MoE in Afghanistan began with provision of basic infrastructure, such as restoring office spaces and furniture, or teaching English and computer literacy. This was essential before longer term and sustained capacity ownership could take place.

Gender Is Also a Human Resource Issue

In many developing contexts, women often refrain from competing with men for high managerial positions due to internalized stereotypes. This is a serious human resource issue. Agencies need to scan all activities for opportunities to increase women's participation, and education is a positive force that can contribute toward that goal. The education sector often is considered "one in which it is acceptable to address gender issues and in which substantially less resistance might be incurred by the promotion of a gender agenda" (Larson, 2008, p. 40).

Put Processes Before Products

In Afghanistan, IIEP's collaboration with the MoE on policy documents and the NESP gave impetus to capacity development and enhanced sectoral donor coordination. In the process, the MoE gained the necessary self-confidence to be able to commit to and engage in further partnerships.

A Plan Is a Statement of Will and Dignity

Some of the policy documents developed as part of the Afghan national strategy have been criticized for being unrealistic. However, in Afghanistan's political process, ambitious national plans signal a will for drastic change. They are statements of national dignity. If a national plan inspires feelings of hope, dignity, or confidence—invaluable resources in a context where everything is a priority and everything a challenge—who can then claim the right to shoot down these aspirations?

NOTES

This chapter has drawn extensively from Sigsgaard, M. (Ed.). (2011). *On the road to resilience: Capacity development with the Ministry of Education in Afghanistan*. Paris: IIEP.

1. PACE-A consists of four international INGOs: CARE, International Rescue Committee, Catholic Relief Services, and the Aga Khan Foundation.

2. Processes involved in the formulation of a sector plan include building trust and team spirit among MoE departments, securing political and financial backing, setting up institutional arrangements and working groups, diagnosing the sector (including when data are lacking), formulating policies and devising the corresponding strategies to implement them, ensuring proper consultation inside and outside the MoE on what is to be done,

establishing reliable base datasets, and developing country-specific projection and simulation models. The products of the planning process include the strategic document itself, budgets, yearly operational plan documents, and monitoring reports of different kinds.

3. Over 200 stakeholder representatives were invited to the EDF—Ministers, commissions, advisers, donors and aid agencies, UN agencies, consultancy firms, NGOs, and civil-military Provincial Reconstruction Teams (PRT), among others. The sheer number of actors in the sector indicates the need for coordination that the NESP helped to address.

4. Tashkeel is the name given to the establishment of staffing structures within the MoE. It is part of the broader Public Administration Reform framework, which seeks to create an efficient, effective, and transparent civil service in Afghanistan through the restructuring of the civil service and the institution of merit-based, nonpartisan recruitment (Afghanistan Research and Evaluation Unit & World Bank, 2010, pp. 65, 83).

5. NESP-I contains eight priority programs: (1) General Education, (2) Teacher Education and Working Conditions, (3) Education Infrastructure Rehabilitation and Development, (4) Curriculum Development and Learning Materials, (5) Islamic Education, (6) Technical and Vocational Education and Training, (7) Literacy and Non-Formal Education, and (8) Education Administration Reform and Development.

6. Adapted from Bird, L. (2010). "A Tribute to Jackie: Trainer, Researcher and Scholar." *Girlhood Studies: An Interdisciplinary Journal, 3*(1), 1–2.

7. The provincial level was less well represented and supported due to security issues.

8. These include the Ministry of Labour, Social Affairs, Martyrs and Disabled, the Ministry of Women's Affairs, and the Ministry of Finance.

9. Adapted from Sigsgaard, M. (Ed.). (2011). *On the road to resilience: Capacity development with the Ministry of Education in Afghanistan.* Paris: IIEP.

CHAPTER 13

"Helping Our Children Will Help in the Reconstruction of Our Country"

Repatriated Refugee Teachers in Post-Conflict Sierra Leone and Liberia

SUSAN SHEPLER

Teachers are key agents in developing robust, quality educational systems (Kirk & Winthrop, 2008a). However, little information is available about teachers in post-conflict environments. Increasing the confidence of teachers with limited levels of education or training and equipping teachers with the skills needed to effectively manage their classrooms (e.g., dealing with the effects of trauma among students) are likely ways to better equip teachers to provide education in post-conflict environments. However, more research is needed to adequately identify and respond to teachers' needs in a variety of post-conflict settings.

This chapter responds to this need. It draws on data from an innovative research project tracing former refugee teachers who received teacher training from the International Rescue Committee (IRC) in refugee camps in Guinea (Shepler, 2010). The IRC's refugee education program in Guinea—of which Jackie Kirk was a part—was designed to meet the needs of an ever-changing refugee population over a 17-year period (1990–2007). From "schools started under mango trees," various institutions and activities were designed to support an educational system with an enrollment of 81,000 students at its peak. A main component of the program was teacher training for legions of volunteer teachers, some of whom had taught for years in schools in Sierra Leone or Liberia before fleeing from war and some who had no previous experience in front of the classroom. The study explored, among other things, whether and how these teachers, once repatriated, contribute to the reconstruction of educational systems post-conflict.

We conducted the research from January to May 2009 with a team of West African research assistants, sponsored by the IRC's LEGACY initiative. We traced over 600 repatriated refugee teachers who had returned to their homes in Sierra Leone and Liberia, in an effort to determine the effects of the training they received—particularly whether they were still working as teachers in their post-repatriation lives, or whether they had made use of their training in other ways. Based on personal narratives, we investigated individual motivations to continue difficult work in the classroom as well as constraints faced at the personal, community, and national levels. We compared the experiences of those currently teaching and those who had left the teaching field, rural and urban residents, and the cultural and political contexts of Sierra Leone and Liberia. Our objective was to advance some theories about systemic and policy barriers to teachers' contributions post-conflict and determine which policies most encourage individual change agents in schools.

BACKGROUND: TEACHERS AS CHANGE AGENTS

Teachers have important roles to play in the structural transformations of societies, particularly in post-conflict contexts. Schools are often one of the first community organizations to start functioning after a crisis (Kirk, 2004c) and can act to bring a sense of normalcy back to everyday life in post-conflict communities (Vongalis-Macrow, 2006, p. 104). However, schools and teachers can be part of the problem as well as part of the solution in post-conflict contexts, because of their role in transmitting social and cultural values (Smith, 2007, p. 22).

Windows of opportunity may open for teachers to transform teaching and learning processes in schools, as well as curricula. Teachers can be agents of change within the education sector and broader society by rethinking what students need to learn in schools, and how and by whom this information should be taught (Kirk, 2004c). In rural Rwanda, Paul Rutayisire (2007) finds that teachers are widely regarded as the most educated members of communities, thus giving them potential influence to contribute to post-conflict justice and reconciliation.

While teachers have the potential to create and promote change within their classrooms, schools, communities, and society at large, they also must work in an environment in which they have the opportunity to introduce such change. When teachers are provided with the information, support, and resources needed to make positive contributions, they will be better able to fulfill their potential of being agents of positive change (Osman & Kirk, 2001).

However, teachers may be limited in their power within their communities to make educational recommendations, due to their age, their sex, or other factors (Kirk & Winthrop, 2008a). For example, while teachers may push for the increased education of girls, elders and other leaders within the community may not abide by teachers' suggestions. Teachers' agency for change on a national level also may be undermined if government policymakers rely on outside agents, such as non-governmental organizations (NGOs), to lead education reconstruction, without actively engaging teachers (Vongalis-Macrow, 2006). Teachers also may be limited by their own lack of secondary education or formal teacher training (Kirk & Winthrop, 2007). Similarly, Smith (2005) highlights the difficulties that teachers may face in bringing about social change in their classrooms, stating:

> It is unrealistic to expect that relatively inexperienced teachers, untrained in the basics of human rights education and other relevant areas [e.g., peace, human rights and democracy, girls' education, education for youth returning from combat] will be able to take forward such areas with students without having developed the necessary skills themselves. (p. 382)

Teachers also may face difficulties in being change agents if they feel disempowered or lack the capacity to deliver due to insufficient training or resources, ongoing crime and violence, or hierarchical management styles within the education sector (Osman & Kirk, 2001).

Although they may not receive financial compensation for their work, teachers in post-conflict environments may continue teaching because of a "sense of satisfaction and appreciation of the importance of being a teacher in their community" (Kirk & Winthrop, 2008b, p. 885). Teachers in conflict-affected areas also may benefit from the opportunity to focus their attention on teaching, rather than on their personal losses resulting from conflict. These psychosocial benefits are highlighted by a study with female teachers in Afghanistan who reported that teaching kept them from being alone and constantly reliving their conflict-induced traumas—rather, the opportunity to teach gave them something else to think about (Kirk, 2004c).

IRC'S REFUGEE EDUCATION PROGRAM

The IRC has supported education for refugees in Guinea since 1991 when the first waves of refugees arrived from Liberia and began setting up informal schools in Guinea. Those refugees were later joined by refugees from Sierra Leone. Enrollment in the IRC education program grew from 12,000 in 1991 to 81,000 at its peak in 1999. By 2008, after 17 years of operation, hundreds of thousands of students, teachers, and administrators had passed through the IRC schools. The IRC's education program in Guinea has been well documented, so it is not necessary to go into great detail here (see, e.g., D. Jones, 2009; Smith & Winthrop,

2002; Tenenbaum, 2004). It is fair to conclude that the IRC education program in Guinea is widely seen as successful and indeed a model for education provision in other refugee situations.

Although the program beneficiaries initially were understood to be the refugee men, women, and children in Guinea who were students in the program, the refugee education program also provided important professional training and development opportunities for male and female teachers and other education personnel such as classroom assistants, head teachers, and education managers. The training and certification of teachers grew to be an important part of the IRC's refugee education program in Guinea. The focus on teacher recruitment, training, and education created a pool of qualified professionals, who, it was hoped, could contribute to the reconstruction, development, and expansion of educational systems in their countries of origin once they repatriated.

Efforts at cross-border certification are an important element of the IRC's efforts on behalf of the teachers it trained and employed. One long-time IRC staffer reports that there were two major certificates that teachers trained in Guinea acquired: the B Certificate and the C Certificate.[1] In the IRC Guinea program, teachers trained up to 1998 were examined and those who passed the examinations were given the IRC's B Certificate. Between 1999 and 2000, IRC Guinea and Liberia worked with the Ministry of Education (MoE) of Liberia to study the training offered by IRC Guinea to see whether MoE Liberia would equate it to any of the MoE certificates. The IRC worked with the Division of Teacher Certification and Accreditation at MoE Liberia. Eventually, MoE Liberia decided to equate the B Certificate issued by the IRC with the C Certificate the MoE issues in Liberia. (That is, the IRC's certificate would allow a teacher to teach at the primary level in Liberia.) IRC Guinea entered into another round of negotiations between 2003 and 2004 with MoE Liberia, with the aim of using the teacher training modules used in teacher training colleges in Liberia to train IRC Guinea teachers. As a result of these negotiations, the MoE permitted the use of its training modules in Guinea and also agreed to examine and accredit teachers who were trained using those modules. Successful teachers were issued the C Certificate directly by MoE Liberia in 2005.

There were similar negotiations with the Ministry of Education in Sierra Leone, but they never led to the same acceptance of IRC certificates as equivalent to any of Sierra Leone's certificates. We heard different explanations for this. One is that Sierra Leone had a more vibrant teacher training and certification program even before the war. Another is that the ministry felt threatened by an NGO stepping into its territory. Yet another is that the IRC was arrogant in the meetings with the Ministry of Education of Sierra Leone. Regardless of the decision not to formally accept IRC teacher training, many of the IRC teacher training precepts have been included in the Distance Education Program currently in operation in Sierra Leone, and IRC Sierra Leone currently is working cordially with education officials at all levels.

THE GUINEA TRACER STUDY

In early 2009, the IRC sponsored a research project to trace the former refugee teachers who had been trained in refugee camps in Guinea and interview them about the influence the training had on their post-repatriation lives and to find out whether they were contributing to the reconstruction of the post-war educational systems in their home countries. The aim was to discover, from the perspective of these teachers, the long-term effects of their training as well as the challenges they faced in their repatriation and reintegration. This study is something unique. Because it does not measure the immediate outputs of an intervention, it cannot really be called an evaluation of the IRC's teacher training program in Guinea. Rather, this work is looking for unspecified collateral benefits of the program, several years after the program's conclusion. Neither is this an assessment of the educational systems of Sierra Leone or Liberia. Our study interviews those who currently are working as teachers as well as those not working as teachers, in order to investigate the reasons some decided to leave the teaching profession and some decided to stay on.

The most challenging aspect of the research was tracing the 2,000 to 4,000 former teachers across Sierra Leone and Liberia. There were very few written records of their whereabouts and it was assumed that the former teachers had resettled widely. A seven-person research team from Sierra Leone and Liberia used snowball sampling, informal networks, and mobile phones to collect 640 semistructured interviews over a period of several months.

At the end of the data collection period, the team met together to discuss themes and code the data. The interviews resulted in a set of individual life narratives rather than a collection of numerical choices in response to predetermined survey questions. It was hoped that the stories would teach us how better to support teachers, and therefore how to support quality educational systems in post-war countries.

Table 13.1. Description of the Sample:
Some Key Demographic Data about the Sample

Male: 82%			Female: 18%	
Liberian: 40%		Sierra Leonean: 60%		
Rural: 24%	Headquarter Town: 64%			Capital City: 13%
Received IRC Certificate: 66%			Did Not Receive IRC certificate: 34%	
Paid Teacher Now: 63%			Not Paid Teacher Now: 37%*	

*This figure includes volunteer teachers and those not working as teachers at all.

Methodologically, assessing the long-term effects of training is not straight-forward. Respondents have been impacted by multiple events over the years, including possible multiple relocations, training from other agencies, and further formal education. I addressed these challenges by focusing on the *individual level* —by looking at skills learned, career trajectories, and challenges faced after repatriation, and by examining the leadership roles undertaken. The individual-level data can tell us much about the structural issues operating at the national level that stand in the way of positive change in the educational system.

Why Teach?

We heard a range of responses when we asked people currently working as teachers why they decided to continue in the teaching field. Many of those surveyed had been teachers before displacement and were continuing their career trajectories where they had left off. In total, 64% of the sample reported some experience working in a school, as a paid or volunteer teacher, before they went to Guinea; 71% of those currently employed as teachers had some experience as a teacher before their displacement.

The first theme we heard was, *teaching is a good job.* Responses included: "I am a born teacher. So it is my own profession. I love it very well," and "Teaching is a good job and a blessing job," where "blessing" means that although the pay may be small, teachers get blessings from God for their good work. A former classroom assistant, now working as an elementary school teacher in Liberia, said, "I love children. I'm not shy and like to be with people. Moreover, teaching is an interesting job because it makes you to learn new things every day." Others expanded on the opportunity for learning and personal development inherent in the teaching profession: "I want to broaden my knowledge and get more experience in life through reading"; "Because it makes my livelihood better. Every day I come in contact with new ideas"; and "It's an honorable job. It makes me come in contact with many people, the president as well as fools."

Echoing the results in the literature review about the psychosocial benefits of teaching for war-affected people, others explained that teaching is an honorable profession. One respondent stated, "It is a good career, and I find it interesting. Moreover, I have an obligation to educate my fellow Sierra Leoneans." Another respondent said:

> I love to educate people, train people so that they can improve their lives to improve the communities. I have taught for 46 years. As people say, [the] Liberia war is attributed to ignorance, poverty, and disease. And it is because people are not educated. So, I think if I contribute my quota to the country through education, I will have done better to uplift the country.

Clearly, respondents had a range of reasons for understanding teaching as a "good" job. Some had a more pragmatic explanation for their continuing work in the classroom, and we found that the next theme for continuing in the teaching field was *the desire to put training to good use*. Some responses along this line were: "I don't want to sit idly. I want to put my knowledge and skills into use"; "Because I have undergone the training. I can't quit the known for the unknown"; "It is my career. I inherited it from my father who was a teacher. I have been trained in it more than any other job so I am here until retirement age"; and "I was a teacher before the war, and I got more training in Guinea. So it didn't make sense to do a new thing." Some teachers felt the need to use their subject-specific training. One decided to keep teaching "because French teachers were in great demand." Another explained, "I am a biology teacher. The reason why I decided to continue is that there is a shortage of science teachers in the school system in Liberia."

Another common theme among teachers was: *teaching is needed for the future of the country*. In response to the question, "Why have you continued to teach?" some of the answers were: "I look at it as a religious duty"; "To train children to build a better Sierra Leone"; "I decided to teach because I know someone taught me, and I don't want to depend on foreigners to teach my children. For those that taught me, most of them have died, so I need to be able to replace them to continue to teach my country"; "Because there is a shortage of trained teachers in Liberia now; if everyone sits down, who will teach our children?"; "Because I feel that helping our children will help in the reconstruction of our country, Liberia"; "There are a lot of inexperienced teachers in the teaching system today so I decided to help mold the minds of our youths using the experience from IRC"; and "Because learning brings about development within a country. And people can only learn when there is a teacher to teach. So I decided to be one of the teachers." These teachers expressed a sense of duty or obligation toward their institutions, communities, countries, or to the younger generation.

Finally, some teachers explained their decision to continue teacher by letting us know that *teaching is a stepping stone or the only job available*. Teaching is often a first job for people right out of college and is seen as a phase that most professionals pass through. Some responses in this vein include: "I want to accumulate income to go for a further course"; "I want to use the teaching as a stepping stone to higher heights"; and "There is no option. Teaching is a sort of waiting room." Others explained that they had no other option, that they felt teaching was the only job available to them, or certainly the easiest to get. Some said that other jobs were gained only through nepotism, and that teaching work was easier to get than other jobs: "I have no option. I don't have family in the NGO office to help me get a job"; and "Well, I have no option. In Sierra Leone it is who knows you that link you to get jobs."

To summarize these responses, we coded all the interviews for answers to the question, "Why are you teaching?" according to the most popular responses (see

Figure 13.1. Responses to the Question, "Why Do You Teach?"

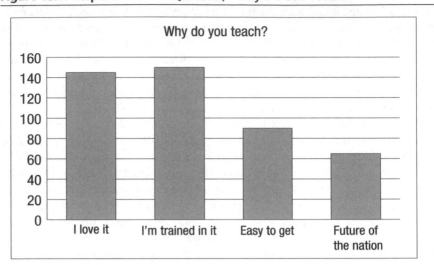

Figure 13.1). Some people gave more than one answer. In addition to asking teachers why they decided to teach, we asked about career goals (i.e., "What kind of work do you want to do in the future?"). Some of the older respondents laughed at the question and pointed at their white hair. The responses are presented below, divided between those who currently are teaching and currently not teaching.

Table 13.2 shows that those who are teaching, for the most part, want to be teaching. Those who are not teaching, for the most part, want to be doing something else.

Why Not Teach?

For the other side of the story, we asked the 37% of the sample not currently teaching why they had left the teaching field. Figure 13.2 presents the results among nonteachers, coding for the most common responses. Again, some respondents gave more than one answer.

Table 13.2. Career Goal by Current Employment

	Teaching	NGO work	Other
Currently teaching	79%	2%	18%
Currently not teaching	34%	14%	52%

Although the general perception is that people choose not to teach because of the low or irregular salary,[2] this was, surprisingly, rarely cited among our respondents. However, "found a better job" often meant they had found a job with better pay. "Hard to get approved" was an important issue, pointing to the fact that there were people who wanted to teach and who were trained to teach, but who could not get on to the government payroll. Again, the team went through the interview transcripts and selected responses to the question, "Why not teach," that they found interesting and/or not represented in the coding categories.

Many left the teaching field for what they considered to be a *better job*, often with an NGO. Indeed, 40 of the respondents currently are working for the IRC in Sierra Leone or Liberia. Some of their responses are: "I didn't really decide to leave teaching. But it is because of promotion. My job responsibilities cannot allow me to be in the classroom." From a man working as education secretary for a Christian mission: "My authorities felt I should leave the classroom to come and fill this position as education secretary." One told us, "I left teaching because my contract ended as a teacher, and later got a job with Save the Children in Liberia. I was serving as community development facilitator." One gave material reasons other than money for his career switch: "Because the NGO job I am doing is attractive. In the classroom there is no motorbike, no computer. So I feel it's better as an NGO worker."

Several explained that although they were not classroom teachers, they still felt they were contributing to the education field, or using their teaching skills with

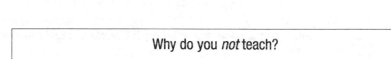

Figure 13.2. Responses to the Question, "Why Do You *Not* Teach?"

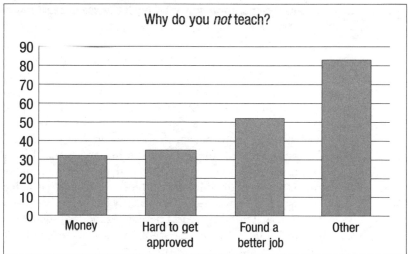

a different student population: "I didn't just leave the teaching *per se*, but because I have the knowledge to train teachers and the same IRC gave me the opportunity to exercise that knowledge in the field"; "I have not directly left the teaching, but I am doing in different perspective. I am a trainer of teachers, and so I give a great deal of knowledge to help the teachers teach their classes"; and "I don't want to continue teaching, but I want to continue supporting education. In fact, I am even thinking of starting my own school near here in a community with no school." Clearly, leaving the classroom should not be equated to leaving the education field. Many of these individuals commented that when the NGO jobs dried up, they were likely to return to the classroom.

Some respondents merely wanted a different career with different challenges: "Every human being wants to grow. Because of the opportunity I got, I decided to leave teaching"; "I wanted to change my lifestyle. I didn't want one program throughout my life"; and "I wanted to try my hand at other things since I have already taught for 10 years." Others were simply ready to retire.

After considering all these reasons, undoubtedly the most important issue was conditions of service for teachers in both Sierra Leone and Liberia. There is a common joke that teachers are not paid in this world but instead they will be paid in the next. Low and infrequent pay is a universally acknowledged aspect of the teaching profession in West Africa, and it is not surprising that this item came up repeatedly. One local research assistant explained to us that he was interviewing an older man, and when asked why he had left teaching, the man became somewhat belligerent, saying, "You, boy, what benefit will you get from it?" Other responses were: "If you remain in teaching, you will die poor"[3]; "Because the government does not pay teachers well. And private schools are not willing to take too many teachers"; "The income is very small and the cost of living is high"; and "Everyone looks for greener pastures. Teacher money is very small." It was not just low pay, another teacher told us: "With Sierra Leone government you may be employed but won't receive salary for over 6 months."

It is common knowledge that teacher pay is low and irregular, but for several people it was the corruption in the educational system that led them away from the profession. Indeed, when discussing the differences between the IRC Guinea educational system and the educational systems in their home countries, people often cited their frustration at the lack of supervision in the Sierra Leonean and Liberian schools. It feels good to know that someone cares whether you are doing a good job in the classroom. Three of the responses in this area were: "I left the teaching due to the status of the school: no staffing at all and no care from even our bosses"; "Because the standard of education in Liberian schools has reduced considerably. The Liberia educational system is completely commercialized where teachers receive bribes from students. With me, I have never received such. And so I decided to leave teaching"; and "I left the classroom because of very low salary and the corrupt practices of school administrators."

Especially for Sierra Leoneans, the fact that their Ministry of Education did not recognize their training in Guinea kept them from getting on the government payroll. Interview excerpts that addressed this issue include: "Well, on my arrival I did not even apply because I knew the Sierra Leone government would not consider me"; and "They say we are untrained and unqualified teachers. We never got paid, so I decided to quit." A school principal gave his perspective on the situation:

> The problem is not lack of qualified teachers. We have about ten teachers here who haven't been approved by the Ministry [of Education]yet, so they are volunteers and I pay them out of school funds. *All* the teacher approvals have to happen in Freetown. It's been 2 years and some are still waiting.

In Liberia, although Ministry of Education policy is to accept the IRC Guinea-issued B Certificate as equivalent to the C Certificate earned in Liberia, people still complained of problems getting on the payroll at the local level. One particularly affecting story was narrated by a frustrated Liberian:

> I came back in 2006 because they asked us to come home and help our country through teaching. I made it possible for the return opening of the Kolahun Central High School. I initiated many other means to bring up the school, but there was no means to pay teachers. So it was decided that the parents should contribute a little to help the teachers, but the DEO [District Education Officer] went against it. So I decided to seek another job with MSF [Médecins sans Frontières], but the DEO wrote against me saying I was trained by the ministry so I was compelled to teach. Now, I stay, but I am not on payroll up to now, as we speak I am not on payroll. How do I survive here? The government incentive recently, I did not receive. This has happened for 3 years now (2006–2009). The DEO is saying that the training received from Guinea is not equivalent to the teacher training here in Liberia, so through that he takes advantage of us.

Table 13.3 shows that among our sample, before displacement, the population of Liberian teachers was less well trained than the population of Sierra Leonean teachers. It shows that similar percentages received the B Certificate while in Guinea. Did different government policies in Liberia and Sierra Leone produce different outcomes? Even with a supposedly easier route to formal employment, a smaller percentage of Liberian than Sierra Leonean former IRC teachers currently are working as teachers.

We discovered that in Liberia, although in theory the IRC training was accepted as equivalent to Liberian training, in practice some former IRC teachers found it difficult to get on the government payroll. Often it was easier to find employment in one of the many community schools popping up all over Liberia.

Table 13.3. Results Disaggregated by Country

Country	No training before	Received B Certificate	Teacher now?
Liberia (n = 234)	68%	69%	52%
Sierra Leone (n = 384)	59%	64%	68%

In Sierra Leone, on the other hand, in theory the IRC training was not accepted by the government, yet in practice some people found their B Certificate to be quite useful. Some described using it to find jobs in private schools or community schools. In the remote areas of Kailahun, where in some schools a majority of the teachers went through the IRC training, it was reported that principals and headmasters were quite eager to hire former IRC teachers, even if they knew it would be difficult to get them on the rolls. Others reported that their IRC certificate helped them get accepted into further training courses (e.g., the Teachers Certificate offered through Distance Education at Eastern Polytechnic).

We can think of the percentage of nonteachers who say their career goal is to teach as a measure of the difficulty of getting a job teaching. Table 13.4 shows that at the moment, in Liberia there are greater barriers to being employed as a teacher, despite the government's acceptance of the IRC training. Of course, some of this difference is explained by the fact that Sierra Leone is more years post-conflict than Liberia and therefore has had time to rebuild its education bureaucracy.

There are several interesting issues here for further research. First is the importance of centralized control. It is our sense that in Liberia there are many more private schools, what might be called community schools in Sierra Leone. There is therefore more decentralized hiring and, we were told, less quality control in the schools. On the other hand, in Sierra Leone even mission schools are under the control of the Ministry of Education. Hiring decisions are much more centralized, which leads to years waiting to get on the payroll, but one could argue that there is therefore much more quality control.

We also noticed that in Sierra Leone many more people pursued further formal teacher training after their return (see Table 13.5).

Table 13.4. Percentage of Nonteachers, by Country, Whose Career Goal Is to Teach

	Number of nonteachers in the sample	Of those, number whose career goal is to teach	Percentage (%)
Liberia	112	48	43
Sierra Leone	124	32	26

Table 13.5. Numbers of Respondents Completing Further Teacher Training after Repatriation in Liberia and Sierra Leone

	Bachelors	Secondary	Primary	Total
Liberia (n = 234)	1 (B.A.)	2 B Cert.	8 C Cert.	11
Sierra Leone (n = 384)	19 (B.A., B.Ed., B.Sc.)	18 HTC	67 TC	104
Total	20	20	75	115

Significantly more Sierra Leoneans than Liberians pursued further training after returning home. This is probably explained primarily by the fact that the Liberia Ministry of Education accepted the IRC Guinea B Certificate and the Sierra Leone Ministry of Education did not. Therefore, many young teachers felt obligated to repeat the material they had already learned in order to get the right piece of paper. Some we talked with found this frustrating, but due to the ease of studying with the Distance Education program in Sierra Leone, most took it in stride. The vast majority reported that the IRC training made their further training easier. Many had even kept their notes from the training in Guinea and used them to study for their new courses.

Our findings make it clear that government-level policy is not sufficient to re-integrate former refugee teachers. If the state does not budget for hiring teachers, it will not matter whether they have certification or not. We also found that teachers still face challenges at the local level, regardless of national-level policy. This finding points to the importance of the local level and the school level in understanding teachers' experiences. It is not enough to give people skills and then expect that they can be entrepreneurial and change the educational system on their own. They need to be supported to work for change from within the system.

Rural and Urban

Two of the reasons cited for leaving the teaching field were as follows: "[My employers] sent me to the bush too much and I didn't have a chance to learn"; and "The ministry told us we had to go to the interior and I want to be in Monrovia to further my education." These responses echo what a recent World Bank report on education in Sierra Leone reports: "Many teachers who graduate from institutions in the capital and district headquarter towns do not return to their home areas to take employment. As a consequence, rural areas are deprived of trained and qualified teachers" (L. Wang, 2007, p. 75). However, our larger results seem to contradict the idea that teachers do not want to work in rural areas. Table 13.6 breaks down responses based on where respondents are living now.

Table 13.6. Training and Employment Profile Disaggregated by Current Location

Location	N	Percent	No training before	Received B Cert.	Teacher now?
Rural	152	24%	65%	68%	72%
Town*	408	64%	63%	65%	65%
City	80	13%	65%	59%	33%
Total	640	100%	63%	66%	63%

*We coded as "town" any place that was not a small village and not the capital city. There is therefore a wide range of variation in this category.

Notice that all three categories (currently living in rural, town, and city) were equally untrained before displacement, but after repatriation we see a different story. Although we cannot really say anything about causation, those who are living in the rural areas now are more likely to teach. Perhaps those who want to teach are more likely to move to the rural areas where teaching jobs are easier to get. Conversely, those in the city are less likely to teach. Perhaps those who come to the city do so for other reasons, to find other types of work or to pursue further training.[4]

A fair number of our respondents were people who started out teaching in rural schools, fled to Guinea and taught there when they had the chance, then repatriated back home and continued teaching. Indeed, the motivations of rural teachers are often different from the motivations of urban teachers. The rural teachers we interviewed were usually in their own or their spouse's home village. They expected to stay there, usually farming for a living, and contributing to the development of their communities by teaching on the side. Urban teachers, on the other hand, were usually young and career minded, using teaching as a stepping-stone to something better.

DO REPATRIATED REFUGEE TEACHERS TAKE ON EDUCATIONAL LEADERSHIP ROLES WITHIN THEIR SCHOOL OR COMMUNITY?

In Schools

We tried to get at the answers to this question by asking teachers, "Besides teaching, what other work do you do in the school?" People gave answers that ranged from principal or vice principal to, "I help organize the sports" or "I run the school garden." Some had formal positions as head of peace clubs, health clubs, or other clubs funded by outside organizations. We coded any of these things as "leadership role in the school" and found that 73% of teachers had some leadership role in their school and 27% reported that their only work at the school was teaching.

The most interesting question to us was whether IRC teachers could be agents of change in their schools. While in Guinea they learned new student-centered learning techniques and other modern teaching and school management methods. How much could a handful of "refugee teachers" turn around the culture of a school mired in old ways of doing things? We heard a few examples of former IRC teachers who, following the model of the IRC teacher training workshops, organized informal inservice trainings for their colleagues who were curious about the new teaching methods.[5]

In Other Organizations

We interpreted education-related roles rather broadly to include community sensitization and mobilization, as well as training of trainers and curriculum development. Many former IRC teachers in our sample have gone on to hold education-related positions, primarily for NGOs (especially IRC), but also for community-based organizations, religious missions, and government. In our sample, 32 respondents now work for the IRC in education-related programs. Four are working on gender-based violence with the IRC. Eleven are working as trainers for other NGOs (including the International Committee of the Red Cross, Concern Worldwide, the Danish Refugee Council, German Development Agency [GTZ], International Organization for Migration, Handicap International, and Ibis). Two started their own NGO. Four are working with NGOs on health-related (mostly HIV/AIDS) training and outreach. Two are education officers for Missions, and two are education ministry employees.

In Their Communities

Several respondents told us they served in their local community teacher association or parent teacher association. Forty respondents said, in response to the question, "How did you use your IRC training outside the classroom?" that they try to convince parents in their communities to send their children to school.

OTHER CAREER TRAJECTORIES

Of course, we were not interested just in change agents in the education sector. We also were looking for other instances of leadership among the former refugee teachers. We found that those not involved in education—either as teachers, administrators, or NGO workers—were engaged in a range of different activities. Nineteen were working for International NGOs in administrative capacities (including GTZ, International Medical Corps, the Norwegian Refugee Council, and others). Ten were working for government or parastatals (including the ministry of mines, the anti-corruption commission, the national statistics office, as a secretary at a teacher training college, and as a local court clerk). Three worked in mining, four worked for the police, and five were in the health field (as nurses or pharmacists). Six of the former refugee teachers described themselves as doing private business or trading (although people doing similar work might call themselves "unemployed"). Two were working in photography, two were security guards, one was driving a motorcycle taxi, and one was a weighing clerk at a rubber buying station. Often respondents told us that they drew on some aspect of their IRC training to help them find their new jobs. For example, some started with the health training in the camps and realized they had an interest in the health field. In addition to the employment data reported above, 5% of those in the sample were students in fields ranging from medicine to peace and conflict resolution to education. Twelve percent of the sample reported themselves to be unemployed. In this context, unemployed likely means not employed in a salaried job.

OTHER WAYS THE IRC TRAINING WAS USED

We also asked our informants, "How did you use the IRC training you received outside the classroom setting?" Figure 13.3 presents the results from our coding of the responses, with some people giving more than one answer.

Figure 13.3. Responses to the Question, "How Did You Use the Training Outside the Classroom?"

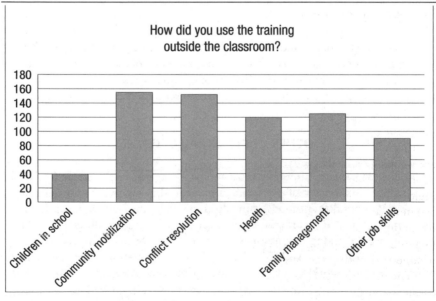

One key finding was that the conflict resolution workshop was cited as particularly useful (even though it was held infrequently). Those surveyed described the ways they had resolved conflict both in the refugee setting and once they returned home. For example, several explained that they had to resolve conflict over land after they returned home. Others explained that they understood now that conflict is natural, and described how they used the lessons they had learned about trying to find a "win–win" solution to conflicts. The fact that the conflict resolution workshop had such an impact on the teachers points to the possibility for other high-impact training courses with an educated refugee population.

We asked those who went on to further education whether the IRC training had been useful in their new courses, and almost all agreed that it had. Some women were particularly grateful for the training, saying that even more than the content, the way the workshops were organized—with equal participation by all—made them feel bold to speak in a group, even among men and people older or better trained than themselves.

CONCLUSION AND RECOMMENDATIONS

In previous reports evaluating the IRC's education program in Guinea, positive results were documented for students; but the positive effects for teachers and for the reconstruction of educational systems in their countries of origin were always assumed and never demonstrated. The goal of this research was to go beyond the assumptions and document former teachers' own experiences and voices from the ground up, and in the process assess the long-term effects of the teacher training for refugee teachers in Guinea. The result was a complex tapestry of personal stories, which taken together shed light on the struggles and triumphs of individuals, as well as some of the structural issues facing former refugees at the local, national, and international levels.

The good news is that two thirds of the surveyed teachers trained by the IRC in Guinea are employed as teachers, often at their old schools. Those who have stayed in the teaching field describe their love of the work, their desire to contribute to the development of their communities and nation, and sometimes simply their lack of other options. Some have found better paying work with NGOs or are working in other professions by choice. Overall, the people we interviewed appreciated the training they received from the IRC in Guinea and pointed to multiple ways in which they made use of the training after their repatriation. The bad news is that some have left the teaching field in disgust. They describe the low pay and poor conditions of service, but also complain about the difficulty of getting onto the teaching rolls, even with the right certification and even in the face of supposed teacher shortages.[6]

The findings from this study suggest that eventual reintegration of displaced teachers and their roles in education reconstruction should be in policymakers' minds from the beginning. It is true that conflict-affected countries' governments are often weak or unstable. There nevertheless should be an effort to work toward refugees' eventual reintegration by collaborating with home institutions. This collaboration could take the form of travel support for Ministry of Education officials to visit refugee settings. The IRC began working to that end for teachers near the end of its time in Guinea, and that is a lesson that certainly should be carried over into other refugee settings. It is also important to investigate the possibility of cross-border certification for teachers in refugee situations, perhaps by moving toward a regional teacher certification system.[7]

Our study concluded that there was not a shortage of trained teachers in Sierra Leone or Liberia, though there is a shortage of trained teachers in classrooms. This suggests that training more teachers alone is not the answer. One high level respondent put it this way: "Training more teachers is like pouring water into a bucket with holes in it." More emphasis should be placed on teacher *retention,* and on how to utilize the former IRC teachers as effective local partners for different projects. At the level of the Ministries of Education, we must ensure that hiring and pay are fair and transparent, and local level corruption must be addressed. And finally, individuals should continue to be supported to be agents of change in their schools and communities.

NOTES

I wish to acknowledge Bidemi Carrol and the LEGACY program of the IRC, which proposed and funded the research on which this chapter is based. Thanks are also due to the research team in West Africa: David Mackieu, Wusu Kargbo, Sia Mani, Fertiku Harris, Pauline Gborlawoe, and Nathaniel Boakai, as well as the many IRC employees who assisted in the execution of the research. Thanks also to Sharyn Routh and Janelle Nodthurft for research assistance.

1. The names come from Liberia's certification system where the C Certificate is for primary school levels and the B Certificate is for higher levels. In Sierra Leone, the primary school certificate is called the Teachers Certificate (TC) and the secondary school certificate is the Higher Teachers Certificate (HTC).

2. See Bennell and Akyeampong (2007) for DfID and L. Wang (2007) for the World Bank on teacher motivation. See reports by Shriberg (2007) for more on the conditions of service for Liberian teachers.

3. Shriberg (2007) points to the same conventional wisdom, even using the same phrase as a heading in her report.

4. The DfID report on teacher motivation in Sub-Saharan Africa and South Asia contains some similar findings, noting that teachers who work at schools in their home areas have a higher level of job satisfaction and a broader commitment to promoting education and development, due to more supportive social networks and knowledge of the community (Bennell & Akyeampong, 2007, p. vii).

5. Shriberg's (2007) study on the conditions of service for Liberian teachers asked a similar question, and it is worth reporting her results here. She concluded, "Teachers trained in the education programs of camps for displaced persons (refugee and/or IDP camps) who have now returned and are working in Liberian schools are making an important contribution to education in postwar Liberia. Overall, 191 (46.6 percent) of the teachers surveyed who are now working in IRC-supported schools had taught while they lived as refugees or IDPs. Of these, 79.7 percent reported that they are sharing their knowledge, skills and training with their fellow teachers" (Shriberg, 2007, p. 21).

6. Nishimuko's (2007) study reports similar findings. In a countrywide sample of classrooms in Sierra Leone, the majority of teachers had some teacher training and more than 80% had over 5 years of experience, yet 96% of teachers were dissatisfied with their salary.

7. This falls in line with what Jackie Kirk (2009a) recommended for students in *Certification Counts: Recognizing the Learning Attainments of Displaced and Refugee Students.* She concluded that the presence of a regional examination body, the West African Examinations Council made for better results for students. A similar regional body for teacher certificates might be useful and allow for international movement of trained teachers to meet immediate demand.

Part IV

NEW DIRECTIONS IN RESEARCH ON EDUCATION AND CONFLICT

Picturing Violence

Participatory Visual Methodologies in Working with Girls to Address School and Domestic Violence in Rwanda

CLAUDIA MITCHELL

A number of years ago, Jackie Kirk and Stephanie Garrow published the lead article in an issue of the South Africa feminist journal *Agenda* called "'Girls in Policy': Challenges for the Education Sector." In one of the sections of the article, they challenge the research and policy community to reverse the image of girls from being speechless to speaking out. As they observe:

> Although the girl child has been at the centre of national government and donor policies on education and other issues for a number of years, she herself [has] tended to be a silent figure. She has been photographed for the cover of attractive donor agency publications, been the subject of a number of meetings and conferences, and has been written about in numerous reports and policy briefs. Strategies to promote her educational opportunities, improve her health, and protect her from abuse, early marriage and female genital mutilation have been developed and implemented by a large number of well-intentioned individuals and organizations. And yet, in most of these instances, the girl child remains speechless. (Kirk & Garrow, 2003, p. 8)

This article was, of course, "just the beginning" in terms of the kind of work that both Jackie Kirk and Stephanie Garrow went on to do in relation to girls' education. But their interest in and attention to visual culture, in particular, inspired much subsequent work, including, for example, the critical work of Catherine Magno and Jackie Kirk that interrogated those very covers of attractive donor publications (see, e.g., Magno & Kirk, 2010). Drawing on focus groups, interviews with policymakers working in girls' education, and critical readings of the visual images in policy documents, they come to the conclusion that the very process of doing this kind of visual work is critical to policy change.

> We all carry assumptions about what we think girls' education in international development is and should be, sight unseen. Interrogating these images has now allowed us to "look" at images of girls' education and in response draw conclusions about what intended and unintended meanings can be drawn from them. The research itself has brought change to individuals, as several participants mentioned that they will never look at photographs the same way again. Policy implications at the institutional level might lead to the purposeful collection of images that respond more directly to emerging policy trends at UNGEI partner organizations. Important areas for further research would include comparative analysis of image groups (e.g., UNICEF images compared with UNESCO images) and respondent groups (e.g., World Vision staff compared with CIDA staff), as well as *involving girls themselves in data collection and analysis.* (Magno & Kirk, 2010, p. 31, emphasis added)

It is the idea of involving girls themselves that I highlight in this chapter through what I describe elsewhere (Mitchell, 2011) as participatory visual research methodologies (PVRM). This approach can contribute to giving girls a voice, particularly in relation to such sensitive areas as gender violence in and around schools and communities in conflict/post-conflict settings. By PVRM, I refer to the use of such approaches as photovoice (Wang, Burris, & Xiang, 1996), where community participants become photographers and documentarians of the issues of concern in their lives; participatory video, where community members are involved in video-making (see Mitchell & de Lange, 2011); drawing (see Theron, Mitchell, Smith, & Stuart, in press); and digital storytelling (Gubrium, 2009), all of which draw on participatory visual tools for engaging often marginalized community members (children and young people, women, victims of poverty) in decision-making processes. Such approaches serve as modes of inquiry, modes of representation, and modes of dissemination. As research tools they help to address some of the inherent power differentials between the researcher and the researched, and, I note here, attempt to see the issues "through the eyes" of participants. Simultaneously, this chapter looks at the ways in which this kind of work can contribute to deepening an understanding of the critical issues that policymakers need to address. In essence, this work seeks to "shift the boundaries" of knowledge production (Marcus & Hofmaener, 2006), as a type of grassroots policymaking.

In the chapter I draw on my work with children and young people in Rwanda, focusing in particular on the voices of girls and young women. Following Jackie Kirk's (2009b) thoughtful and urgent work on "starting with oneself," I use examples from my own fieldwork as a way to reflect on some of the challenges and successes in working with participatory visual methods. Visual studies, it seems to me, invite reflection by the very nature of working with visual images. As Susan Sontag (2003) observes, visual images have the power to haunt us, and it is perhaps that haunting that seems critical to helping us take our research into social action.

THE CONTEXT OF RWANDA

Between 2005 and the present I have been involved in a number of participatory visual research initiatives related to safety and security in the lives of women and children in Rwanda (see Mitchell, de Lange, & Moletsane, 2011; Mitchell & Kanyangara, 2006; Umurungi, Mitchell, Gervais, Ubalijoro, & Kabarenzi, 2008). Of central importance have been the risks of violence against children in Rwandan society as a result of the genocide. Although it is now some 16 years after the genocide, the "afterlife" of the genocide is still very much present. To discuss Rwanda as a post-conflict society, particularly in the context of other chapters in this volume, is far from straightforward, but perhaps the significance of this idea of afterlife in and of itself is something that needs to be explored.

As Patrick Kanyangara and I found in a participatory visual study with several hundred schoolchildren in Rwanda where we used drawings and performance, young people are still dealing with the legacy of the genocide (Mitchell & Kanyangara, 2006). Some of them head families. This often leads to an economic precariousness whereby the child heading up a family cannot bring up his or her younger brothers and sisters. According to the first available national statistics, child-headed households constituted 13% of Rwandan families in 1996. Over time, their number has decreased somewhat but the ravages of AIDS seem to be perpetuating this situation: More than 100,000 households are still headed by children (Ministry of Finance and Economic Planning, 2002; 2007). In a study aimed at learning about the conditions in which these young heads of household live, interviews conducted with a sample that covered the entire country led to the conclusion that their rights are regularly disregarded and their health and education needs ignored by the community (ACORD, 2001, p. 26).

In addition to this, there are a number of families that care for orphans. In such conditions, some children reported that they are neglected, are not educated, and are employed as houseboys or housegirls (Mitchell & Kanyangara, 2006). Since girls who are heads of families enjoy no protection, they live in a climate of permanent insecurity and are vulnerable to attempts at intimidation and sexual assault, particularly at night. Girls who have been left orphaned but have been absorbed into other families are more likely to have been deprived of education, as they often are expected to take on childcare roles or find work as domestic servants. Young women may have been forced to sell sex to provide for themselves, and they constitute one of the most vulnerable groups regarding HIV transmission. Of the more than 3,000 rapes recorded by the Rwandan police in 2005 and again in 2006, 78% involved those under the age of 18. Police reports, which have categorized children as (1) under 10, (2) between 10 and 14, and (3) above age 14, have further noted the ways in which cases of sexual violence vary according to the ages of the victims. Their reports indicate that 33.7% of rapes involved children under the age of 10. Children most often are abused by those who should protect them, including caregivers, teachers, employers, Local Defense Forces, and personnel at orphanages and childcare centers, with the exception of children on the streets, who also report physical and sexual violence by strangers. Furthermore, it should be remembered that during the genocide some fundamental taboos such as murder were infringed and even turned into an obligation. Some children (now adults) witnessed murders committed by their parents, while others saw their parents being killed, tortured, and humiliated. At the same time, adults experienced so much violence during the genocide in Rwanda that they might trivialize violent acts committed against children and their physical and psychological consequences.

From the above, it is clear that the security situation of children in the current Rwandan society is worrisome. But the most serious problem lies in the fact that children in most cases are abused by adults who may do all they can to conceal these violent acts. Rwanda has made great strides in terms of its policies and laws pertaining to gender and gender violence, which could serve to protect children. The recent Economic Development and Poverty Reduction Strategy itself called for an extensive analysis of gender in relation to the lives of girls and women across all sectors, and the various sectors currently are developing gender policies. The newly formed Gender Observatory is a structure that will help to monitor what is happening in relation to the implementation of these various policies. A critical gap remains, however, in understanding the lived experiences of girls, particularly in rural areas, where their lives do not neatly divide into "health sector," "education sector," or "agriculture sector." Thus, for example, the education sector may have identified that girls (more than boys) fail to attend school because they are called on to work in the fields. However, the agriculture sector may be supporting programs requiring extra work from female-headed household workers (and perhaps even ignoring the age of the workers) because the focus is on crop productivity or access to markets. The challenge, then, is to see the issues from the vantage point of girls and young women themselves.

PARTICIPATORY VISUAL METHODOLOGIES

In this section, I highlight the use of two visual methods—photovoice and drawing
—presenting them each as a case study. As noted above and as explored elsewhere
(see de Lange, Mitchell, & Stuart, 2007; Mitchell, 2009; Mitchell, Walsh, & Moletsane, 2006; Moletsane, Mitchell, Smith, & Chisholm, 2008), the significance of the
visual (drawings, video making, and photography) in breaking the silence related
to gender violence in and around schools is critical. Here I highlight how the visual
helped to "open the eyes" of policymakers.

Case Study 1: Photovoice: What Can a Girl Do with a Camera?

Borrowing from the formulation put forward by Spence and Solomon (1995),
"What can a woman do with a camera?" I pursued the question: What happens
when participants are given cameras to document their experiences "through
their eyes"? This work is informed by the well-established feminist visual project
of Caroline Wang and Mary Brinton Lykes, pioneers in the area of photovoice.
Caroline Wang, who "patented" the term *photovoice*, coordinated a large project in
China with rural women. As described in *Visual Voices: 100 Photographs of Village
China by the Women of Yunnan Province* (Yi, et al., 1995), the work aimed at three
interwoven elements: individual change, the quality of life in the community, and
policy changes aimed at achieving social equity (see also Wang & Burris, 1994;
Wang, Burris, & Xiang, 1996). Inspired by Wang's project in China, Mary Brinton
Lykes's work in Guatemala over the past 20 years has taken place in the context
of women silenced by violence and pervasive fear (see, e.g., Lykes, 2001a, 2001b;
Asociación de la Mujer Maya Ixil (ADMI) & Lykes, 2000). One of the objectives of
the study described here is to suggest that this visual method, photovoice, can fill
the gap between (1) information gained using surveys, and (2) the requirements
of planning an action addressing complex issues in relation to health/AIDS and
education for vulnerable groups in Rwanda. Analysis of the voices of young girls
living on the street in this study also document young girls' choices and their capacities (or their "insider expertise") to provide insight into the challenges, desired
solutions, and realities that they prioritize.

The fieldwork for the study was conducted in the UMWALI Center located in
an urban district in the North Province of Rwanda, the former Ruhengeri province. That Center aims at gathering together girls living on the street and tries to
reintegrate them into a normal life, including attention to initiating them into
some small income-generating projects. In total, 16 girls living on the street and
ranging in age from 11 to 14 years were involved. The overall focus was on photo-
graphing what they saw as images of "feeling safe and not so safe," particularly in
relation to the possibilities of gender violence in their environment. Divided into

four small groups of four, the participants were given disposable cameras and had approximately 45 minutes to take their pictures. The data production workshops took place over 2 days. All the work was organized "on location" at one Center. While the details of the project are described in more detail elsewhere (Umurungi et al., 2008), here I want to focus on one set of images produced by the girls and discuss them in the context of a type of grassroots policymaking. The girls' photographs of "feeling unsafe" included pictures of the local stadium in Ruhengheri, which is not that far from the Center where they congregated or from public toilets that the girls also used. Many of their photographs were also of houses where football players live (see Figure 14.1). The captions on some of their photos read: "I am scared of these players; I do not believe in them, they can be perpetrators"; "Those are football players' lodges. Towards the evening when it is getting dark the area becomes dangerous, they can abuse me there"; and "This picture shows the toilets of the stadium, I used to sleep in the stadium but street boys intended to abuse me in these toilets several times."

Figure 14.1. "Unsafe Place"

What came out of the girls' photos that was important in relation to social action is the fact that at the very same time that the girls were taking these photographs, an international nongovernmental organization (NGO) working in Rwanda was in the process of developing a campaign for addressing gender violence through the use of the voices of sports heroes. The idea behind the campaign was one of drawing on the high visibility of sports heroes to appeal to the general population to change their actions. Ironically, these were the very people that the girls identified as being the perpetrators of gender violence. As a result of this project, my colleagues and I were able to show the girls' photos and captions to the NGO and engage in the "turning of the tide" in terms of how they planned to proceed, moving away from a campaign that drew on the voices of sports heroes to a strategic plan to work with the Ministry of Youth and Sport to provide sensitizing sessions on what counts as gender violence and responsible behavior. The girls had spoken.

Case Study 2: Drawings

The use of drawings in social research is located within several broad yet overlapping areas of contemporary study. These include arts-based or arts-informed research (Knowles & Cole, 2008); work within participatory visual methodologies (de Lange, Mitchell, & Stuart, 2007; G. Rose, 2001); textual approaches in visual studies in the social sciences (Mitchell, 2011); and the tradition of using drawings in psychology. As explored elsewhere (Theron, Mitchell, Smith, & Stuart, in press), what is particularly significant about drawings, as method, is their simplicity. All you need is a paper and a pencil or pen. If there is simplicity in collecting the data through drawings, there is complexity in the interpretive process. Does one ask for captions? Use the drawing as a type of elicitation? What do the drawings really mean? I like the immediacy of drawings and their potential to move audiences. In work that I was carrying out in Rwanda on developing a policy on violence against women and children, I spent time with young people in all regions of the country. With a small team, we met groups of young women in communities and carried out 2-day consultative workshops. In the workshops they brainstormed the issues related to gender-based violence (GBV), performed through role play, and drew pictures in response to the prompt: "Gender-based violence: Problems and solutions." I was interested in the ways in which the participants in the workshops were themselves able to participate in the analysis of the issues, not just through their own drawings of both challenges and solutions, but also in relation to looking across the drawings when I set them up as a display at the back of the hall or classroom where we were working.

I would be remiss if I did not point out that although drawing may seem to be simple, there are some complexities. When I first introduced the idea of drawing to one group of young people in rural Rwanda, they simply stared at me, even with all the input of my colleagues who spoke Kinyarwanda and who were from the local area. Finally one person spoke up and said that they didn't know how to draw. At first I thought there was a concern that their drawings would not be good enough, but what I realized is that many of the participants had had very few opportunities to attend school and little access to paper or pencils. One young man in his early 20s, and older than most of the participants, commented that he was only in grade 2 at school and that he had experienced a lost childhood. In this case we began with role play, and then proceeded to the drawings and simply assured participants to just put on paper what they could.

In total, we collected several hundred drawings. While my colleagues and I presented statistical and other data to various groups of stakeholders and policymakers in Rwanda, it was the drawings that made up the most concrete and evocative data that we could take to these various audiences to "haunt" them, as Sontag (2003) described. One of the drawings that was particularly powerful in this work was "baby" (see Figure 14.2). The girl who drew this picture was showing the tragedy and the waste of two lives—the baby in the toilet and the desperate young mother. This drawing highlights the significance of unwanted pregnancy,

Figure 14.2. "Baby"

often as a result of sexual violence, and of course infanticide as a form of violence against children—although in this case it is a child (the young mother) who has been violated in the first place. When I showed this image in larger-than-life format in a PowerPoint presentation to policymakers, I could see that it was difficult for them to look away. While the policymakers were aware that desperate pregnant girls and young women were engaging in the practice of disposing of babies in toilets, somehow the image itself was haunting.

In the case of the photograph of the sports heroes' homes, I can say with some confidence that there was policy change at least at the level of planning a campaign. In the case of the drawing of the baby in the toilet, I have less concrete evidence. But what was clear from the response of the audience was a sense that the girls had been heard.

SOME CRITICAL ISSUES IN WORKING WITH PARTICIPATORY VISUAL METHODOLOGIES

What the two case studies highlight is not just the "giving of voice" to girls, but ways of ensuring that they are heard (and seen) by policymakers. In both cases, this objective meant taking the images back to various groups that had responsibility for girls living on the street. Two critical issues relate to dissemination and ethical issues.

Modes of Dissemination

As I explore elsewhere (Mitchell, 2011), ensuring dissemination may mean expanding our repertoire of skills as researchers so that we examine practical ways of ensuring that images are displayed in ways that reach audiences. In both cases above, the dissemination was done through PowerPoint presentations in order to reach policymakers at the national level. I also have been exploring the ways that local exhibitions involving clotheslines and other "low tech" approaches might be used, especially in communities. In such cases, the participants themselves, in this case the girls, can be engaged in "showing and telling." Moreover, local collaborators such as NGOs, which themselves are interested in documenting their work and reaching audiences, can be involved in addressing their community-outreach mandates.

Ethical Issues and the Politics of Doing Less Harm

At the same time, the idea of public display, especially in the area of ethical issues, is a critical one, particularly in the context of GBV. How do we make sure that those who are willing to speak out through their photos and pictures are not further victimized? As Fiona Leach (2006) observes, researchers working in this area have a particular responsibility. When it comes to photographs, my colleagues and I build in a component in our photovoice workshops called "No Faces," where we offer visual examples of what participants might photograph instead of faces and what the ethical issues might be. In adding this No Faces session to preparation for photovoice work, there is the possibility of engaging participants in reflection and discussion about human rights—not just their own, but also the rights of others not to be photographed. In the case of the girls living on the street, many of their photos and drawings were actually of places and devoid of people (e.g., the houses of the sports heroes or pictures of toilets). It is their captions that reveal their reasons for taking the pictures. In other cases, participants have seen that they could just take a picture of a hand or "from the waist down." It is in discussion that they might talk further about how even a hand or a shoe could be revealing, especially in a rural area or in a camp.

Another obvious ethical consideration relates to the actual process of taking photographs. In the case of the girls living on the street, they were accompanied at all times by one of the researchers. This was important to ensure their protection. It was also, however, an opportunity to develop a more collaborative relationship between the research team and the girls. In another project that took place in an informal settlement and market in South Africa, the teacher who was heading up the study realized that the pictures the children were taking in order to document poverty could be potentially revealing of local people, and as he accompanied them, he was able to learn much more about the community. He also was able to serve a protectionist role. He commented that the traders in the market were particularly "under attack" because they were employing children who should have been at school and they might have threatened or attacked the photographers (Mitchell et al., 2006). The teacher in this case explained the issues and why it was important that the children took pictures of the market.

Anonymity and confidentiality are important in all work with children. Clearly, participants need to be informed of their rights and the fact that they do not have to participate. They also have to be assured that their identities will not be revealed and that their work will be kept confidential. As I highlight elsewhere, issues of confidentiality and anonymity are sometimes difficult to convey to children, particularly when they have not had the chance to go to school, and where the research team itself is made up of outsiders. Thompson (2009) developed a visual consent form, as she calls it, as a way to increase the possibility that participants will understand. Clearly, one aspect of ensuring protection for children, particularly in the context of GBV, is not to allow their real names to appear on the image. This can be of concern, of course, particularly in the context of drawings, where the person drawing may have a particular sense of ownership of what they have drawn (Mak, 2006).

TOWARD A GLOBAL UNDERSTANDING OF GIRLS' PERSPECTIVES ON GENDER VIOLENCE: ON THE POLITICS OF VISUAL CULTURE

Beyond the specific and often local uses of visual images of gender violence produced by children, and especially by girls, I want to suggest that there are broader uses of this work. These uses can be both by organizations such as UNICEF and Save the Children, which as a matter of "best practice" recognize the significance of the voices of children in identifying and addressing social issues, as well as by research groups and other configurations of researchers who regularly make use of visual data produced by children.

If one googles "children's drawings," one will come up with references to a fascinating array of different collections, ranging from drawings produced by children in the Terezin Concentration Camp, at the Jewish Museum in Prague, to the World Awareness Children's Museum whose mission it is to "foster awareness, understanding, and appreciation of worldwide cultural diversity for children and adults" (World Children's Museum, 2009). One can even access virtual collections such as the drawings produced by children during the Spanish Civil War (see, e.g., Columbia University's Children's Drawings of the Spanish Civil War, http://www. columbia.edu/cu/lweb/eresources/exhibitions/children/). The google references generally include the size of the collections: 2,000 pieces of art created from over 100 countries at Paintbrush Diplomacy; 1,300 words in the Stone Soup Museum of Children's Art; 4,500 children's drawing from Terezin. And if you visit the virtual collections, you will discover that it is often possible to know the age, sex, and location of the child producer, along with, in some cases, even the name. The circumstances in which the drawings were collected are also part of the information provided. In the case of the Terezin drawings, Mrs. Friedl Dicker Brandeis taught art classes to children at the camp before she was sent to Auschwitz. She was able to hide two suitcases full of the children's drawings. Some of this work complements what is also present in published book collections, as can be seen in "*I Never Saw Another Butterfly*": *Children's Drawings and Poems from Terezin Concentration Camp, 1942–1944* (Volavkova, 1978) or in Geist and Carroll's *They Still Draw Pictures: Children's Art in Wartime from the Spanish Civil War to Kosovo* (2002). I am not aware of any public or private archives of drawings that are specific to GBV in its various manifestations of physical, psychological, and sexual abuse, particularly in and around schools in conflict and post-conflict settings. Glenys Clacherty's (2006) work with the drawings of refugee children perhaps comes closest to offering a public collection.

What happens to the visual images produced in various projects and how, in the case of GBV, can these images have greater impact? The issue of who actually might work with these drawings through the use of, for example, a participatory archive needs to be raised, but as other work with participatory archiving with communities suggests, this is clearly a new area for analysis and dissemination (de Lange, Mnisi, Mitchell, & Park, 2010; Mnisi, de Lange, & Mitchell, 2010). The participatory archive, as Huvilo (2008) and Shilton and Srinivasan (2008) note, is a relatively new concept and refers to the ways in which community users can be engaged in designing the archive as well as in coding and re-coding the data. As Shilton and Srinivasan (2008) observe, the reason for creating a new participatory method is to prevent, as much as possible, the distortion of cultural histories of marginalized populations. How might police offices or others who address gender violence in Rwanda interact with collections? How would the young producers in Rwanda (most between the ages of 13 and 18) who drew the images noted above interact with an archive of the images? Would images in a digital archive alter their meaning? Would the process of reviewing their own images and those of their peers be traumatic? How could the whole process of dialogue and discussion about the meaning of the collection or the process of creating new stories through the use of a digital storytelling activity help young people to re-imagine a new future? Work on the use of collections of drawings by the producers themselves, along with users such as teachers and police officers, in addressing gender violence has the potential to alter the balance of power between researchers and communities.

A VISION FOR THE FUTURE

Jackie Kirk and Stephanie Garrow (2003) conclude their article on girls and policymaking by calling for those working with girls to develop "highly flexible approaches which build the capacity of girls to best address the issues of most concern to them" (p. 14).

As we move toward 2015 and the global expectations for realizing the various Millennium Development Goals related to equity and girls' access to education and educational resources, it is critical that girls' voices, girls' perspectives, and the processes of girls' engagement are fully appreciated. It is more than just an issue of "giving voice," however, as I have tried to highlight in this chapter. It is also an ethical process, and one that goes beyond what might be seen as tokenistic "uses" of girls' voices. This discussion should suggest that in taking seriously the voices of children in our research, we need to employ technologies, techniques, and methods that allow us to fully honor the trust that young artists bestow upon researchers. As Kirk and Garrow (2003) observe, "To be effective and sustainable, such processes rather than superficial changes in the mechanics of operation, need to reflect fundamental shifts in individual mindset and organizational culture" (p. 14). When I think of the cardboard boxes of data, the crammed and locked file cabinets (as per our agreements with Research Ethics Boards), the elaborate projects headed up by global organizations that yield vast quantities of rich data not always studied beyond the life of a project, and the untapped potential of the images for "play and replay," I want us as a research community to revisit the ethical dimensions of doing research with children. Stashing drawings into two suitcases, as Mrs. Friedl Dicker Brandeis did to protect the drawings done by the children of Terezin, ensured that one day the images would be made public. I am not arguing that all images from our collection should "go public" or that there is only one way of invoking the participation of the producers. Indeed, more conventional exhibitions and the use of participatory archiving are only two ways of doing this. What I am calling for is the use of tools and platforms that fully engage the participation of the producers and users so that the images end up as more than attractive covers on reports.

CHAPTER 15

From Child-Friendly Schools to Child-Friendly Research Methods

Lessons Learned on Child-Centered Research from UNICEF's Learning Plus Initiative

STEPHANIE BENGTSSON
LESLEY BARTLETT

During the late 20th century, the role of children[1] within social research began to be re-imagined around their inclusion as "subjects rather than objects of inquiry" (Christensen & James, 2008, p. 1; see also Greig, Taylor, & MacKay, 2007; Woodhead & Falkner, 2008). This shift resulted in part from the evolution of the global children's rights movement, which was conceived in the aftermath of World War I. In recent decades, some aid agencies working with children have responded to this shift, promoting policies and programming based on what is known as "child-friendly" research, or research *with* children, rather than simply *about* or *on* children (Hart & Tyrer, 2006). This chapter explores a UNICEF research project that attempted to meaningfully incorporate children's voices.

In 2007 we were invited by UNICEF to design and lead a five-country research study for the Learning Plus Initiative in Africa, an initiative aimed at promoting "Child-Friendly Schools."[2] With colleagues from the United States and five focal African countries, we developed a research project that included children's perspectives. The overall purpose was to examine obstacles to the inclusion of essential services in schools in Lesotho, Nigeria, Rwanda, Swaziland, and Tanzania. Our study aimed to answer the following questions:

- What risks and threats to educational quality, care, and protection (specifically risks and threats to inclusion, participation, and gender equity) exist in schools and their surrounding communities?
- What strategies are used to overcome these risks and threats?
- Specifically, what policies, practices, and intersectoral partnerships exist to facilitate schools as centers of quality education, care, and protection?

Prior to the global shift in research, this study would likely have involved only classroom and school observations; interviews with teachers, principals, and possibly parents; and a survey of these various stakeholders. However, as the ultimate goal of Learning Plus is to ensure that schools are functioning as centers of care and support for *children*, UNICEF suggested that children's perspectives be central to the study. As children were the key stakeholders in Child-Friendly Schools, UNICEF felt that understanding how the children both perceived and participated in essential service provision was fundamental to the success of the initiative.

This chapter highlights lessons learned from designing and using child-friendly research methods in what we refer to as challenging contexts, where service delivery is difficult because the area is post-conflict and undergoing reconstruction, post-natural disaster, and/or affected by poverty, HIV/AIDS, civil unrest, drought, or other factors. We argue that many of the methodological insights gained from this study can be effectively transferred to crisis contexts, such as emergencies created by violent conflict or natural disaster, where there is a dearth of child-friendly research. We believe that researchers in these contexts could benefit greatly from becoming proficient in child-friendly research and modifying methods that have been developed and evaluated in more stable contexts.

The chapter is organized as follows. First, we review literature regarding child-friendly research, beginning with the roots of children's rights in crisis contexts, and argue from a rights-based perspective for more child-friendly research in such contexts. Second, we discuss theoretical, methodological, and ethical challenges of this work as set out in the literature. Third, we describe how we incorporated child-friendly methods in the project and discuss our insights. Finally, we conclude that while there are problems associated with child-friendly research, the benefits far outweigh the costs.[3]

ROOTS OF CHILDREN'S RIGHTS IN CRISIS CONTEXTS

An understanding of the roots of the children's rights movement in conflict lays an important foundation for a study of the lessons learned from an initiative such as

Learning Plus. In particular, it emphasizes the importance of taking a rights-based approach to research in all humanitarian and development settings, which consequently forces us as researchers to consider how best to protect the rights of our youngest research participants. If we use the United Nations (UN) Convention on the Rights of the Child (CRC) to guide our work in education, we find that not only do children have the right to a quality education (Article 28), but they also have the right to express themselves "freely in all matters affecting [them]" (Article 12). These rights do not disappear during a crisis, but in fact become all the more necessary. In other words, it is when rights are at the greatest risk of being violated that they must be most fiercely protected.

In 1919, Eglantyne Jebb founded the Save the Children Fund, whose inaugural relief scheme provided food for starving children in Austria. She went on to draft the first Declaration of the Rights of the Child, endorsed by the League of Nations General Assembly in 1924 as the World Child Welfare Charter. The charter aimed to ensure that the international community considered children's rights first and foremost when planning relief efforts (and later development). The document set out five key rights concerning children's well-being. Among these rights there are specific directives aimed at helping the most vulnerable. For example, the fourth right states: "The child must be put in a position to earn a livelihood, and must be protected against every form of exploitation." The formulation of these rights implies the presence of an adult who "gives," "feeds," "nurses," "puts the child in a certain position," and "brings the child up" and, as such, implies treating children as objects rather than subjects of development. Taking a children's rights-based approach to research at the time would likely not have involved active engagement with children's perspectives.

Shortly after its founding at the end of World War II, the UN started the International Children's Emergency Fund (now the International Children's Fund, UNICEF), which aimed to provide emergency food and healthcare for children affected by the war (P. Jones, 2006). In 1959, the UN expanded the Declaration of the Rights of the Child to include the rights to a name, a nationality, and an education. Three decades later, the UN General Assembly adopted the CRC. With all nations as signatories (save the United States and Somalia), and an explicit mention of freedom of expression, this document "signals that a clear, discursive space has been delineated for children. They have an autonomy that exists outside family, school and institutions and a voice conditioned neither by competence nor chronological age" (Kellett, Robinson, & Burr, 2004, p. 35). According to the CRC, researchers working with children's issues should find meaningful ways of incorporating children's voices into work that affects them. Several scholars writing on child-friendly research explicitly link this approach to the expanding children's rights movement (Kellett et al., 2004; Woodhead & Falkner, 2008). For example, Woodhead and Falkner (2008) argue that research in Great Britain increasingly has incorporated the perspectives of children, largely because of how important the right of children to express their views and feelings has become on the global agenda.

This drive to listen meaningfully to children's voices has led researchers to look for inspiration from the burgeoning body of participatory research with adults, designed to incorporate perspectives of communities more consequentially into research that directly affects them. For example, the Mosaic approach, which initially was aimed at working with preschool-aged children but has since been modified for use with older children, involves using a range of methods based on children's lived experiences and builds on participatory rural appraisal (PRA) (Clark & Moss, 2001, in Greig et al., 2007). The approach imagines the research question as a puzzle, which can be answered by piecing together data from a series of different tools for "listening" to children, both verbally and visually (Greig et al., 2007). Such tools could include observation, mapping, photography, group discussions, drawings, and so on. It is hardly surprising that PRA, which aims to include the most vulnerable communities in their own development, became such an influence for doing research *with* children, as children so often are perceived as being among the most vulnerable within a population.

ACADEMIC RESEARCH *WITH* CHILDREN AND YOUNG PEOPLE

Despite the clear link between children's rights and emergencies, there is a dearth of academic research from crisis contexts that includes children's perspectives. This is particularly true for research in the field of education in emergencies (Hart & Tyrer, 2006; Winthrop & Kirk, 2008). The so-called "emergency alibi," where "emergencies are seen as events that require swift action, rather than opportunities for critical reflection," might explain the lack of child-friendly research (Martone & Neighbor, 2004, p. 11). In other words, if we think we know roughly what is in the best interests of children, we should proceed with urgency, because we do not have time to listen to what they have to say. This can be viewed as an unintended consequence of the CRC—a set of universal rights can lead to a universalized notion of what is in the best interests of children when, in fact, these rights are inextricably bound to cultural, political, and social contexts (Miles & Hossain, 1999; Rwezaura, 1994). Also, in crises there is a tendency to prioritize the rights that correspond to the concept of "basic needs" (e.g., food) over others (e.g., freedom of expression), according to Maslow's hierarchy of needs as outlined in Huitt (2007), so that we essentially return to the understanding of children's rights that predated the CRC.

A few studies of education in crisis contexts do showcase children's voices. Obura (2003) discusses education management strategies in Rwanda since the 1994 genocide. She devotes an entire section to presenting "the voices of children" in order to understand "their perceptions and experiences in terms of schooling in Rwanda today" (Obura, 2003, p. 151). Winthrop and Kirk (2008) explore how primary school students conceptualize their own well-being relative to their experiences with school through the International Rescue Committee's Healing Classrooms Initiative in Ethiopia, Afghanistan, and Sierra Leone. Both studies involve student interviews and are based on the idea that policy and practice affecting students need to incorporate their perspectives, because they give valuable insight into their experiences. By meaningfully including children's perspectives, researchers not only ensure the fulfillment of children's rights, but they also improve the "credibility of the knowledge" derived from their research (Fraser, 2004, p. 26).

In so-called Western contexts, academic literature on meaningful engagement with children in research has burgeoned in the past 2 decades. Scholars from a range of different fields—including psychology, education, anthropology, and sociology—are exploring (1) conceptual and theoretical approaches, (2) ethics, and (3) methods involved in more child-centered research (Christensen & James, 2008). A brief discussion of these three key areas follows, highlighting ideas from challenging and crisis contexts where possible.

A CONCEPTUAL FRAMEWORK
FOR "CHILD-FRIENDLY" RESEARCH

Traditionally, educational approaches to research in challenging and crisis contexts have taken the educational system as the unit of analysis (Winthrop & Kirk, 2008). These approaches, even when considering education as a multilevel system, rarely take children's perspectives into account, preferring instead to rely on researchers' observations and responses from "expert adults" at each level. Child-friendly approaches to education research involve acknowledging the individual child at the center of the system, just as UNICEF's Child-Friendly Schools initiative does. Figures 15.1 and 15.2 show traditional and child-friendly approaches, respectively, to education research.

However, simply placing the child at the center of research does not make a study child-friendly. Engaging in research *with* rather than *about* children requires researchers to consider two key interrelated factors: power dynamics and communication. Christensen and Prout (2002, as cited in Robinson & Kellett, 2004, p. 85) outline four ways children have been viewed in research, moving from least to most empowered:

- the child as object,
- the child as subject,
- the child as social actor,
- the child as participant/co-researcher

Figure 15.1. Traditional Approach to Education Research

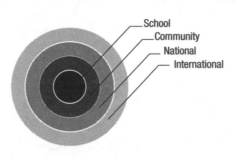

School
Community
National
International

Figure 15.2. Child-Friendly Approach to Education Research

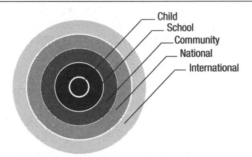

Child
School
Community
National
International

For research to be child-friendly, the researcher must view the child in one of the latter three ways. Of course, extenuating circumstances can limit how the researcher is able to interact with the child, reminding us that "the most appropriate kind of participation will depend on the focus and objectives of the project concerned" (Chronic Poverty Research Centre, 2005–2010, para. 1). Generally, the larger the scope of the project, and the shorter the time frame, the harder it is to treat children as social actors, full participants, and co-researchers.

On a related note, Fraser (2004) asks researchers to contemplate whether research with children should differ from research with adults. The response to this question potentially has enormous implications for the direction the research will take. Often researchers who view children as social actors do not distinguish sharply between adults and children and thus do not find it necessary to change research methods depending on the age of the research subject (Robinson & Kellett, 2004). Others argue that methodologies *do* need to be adapted in work with children, not because of the children's developmental stage, but because "the way in which research can be negotiated with children and young people will differ according to habits and mores which the child or young person has learned. Moreover this involves a degree of acceptance of the power relationships to which the child or young person is already subject" (Fraser, 2004, p. 24). This debate comes down to a question of communication between researcher and researched. Is the researcher able to communicate the research aims to the researched in an intelligible way? Is the researcher able to design data collection methods that allow the researched to communicate their perspectives intelligibly?

ETHICS

Possibly the most dramatic change in the ethical dimension of research with children over the past 3 decades has been a move to contemplate the relationship between researcher and researched, and a consequent effort to treat children with respect (Alderson, 2004). Ensuring the meaningful participation of children, however great or small, rather than simply using them for "decoration and tokenism" is crucial (Hart, 1997, in Clark, McQuail, & Moss, 2003). In other words, asking children to participate for the sake of appearances to further other agendas (political, funding, etc.) is not ethical. There must be a direct and sound correlation between tasks children are asked to perform as part of studies and the findings and policy recommendations derived from those studies.

Studies with children must take into account three major ethical considerations, in addition to integrity of results: informed consent, avoidance of deception, and privacy and confidentiality (Christians, 2005). Some researchers argue there should be no difference in ethical standards for adults and for children, because all social actors are entitled to the same set of rights (Robinson & Kellett, 2004). Others (and we count ourselves among them) argue that while, broadly speaking, the same ethical standards should apply, special considerations need to be made to ensure that research with children is truly ethical. Establishing how to gain informed consent from child participants is particularly challenging. The researcher needs to frame research aims and participants' rights so as to "make sense" to the children involved, because she needs to ensure that children are participating freely and do not feel in any way coerced (Fraser, 2004, p. 23). There is a tension here in giving as much information as possible to avoid deception of participants, without discouraging participation because explanations seem long-winded or confusing (Hill, 2005). For children who are unable to read, researchers must be able to explain the informed consent process. Care should be taken in choosing language that is child-friendly, which varies from context to context.

METHODS

These ethical considerations lead directly to two methodological insights. First, research methods must be age-appropriate and culturally appropriate to help ensure that children feel comfortable participating in the research (Chronic Poverty Research Centre, 2005–2010; Hart & Tyrer, 2006). Collaboration with local researchers may be key in this regard. Failing to consider the cultural framework of the project can lead to the discomfort of participants and ultimately inaccurate findings (Chronic Poverty Research Centre, 2005–2010; Fraser, 2004; Hart & Tyrer, 2006). Second, the research should be engaging and fun. Not only does this help maximize potential benefits for children by giving them an enjoyable activity to participate in, but it also can help give more credible results. Hill (2006) suggests that when children find the research method "boring," as can be the case with, for example, questionnaires, this "can evoke 'subversive' responses" (p. 80). Even when not attempting to be subversive, children sometimes give false responses when asked to participate in a more formal-seeming study, either because they think these responses are what the researcher had in mind, or because they fear punishment for "getting the answer wrong." Finally, as Clark, McQuail, and Moss (2003) point out, a range of diverse research activities that are fun encourages voluntary participation by children from different age groups.

As this discussion implies, there is no objective master list of child-friendly methods that can be followed like recipes when working with children. Rather, a burgeoning body of research with children can provide inspiration when designing studies. These studies tend to involve the development and use of a number of different methods, "not just for the purpose of triangulation, but rather to create manifold perspectives and to listen more effectively" (Clark et al., 2003). However, Greene and Hill (2005) warn that there should always be a clear rationale behind each method (p. 16). Different methods must complement one another as much as possible. In other words, can the data captured by each method be used together to successfully answer the overarching research question(s)?

In the following section, we discuss our own attempts to include children's perspectives in the design of UNICEF's Learning Plus study. We begin with an overview of the study and then move into a discussion of our understanding of child-friendly research and how this informed our approach. We next describe the research methods developed and the rationale behind their design. Where relevant, we include specific examples of findings, challenges faced, and insights gained from developing and using the method in question.

DESIGNING A RESEARCH STUDY WITH A CHILD-FRIENDLY COMPONENT

The Learning Plus study aimed to inform policy and practice that would transform schools into centers of care and support, particularly for vulnerable children. It was a mixed-methods study, involving intra- and international partnerships among six universities and UNICEF (see Figure 15.3).

After conducting an extensive literature review with our New York-based colleagues and African research partners, we determined the need for a list of indicators that could measure the current state and quality of service provision and could later be utilized to measure progress. Quality of services was operationalized according to three guiding principles: inclusiveness (physical and social), participation (of children and adults at the school), and gender equity. We developed an index of indicators for what an ideal Learning Plus school would look like across the dimensions of both policy and practice.[4] A range of methods was designed based on the index, including observation checklists, questionnaires, interviews, and focus groups. A workshop was held in Rwanda in February 2008. This workshop was a crucial component of the process because it allowed us to work with our African

Figure 15.3. Intra- and International Partnerships Involved in the Learning Plus Study

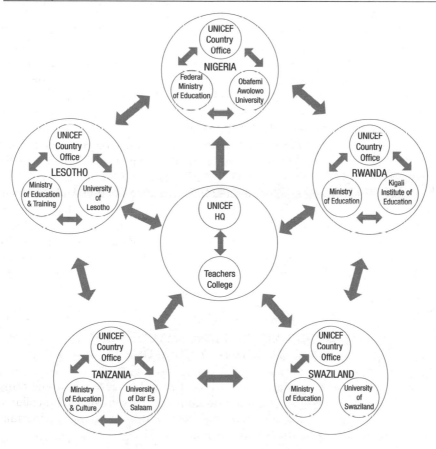

counterparts and UNICEF officers to help ensure the cultural appropriateness and feasibility of the methods designed and to make important modifications.

DESCRIPTION OF THE CHILD-FRIENDLY METHODS

We were influenced strongly by the Mosaic approach when designing the child-friendly component of the study. However, the sheer scale and short time frame of the study restricted the extent to which children could participate in the research and did not allow them to be full participants or co-researchers. Our design was based on a view of children as somewhere between subjects and social actors. Although we took a child-centered approach to our design, we did maintain a more traditional power dynamic between adults and children, because we asked local researchers in collaboration with school administrators to determine which children to include and exclude. Further, we made certain judgments about the maturity and cognitive abilities of the children, and tailored our instruments accordingly (Robinson & Kellett, 2004).

After discussions with our African partners, we realized that our attempts to draft comprehensive informed consent documents for our series of child-friendly instruments would likely have the reverse effect of the desired one. The partners warned us that participants might mistrust our aims, because these documents would seem foreign to children and adults alike. We thus drafted a much-simplified version, delivered orally by researchers, to ensure maximum participation and comfort of informants. An example is presented in Box 15.1.

What follows is a brief description of the methods designed, which includes the rationale for each method, comments about the design (including any modifications made during the workshop), and, where appropriate, findings illustrating how the instruments work. The methods are summarized in Table 15.1.

Tour/Camera Activity

While researchers conducted their own tours of the schools using observation checklists, we felt it would be important to obtain children's perspectives on

---

Box 15.1. Informed Consent (Tour/Camera Activity)

We hope it will be interesting and fun if you are given the chance to help us take photos of different places in your school that mean something to you. We think it is important that the people who make big decisions about schools and education (usually adults!) learn what matters to you and why, to help them make better decisions. *You won't get into trouble for any of the photos that you take! If you don't want us to show anyone outside of our team any of your photos, tell us and we will keep them to ourselves!*

different places, specifically their relationships with physical and social spaces around the school. Consequently, building on the work of Greig and colleagues (2007) and Barker and Weller (2003a, 2003b), we designed the tour/camera activity.

Researchers selected a group of students and asked the students to take them to different places on the school grounds, such as "places where you feel you DON'T belong" and "places that you think need to be improved or changed" (see Figure 15.4). At each location, students assisted the researchers in taking pictures and described why they had taken the re searchers to that specific place (see Figure 15.5). This description of *why* was crucial because, as Barker and Weller (2003a) put it, researchers often end up "giving their own 'adultist' interpretation and assumptions to the pictures" instead of giving children the opportunity to explain their decisions (p. 42). This was highlighted for us during a school visit in Rwanda. When children were asked to take researchers to a place that they did not like or felt scared in, the children led them to the patch of land that the school shared with the local courthouse, and began to take photographs. There were individuals there wearing prisoners' uniforms. We were ready to write about how the school needed a fence between their property and the courthouse because children were scared of the prisoners. However, when asked, the children explained that they were scared of the electricity pole that was there. We thus stressed to researchers the importance of communicating with the children and taking detailed notes of what *they* had to say. Researchers were asked to keep this in mind during data analysis as well. While we encouraged them to look closely at the photographs, we reminded them that the photographs were meant to serve mainly as a mediation point, and that what should be coded were the children's explanations.

Tour/Paper Plate Activity

We wanted to come up with a similar activity to the one outlined above to engage younger children. Drawing on Clark and colleagues (2003), we asked children to decorate plates with a smiling face and a frowning face, which the children

Table 15.1. Child-Friendly Research Methods

Older students (last few grades of primary)	Younger students (first few grades of primary)
Tour/Camera Activity	Tour/Paper Plate Activity
Sending a Message—Writing Activity	Sending a Message—Drawing Activity
A New Student—Writing Activity	A New Student—Drawing Activity
Focus Group for Older Students*	Teddy Bear—Focus Group for Younger Students

*We will not discuss the focus group for older students, because it did not involve any specific child-friendly design elements.

Figure 15.4. Rwandan Children Discuss Where to Take Researchers for the Tour of Their School

Figure 15.5. Researchers Assist Rwandan Student in Taking a Photograph of the School Grounds

used to show how they felt about their surroundings during a tour of the facility with researchers.

In our instructions to local researchers, we asked them to use the observation checklist and responses from the tour/camera activity to decide a route around the school. At key locations, they would ask children to hold up happy plates if they liked the place, and sad plates if they did not. The children were asked to close their eyes in order to prevent them from being influenced by their peers. After counting the number of happy and sad plates, the researchers would ask students what they did/did not like about the place in question, again to ensure that children's views were captured.

One major finding across all countries was that there was a lack of adequate toilet facilities. The Swazi researchers reported that when they took the children to the toilets at some schools and asked them to hold up their plates, there was some confusion as approximately half the students held up happy plates and half held up sad plates. The children who held up the sad plates explained that the toilets were dirty, unsafe, and smelled bad. The children who held up the happy plates agreed that this was the case, but had held up the happy plates because they liked having a place to go to relieve themselves! This demonstrates that school toilets were something they valued highly, but that the quality of those facilities needed to be drastically improved.

Sending a Message—Writing Activity

Adapting an activity proposed by Mahbub (2008) and Messiou (2002), we asked students to write letters that would be sent "to America where there are some people who are really excited to hear about your school and have asked some questions to find out about it." They were invited to write anonymously about their school, describing a typical school day, their favorite things, or bad things that happened at school, to provide useful first-person narrative accounts of children's school experiences. We reasoned that the children would be put at ease to write what they felt because the messages were anonymous and being sent away from school authorities.

A few modifications were made to this instrument as a result of the Rwanda workshop. At first, we used the idea of a "message in a bottle." However, local researchers felt that the bottle would not translate as a relevant cultural symbol, and that this might cause confusion about the purpose of the research. We decided to use big envelopes instead of bottles to collect the messages. Second, when we tested the instrument in a school, the participants were visibly uncomfortable. When one Rwandan researcher asked why the students were upset, they said that they were worried about the essay being an examination. We therefore included a note to researchers about engaging in some activity in the first few minutes of meeting the students to put them at ease and about giving a detailed introduction to the exercise so that it came across more as a letter-writing activity than a test. We also asked researchers to stress that the children would not get into trouble for any of their responses, and that they should keep their letters anonymous.

Sending a Message—Drawing Activity

We designed a drawing activity because we wanted to give younger students "another avenue . . . to express their views and experiences" (Clark et al., 2003, p. 33). Students were invited to draw pictures of adults who worked at their school; something nice that had happened to them or something they liked about school; something they did not like about school; and something they felt the school needed or should have. Researchers were expected to ask questions and take detailed notes as the students drew.

During the Rwanda workshop, one researcher expressed concern about the validity of this method: He felt that using drawing to express oneself was a very "Western" idea and would not necessarily work in an "African" context. However, another researcher disagreed, stating that he felt the children would enjoy the activity and that we would likely get solid findings as a result. While we decided to keep the method, we emphasized the importance of researchers communicating with students about what they were drawing and why (as described in Mahbub, 2008).

For drawing activities to be most useful in research, the artist's own interpretations should be included. Very few researchers wrote detailed notes about what the children said about their drawings, or, more specifically, why they drew things a certain way. As a result, this analysis failed to get at what meanings the children were making of their lived school experiences. In order to generate the kind of data we sought, this activity required more training, more opportunities to practice, and more specific guidance.

New Student Activity—Writing and Drawing Activities

As inclusion was a guiding principle of this study, we wanted to explore students' attitudes toward vulnerable children. We decided to use persona dolls, which have proven valuable tools for aid agencies (e.g., Save the Children) and teachers to communicate with children and allow them to express feelings about vulnerable children (Clark et al., 2003). Building on the Portsmouth Ethnic Minority Achievement Service (2008), we designed the new student activity.

Students were shown a doll that was introduced to them by the researcher as a new student. The researcher described the name, age, cultural background, language, likes, dislikes, and so forth, of the doll, and went on to explain why the child was vulnerable (deciding on a category of vulnerability most applicable to the local context). Students were asked to write anonymous descriptions of how they felt about the child, whether they wanted to be friends with the child, and how they felt the child would be treated at school. Younger students unable to express themselves as clearly through writing were asked to draw a picture of the child at school, thinking about whether they wanted to be friends with the child and how they felt the child would be treated. As with the drawing activity described above, researchers were asked to communicate with the younger students about what they were drawing.

Figure 15.6 and its accompanying excerpt (shown in Box 15.2, on page 267) offer a wonderful example, from the Lesotho country report, demonstrating how data captured through these instruments led to some important findings regarding policies and practice concerning inclusion.

Thus, as can be seen from the Lesotho country report, while the policy environment in the country did not foster inclusion of students with physical disabilities, child-friendly methods made it clear that the students were quite open to that possibility. In addition, these methods gleaned important information in Rwanda about teacher mistreatment of students who were disabled, orphaned, or HIV-positive, which would likely not have come to light had the children not been consulted.

Teddy Bear Activity

Our final method—a focus group for younger students using a teddy bear mediator—was designed to correspond to the focus groups that were run with older students. For this activity, a teddy bear was used as a mediator to find out about the school, building on the work of Clark and colleagues (2003).

Researchers introduced the teddy bear to students as a friend who wanted to help make things better for children around the world by finding out about different children's school experiences. The researchers would pretend the bear was "whispering" questions to them, which would be relayed to the children. We developed a script for the researchers to ensure that a number of issues around children's likes and dislikes, safety and security, nutrition, and physical and mental health were covered. To make the activity as culturally appropriate as possible and to make the children feel comfortable, we asked the local researchers to come up with a typical name for the bear. During the Rwanda workshop, a number of local researchers suggested using a toy hare instead of a teddy bear, because the hare is a popular character in folklore, and thus they felt the children would relate better to a hare. Minor modifications such as these enhanced the cultural relevance of the research activities in important ways.

As can be seen from the following Swazi example, the teddy bear can be a useful mediator in understanding the experiences of younger children at the school:

Figure 15.6. Drawing by a Basotho Child of the New Student Represented by the Persona Doll

All children involved in the teddy bear activity reported that what they like most about school is learning in class and playing with friends at break time. When asked to comment on their drawings, the students commented, "We like being taught how to read, write and speak English and playing with friends." The children also identified a number of things that are bad at the school. The commonly cited bad things were teachers who beat students. "They beat us anywhere they like," said one student. Students also indicated that they did not like teachers who punish students by not allowing them to go for their break or lunch time, teachers who call students by names and embarrass them in front of other students, the school uniform, eating the same diet every day, the broken chairs and desks, the male teachers who propose love to girls, the dirty and smelly toilets, fetching water from the river, students who abuse drugs, teachers who sleep in class and teacher who come to school drunk. (Mazibuko & Gathu, 2009, p. 70)

This excerpt from the Swazi country report demonstrates how child-friendly methods elicit a perspective quite distinct from the one offered by teachers and administrators about the environment at the school: Physical safety at school and getting to school was a major concern expressed by children, in contrast to reports

---

Box 15.2. "New Student" Narrative

Children invariably drew a blind student holding a walking stick and said they would like to have him in their school and be friends with him. Most said they wanted to be friends with him because "we never had a blind friend before" but a few also said because "he's a human being." The name "Tuti Tombela," apparently used by the researcher resulted in much laughter by the children because they found it unusual. But the children said they would like to be friends with him, and other children would too. They would not mind the fact that Tuti was disabled and that all children would take care of him and wash him. However, one child felt that Tuti would be unhappy at her school because other children would regard him as "unfit." Although sympathetic, the child indicated that they would be afraid of him and they would find him rather disgusting. Another boy confirmed that some children would make fun of Tuti, but that he still felt that Tuti needs to attend school so that he can take care of himself. Therefore, while some advised that Tuti should not go to school and embarrass himself, others said that his father should allow Tuti to go to school because [otherwise it] would be infringing on Tuti's rights to education (Lefoka, Nyabanaba, & Sebatane, 2009, p. 66).

---

from administrators and teachers. Further, the method revealed that children derived psychosocial support largely from peers. However, the Swazi researchers reported that at some schools the teddy bear activity was less successful because the children were not convinced that a toy could talk, and thus seemed hesitant to talk freely. This could be because the children were too old for this activity, or because the researchers had not received sufficient training in how to successfully use the teddy bear as a mediator.

CONCLUSION

Across the five cases, the researchers found these child-friendly methods—when used in conjunction with observation checklists, surveys, and interviews with ministry officials, administrators, teachers, parents, and other stakeholders—useful in comparing and contrasting the state of inclusion, participation, and gender equity in policy and in practice. The child-friendly research methods proved particularly valuable, as they revealed interesting findings such as the quality and frequency of a school feeding program, students' fears about safety, the importance of peer psychosocial support, the value placed on working latrines by students, and students' attitudes toward inclusion. In some cases, the data collected from children yielded significant surprises (e.g., about teachers pressuring children for sex); in other cases, the perspectives of children contradicted official reports in ways that required further investigation.

Qualitative research with children is complicated (Greig et al., 2007). By far the biggest challenge we faced when designing these methods was the knowledge that we would not engage with the children ourselves. The success of child-friendly methods depends on the rapport between the researcher and the children. In fact, not only does the researcher need to be adept at conducting qualitative research, but she also needs to be "good with children." A lot of this comes down to practice and exposure. The most successful component of the research design process was the Rwanda workshop, facilitated by the Teachers College researchers and UNICEF headquarters, which brought together researchers from each of the five countries, UNICEF country officers, and, in some cases, government officials. The workshop format prioritized the active participation of all attendees, who had the opportunity to discuss and revise the instruments that had been developed by the New York team. This process resulted in delightfully open discussion among stakeholders and important changes to the instruments.

Had there been more time and resources, it would have been wonderful to extend the workshop to involve the local researchers in the design, rather than simply the modification, of the child-friendly methods themselves, and to provide researchers with more extensive training in each method. Childhood varies according to cultural context and so it would be important to include cultural awareness and appropriateness from the start (Kellett, Robinson, & Burr, 2004; Rwezaura, 1994). In fact, judging by the findings from all five country reports, the child-friendly method with which researchers were most comfortable and that resulted in the strongest analysis was the new student activity, and this was the method that required the most ownership on the part of the local researchers, because it required researchers to come up with a persona for the doll that they thought the children would respond to and that would be most relevant in each unique context.

Our key recommendation for those wishing to conduct research with children in educational settings in the future, particularly in challenging and crisis contexts, is to involve local researchers as much as possible, as early on in the process as possible. Local researchers can give valuable insights into the construction of childhood in their respective cultural contexts. Of course, as discussed above, this may require a significant investment in training—including training in research design, working with children, data collection, and analysis. The advantage of making a significant investment in research training is that hubs of expertise can then be established, which can be drawn from in the future. If there is no one available in the immediate community, researchers from colleges and universities in the country or in the region should be considered. Training teachers in carrying out action research utilizing child-friendly methods would be a useful long-term investment to help ensure that educational research is directly relevant to informing educational practice.

In closing, we hope that other researchers working in challenging and crisis contexts can learn from our missteps and our successes with child-friendly research. If we are serious about children's rights, we need to remember that this rights movement has its roots in trying to help children affected by emergencies, and that we have a duty to continue to come up with creative ways to involve children in their own development.

NOTES

1. For the purposes of this chapter, in accordance with international norms, a *child* is defined as a person who is under the age of 18.

2. For a brief description of UNICEF's Child-Friendly Schools, please visit http://www.unicef.org/girlseducation/files/CFS1Web.pdf.

3. While we do present some findings, this chapter is primarily a methodological one, and, as such, the findings serve mainly as examples of how the methods function. For the findings from the study, please see UNICEF (2010b).

4. This index drew from the Index for Inclusion, the INEE Minimum Standards for Education in Emergencies, Chronic Crises, and Early Reconstruction, and the Sphere Project. It was intended to be a conceptual framework that would provide a comprehensive picture of an ideal Learning Plus school, one that delivers quality education, in close coordination with other sectors, including psychosocial support, physical health, water and sanitation, nutrition, and safety and security.

CHAPTER 16

Innovative Methods in Education in Emergencies Research
A Randomized Trial Assessing Community-Based Schools in Afghanistan

DANA BURDE

Doctors rely routinely on randomized trials to test the effectiveness of medical treatments. Reports of these randomized studies appear in daily newspapers and are considered the "gold standard" to determine the efficacy of a new medication. Although randomized trials were used first in medical science, they have assumed a prominent role in the social sciences and recently have gained popularity among education funders and researchers. Education research in the United States is now heavily influenced by randomized methods.

The use of randomized trials also has surged in international social science studies. A recent profile in *New Yorker* magazine credits Esther Duflo, an economist at the Massachusetts Institute of Technology, and her institute, the Poverty Action Lab, with promoting randomized trials widely among international development organizations (Parker, 2010). Institutions such as the World Bank promote educational research worldwide that employs these methods (Kremer, 2003) and, with randomized trials becoming more familiar, international nongovernmental organizations (NGOs) such as the International Rescue Committee are beginning to use these methods for their program assessments, to measure the impact of their education programs in difficult environments around the world.

In this chapter, I discuss the promise of randomized trials to illuminate the impact of education in emergencies programs[1] on the communities they are intended to serve. Randomized trials have been employed infrequently to study humanitarian programs and never, to my knowledge, to study education in emergencies programs. The chapter proceeds in the following way: I start with an overview of randomized trials as a key feature of evidence-based research and debates about their strengths and weaknesses. I review some of the reasons for the slow incorporation of randomized trials into education in emergencies research. Next, I present my experience conducting a randomized trial as part of a mixed-methods study in Afghanistan. In this study, we randomly assigned community-based schools (CBSs) to remote Afghan villages in 2007, comparing treatment with control villages to test the impact of the program on children's educational outcomes and household-level indicators (control villages received schools in 2008). I argue that with appropriate preparation, randomized trials can be conducted successfully under some of the most challenging conditions and in some of the most hard-to-reach areas of the world. As a complement to qualitative data, they can provide a deeper and more complete understanding of effective elements of education in emergencies programs.

THE CASE AGAINST RANDOMIZED TRIALS

Randomized trials are research designs that study the impact of an intervention by dividing a population into two groups and randomly administering a treatment to one group, but not the other. For example, consider a new reading instruction. The control group receives the status quo while the treatment group receives the new instruction. Assuming that the whole sample is large enough to be statistically similar in all relevant ways (i.e., population differences are evenly distributed across the sample), the only difference between the groups will be the new reading program. Therefore, any change measured between the groups at the end of the study can be attributed to the intervention rather than to other factors such as, for example, wealth, health, interest in reading, or parents who are deeply committed to education. A randomized trial does not assume that these differences are absent, but that proper sampling ensures they appear equally in both groups, thus allowing the researchers to control for their effect. Proponents believe that these are the best research methods for understanding program impact and that if a randomized trial can be implemented properly it should be (Angrist, 2004; Cook, 2003; Duflo, quoted in Parker, 2010; Kremer, 2003).

Critics object to these studies on several counts. First, they argue that randomized trials limit the scope of research, confining studies to only narrow questions that focus on program effectiveness (Lareau, 2009; Lather, 2004; Phillips, 2009; Ranis, 2009). They argue further that these questions are rarely the most interesting to researchers. Since randomized trials focus on cause and effect relationships, an overemphasis on randomized trials constrains creativity and turns inquiries away from understanding "why" and "how" a social phenomenon works or happens (Ranis, 2009; Walters & Lareau, 2009).

The second criticism addresses fidelity to design and implementation. Critics argue that in order to be effective, randomized trials need to be implemented with a level of accuracy that is difficult to achieve. The treatment intervention must be sufficiently discrete so that the control group does not inadvertently receive treatment, thus contaminating the sample. If treatment and control groups are in close proximity, it may be difficult to ensure, for example, that only the teachers in the treatment group receive the new reading training and that the control group is not "contaminated" by the treatment (Henig, 2008; Hess & Henig, 2008; Lareau, 2009).

Finally, critics question the ethics of conducting a randomized trial if one portion of the sample must be denied treatment in order to study the impact of a particular intervention. These critics argue that denying an intervention to the control group potentially leaves a population underserved, an even bigger concern in relation to humanitarian programs. Given skepticism regarding the value of the questions that randomized trials address, a trade-off like this is too great to warrant this type of study design (Clegg & Slife, 2008; Hess & Henig, 2008; Klees, 2008; Steiner-Khamsi, 2009).

These critics have legitimate concerns. Additional reasons humanitarian actors have been slow to incorporate randomized trials into education in emergencies research have to do with complicated logistics and a reluctance to conduct research of any type in such a challenging environment. Research teams require security networks. Aid workers may decry spending money on research when conditions in emergency circumstances are dire and many other needs are prominent. When hundreds of thousands of children lack school buildings or textbooks, it can be difficult to justify spending funds on research studies. Yet amid a barrage of criticism of their work, international bilateral aid agencies and NGOs are increasingly eager to demonstrate the impact of their programs. And aid agencies are increasingly interested in employing these rigorous methods to assess program impact (according to personal conversations with staff from various international NGOs based in the United States).[2]

It is important not to overstate the case against randomized trials. Randomized trials can be useful, particularly in measuring the impact of education interventions, and they are, as yet, underused to assess education in emergencies interventions. As I will show in the next section, the concerns with randomized trials in general, and in humanitarian situations in particular, can be overcome. Moreover, my research in Afghanistan suggests a number of benefits from randomized trials. I argue that although they are not relevant for every interesting research question, they can be conducted in challenging conditions, and they can provide important insights into cause and effect relationships, responding to some of the most urgent and critical questions that educators working in difficult environments have about their programs. When randomized trials are complemented by qualitative methods, they are even more effective. In the next section, I give a detailed account of the randomized trial that my co-investigator and I carried out in Afghanistan, and the strengths and weaknesses of the method.[3]

STUDY OF COMMUNITY-BASED SCHOOLS IN AFGHANISTAN

This study worked with a large international U.S.-based NGO, Catholic Relief Services (CRS), to randomly assign their CBSs to eligible villages in a remote rural area of Afghanistan and to measure the effects of community-based schooling on children, households, and villages. Launching this study successfully required significant negotiations with NGO partners and the Afghan government, several years of work toward garnering grants, and a successful pilot study to test field procedures before all agreements were reached and the full funding secured to carry out the large-scale randomized trial. This section summarizes the background and significance of the research question, the randomized trial design and execution, and the qualitative methods that complemented it.

Background and Significance

In 2004, when what I call the "education in emergencies movement" was beginning to expand, I sought to understand the impact of education in emergencies programs on populations affected by conflict. Although trained primarily in qualitative methods, specifically case studies and ethnographies, I decided to carry out a randomized trial with a co-investigator (an economist) because of the robustness this kind of method offered for testing social service interventions. Three key issues underscore the importance of conducting this randomized trial of CBSs in Afghanistan.

First, community-based education—wherein schools are based in mosques or homes and teachers are members of the community—is an increasingly popular humanitarian intervention in countries emerging from conflict. Where the educational system has collapsed or government capacity is weak, CBSs are used to provide education services quickly. This humanitarian policy is buttressed by three broader international trends: (1) decreased government budgets devoted to social services; (2) increased focus on universal education principles; and (3) international conventions that call for community participation in education. Community-based schools are widely used as a way for governments to move toward universal primary enrollment in the context of limited budgets (Bray, 2000; P. Rose, 2003) or system breakdowns (Burde, 2004).

Second, international agencies promote community-based education both for its potential impact on social and educational outcomes and for its influence on the systems through which educational services are delivered. Communities participating in these programs typically provide classroom space as well as administrative support from community associations. International agencies believe that working through community associations (e.g., parent teacher associations, community education committees) may promote structural reform while enhancing the indirect social benefits for children and their families by embedding schools in their communities. In countries recovering from conflict, community associations are considered an essential element for enhancing participation among marginalized communities, strengthening a community's commitment to education, and increasing community cohesion. International aid agencies support these education programs to improve child welfare, to increase girls' enrollment, and to protect children (Canadian International Development Agency, 2001; Machel, 1996; Nicolai & Triplchorn, 2003; Sinclair, 2002).

Finally, although qualitative case studies are numerous, there is scant robust, quantitative data collected on these programs. The research questions in this study include both school-based issues related to enrollment, attendance, and achievement among boys and girls, as well as questions regarding the relationship between schools and the communities in which they are located.

Pilot Study

A qualitative pilot study was a critical first step to create the necessary conditions for the full-scale study. In 2005–2006 the pilot study examined the differences in adolescents' outcomes (protection and life chances) across two NGO schools, one government school, one religious school, and a group of unenrolled children. A total of 49 adolescents (12–14 years old) were given an attitude and behavior survey, 5 classrooms were observed, approximately 90 students were administered achievement tests, and 6 adolescents were interviewed using a semistructured qualitative interview protocol. The pilot study was a critical component preceding the randomized trial for the following reasons: (1) Relationship building: it allowed me to build a relationship with CRS, the NGO implementing the program that would later become the randomized intervention under study; (2) Contextual understanding: questions examined in the randomized trial were guided by the questionnaires used in the pilot study, and training provided to local CRS staff helped develop capacity that was critical to training a large survey team the following year; and (3) Field procedures: the way in which the randomized trial was managed and administered was based on information learned during the pilot study. The multiple complexities (language, culture, conflict, extreme weather) inherent in a foreigner's work in Afghanistan required particularly heavy investment in advance of the large-scale study, and CRS provided significant field support to facilitate the research.

CRS is an international U.S.-based NGO that supports relief and development programs in countries around the world. CRS has worked in Afghanistan since 2001, just after the fall of the Taliban. CRS works in several provinces around Kabul, but the bulk of its work takes place in the center and west of the country, in Herat and Ghor Provinces. Because the security situation had deteriorated by 2006 (riots, increased suicide attacks, ongoing kidnapping threats), I arranged to work directly with CRS to carry out the pilot study in the Panjshir valley. CRS provided housing, vehicles, drivers, program staff, office space, office infrastructure, and security tracking (satellite phones and a call-in system).

I trained Afghan staff[4] in basic research methods, randomized trials, informed consent, and standardized interviewing techniques. Reviewing the attitude and behavior survey line by line with CRS local Afghan education staff increased the survey's relevance and meaning. Staff discussed, for example, which measures would provide the best indication of economic status and debated questions that some believed were too sensitive to ask children. The achievement tests for math and Dari language were also critical instruments designed for the study, as no national achievement tests existed at the time in Afghanistan.

Rumor, suspicion of Western secular ideas and values, and nationalism posed security risks and barriers to research. I was advised to scrap informed consent forms[5] because the concept of "confidentiality" raised suspicions among parents and teachers. In a society where behavior is strictly regulated, references to keeping conversations private may raise suspicions about inappropriate behavior (otherwise why would confidentiality be necessary?). Study *supporters* (teachers, mullahs, government administrators) commented on Western attempts to brainwash Afghans, to convert Muslims to Christianity,[6] or to weaken madrasas by cutting off funds and replacing them with NGO schools. Some asked who was behind the study, and whether I was "sympathetic to the Afghan nation."

To facilitate the research and ease security concerns, I developed a network of contacts throughout the country among those with regional, national, and international interests in the study results. Data from the pilot study were entered into a preliminary database, and I gave briefings to the Ministry of Education, UNICEF, CRS, CARE, the Afghan Research and Evaluation Unit (AREU), and USAID. The Minister of Education was interested in the future of the study and committed to research-based approaches toward policy design and implementation. International agencies were interested in the study results, but were particularly interested in studying the effects of their interventions on their hoped-for outcomes. They expressed interest in better understanding the effects of their own programs.

Based on the results of the pilot study and feedback from local and international staff, I and my co-investigator modified the study to provide a robust comparison between children enrolled in NGO schools and unenrolled children, reduced the emphasis on comparing across four categories of schools, and revised the research questions so that they were more closely linked to the intervention that CRS conducts in Ghor and Herat.

The Program

CRS is part of the Partnership for Advancing Community Education in Afghanistan (PACE-A) consortium. PACE-A is a 5-year, $24 million USAID-funded program that began in June 2006 and is meant to "expand quality learning and life opportunities for marginalized communities and their children in Afghanistan" (PACE Summary, 2006, p. 1) via a consortium of NGOs tasked with providing hundreds of CBSs for children between the ages of 6 and 11 in 19 provinces across Afghanistan. The CRS portion of the program was ambitiously intended to reach approximately 80 villages in Ghor and Herat Provinces by the end of 2008.

Ghor Province is among the most remote and inaccessible regions, covering a mountainous plateau subject to harsh winters and relatively mild summers. When this study was carried out, conflict in Ghor was sporadic and intertribal rather than Taliban-related. Roughly 90% of the 485,000 inhabitants of the province live in rural villages organized by tribe or clan. Few of these villages have government schools. This is not a result, exclusively, of Afghanistan's multiple conflicts—these villages have never been reached by the government educational system. At the same time, parents consider education critical to the development and socialization of their children and go to great lengths to enroll them in school. A small minority of villagers cope with the barriers by sending their children, almost exclusively their boys, to the closest government school. On average these children walk 2 hours one-way to get to school. Once there, the school day typically lasts 2.5 hours. After school, the children return home, again on foot.

In establishing community schools in remote areas where children previously have not had access to education, CRS has several goals: to increase access to education generally, and particularly for girls; to strengthen community-based associations such as parent teacher associations and community education committees; to provide education that meets a certain standard of quality; and to avoid the pitfalls that have hindered other community-based school programs in the past by developing close and careful coordination with the Afghan Ministry of Education (MoE). Beyond these goals, it is widely expected that community associations will enhance general support for education, and that the program will provide indirect benefits to children, such as protection and life chances. CRS believes that educating teachers to use alternative forms of discipline (instead of corporal punishment) may reduce violence in the classroom, and that the more intimate atmosphere of a community school, supported by community associations, may encourage positive social and educational outcomes.

Prior to establishing schools, CRS identifies the district as secure enough for its staff to work in without excessive risk. Next, CRS chooses the highest priority communities based on need and the following criteria: (1) distance from a government school (at least 3 kilometers); (2) level of interest expressed by a community in a CBS and willingness to send girls; (3) availability of potential teachers (especially women); (4) community willingness to mobilize resources (teachers' salaries and classrooms); and (5) support from the MoE. When the program begins, CRS first mobilizes community support. Community members identify an existing space to host the school (room in a home or mosque) and help support the teacher, who usually comes from the community. CRS provides training to these teachers, materials for the classroom (government curriculum), and regular monitoring to track progress over time.

To carry out the randomized trial, we (the researchers) asked CRS to conduct a broad needs assessment that would identify all of the villages that would be eligible for schools in the first and second years of the program (rather than identifying only the group for year one). Once they had the list of eligible villages for both years, we would determine randomly which villages would receive schools in 2007 versus 2008. Thus, all villages in the sample would eventually receive schools, but the 2007 villages would get them first. These schools would then encompass a "treatment group" that could be compared with a "control group" after 1 year of the intervention had been completed. In this way, we responded to one of the key ethical concerns about randomized trials: no one was denied education. Instead, CRS identified equally needy groups and allocated schools in a way that was both fair and optimal for studying the program impact over the 2 years that it would take to start the program anyway.

Still, CRS staff expressed concern both about spending money on research when villages needed services, and about changing their standard needs assessment procedures in order to provide 2 years' worth of eligible villages rather than one "most needy" group. We explained that the grant money used was available only for research and therefore the study did not reduce resources that otherwise would have been available for programs. We also argued that randomization was a fair way to allocate schools among eligible villages, given the constraints associated with needs assessments, specifically the difficulty of selection based on need without bias.

Randomized Trial Research Design

We had to modify our original design in a number of ways in the field—a testament to the flexibility required for all education in emergencies research. In the original design, 80 to 100 villages were slated to receive a CRS school. Of these, half were intended to be randomly assigned to receive a CRS school in 2007. Those villages were to be divided into four treatment groups: the first was to receive only the standard CRS training given to all CRS schools; a second group was to receive an extra training module for the community association that encourages girls' education; the third was to receive a module on alternatives to corporal punishment; the fourth was to receive both special components. This two-level randomization design was intended to allow us to evaluate both the effects of the CRS schools in general and the effects of *variations* in the CRS program.

In fact, given numerous constraints, the sample size shrank before the study began to 34 villages. Schools were randomly assigned to these 34 villages in two districts. From CRS reports, we were able to assume that all villages in both districts were relatively similar. In order to address possible regional differences within the province, we stratified the sample at the district level. Deteriorating security resulted in additional attrition in the southern district toward the end of the first completed round of data collection. The final sample consisted of 31 villages, 805 households, and 1,490 children. Security problems affected treatment and control groups equally; thus the number of villages assigned to each group remained roughly the same.

Originally, we intended to collect the data in two phases: baseline and final. Because of the problems with security and the decline in number of villages, however, we carried out data collection over three phases: baseline in Spring 2007,[7] follow-up in Fall 2007, and final in Spring 2008. We believed that expecting results within a short interval was appropriate given the nature of the work (rapid delivery of services) and the contrast between children's experiences before they went to school and after they started school. Finding such results within a few months is also consistent with experimental results from programs implemented in more stable areas in the world (see, e.g., Banerjee, Cole, Duflo, & Linden, 2007; He, Linden, & MacLeod, 2006).

Original Hypotheses

The proposed research design was intended to allow us to test the following primary hypotheses:

- Hypothesis one, attendance/enrollment: Children living in a village that receives a CRS school will be more likely to enroll in school and will attend more regularly than children in other villages.
- Hypothesis two, learning: Children who live in villages that receive a CRS school will perform better on academic achievement tests on math and language skills than children in other villages.
- Hypothesis three, indirect social outcomes: Children who live in villages that receive a CRS school will report higher levels of social integration (e.g., more reported ties to other children on social network measures), higher levels of security (e.g., reporting comfort in walking in the community), and higher levels of safety (e.g., fewer reports of abuse) than children who live in other villages.
- Hypothesis four, comparative experiences:

  a. Compared with communities without this module, in communities given the training module encouraging support for girls' education, girls will be more likely to attend school.

    b. Compared with children attending other CRS schools, children attending CRS schools in which the teacher receives training on disciplinary alternatives to corporal punishment will report less corporal punishment.

    c. Children who, absent the CRS program, would have had no education or attended a government or Qur'anic school, but who were able to attend a CRS school, will report better outcomes on the above measures than children who had these alternative experiences in villages without a CRS school.

We were able to execute the study to respond to hypotheses one through three successfully. Because of the smaller-than-intended sample size, and because of the obstacles encountered, as described above, the actual design that we were able to carry out included the basic comparisons between treatment and control groups, but did not include the intended comparisons of variations within treatment. Table 16.1 represents the actual study conducted.

Research Protocol: Study Execution

The research protocol comprised five stages: (1) preparation, staff training, and randomization; (2) Spring 2007 baseline survey (including household data, child questionnaire, attitude and behavior survey, achievement test); (3) Fall 2007 mid-term survey (including attendance/enrollment check, household data, child questionnaire, achievement test, friendship networks, teacher survey, monitoring); (4) Spring 2008 final survey (household data, child questionnaire, achievement test, teacher survey); and (5) Summer 2008 round of qualitative data collection (semistructured interviews with teachers, village leaders, school management committee members). A second round of qualitative interviews was planned for September 2008, but was cancelled because of deteriorating security.

Table 16.1. Actual Study Conducted

	CRS school in 2007 n = 31 villages; n = 805 households; n = 1,490 children aged 6–11	
	Yes in 2007	No in 2007 (Would have schools in 2008)
Type of CRS School	Group 1: Normal CRS Class 13 Villages 635 Households	Group 2: No CRS Schools 18 Villages 628 Households

The attitude and behavior survey was a condensed version of the one field-tested in the pilot study with children aged 11–14; it included about 30 of the original 120 questions. It was administered only to children aged 9–11 and only during the baseline data collection. We discovered that the children were unable to respond to these basic questions regarding their activities,[8] and as a result we expanded the questionnaire for the head of the household, adding additional questions about the children. The achievement test was a simple math and language test based on experiences in the pilot study with both enrolled and unenrolled children. The math test was delivered with oral prompts (reading the questions) and written prompts (pictures). The language portion also was delivered with oral (reading) and written (letter identification, simple words) prompts. The level of difficulty of questions was varied enough to discriminate among different levels of achievement.

The survey team consisted of approximately 18 Afghan researchers managed by an Afghan Research Supervisor.[9] The team received extensive training in standardized interviewing before conducting door-to-door surveys. For all three rounds of data collection, the team surveyed every household in every village in the study, interviewing every head of household, and administering achievement tests for every child between the ages of 6 and 11. The surveyors returned repeatedly to locate and interview any children who were missing from the village. They visited government schools to determine whether children enrolled in the study attended government area schools. Each round of surveying took between 6 and 8 weeks to complete.

The data were collected to measure both longitudinal change and impact compared across treatment and control villages. To determine longitudinal impact, all of the respondents (both heads of households and children) were coded and tracked (matched) throughout the rounds of data collection. Matches were determined according to several indicators, including primarily global positioning system (GPS) coordinates. The surveyors also recorded GPS coordinates for school locations (both government and CBSs) so that effects of distance to school could be measured on boys' and girls' educational outcomes.

Qualitative Component of Large-Scale Study

The randomized trial was complemented by a qualitative component. While the quantitative data collected during the randomized trial helped us answer important questions about impact, the qualitative portion addressed some of the "why" questions that our randomized trial could not answer. In our study, we explored one case, the CRS program, in multiple sites (villages in Ghor). The qualitative case component was intended to help us understand more about:

- the *program*, that is, CRS's PACE-A program;
- the *place*, that is, country, province, districts, and villages in which we were collecting data;

- the various *institutions* that were part of our study or influenced it: that is, households, families, schools (government and CBS), mosques, School Management Committees (SMCs), village shuras, MoE; and
- the *individuals* that were part of our study or influenced it, that is, children, parents/heads of households, teachers, village headmen (arbobs), CRS education staff members, CRS managers, PACE-A directors.

Information for the case study came from a variety of sources: documents, observations, and interviews. I list four main categories here that we explored in our semistructured interview protocols in order to understand the randomized results in more detail. These categories correspond to the categories of questions we explored in our quantitative questionnaires:

- demographics (family structure, economic activities, exposure to conflict);
- educational indicators and outcomes (attitudes toward education; children's enrollment, attendance, and achievement);
- discipline and safety (in school and at home); and
- community (civic awareness, trust in institutions, voice, tolerance).

We explored variations on these topics through the interviews with parents, teachers, mullahs, SMC members, and village headmen (arbobs).

PRELIMINARY FINDINGS

At the time of this writing, data analysis of this study was incomplete, and therefore we could not include a full summary of the findings. I provide here a summary of our first set of analyses. The CRS program was successful in its faithful and rigorous application of a randomized approach to its education intervention in Ghor Province, and, as a result, we were able to isolate our questions of interest and study their impact. The randomized trial design allows us to make strong statements about the ability of the program to eliminate gender disparity in education in remote Afghan villages. We have clear findings on the questions related to the most direct program impact—enrollment, attendance, and achievement. We found that CBSs have a dramatic effect on children's academic participation and performance, and have tremendous potential for reducing existing gender disparities in rural areas in Afghanistan. Children are almost 50% more likely to attend school if there is a CBS available to them. Most important, the rate of girls' attendance increases by 15 percentage points more than that of their male counterparts (for a detailed discussion of these findings, see Burde & Linden, 2010).

Proximity to school was the key reason cited by parents, teachers, and community leaders for these dramatic results. See Figure 16.1 for a representation of enrollment and proximity to school.

In the qualitative interviews that complemented the survey data, respondents repeatedly noted distance as the primary reason their children did not attend government schools. Distance impacted girls and very young boys more significantly than boys age 9 or older. Interviewees cited insecurity and propriety as the main reasons they kept girls home from school. It was not because they consider it improper or culturally inappropriate for girls to attend school, but rather because they consider it dangerous and culturally inappropriate for girls to walk long distances unaccompanied to go anywhere. Impropriety in these villages is defined, among other things, by unaccompanied travel among strangers (meaning men since women's public roles are restricted). Thus, *education* for girls is socially acceptable, but the *travel* required to attend most schools is not. This is critical information. Many foreigners assume that Afghans do not want to educate their girls or are hesitant at best. However, our findings show that when issues of distance are addressed, at the primary level (up to and including age 11), parents are eager to send their girls to school and do so in essentially equal numbers as their boys. In contrast to centrally located schools, attending school inside their villages does not challenge norms of propriety for girls because the schools are in close proximity and villages are small.

Figure 16.1. Enrollment and Proximity

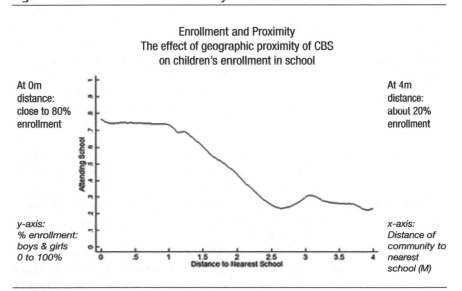

Source: Reproduced from Burde & Linden, 2010

DISCUSSION

These findings are robust, and the study was not weakened by the drawbacks that critics point to when they cite their concerns about randomized trials. First, although our question was narrow and targeted, our study focused on some of the questions that were most relevant for measuring the impact of this community-based school program.

Second, the treatment and control groups were separated adequately, and we do not believe that any contamination occurred. Because we randomized villages in clusters, the villages that received schools were sufficiently distant from those that had not yet received them to avoid most if not all interaction between them. We know that no children from control villages attended CBSs in treatment villages, and none of the control villages received schools, materials, or teacher training. In the event, however, that spillover effects occurred, we can use statistical methods to account for this.

Third, although ethical concerns are significant, we do not believe that this study violated our ethics. Whether or not the study took place, CRS would not have been able to provide community-based schools at the same time to all of the villages in our sample. As noted above, they had planned to phase in the schools over time using a standard needs assessment approach to determine which villages should receive schools first. NGO needs assessments are relatively unsystematic and imprecise, particularly in volatile environments. NGO staff may identify villages based on criteria beyond need—for example, personal connection, proximity, or a vocal constituency. Thus, provided that all villages eventually received the service in question, randomly selecting the villages that received services first should not be any more detrimental to communities than a standard needs assessment would be. All villages in the sample received schools by the second year of the program.

Finally, despite the success of the randomized trial, it is important to note that our qualitative methods were critical to understanding more than the basic program results. That is, while the randomized trial shows that children were enrolled and attended school, and that they learned while there, it does not reveal why this is the case. Understanding why parents are willing to send their children to school—girls as well as boys—requires qualitative data that shed light on cultural norms, security, and community relations. Through qualitative interviews with community members and key stakeholders, we are able to provide a level of detail, depth, nuance, and vividness (Rubin & Rubin, 2005) that the results from the randomized trial alone cannot show.

Although I argue that our research design was successful at addressing or avoiding the common pitfalls of randomized trial designs, we faced logistical challenges that were nearly insurmountable. Insecurity in countries affected by conflict is uneven. Peaceful neighborhoods exist within explosive cities, and calm provinces may endure in corners of a restive country. Within conflict-affected areas, there is also significant variation. One area may be plagued by criminal violence, while another may be characterized by ideological or ethnic conflict. Some may experience all three kinds of violence. As noted above, Ghor Province is relatively calm. It does not face the threat of the Taliban that is now prevalent in many parts of Afghanistan, yet it remains a lawless area, governed by various local strongmen who feud and shift allegiances periodically. In addition, because of its altitude, it experiences some of the most severe weather in the country—deep freezes and heavy snows in the winter, floods in the spring.

Carrying out a complicated study under such difficult circumstances was challenging. I signed a Memorandum of Understanding with CRS at the start of the study that included a security agreement, and I relied almost entirely on CRS's security network to make our travel decisions. CRS had longstanding and close relationships with the communities in which it worked, but this did not prevent a serious incident from occurring, and a number of CRS staff and most of our survey team were caught in the crossfire. Given the nature of the conflict in Ghor—the lack of Taliban and the absence of U.S. troops—neither we nor CRS were perceived to be parties to the conflict. Rather we were caught up in existing local tribal dynamics and social norms that used violence against visitors (us) to make a point against the perceived host (a rival strongman). The perpetrators' intention was to warn, not to harm, and our team was very lucky to emerge from this incident only shaken, not injured. My friend and colleague, Jackie Kirk, was working on the PACE-A program for the International Rescue Committee in the eastern part of Afghanistan when she and her colleagues were killed by the Taliban. It is beyond the scope of this chapter to discuss the tipping point when conditions deteriorate to such an extent that delivering aid, or studying it, is no longer feasible. This is an urgent area for future research.

CONCLUSION

In this study, we overcame barriers to research—both the resistance on the part of the humanitarian aid community to carrying out a research study in such a difficult environment and the difficulties that we encountered in this environment. In addition, we conducted the study without being overly encumbered by the constraints cited by the critics of randomized trials—narrow questions, fidelity to design, or ethical issues. Indeed, it is the randomized trial that has permitted us to provide authoritative answers to key questions about community-based schooling and education in emergencies. While we support the choice of a randomized trial, the study was successful, in part, because it took a mixed-methods approach. The qualitative data that complemented the quantitative portion of the study allowed us both to develop our research instruments as well as to explore "how" and "why" questions that uncovered major events in the course of the program and descriptive details of village life that helped explain why our questionnaires produced the results that they did.

We presented the findings to key stakeholders in education in Afghanistan, including European and U.S. bilateral donors, international and national NGOs, and the Afghan MoE. We showed how children's attendance varies with distance from school, and how this outcome varies between boys and girls. Close to 80% of the Afghan population lives in rural areas, most of them in villages with 500 or fewer inhabitants. Providing access to education for this widely dispersed, rural population poses an enormous challenge for the MoE. The MoE understood from our presentation that building central schools will not serve girls or young boys in many areas. For now, primary schools must be placed in villages in order to reach all Afghan children, girls as well as boys. Similarly, CRS and PACE-A circulated these results widely among U.S. policymakers and Afghan partners.

To what extent the favorable reception of our findings to date is associated with the use of a randomized trial is difficult to discern. Perhaps because quantitative findings make possible, in a way that qualitative studies are not able to do, systematic, numeric assessments of phenomena that affect large groups of people, quantitative or mixed-methods studies may command more attention from policymakers, lawmakers, and casual consumers of research studies who attribute importance to quantifiable results. Qualitative studies provide information that is no less crucial. Yet, particularly in assessing program impact, well-administered randomized trials offer strong explanations for cause and effect relationships. Finally, given that most donors request regular quantifiable assessments of the impact of the programs they fund, donors and policymakers welcome results based on experimental designs.

As education programs for populations affected by conflict and disaster continue to expand, it is essential that academics study many aspects of these programs—processes as well as impact—asking important questions that are best answered using either rigorous qualitative or quantitative methods or both combined. Given practitioners' urgency in learning whether and to what extent they have affected the populations they intend to serve, randomized trials are particularly well-suited to respond to questions that relate to impact. Where humanitarians launch innovative education programs, academics also should play a key role, creating checks and balances in the aid system by measuring the impact of the programs, producing comprehensive studies, and contributing to the growth of collective knowledge.

NOTES

Thank you to all of the Catholic Relief Services staff, colleagues at Columbia University, Afghan survey team, research assistants, and others who made this study possible. For a detailed list of study supporters, please see Burde and Linden (2010). And thanks to Elisabeth King and Leigh Linden for their very useful comments on an earlier draft of this chapter. Funding for the large-scale study was provided by the National Science Foundation, the Spencer Foundation, and the Weikart Family Foundation. Funding for the pilot study was provided by the Columbia University Institute for Social and Economic Research and Policy, the Weikart Family Foundation, and the U.S. Institute of Peace.

1. "Education in emergencies programs" refers to education interventions typically carried out by international NGOs and funded by bilateral organizations in countries affected by conflict or disaster.

2. See also 3ie (www.3ieimpact.org) and its partnerships with British and Australian government aid agencies.

3. Leigh Linden, Assistant Professor of Economics and International Affairs at Columbia University was my co-principal investigator on this study beginning in 2007, after the pilot study ended.

4. Four staff were full-time employees of CRS on "loan" to the pilot project; two were hired specifically for the project.

5. Researchers at U.S. universities are required to receive "informed consent" from subjects. This is meant to safeguard the rights of study participants.

6. CRS is a humanitarian agency working with all people regardless or race or creed and is in no way involved in religious conversion.

7. We were unable to complete baseline data collection because of security interruptions.

8. The children in the pilot study were slightly older (1–2 years) and lived in less remote areas than those in this study, so perhaps this accounts for the difference in their ability to articulate responses.

9. The Afghan survey team carried out exceptionally good work, led by the Research Supervisor, Dr. Saeed Mahmoodi, who paid remarkable attention to detail and remained astonishingly calm under pressure.

References

Afghanistan Research and Evaluation Unit (AREU) & World Bank. (2010). *The A to Z guide to Afghanistan assistance 2010*. Retrieved from http://www.areu.org.af/index.php?option=com_docman&task=doc_download&gid=762&Itemid=26

Agency for Co-operation and Research in Development (ACORD). (2001). *The situation of child heads of households in Rwanda: A significant challenge*. Kigali: Author.

Aguilar, P., & Retamal, G. (2009). Protective environments and quality education in humanitarian contexts. *International Journal of Educational Development, 29*(1), 3–16.

Akresh, R., & de Walque, D. (2010). *Armed conflict and schooling: Evidence from the 1994 Rwandan genocide*. Washington, DC: World Bank Development Research Group.

Alderson, P. (2004). Ethics. In S. Fraser, V. Lewis, S. Ding, M. Kellett, & C. Robinson (Eds.), *Doing research with children and young people* (pp. 97–112). London: Sage.

Al-Haj, M. (2005). National ethos, multicultural education, and the new history textbooks in Israel. *Curriculum Inquiry, 35*(1), 47–71.

Allport, G. W. (1958). *The nature of prejudice*. Garden City, NY: Doubleday Anchor Books.

Anastacio, A., & Stannard, H. (2011). People come and go but systems remain: Strengthening the MoE system for community education. In M. Sigsgaard (Ed.), *On the road to resilience: Capacity development with the Ministry of Education in Afghanistan* (pp. 117–132). Paris: IIEP.

Angrist, J. (2004). American education research changes tack. *Oxford Review of Economic Policy, 20*(2), 198–212.

Apfel, R. J., & Simon, B. (2000). Mitigating discontents with children in war: An ongoing pyschoanalytic inquiry. In A. C. G. M. Robben & M. M. Suárez-Orozco (Eds.), *Cultures under siege: Collective violence and trauma* (pp. 102–130). Cambridge: Cambridge University Press.

Appadurai, A. (1996). *Modernity at large*. Minneapolis: University of Minnesota Press.

Arafat, C., & Boothby, N. (2003). *A psychosocial assessment of Palestinian children*. Ramallah: Secretariat of the National Plan of Action for Palestinian Children, Save the Children.

Arefee, M. A. (2011). Capacity development, challenges, achievements, and next steps from the MoE's perspective. In M. Sigsgaard (Ed.), *On the road to resilience: Capacity development with the Ministry of Education in Afghanistan* (pp. 89–116). Paris: IIEP.

Asociación de la Mujer Maya Ixil (ADMI) y M. Brinton Lykes. (2000). *Voces e Imágenes: Mujeres Maya Ixiles de Chajul. Voices and Images: Mayan Ixil Women of Chajul*. Iqul Tuch'Ivatzib'al: Inq'a Ixoq aj Tenam Tx'aul. Chajul, Guatemala: ADMI.

Avery, P. G., Johnson, D. W., Johnson, R. T., & Mitchell, J. M. (1999). Teaching an understanding of war and peace through structured academic controversies. In A. Raviv, L. Oppenheimer, & D. Bar-Tal (Eds.), *How children understand war and peace: A call for international peace education* (pp. 261–277). San Francisco: Jossey-Bass.

Bagoyoko, N., & Gibert, M. V. (2009). The linkage between security, governance and development: The European Union in Africa. *Journal of Development Studies, 45*(5), 789–814.

Baines, E., Brown, S., & Thomson, S. M. (2008). Inside Rwanda's gender revolution. *The Guardian*. Retrieved from http://www.guardian.co.uk/commentisfree/2008/oct/13/rwanda-gender

Bamusanire, E., Byiringiro, J., Munyakazi, A., & Ntagaramba, J. (2006a). *Primary social studies 4: Pupil's book*. Kigali: Macmillan Rwanda.

Bamusanire, E., Byiringiro, J., Munyakazi, A., & Ntagaramba, J. (2006b). *Primary social studies 5: Pupil's book*. Kigali: Macmillan Rwanda.

Bamusanire, E., Byiringiro, J., Munyakazi, A., & Ntagaramba, J. (2006c). *Primary social studies 6: Pupil's book*. Kigali: Macmillan Rwanda.

Banerjee, A., Cole, S., Duflo, D., & Linden, L. (2007). Remedying education: Evidence from two randomized experiments in India. *Quarterly Journal of Economics, 122*(3), 1235–1264.

Barakat, B., Karpinska, Z., & Paulson, J. (n.d.). *Desk study: Education and fragility*. Paper presented to INEE Working Group on Education and Fragility, Paris.

Baranyi, S., & Powell, K. (2005a). *Bringing gender back into Canada's engagement in fragile states: Options for CIDA in a whole of government approach*. Ottawa: North-South Institute.

Baranyi, S., & Powell, K. (2005b). *Fragile states, gender equality and aid effectiveness: A review of donor perspectives*. Ottawa: North-South Institute.

Barker, J., & Weller, S. (2003a). "Is it fun?" Developing children centred research methods. *The International Journal of Sociology and Social Policy, 23*(1/2), 33–58.

Barker, J., & Weller, S. (2003b). "Never work with children?" The geography of methodological issues in research with children. *Qualitative Research, 3*(2), 207–227.

Bartulovic, A. (2006). Nationalism in the classroom: Narratives of the war in Bosnia Herzegovina (1992–1995) in the history textbooks of the Republic of Srpska. *Studies in Ethnicity and Nationalism, 6*(3) 51–72.

Bennell, P., & Akyeampong, K. (2007). *Teacher motivation in Sub-Saharan Africa and South Asia* (Educational Paper No. 71). London: DfID.

Bernard, C., Jones, S., Oliker, O., Thurston, C., Steamsand, B., & Cordell, K. (2008). *Women and nation-building* Santa Monica, CA: Rand Center for Middle East Public Policy.

Betancourt, T., Winthrop, R., Smith, W., & Dunn, G. (2002, October). Emergency education and psychosocial adjustment: Displaced Chechen youth in Ingushetia. *Forced Migration Review, 15*, 28–30.

Betts, A. (2005). *International cooperation and the targeting of development assistance for durable solutions: Lessons from the 1980s* (Working Paper No. 107). Geneva: UNHCR.

Bird, L. (2003). *Surviving school: Education for refugee children from Rwanda, 1994–1996*. Paris: International Institute for Education Planning (IIEP).

Bird, L. (2010). A tribute to Jackie: Trainer, researcher and scholar. *Girlhood Studies: An Interdisciplinary Journal, 3*(1), 178–179.

Bloom, A. (Ed. & Trans.). (1991). *The Republic of Plato* (2nd ed.). New York: Basic Books.

Bonham Carter, R. (2007). Five girls killed in mortar attack on school in Baghdad. Retrieved from http://www.unicef.org/emerg/iraq_38180.html

Boyden, J. (2000, September 10–13). *Social healing in war-affected and displaced children.* Paper presented at the International Consultation on Children in Adversity, Oxford.

Bradbury, M. (1995). Aid under fire: Redefining relief and development assistance in unstable situations. London, HMSO.

Bragin, M. (2004). *Education for all in the conflict zones of Uganda: Opportunities, challenges and a way forward* (Draft discussion document). Kampala: Basic Education and Policy Support, Ministry of Education and Sports, Republic of Uganda.

Brannelly, L., Ndurahutse, S., & Rigaud, C. (2009). *Donors' engagement: Supporting education in fragile and conflict-affected states.* Paris: IIEP/Center for British Teachers (CfBT).

Bray, M. (2000). *Community partnerships in education: Dimensions, variations and implications* (EFA thematic study). Dakar: UNESCO.

Bridgeland, J., Wulsin, S., & McNaught, M. (2009). *Rebuilding Rwanda: From genocide to prosperity through education.* Washington, DC: Civic Enterprises.

Brigety, R. E. (2008). Humanity as a weapon of war: Sustainable security and the role of the U.S. military. Washington, DC: Center for American Progress.

Brouwer, A. M. (2005). *Supranational criminal prosecution of sexual violence: The ICC and the practice of the ICTY and the ICTR.* Antwerp, Belgium: Intersentia.

Brown, G. (2009, September 4). *Afghanistan—National security and regional stability.* Speech delivered at the International Institute for Strategic Studies, London.

Brown, G. (2010). *Education and violent conflict* (Background paper prepared for the UNESCO Education for All global monitoring report 2011, The hidden crisis: Armed conflict and education). Paris: UNESCO.

Bruce, B. (2001, Fall). Toward mediating the impact of forced migration and displacement among children affected by armed conflict. *Journal of International Affairs, 55,* 35–58.

Buckland, P. (2005). *Reshaping the future: Education and postconflict reconstruction* Washington, DC: World Bank.

Buckley-Zistel, S. (2006). Dividing and uniting: The use of citizenship discourses in conflict and reconciliation in Rwanda. *Global Society, 20*(1), 101–113.

Bulír, A., & Hamann, A. (2003). Aid volatility: An empirical assessment. *IMF Staff Papers, 50* (1), 64–89.

Burde, D. (2004). Weak state, strong community: Promoting community participation in post-conflict countries. *Current Issues in Comparative Education, 6*(2), 73–87.

Burde, D., & Linden, L. L. (2009). *The effect of proximity on school enrollment: Evidence from a randomized controlled trial in Afghanistan.* Retrieved from http://www.cgdev.org/doc/events/10.21.09/Proximity_and_Enrollment_2009-05-02.pdf

Burde, D., & Linden, L. (2010). *The effect of village-based schools: Evidence from a randomized controlled trial in Afghanistan* (Working paper). New York: New York University, Steinhardt School of Culture, Education, and Human Development.

Burnside, C., & Dollar, D. (2000). Aid, policies and growth. *American Economic Review, 90*(4), 847–868.

Bush, K. D., & Saltarelli, D. (2000). *The two faces of education in ethnic conflict: Towards a peacebuilding education for children.* Florence, Italy: UNICEF Innocenti Research Centre.

Canadian International Development Agency (CIDA). (2001). *CIDA's action plan for child protection: Promoting the rights of children who need special protection measures.* Ottawa: Author.

Castagno, R. (2006). *Cinematic popular culture and educators' rational reconstructions.* New York: Teachers College Press.

Chambers, R., & Conway, G. R. (1991). *Sustainable rural livelihoods: Practical concepts for the 21st century* (Discussion Paper No. 296). Brighton, UK: Institute of Development Studies.

Chauvet, L., & Collier, P. (2007). *Education in fragile states.* Background paper prepared for the *Education for All global monitoring report 2008: MDGs and the environment: Agenda for inclusive and sustainable development.* Paris: UNESCO.

Cheney, K. E. (2007). *Pillars of the nation: Child citizens and Ugandan national development.* Chicago: University of Chicago Press.

Christensen, P., & James, A. (2008). Researching children and childhood: Cultures of communication. In P. Christensen & A. James (Eds.), *Research with children: Perspectives and practices* (2nd ed., pp. 1–8). New York & London: Routledge.

Christian Aid. *The politics of poverty: Aid in the new cold war* (Report). (2004). London: Author.

Christians, C. G. (2005). Ethics and politics in qualitative research. In N. K. Denzin & Y. S. Lincoln (Eds.), *The Sage handbook of qualitative research* (3rd ed. pp., 139–164). Thousand Oaks, CA, London, & New Delhi, India: Sage.

Chronic Poverty Research Centre. (2005–2010). Toolbox: Overarching issues: Research with children and young people. Retrieved from http://www.chronicpoverty.org/page/toolbox-research-and-children

Clacherty, G. (2006). *The suitcase stories: Refugee children reclaim their identities.* New York: UN Refugee Agency.

Clark, A., McQuail. S., & Moss, P. (2003). *Exploring the field of listening to and consulting with young children* (Research Report No. 445). London: Department for Education and Skills.

Clark-Kazak, C. R. (2009a). Representing refugees in the life cycle: A social age analysis of United Nations High Commissioner for Refugees annual reports and appeals 1999–2008. *Journal of Refugee Studies, 22*(3), 302–322.

Clark-Kazak, C. R. (2009b). Towards a working definition and application of social age in international development studies. *Journal of Development Studies, 45*(8), 1307–1324.

Clark-Kazak, C. R. (2011). *Recounting migration: Political narratives of Congolese young people in Uganda.* Montreal: McGill-Queen's University Press.

Clegg, J. W., & Slife, B. D. (2008). Research ethics in the postmodern context. In D. Mertens & P. Ginsberg (Eds.), *The handbook of social research ethics* (23–38). New York: Sage.

Clemens, M., & Radelet, S. (2003). *The millennium challenge account: How much is too much, how long is long enough?* (CGD Working Paper No. 23). Washington, DC: Center for Global Development.

Cole, E. A. (2007a). Reconciliation and history education. In E. A. Cole (Ed.), *Teaching the violent past: History education and reconciliation* (pp. 1–30). New York: Rowman & Littlefield.

Cole, E. A. (2007b). Transitional justice and the reform of history education. *International Journal of Transitional Justice, 1*(1), 115–137.

Collier, P. (1999, April 26–27). *Doing well out of war.* Paper prepared for the Conference on Economic Agendas in Civil Wars, London, World Bank. Retrieved from http://www.arts.ualberta.ca/~courses/PoliticalScience/474A1/documents/CollierDoingWellOutofWarApril99.pdf

Collier, P. (2007). *The bottom billion: Why the poorest countries are failing and what can be done about it.* Oxford: Oxford University Press.

Collier, P. (2009). The political economy of state failure. *Oxford Review of Economic Policy, 25*(2), 219–240.

Collier, P., & Dollar, D. (2002). Aid allocation and poverty reduction. *European Economic Review, 26,* 1475–1500.

Collier, P., & Hoeffler, A. (2004). Greed and grievance in civil war. *Oxford Economic Papers, 56*(4), 563–595.

Cook, T. D. (2003). Why have education evaluators chosen not to do randomized experiments? *Annals of the American Academy of Political and Social Science, 589*(1), 114–149.

Craig, D. (2000). "A" is for Allah, "J" is for Jihad. *World Policy Journal, 19*(1), 90–94.

Cranton, P. (2006). *Understanding and promoting transformative learning: A guide for educators of adults* (2nd ed.). San Francisco: Jossey-Bass.

Crisp, J. (2003). *No solution in sight: The problem of protracted refugee situations in Africa.* Geneva: UNHCR.

Crombe, X. (2006). Humanitarian action in situations of occupation: The view from MSF. *Humanitarian Exchange Magazine* (33), Retrieved from http://www.odihpn.org/report.asp?id=2794.

Das, V., Kleinman, A., Lock, M., Ramphele, M., & Reynolds, P. (Eds.). (2001). *Remaking a world: Violence, social suffering and recovery.* Berkeley: University of California Press.

Davies, L. (2004). *Education and conflict: Complexity and chaos.* London: Routledge.

Davies, L. (2008). *Educating against extremism.* Stoke-on-Trent, UK: Trentham Books.

Davies, L. (2009). *Capacity development in education in fragile contexts* (Working paper for ETF/GTZ/INEE). doi: 10.2816/12196

Davies, L. (2010). *Understanding education's role in fragility: Synthesis report on Afghanistan, Bosnia-Herzegovina, Cambodia and Liberia* (Report for INEE). Paris: UNESCO.

Davies, L. (2011). Learning to trust: Legitimacy, transparency and professionalism in education in fragile contexts. In H. Weiland (Ed.), *Education in fragile contexts: Government practices and political challenges.* Freiburg, Germany: Arnold Bergstrasse Institute.

Davies, L., Harber, C., Schweisfurth, M., Williams, C., & Yamashita, H. (2008). *Educating in emergencies in South Asia: Reducing the risks facing vulnerable children.* Birmingham, UK: Centre for International Education and Research/UNICEF South Asia.

De Berry, J. (2003). *The children of Kabul: Discussion with Afghan families.* Save the Children Federation.

De Grauwe, A. (2009). *Without capacity, there is no development.* Paris: IIEP. Retrieved from http://www.iiep.unesco.org/fileadmin/user_upload/Cap_Dev_Rethinking/pdf/CapDev_Synthesis.pdf

De Grauwe, A., & Gay, D. (2010). The uselessness and usefulness of plans. *UNESCO IIEP Newsletter, 28*(2), 1–2. Retrieved from http://www.iiep.unesco.org/fileadmin/user_upload/Info_Services_Newsletter/pdf/eng/2010/2010_2En.pdf

De Lange, N., Mitchell, C., & Stuart, J. (Eds.). (2007). *Putting people in the picture: Visual methodologies for social change.* Amsterdam: Sense.

De Lange, N., Mnisi, T., Mitchell, C., & Park, E. (2010). Giving life to data: University community partnerships in addressing HIV and AIDS through building digital archives. *E-learning and Digital Media, 7*(2), 160–171.

De Vriese, M. (2006). *Refugee livelihoods: A review of the evidence* (No. EPAU/2006/04). Geneva: UNHCR.

Delap, E. (2005). *Fighting back: Child and community-led strategies to avoid children's recruitment into armed forces and groups in West Africa.* London: Save the Children.

Des Forges, A. (1999). *Leave none to tell the story.* New York: Human Rights Watch.

DfID (Department of International Development)(2005a). *Fighting poverty to build a safer world: A strategy for security and development.* London: Author.

DfID. (2005b). *Girls' education: Towards a better future for all.* London: Author.

DfID. (2005c). *Why we need to work more effectively on fragile states.* London: Author.

DfID (2010) *Learning for all: DfID's education strategy 2010–2015.* London: Author.

Dryden-Peterson, S. (2003). *Education of refugees in Uganda: Relationships between setting and access.* Kampala, Uganda: Refugee Law Project.

Dryden-Peterson, S. (2006). The present is local, the future is global? Reconciling current and future livelihood strategies in the education of Congolese refugees in Uganda. *Refugee Survey Quarterly, 25*, 81–92.

Dryden-Peterson, S. (2010). *Barriers to accessing primary education in conflict-affected fragile states: Literature review.* London: Save the Children.

Duerr, A., Posner, S. F., & Gilbert, M. (2003). Evidence in support of foster care during acute refugee crises. *American Journal of Public Health, 93*(11), 1904–1909.

Duffield, M. (1997). NGO relief in war zones: Towards an analysis of the new aid paradigm. *Third World Quarterly, 18*(3), 527–542.

Duffield, M. (2001a). *Global governance and the new wars: The merging of development and security.* London: Zed Books.

Duffield, M. (2001b). Governing the borderlands: Decoding the power of aid. *Disasters, 25*(4), 308–320.

Duffield, M. R. (2007). *Development, security and unending war: Governing the world of peoples.* Cambridge: Polity.

Duffield, M. (2008). Global civil war: The non-insured, international containment and post interventionary society. *Journal of Refugee Studies, 21*(2), 145–165.

Duffield, M. (2010). The liberal way of development and the development-security impasse: Exploring the global life-chance divide. *Security Dialogue, 41*(1), 53–76.

Easterley, W. (2006). *The white man's burden: Why the west's effort to aid the rest has done so much ill and so little good.* New York: Penguin.

Edwards, S., & van Wijnberg, S. (1989). Disequilibrium and structural adjustment. In H. Chenery & T. N. Srinivasan (Eds.), *Handbook of development economics* (pp. 1481–1533). Amsterdam: North-Holland.

EFA-FTI. (2008). Fast Track Initiative (FTI) Support to Fragile Situations. The FTI Progressive Framework: Discussion Document & Guidelines. Washington, DC: EFA- FTI Secretariat.

EFA-FTI. (2010). Home. Retrieved from http://www.educationfasttrack.org/home/

EFA-FTI Secretariat. (2004). *Framework for the EFA Fast Track Initiative.* Washington, DC: Author.

Elder, G. H., Jr. (1998). The life course as developmental theory. *Child Development, 69*(1), 1–12.

English, R. (2010). Counterinsurgency in Afghanistan. *Terrorism and Political Violence, 22*(1), 120–124.

Enloe, C. H. (1989). *Bananas, beaches and bases: Making feminist sense of international politics.* London: Pandora.

Enloe, C. H. (2000). *Maneuvers: The international politics of militarizing women's lives.* Berkeley: University of California Press.

Erikson, E. H. (1950). *Childhood and society.* New York: Norton.

European Union. (2003). *A secure Europe in a better world.* Brussels: Author.

Eurotrends. (2010a). *Study on governance challenges for education in fragile situations: Cambodia country report.* Brussels, Belgium: European Commission.

Eurotrends. (2010b). *Study on governance challenges for education in fragile situations: Liberia country report.* Brussels, Belgium: European Commission.

Fayolle, A. (2006). Out of the trap: How to improve financing for fragile states. *Finance and Development, 43*(4). Retrieved from http://www.imf.org/external/pubs/ft/fandd/2006/12/fayolle.htm

Fearon, D. (2008). The rise of emergency aid relief. In M. N. Barnett & T. G. Weiss (Eds.), *Humanitarianism in question* (pp. 49–72). Ithaca, NY: Cornell University Press.

Fearon, J. D., & D. Laitin. (2003). Ethnicity, insurgency, and civil war. *American Political Science Review, 97*(1), 75–90.

Fraser, S. (2004). Situating empirical research. In S. Fraser, V. Lewis, S. Ding, M. Kellett, & C. Robinson (Eds.), *Doing research with children and young people* (pp. 15–26). London: Sage.

Fredriksen, B. (2009). Rationale, issues, and conditions for sustaining the abolition of school fees. In World Bank & UNICEF (Eds.), *Abolishing school fees in Africa: Lessons from Ethiopia, Ghana, Kenya, Malawi, and Mozambique* (pp. 1–41). Washington, DC: World Bank.

Freedman, S. W., Weinstein, H. M., Murphy, K., & Longman, T. (2008). Teaching history after identity-based conflicts: The Rwanda experience. *Comparative Education Review, 52*(4), 663–690.

FTI. (2008). *Fast Track Initiative (FTI) support to fragile situations: Progressive framework.* Retrieved from http://www.ineesite.org/uploads/documents/store/pfguidelines.pdf

Fuhrer, H. (1994). *The story of development assistance: A history of the development assistance committee and the development co-operation directorate in dates and figures.* Paris: OECD.

Fuller, B. (1991). *Growing up modern: The western state builds third-world schools.* London: Routledge.

Fund for Peace. (2010). *Failed states index 2010.* Retrieved from http://www.fundforpeace.org/web/index.php?option=com_content&task=view&id=452&Itemid=900

Furth, H. (1996). *Desire for society: Children's knowledge as social imagination.* New York: Plenum Press.

Gale, L. (2006). The refugee "family"—Child fostering and mobility among Sierra Leonean refugees. *The International Journal of Sociology of Family, 32*(2), 273–287.

Geist, A., & Carroll, P. (2002). *They still draw pictures: Children's art in wartime from the Spanish civil war to Kosovo.* Champaign: University of Illinois Press.

Geltman, P., & Stover, E. (1997). Genocide and the plight of Rwanda's children: Letter from Kigali. *Journal of the American Medical Association, 277*(4), 289–294.

Gender and Peacebuilding Working Group & Women's Commission for Refugee Women and Children (GPWC & WC). (2005). *Adolescent girls affected by violent conflict: Why should we care?* Ottawa: GPWG.

Ghani, A., & Lockhart. C. (2008). *Fixing failed states: A framework for rebuilding a fractured world.* New York: Oxford University Press.

Glad, M. (2009). *Knowledge on fire. Risks and measures for successful mitigation.* Kabul: CARE and the Ministry of Education of Afghanistan. Retrieved from http://www.care.org/newsroom/articles/2009/11/Knowledge_on_Fire_Report.pdf

Global Campaign for Education. (2009). *Education on the brink: Will the IMF's new lease on life ease or block progress towards education goals?* Johannesburg, South Africa: Author.

Gourevitch, P. (1998). *We wish to inform you that tomorrow we will be killed with our families.* New York: Picador USA.

Gourevitch, P. (2009). The life after: Fifteen years after the genocide in Rwanda, the reconciliation defies expectations. *The New Yorker, 85*(12), 37–49.

Governance and Social Development Resource Centre (GSRDC). (2010). *Recovering from violent conflict.* Retrieved from http://www.gsdrc.org

Government of Canada (GoC). (2005). A role of pride and influence in the world. In *Canada's international policy statement.* Ottawa: Author.

Government of North-West Frontier Province (NWFP), UNICEF, & Save the Children. (2005). *Disciplining the child: Practices and impacts.* Peshawar, Pakistan: Government of NWFP.

Greenberg, M. T., Weissberg, R. P., O'Brien, M. U., Zins, J. E., Fredericks, L., Resnik, H., & Elias, M. J. (2003, (June–July). Enhancing school-based prevention and youth development through coordinated social, emotional, and academic learning. *American Psychologist, 58,* 466–474.

Gregory, D. (2008). "The rush to the intimate"—Counterinsurgency and the cultural turn. *Radical Philosophy* (150), 8–23.

Greene, S., & Hill, M. (2005). Researching children's experiences: Methods and methodological issues. In S. Greene & D. Hogan (Eds.), *Researching children's experience: Methods and approaches* (pp. 1–21). London: Sage.

Greig, A., Taylor, J., & MacKay, T. (2007). *Doing research with children* (2nd ed.). London: Sage.

Gubrium, A. (2009). Digital storytelling: An emergent method for health promotion research and practice. *Health Promotion and Practice 2,* 186–191.

Habermas, J. (1971). *Knowledge and human interests.* Boston: Beacon Press.

Hansen, H., & Tarp, F. (2000). *Aid and growth regressions* (CREDIT Research Paper No. 7). Nottingham: Centre for Research in Economic Development and International Trade, University of Nottingham. Retrieved from http://cbtrc.org/economics/credit/research/papers/cp.00.7.pdf

Harber, C. (1996). Educational violence and education for peace in Africa. *Peabody Journal of Education, 71*(3), 151–169.

Harber, C. (2004). *Schooling as violence: How schools harm pupils and societies.* London & New York: RoutledgeFalmer.

Hart, J. (2006). Saving children: What role for anthropology? *Anthropology Today, 22*(1), 5–8.

Hart, J., & Tyrer, B. (2006). *Research with children living in situations of armed conflict: Concepts, ethics & methods* (RSC Working Paper No. 30). Retrieved from http://www.rsc.ox.ac.uk/PDFs/workingpaper30.pdf

Hart, R. A. (1992). *Children's participation: From tokenism to citizenship.* Florence, Italy: UNICEF International Child Development Centre (now Innocenti Research Centre).

Hayden, T. (2009). Kilcullen's long war: An influential Pentagon strategist plans a fifty-year counterinsurgency campaign. *Nation, 289*(14), 22–24.

He, F., Linden, L., & MacLeod, M. (2006). *Teaching subjects that teachers don't know: English education in India.* Unpublished manuscript, Columbia University, New York.

Henig, J. (December 2008/January 2009). The spectrum of education research. *Educational Leadership, 66*(4), 6–11.

Hess, F., & Henig, J. (2008). "Scientific research" and policy-making: A tool not a crutch. *Education Week.* Retrieved from http://www.frederickhess.org/5123/scientific-research-and-policy-making

Hill, M. (2005). Ethical considerations in researching children's experiences. In S. Greene & D. Hogan (Eds.), *Researching children's experience: Methods and approaches* (pp. 61–86). London: Sage.

Hill, M. (2006). Children's voices on ways of having a voice: Children's and young people's perspectives on methods used in research and consultation. *Childhood, 13*, 69–89.

Hoffman, B. (2009). A counterterrorism strategy for the Obama administration. *Terrorism and Political Violence, 21*(3), 359–377.

Horst, C. (2006a). Introduction: Refugee livelihoods: Continuity and transformations. *Refugee Survey Quarterly, 25*(2), 6–22.

Horst, C. (2006b). *Transnational nomads.* Oxford: Berghahn.

Hovil, L. (2007). Self-settled refugees in Uganda: An alternative approach to displacement? *Journal of Refugee Studies, 20*(4), 599–620.

Hromadžic, A. (2008). Discourses of integration and practices of reunification at the Mostar Gymnasium, Bosnia and Herzegovina. *Comparative Education Review, 52*(4), 541–563.

Huitt, W. (2007). Maslow's hierarchy of needs. *Educational psychology interactive.* Valdosta, GA: Valdosta State University. Retrieved from http://www.edpsycinteractive.org/topics/regsys/maslow.html

Human Rights Watch. (2006). *Lessons in terror: Attacks on education in Afghanistan.* Washington, DC: Author.

Huntington, S. P. (1993). The clash of civilizations. *Foreign Affairs, 72*(3), 22–49.

Huntington, S. P. (1996). *The clash of civilizations and the remaking of world order.* New York: Simon & Schuster.

Huvilo, I. (2008). Participatory archive: Towards decentralised curation, radical user orientation, and broader contextualisation of records management. *Archival Science, 8*, 15–36.

IASC (Inter-Agency Standing Committee) Task Force on Gender and Humanitarian Assistance. (2005). Guidelines for gender-based violence in humanitarian settings: Focusing on prevention of and response to sexual violence in emergencies. Geneva: Author. Retrieved from http://www.humanitarianinfo.org/iasc/publications/asp

IASC. (2007). IASC cluster working groups. Retrieved from http://www.humanitarianinfo.org/iasc/content/Cluster/default.asp?mainbodyID=5&publish=0

ICA (Interagency Conflict Assessment). (2009). *Cambodia: Adjustment or instability?* Washington, DC: U.S. Department of State.

ICG (International Crisis Group). (2002). *Pakistan, madrasas, extremism and the military.* Islamabad/Brussels: Author.

INEE (Inter-Agency Network for Education in Emergencies). (2004). *Minimum standards for education in emergencies, chronic crises and early reconstruction.* Paris: Author.

INEE. (2009). *The multiple faces of education in conflict-affected and fragile contexts.* New York: Author.

INEE. (2010, February). *Strategic research agenda for education in emergencies, chronic crises, early recovery and fragile contexts.* Prepared by the Conflict and Education Research Group at Oxford University and the Teachers College International Education Research Group. Retrieved from http://www.ineesite.org/index.php/post/strategic_research_agenda_soft_launch/

INEE GTT (Inter-Agency Network for Education in Emergencies Gender Task Team). (n.d.). Gender strategies for education in emergencies, chronic crises, and early reconstruction contexts: Recruiting and supporting women teachers. Retrieved from http://www.ineesite.org/ineedownloads/viewall.asp?pid=1387 &cp=18

IBE (International Bureau of Education). (2006). Curriculum change and social cohesion in conflict affected societies. Retrieved from www.ibe.unesco.org/conflict/ConflictSCohe-sion.htm

IIEP (International Institute for Educational Planning). (2006a). *Guidebook for planning education in emergencies and reconstruction*. Paris: UNESCO.

IIEP. (2006b). Afghanistan: Preparation of a strategic education development plan and related capacity development [Project proposal submitted to the Norwegian government by IIEP]. Unpublished internal document. Paris: UNESCO.

International Save the Children Alliance. (2006). *Rewrite the future: Education for children in conflict-affected countries*. London: Author.

Inter-Parliamentary Union. (2011). *Women in national parliaments*. Geneva: Author.

Jacobsen, K. (2002). Livelihoods in conflict: The pursuit of livelihoods by refugees and the impact on the human security of host communities. *International Migration, 40*(5), 95–123.

Jacobsen, K. (2005). *The economic life of refugees*. Bloomfield, CT: Kumarian Press.

Johnson, D. W., & Johnson, R. T. (1994). Constructive conflict in schools. *Journal of Social Issues, 50*(1), 117–137.

Jones, P. (2006). Elusive mandate: UNICEF and educational development. *International Journal of Educational Development, 26*, 591–604.

Jones, D. (2009). *Starting schools under the mango trees: A study of the Guinea refugee education program*. New York: International Rescue Committee, LEGACY Initiative.

Jung, D. (2003). *Shadow globalization, ethnic conflicts and new wars: A political economy of intra-state war*. London: Routledge.

Kaag, M. (2004). Ways forward in livelihood research. In D. Kalb, W. Pansters, & H. Siebers (Eds.), *Globalization and development: Themes and concepts in current research* (pp. 49-74). Boston: Kluwer Academic.

Kaldor, M. (1999). *New and old wars: Organized violence in a global era*. Cambridge, Polity.

Kanyarukiga, S., van der Meer, E., Paalman, M., Poate, D., & Schrader, T. (2006). *Evaluation of DfID country programmes: Country study Rwanda 2000–2005*. London: Department for International Development.

Karam, A. (2001). Women in war and peace-building: The roads traversed, the challenges ahead. *International Feminist Journal of Politics, 3*(1), 2–25.

Keenan, J. (2008). US militarization in Africa: What anthropologists should know about AFRICOM. *Anthropology Today, 24*(5), 16–20.

Kellett, M., Robinson, C., & Burr, R. (2004). Images of childhood. In S. Fraser, V. Lewis, S. Ding, M. Kellett, & C. Robinson (Eds.), *Doing research with children and young people* (pp. 27–42). London: Sage.

The key to peace: Unlocking the human potential of Sudan [Inter-agency paper]. (2002). Nairobi, Kenya: CARE.

King, E. (2008). *The role of education in violent conflict and peacebuilding in Rwanda*. University of Toronto, Toronto.

King, E. (2009). From data problems to data points: Challenges and opportunities of research in postgenocide Rwanda. *African Studies Review, 52*(3), 127–148.

King, E. (2010a). *From classrooms to conflict? Rethinking education in Rwanda and beyond*. Unpublished manuscript.

King, E. (2010b). Memory controversies in post-genocide Rwanda: Implications for peacebuilding. *Journal of Genocide Studies and Prevention, 5*(3), 293–309.

King, E. M., & van de Walle, D. (2007). Girls in Lao PDR: Ethnic affiliation, poverty, and location. In M. Lewis & M. Lockheed (Eds.), *Exclusion, gender and education: Case studies from the developing world* (pp. 31–70). Washington, DC: Center for Global Development.

King, K. (2007). Multilateral agencies in the construction of the global agenda on education. *Comparative Education, 43*(3), 377–391.

Kirk, J. (2004a). *IRC healing classrooms initiative: An initial study in Ethiopia.* Unpublished manuscript. New York: International Rescue Committee.

Kirk, J. (2004b). *IRC healing classrooms initiative: An initial study in Sierra Leone.* Unpublished manuscript. New York: International Rescue Committee.

Kirk, J. (2004c). Promoting a gender-just peace: The roles of women teachers in peacebuilding and reconstruction. *Gender and Development* 12(3), 50–59.

Kirk, J. (2004d). Teachers creating change: Working for girls' education and gender equity in South Sudan. *EQUALS, Beyond Access: Gender, Education and Development 9,* 4–5.

Kirk, J. (2005a). *IIEP gender workshop report, March 2005, Kabul.* Unpublished internal document. Paris: UNESCO.

Kirk, J. (2005b). Violence against girls in school. In J. Ward (Ed.), *Broken bodies, broken dreams: Violence against women exposed* (pp. 72–83). Geneva: United Nations OCHA/IRIN.

Kirk, J. (2006a). *Education in emergencies: The gender implications* (UNESCO Bangkok Advocacy Brief). Bangkok, Thailand: United Nations Educational, Scientific, and Cultural Organization. Retrieved from http://www2.unescobk.org/elib/publications/ 092/

Kirk, J. (2006b). Roles, potential and challenges for donors of the INEE minimum standards in education in emergencies, chronic crises and early reconstruction. Retrieved from http://www.ineesite.org/minimum_standards/CIDA-INEE. pdf

Kirk, J. (2007). Education and fragile states. *Globalisation, Societies and Education, 5*(2), 181–200.

Kirk, J. (2008a). Addressing gender disparities in education in contexts of crisis, post crisis, and state fragility. In M. Tembon & L. Fort (Eds.), *Girls' education in the 21st century: Gender equality, empowerment, and economic growth* (pp. 153–180). Washington, DC: World Bank.

Kirk, J. (2008b). Gender, sexuality and education: Examining issues in conflict contexts. In M. Dunne (Ed.), *Gender, sexuality and development: Education and society in Sub-Saharan Africa* (pp. 203–214). Rotterdam, the Netherlands: Sense.

Kirk, J. (2008c). *Building back better: Opportunities and challenges for education in Pakistan after the 2005 earthquake.* Paris: United Nations Educational, Scientific, and Cultural Organization & International Institute for Educational Planning.

Kirk, J. (Ed.). (2009a). *Certification counts: Recognizing the learning attainments of displaced and refugee students.* Paris: International Institute for Educational Planning.

Kirk, J. (2009b). Starting with the self: Reflexivity in studying women teachers' lives in development. In K. Pithouse, C. Mitchell, & R. Moletsane (Eds.), *Making connections: Self-study and social action* (pp. 115–126). London & New York: Peter Lang. (Reprinted from J. Kirk. (2005). Starting with the self: Reflexivity in studying women teachers' lives in development by. In C. Mitchell, S. Weber, & K. O'Reilly-Scanlon [Eds.], *Just who do we think we are? Methodologies for autobiography and self-study in teaching* [pp. 231–241]. London & New York: RoutledgeFalmer.)

Kirk, J., & Garrow, S. (2003). "Girls in policy": Challenges for the education sector. *Agenda, 56,* 4–15.

Kirk, J., Ogango, M., & Pia, P. (2005). *Sudan basic education program (SBEP) peace education strategy: Strengthening local capacities for peace through education activities.* Unpublished manuscript.

Kirk, J., & Sommers, M. (2005). Menstruation and body awareness: Critical issues for girls' education. *Equals* (Newsletter for Beyond Access: Gender, Education and Development), *15*, 4–5. Retrieved from http://k1.ioe.ac.uk/schools/efps/GenderEducDev/ Equals%20 Issue%20No.%2015.pdf

Kirk, J., & Taylor, S. (2004). *Gender, peace and security agendas: Where are girls and young women?* (Prepared for Gender and Peacebuilding Working Group of the Canadian Peacebuilding Coordinating Committee). Retrieved from http://action.web.ca/ home/ cpcc/en_resources.shtml?x=73620

Kirk, J. & Taylor, S. (2007). Ending Sexual Violence against Women and Girls in Conflict Contexts: UN Security Council Resolution 1325. *Forced Migration Review 27*, 13-14. 27, 13–14. http://www.fmreview.org/FMRpdfs/FMR27/06.pdf

Kirk, J., & Winthrop, R. (2005). Addressing gender-based exclusion in Afghanistan through home-based schooling for girls. *Critical Half, 3*(2), 27–31.

Kirk, J., & Winthrop, R. (2006). Eliminating the sexual abuse and exploitation of girls in refugee schools in West Africa: Introducing female classroom assistants. In F. Leach & C. Mitchell (Eds.), *Combating gender violence in and around schools* (pp. 207–215). Stoke-on-Trent, UK: Trentham Books.

Kirk, J., & Winthrop, R. (2007). Promoting quality education in refugee contexts: Supporting teacher development in northern Ethiopia. *International Review of Education, 53*, 715–723.

Kirk, J., & Winthrop, R. (2008a). Female classroom assistants: Agents of change in refugee classrooms in West Africa? In M. Maslak (Ed.), *The structure and agency of women's education* (pp. 161–178). Albany: State University of New York Press.

Kirk, J., & Winthrop, R. (2008b). Home-based school teachers in Afghanistan: Teaching for tarbia and student well-being. *Teaching and Teacher Education, 24*, 876–888.

Kirk, J., & Winthrop, R. (2009). Moving from innovation to policy: IRC's work with community based education in Afghanistan. In S. Nicolai (Ed.), *Opportunities for change: Education innovation and reform during and after conflict* (pp. 103–114). Paris: IIEP. Retrieved from, http://www.iiep.unesco.org/fileadmin/user_upload/Info_Services_Publications/pdf/2009/Nicolai_Opportunities_for_change.pdf

Kirk, J., & Winthrop, R. (n.d.). The International Rescue Committee's healing classrooms initiative: Teacher development for student well-being—preliminary findings (draft title). Unpublished internal document.

Kirk, J., et al. (2005). *The MoE/SBEP Gender Equity Support Program (GESP): An early impact assessment* (Draft briefing). Nairobi, Kenya: Sudan Basic Education Program (SBEP).

Klees, S. (2008). Reflections on theory, method, and practice in comparative and international education. *Comparative Education Review, 52*(3), 301–328.

Knowles, G., & Cole, A. (2008). *Handbook of the arts in qualitative research.* London & New York: Sage.

Kos, A. M. (2005). Supplement: Training teachers in areas of armed conflict: A manual. *Intervention, 3*(2), 15–24.

Kremer, M. (2003). *Randomized evaluations of educational programs in developing countries: Some lessons.* Washington, DC. World Bank.

Kunder, J. (2005, April 19). Testimony of James Kunder, Assistant Administrator for Asia and the Near East, U.S. Agency for International Development, before the Senate Foreign Relations Committee.Available at http://pdf.usaid.gov/pdf_docs/PDACF407.pdf

Lareau, A. (2009). Narrow questions, narrow answers: The limited value of randomized control trials for educational research. In P. Walters, A. Lareau, & S. Ranis (Eds.), *Educational research on trial* (pp. 154–161). New York: Routledge.

Larson, A. (2008). *A mandate to mainstream: Promoting gender equality in Afghanistan.* Kabul: AREU. Retrieved from http://www.areu.org.af/index.php?option=com_docman&task=doc_download&gid=613&Itemid=26

Lather, P. (2004). This IS your father's paradigm: Government intrusion and the case of qualitative research in education. *Qualitative Inquiry, 10*(1), 15–34.

Lawrence-Lightfoot, S., & Davis, J. H. (1997). *The art and science of portraiture.* San Francisco: Jossey-Bass.

Leach, F. (2006). Researching gender violence in schools: Methodological and ethical considerations. *World Development, 34*(6), 1129–1147.

Leach, F., Fiscian, V., Kadzamira, E., Lemani, E., & Machakanja, P. (2003). *An investigative study of the abuse of girls in African schools* (Education Research Rept. No. 54). London: DfID.

Leach, F., & Mitchell, C. (Eds.). (2006). *Combating gender violence in and around schools.* Trent on Stokes: Trentham Books.

Leader, N., & Colenso, P. (2005). *Aid instruments in fragile states* (PRDE Working Paper No. 5). London: DfID. Retrieved from http://ageconsearch.umn.edu/bitstream/12818/1/pr050005.pdf

Lefoka, P., Nyabanyaba, T., & Sebatane, E. (2009). Learning plus basic education initiative study (Lesotho report). Unpublished manuscript commissioned by UNICEF.

Levin, V., & Dollar, D. (2005). *The forgotten states: Aid volumes and volatility in difficult partnership countries 1992–2002* (Paper for DAC learning and advisory process on difficult partnerships). Retrieved from http://siteresources.worldbank.org/INTLICUSSPANISH/Resources/34687926.pdf

Levine, D., & Bishai, L. (2010). *Civic education and peacebuilding* (U.S. Institute of Peace special report). Washington, DC: U.S. Institute of Peace.

Lewin, K. M. (2009). Access to education in Sub-Saharan Africa: Patterns, problems and possibilities. *Comparative Education, 45*(2), 151–174.

Lewis, M., & Lockheed, M. (2006). *Inexcusable absence: Why 60 million girls still aren't in school and what to do about it.* Washington, DC: Center for Global Development.

Lewis, M., & Lockheed, M. (2007). Social exclusion: The emerging challenge in girls' education. In M. Lewis & M. Lockheed (Eds.), *Exclusion, gender and education: Case studies from the developing world* (pp. 1–27). Washington, DC: Center for Global Development.

Longwe, S. (1998). Education for women's empowerment or schooling for women's subordination. *Gender and Development, 6*(2), 19–26.

Lopes-Cardozo, M. (2008). Sri Lanka: In peace or in pieces? A critical approach to peace education in Sri Lanka. *Research in Comparative and International Education, 3*(1), 19–34.

Lopes-Cardozo, T. M., & Novelli, M. (2010). *The Netherlands aid to education in conflict affected countries* (Background paper prepared for the *Education for All global monitoring report 2011, The hidden crisis: Armed conflict and education*). Paris: UNESCO.

Lopez, A. M. (2010). The new counterinsurgency era: Transforming the US military for modern wars. *Political Science Quarterly, 125*(2), 347–348.

Loughry, M., & Eyber, C. (2003). *Psychosocial concepts in humanitarian work with children: A review of the concepts and related literature.* Washington, DC: National Research Council.

Lundborg, P. (1998). Foreign aid and international support as a gift exchange. *Economics and Politics, 10*(2), 127–142.

Lykes, M. B. (2001a). Activist participatory research and the arts with rural Mayan women: Interculturality and situated meaning making. In D. L. Tolman & M. Brydon Miller (Eds.), *From subject to subjectivities: A handbook of interpretive and participatory methods* (pp. 183–199). New York: New York University Press.

Lykes, M. B. (2001b). Creative arts and photography in participatory action research in Guatemala. In P. Reason & H. Bradbury (Eds.), *Handbook of action research: Participative inquiry and practice* (pp. 363–371). Thousand Oaks, CA: Sage.

MacEwen, L.; Choudhuri, S. & Bird, L. (2010). *Education sector planning: Working to mitigate risk of violent conflict* (Background paper prepared for the *Education for All Global Monitoring Report 2011, The hidden crisis: Armed conflict and education*). Paris: UNESCO. Retrieved from http://unesdoc.unesco.org/images/0019/001907/190707e.pdf

Machel, G. (1996). *Impact of armed conflict on children.* New York: United Nations.

Machel, G. (2000). *The impact of armed conflict on children: A critical review of progress made and obstacles encountered in increasing protection for war-affected children.* Available online at http://www.saiv.net/SourceBook/Storage/documents/doc_armedconflict_children.pdf

Machel, G. (2001a). *The Machel review 1996–2000: A critical review of progress made and obstacles encountered in increasing protection for war-affected children.* New York: United Nations.

Machel, G. (2001b). *The impact of war on children.* London: C. Hurst.

Magno, C., & Kirk, J. (2010). Sight unseen: "Re-viewing" images of girls' education. *Girlhood Studies: An Interdisciplinary Journal, 3*(1), 9–33.

Mahbub, T. (2008). Inclusive education at a BRAC school—Perspectives from the children. *British Journal of Special Education, 35*(1), 33–41.

Mak, M. (2006). Unwanted images: Tackling gender-based violence in South African schools through youth artwork. In. F. Leach & C. Mitchell (Eds.), *Combating gender violence in and around schools* (pp. 113–123). Stoke-on-Trent, UK: Trentham Books.

Manchanda, R. (2001). Ambivalent gains in South Asian conflicts. In S. Meintjes, A. Pillay, & M. Turshen (Eds.), *The aftermath: Women in post-conflict transformation* (pp. 99–120). London: Zed Books.

Mansory, A. (2007). *Drop out study in basic education level of schools in Afghanistan.* Kabul: Swedish Committee for Afghanistan.

Marcus, T., & Hofmaener, J. (Eds.). (2006). *Shifting the boundaries of knowledge.* Pietermaritzburg, South Africa: UKZN Press.

Marshall, D. (1999). The construction of children as an object of international relations: The Declaration of Children's Rights and the Child Welfare Committee of the League of Nations, 1900–1924. *International Journal of Children's Rights, 7*, 103–147.

Martone, G., & Neighbor, H. (2004). Aid agencies must think about how people are living, not dying. *Humanitarian Affairs Review.* Retrieved from http://www.reliefweb.int/rw/lib.nsf/db900SID/AMMF-6NHKBM?OpenDocument

Mathews, D. (2001). *War prevention works: 50 stories of people resolving conflict.* Oxford: Oxford Research Group.

Mazibuko, E. Z., & Gathu, K. (2009). Learning plus basic education initiative study (Swaziland report). Unpublished manuscript commissioned by UNICEF.

McClure, K. R. (2009). Madrasas and Pakistan's education agenda: Western media misrepresentation and policy recommendations. *International Journal of Educational Development, 29*(4), 334–341.

McGillivray, M. (2006). *Aid allocation and fragile states* (Discussion Paper No. 2006/01). Helsinki, Finland: UNU-WIDER. Retrieved from http://www.wider.unu.edu/stc/repec/pdfs/rp2006/dp2006-01.pdf

Menocal, A., & Othieno, T. (2008). *The World Bank in fragile situations*. London: ODI. Retrieved January 10,2011, from http://www.odi.org.uk/resources/download/3319.pdf

Messiou, K. (2002). Marginalisation in primary schools: Listening to children's voices. *Support for Learning, 17*(3), 117–121.

Mezirow, J. (1981). A critical theory of adult learning and education. *Adult Education Quarterly, 32*(1), 3–24.

Mezran, K. (2009). Counterinsurgency and the global war on terror: Military culture and irregular war. *Globalizations, 6*(1), 164–166.

Miles, M., & Hossain, F. (1999). Rights and disabilities in educational provision in Pakistan and Bangladesh: Roots, rhetoric, reality. In F. Armstrong & L. Barton (Eds.), *Disability, human rights and education: Cross-cultural perspectives* (pp. 67–86). Buckingham, U.K. & Philadelphia, PA: Open University Press.

Miller, D., & Mills, T. (2010). Counterinsurgency and terror expertise: The integration of social scientists into the war effort. *Cambridge Review of International Affairs, 23*(2), 203–221.

MINECOFIN. (2000). *Rwanda vision 2020*. Kigali: Ministry of Finance and Economic Planning.

Ministry of Education, Afghanistan. (2007). *National education strategic plan for Afghanistan 1385–1389*. Retrieved from http://www.iiep.unesco.org/fileadmin/user_upload/News_And_Events/pdf/2010/Afghanistan_NESP.pdf

Ministry of Education, Afghanistan. (2011). *Education Interim Plan 2011-13*. Version 5. Retrieved from http://www.educationfasttrack.org/media/library/AfghanistanInterimEducationPlan.pdf

Ministry of Finance and Economic Planning, Rwanda. (2002). *A profile of poverty in Rwanda: An analysis based on the results of the Household Living Condition survey 1999–2001*. Kigali: Author.

Ministry of Finance and Economic Planning, Rwanda. (2007). *Economic development and poverty reduction strategy 2008–2012*. Kigali: Author.

Ministry of Higher Education (MoHE), Afghanistan. (2004). Strategic action plan for the development of higher education in Afghanistan. Kabul: Ministry of Higher Education. Retrieved from http://planipolis.iiep.unesco.org/upload/Afghanistan/Afghanistan_higher_education_strategic_plan.pdf

Minow, M. (1998). *Between vengeance and forgiveness: Facing history after genocide and mass violence*. Boston: Beacon Press.

Mirembe, R., & Davies, L. (2001). Is schooling a risk? Gender, power relations, and school culture in Uganda. *Gender and Education, 13*(4), 401–416.

Mitchell, C. (2009). Geographies of danger: School toilets in Sub-Saharan Africa. In O. Gershenson & B. Penner (Eds.), *Ladies and gents: Public toilets and gender* (pp. 62–74). Philadelphia: Temple University Press.

Mitchell, C. (2011). *Doing visual research*. London & New York: Sage.

Mitchell, C., & de Lange, N. (2011). Community based video and social action in rural South Africa. In L. Pauwels & E. Margolis (Eds.), *Handbook on visual methods*. London: Sage.

Mitchell, C., de Lange, N & Moletsane, R. (2011). Before the camera rolls. In L. Theron, C. Mitchell, A. Smith, & J. Stuart (Eds.), *Picturing research: Drawing(s) as visual methodology* (pp. 219–231). Rotterdam: Sense.

Mitchell, C., & Kanyangara, P. (2006). *Violence against children and young people in and around schools in Rwanda: Through the eyes of children and young people*. Kigali: National Youth Council, UNICEF.

Mitchell, C., Walsh, S., & Moletsane, R. (2006). "Speaking for ourselves": A case for visual arts-based and other participatory methodologies in working with young people to address sexual violence. In F. Leach & C. Mitchell (Eds.), *Combating gender violence in and around schools* (pp. 103–111). Trent-on-Stokes: Trentham Books.

Mnisi, T., de Lange, N., & Mitchell, C. (2010). *Learning to use visual data to "save lives" in the age of AIDS? Communitas: Journal for Community*, 15, 183-201

Moletsane, R., Mitchell, C., Smith, A., & Chisholm, L. (2008). *Mapping a Southern African girlhood*. Rotterdam, the Netherlands: Sense.

Molyneux, M. (1985). Mobilisation *without* emancipation? Women's interests, states and revolution in Nicaragua. *Feminist Studies, 11*(2), 227–254.

Moran, M. (2006). *Liberia: The violence of democracy*. Philadelphia: University of Pennsylvania Press.

Moreno Torres, M., & Anderson, M. (2004). *Fragile states: Defining difficult environments for poverty reduction*. London: DfID.

Moser, C. (1989). Gender planning in the third world. *World Development, 17*(11), 1799–1825.

Mukarugomwa, V. (2007). *Gender-based violence in and around schools in Rwanda*. Kigali: Action Aid International Rwanda.

Mundy, K. (2002). Retrospect and prospect: Education in a reforming World Bank. *International Journal of Educational Development, 22*(5), 483–508.

Mundy, K. (2006). Constructing education for development: International organizations and education for all. *Comparative Education Review, 50*(2), 296–298.

Münkler, H. (2005). *The new wars*. Oxford: Polity.

Muramila, G. (2007, September 30). Primary school enrollment rises. *New Times* (1303).

National Museum of Rwanda. (n.d.). Murambi Genocide Memorial Center. Retrieved from http://www.museum.gov.rw/2_museums/murambi/genocide_memorial/pages_html/page_intro.htm

Nicolai, S. (2004). *Learning independence: Education in emergency and transition in Timor Leste since 1999*. Paris: IIEP.

Nicolai, S. (Ed.). (2009). *Opportunities for change: Education innovation and reform during and after conflict*. Paris: IIEP.

Nicolai, S., & Triplehorn, C. (2003). *The role of education in protecting children in conflict*. London: Overseas Development Institute.

Nishimuko, M. (2007). Problems behind Education for All (EFA): The case of Sierra Leone. *Educate, 7*(2), 19–29.

Nyamwassa, G., Karegeya, C., Rudasingwa, D., & Gahima, M. (2010, September 5). Rwanda needs deeper reforms. *Daily Monitor*.

Obura, A. (2001). *Knowing the pen: Girls' education in the southern part of Sudan*. Nairobi, Kenya: United Nations Children's Fund and Operation Lifeline Sudan.

Obura, A. (2003). *Never again. Educational reconstruction in Rwanda*. Paris: IIEP.

Obura, A. (2005). *Planning a systemic response to the needs of orphans and other vulnerable children in Rwanda: Draft report*. Kigali: MINEDUC.

Obura, A., & Bird, L. (2009). *Education marginalisation in post conflict settings: A comparison of government and donor responses in Burundi and Rwanda* (Background paper prepared for the *Education for All global monitoring report 2010, Reaching the marginalized*). Paris: UNESCO. Retrieved from http://unesdoc.unesco.org/images/0018/001866/186602e.pdf

ODI (Overseas Development Institute). (2005, May). *Scaling-up versus absorptive capacity: Challenges and opportunities for reaching the MDGs in Africa* (Briefing paper). London: Author.

OECD (2007a). *Glossary of Statistical Terms: Fragile States*. Retrieved from http://stats.oecd.org/glossary/detail.asp?ID=7235

OECD. (2007b). *Principles for good international engagement in fragile states and situations*. Paris: OECD.

OECD. (2007c, April 3–4). *Fragile states: Policy commitments and principles for good international engagement in fragile states and situations*. Presented at DAC high-level meeting in Paris.

OECD. (2008). *Service delivery in fragile states: Key concepts, findings, and lessons*. Retrieved from www.oecd.org/dataoecd/17/54/40886707.pdf

OECD-DAC. (1997). *Guidelines on conflict, peace and development cooperation*. Paris: OECD.

OECD-DAC. (2001). *Helping prevent violent conflict: The DAC guidelines*. Paris: OECD. Retrieved from http://www.oecd.org/dataoecd/15/54/1886146.pdf

OECD-DAC. (2008). *Resource flows to fragile and conflict-affected states: Annual report 2008*. Paris: OECD.

OECD-DAC. (2010). Stat extracts: Creditor reporting system. Retrieved from http://stats.oecd.org/Index.aspx?DatasetCode=CRSNEW

O'Malley, B. (2007). *Education under attack*. Paris: UNESCO.

O'Malley, B. (2010). *Education under attack 2010*. Paris: UNESCO.

Osman, R., & Kirk, J. (2001). Teaching as agents of change: A teaching and learning experience through and about change. *Perspectives in Education, 19*(1), 172–180.

Parker, I. (2010, May 17). Profiles: The poverty lab. *The New Yorker*, pp. 79–89.

Partnership for Advancing Community-based Education in Afghanistan (PACE). (2006). *Project summary*. Kabul: CARE.

Pašalic-Kreso, A. (2008). The war and post-war impact on the educational system of Bosnia and Herzegovina. *International Review of Education, 54*(3–4), 353–374.

Pettigrew, T. F. (1998). Intergroup contact theory. *Annual Review of Psychology, 49*, 65–85.

Phillips, D. C. (2009). A quixotic quest? Philosophical issues in assessing the quality of education research. In P. Walters, A. Lareau, & S. Ranis (Eds.), *Educational research on trial* (pp. 163–195). New York: Routledge.

Picciotto, R. (2005). Memorandum submitted by Professor Robert Picciotto, International Development Department at the House of Commons, Retrieved from http://www.publications.parliament.uk/pa/cm200405/cmselect/cmintdev/464/5031502.htm

Pigozzi, M. J. (1996). *Education in emergencies and for reconstruction: Guidelines with a developmental approach*. New York: UNICEF.

Pinheiro, P. S. (2006). *World report on violence against children*. Geneva, United Nations. Retrieved from http://www.violencestudy.org

Portsmouth Ethnic Minority Achievement Service. (2008). Guidance on using persona dolls. Retrieved from http://www.blss.portsmouth.sch.uk/earlyears/eypdolls_tr.shtml

Postman, N., & C. Weingartner. (1967). *Teaching as a subversive activity*. New York: Basic Books.

Powell, C. (2001, October 21). Remarks to the National Foreign Policy Conference for Leaders of Nongovernmental Organizations, Washington, DC. Retrieved from http://avalon.law.yale.edu/sept11/powell_brief31.asp

Qahir, K. (2008). Training refugee Afghan women teachers in the female education program, Pakistan. In J. Kirk (Ed.), *Women teaching in South Asia* (pp. 196-220). New Delhi: Sage India.

Ranis, S. (2009). Blending quality and utility: Lessons learned from the education research debates. In P. Walters, A. Lareau, & S. Ranis (Eds.), *Educational research on trial* (pp. 125–141). New York: Routledge.

Ratcliffe, M., Patch, J., & Quinn, D. (2009). Expanding primary access in Cambodia: 20 years of recovery. In S. Nicolai (Ed.), *Opportunities for change: Education innovation and reform during and after conflict* (pp. 127–138). Paris: IIEP.

Reality of Aid. (2008). *The Reality of Aid 2008: Aid effectiveness, democratic ownership and human rights*. Quezon City, Philippines: Ibon Books.

Reyntjens, F. (2004). Rwanda, ten years on: From genocide to dictatorship. *African Affairs, 103*, 177–210.

Richards, P., Archibald, S., Bruce, B., Modad, W., Mulbah, E., Varpilah, T., & Vincent, J. (2005). *Community cohesion in Liberia: A post-war rapid social assessment* (Social Development Papers No. 21). Washington, DC: World Bank.

Roberts, A. (2000). Humanitarian issues and agencies as triggers for international military action. *International Review of the Red Cross* (839), 673–698.

Robinson, C., & Kellett, M. (2004). Power. In S. Fraser, V. Lewis, S. Ding, M. Kellett, & C. Robinson (Eds.), *Doing research with children and young people* (pp. 81–96). London: Sage.

Rogers, W. (2003). What is a child? In M. Woodhead & H. Montgomery (Eds.), *Understanding childhood: A multidisciplinary approach* (pp. 1–23). Milton Keynes, UK: Open University.

Republic of Rwanda (RoR). (1995). *Document final provisoire: Conférence sur la politique et la planification de l'éducation au Rwanda*. Kigali: Ministère de l'Enseignement Primaire et Secondaire & Ministère de l'Enseignement Supérieur, de la Recherche Scientifique et de la Culture.

RoR. (1997). *Study of the education sector in Rwanda*. Kigali: Ministry of Education, UNESCO & UNDP.

RoR. (2002). *Poverty reduction strategy paper (PRSP)*. Kigali: International Monetary Fund.

RoR. (2006). *Rwanda genocide ideology and strategies for its eradication*. Kigali: Senate of Rwanda.

RoR. (2007). *Economic development and poverty reduction strategy, 2008–2012*. Kigali: Ministry of Finance and Economic Planning.

RoR. (n.d.). *La scolarisation féminine*. Kigali: Ministère Rwandais de la Santé Publique & des Affaires Sociales, Direction de la Promotion Féminine.

Rose, G. (2001). *Visual methodologies*. London & New York: Sage.

Rose, P. (2003). Community participation in school policy and practice in Malawi: Balancing local knowledge, national policies and international agency priorities. *Compare, 33*(1), 47–64.

Rose, P. (2009). Scaling-up aid to education: Is absorptive capacity a constraint? *Prospects, 39*, 109–122.

Rose, P., & Greeley, M. (2006). *Education in fragile states: Capturing lessons and identifying good practice* (Prepared for the DAC Fragile States Group Service Delivery Workstream Sub-Team for Education Services). Paris: OECD.

Ross, M. H. (2002). The political psychology of competing narratives: September 11 and beyond. In C. Calhoun, P. Price, & A. Timmer (Eds.), *Understanding September 11* (pp. 303–320). New York: New Press.

Rubin, H., & Rubin, I. (2005). *Qualitative interviewing: The art of hearing data.* Thousand Oaks, CA: Sage.

Rutayisire, P. (2007). The role of teachers in the social and political reconstruction of post-genocide Rwanda. In F. Leach & M. Dunne (Eds.), *Education, conflict and reconciliation: International perspectives* (pp. 115–130). Oxford: Peter Lang.

Rwezaura, B. (1994). The concept of the child's best interests in the changing economic and social context of Sub-Saharan Africa. *International Journal of Law and the Family, 8*, 82–114.

Sachs, J. (2005). *The end of poverty: How we can make it happen in our lifetime.* London: Penguin.

Said, E. (2001, October 22). The clash of ignorance. *The Nation.* Retrieved from http://www.thenation.com/doc/20011022/said

Saigol, R. (1995). *Knowledge and identity: Articulation of gender in educational discourse in Pakistan.* Lahore: ASR Publications.

Saigol, R. (2000). *Symbolic violence: Curriculum, pedagogy and society.* Lahore, Pakistan: Society for the Advancement of Education.

Salomon, G. (2002). The nature of peace education: Not all programs are created equal. In G. Salomon & B. Nevo (Eds.), *Peace education: The concept, principles, and practices around the world* (pp. 3–13). London: Erlbaum.

Save the Children. (2003). *The children of Kabul.* Washington, DC: Author.

Save the Children. (2007). *Last in line, last in school: How donors are failing children in conflict-affected fragile states.* London: Author.

Save the Children. (2008). *Learning from those who live it: An evaluation of children's education in conflict-affected fragile states, Save the Children, Rewrite the Future Global Evaluation Report 2008.* London: Author.

Save the Children. (2009). *Last in line, last in school: Donor trends in meeting education needs in countries affected by conflict and emergencies.* London: Author.

Save the Children. (2010). *The future is now: Education for children in countries affected by conflict.* London: Author.

Schleicher, A. (2007, October 2–3). Education: A critical path to gender equality and women's empowerment. Paper presented at the global symposium, Education: A critical path to gender equality and women's empowerment, Washington, DC.

Scott, J. (1990). *Domination and the arts of resistance: Hidden transcripts.* New Haven, CT: Yale University Press.

Seitz, K. (2004). Education and conflict. The role of education in the creation, prevention and resolution of societal crises—Consequences for development cooperation. Eschborn, Germany: GTZ.

Sen, A. (2006). *Identity and violence, the illusion of destiny.* New York & London: Norton.

Shah, S. M. (2010). Is capacity being built? A study of the policymaking process in primary and secondary education subsector. Kabul: AREU.

Shepler, S. (2010). *Does teacher training for refugees contribute to post-conflict reconstruction of educational systems? Evidence from West Africa.* New York: International Rescue Committee, LEGACY Initiative.

Shilton, K., & Srinivasan, R. (2008). Participatory appraisal and arrangement for multicultural archival collections. *Archivaria, 63*, 87–101.

Shriberg, J. (2007). *Teaching well? Educational reconstruction efforts and support to teachers in postwar Liberia.* New York: International Rescue Committee, Child and Youth Protection and Development Unit.

Sigsgaard, M. (2009). *Education and fragility in Afghanistan: A situational analysis.* Paris: IIEP & INEE. Retrieved from http://www.iiep.unesco.org/fileadmin/user_upload/Info_Services_Publications/pdf/2009/Afghanistan.pdf

Sigsgaard, M. (Ed.). (2011). *On the road to resilience: Capacity development with the Ministry of Education in Afghanistan.* Paris: IIEP. Retrieved from http://www.iiep.unesco.org/fileadmin/user_upload/Info_Services_Publications/pdf/2011/Afghanistan_Resilience.pdf

Sinclair, M. (2001). Education in emergencies. In J. Crips, C. Talbot & D. Cipollone (Eds.), *Learning for a future: Refugee education in developing countries* (pp. 1-83). Geneva: UN High Commissioner for Refugees.

Sinclair, M. (2002). *Planning education in and after emergencies.* Paris: IIEP.

Slim, H. (1996). Military humanitarianism and the new peacekeeping: An agenda for peace? *IDS Bulletin, 27*(3), 86-95.

Smith, A. (2005). Education in the twenty-first century: Conflict, reconstruction, and reconciliation. *Compare, 35*(4), 373–391.

Smith, A. (2007). Education and conflict: An emerging field of study. In F. Leach & M. Dunne (Eds.), *Education, conflict and reconciliation: International perspectives* (pp. 19–32). Oxford: Peter Lang.

Smith, A., & Vaux, T. (2003). *Education, conflict and international development.* London: UK Department for International Development.

Smith, W., & Winthrop, R. (2002). *Internal evaluation of IRC education programs 1999–2002.* New York: International Rescue Committee.

Sontag, S. (2003). *Regarding the pain of others.* London: Picardor.

Spence, J., & Solomon, J. (Eds.). (1995). *What can a woman do with a camera?* London: Scarlet Press.

Spink, J. (2005). Education and politics in Afghanistan—The importance of an education system in peacebuilding and reconstruction *Journal of Peace Education, 2*(2), 195–207.

Steiner-Khamsi, G. (2009). Knowledge-based regulation and the politics of international comparison. *Nordisk Pedagogik, 29*, 61–71.

Stephens, J., & Ottaway, D. B. (2002). The ABCs of Jihad in Afghanistan. *Washington Post.*

Stewart, F. (Ed.). (2008). *Horizontal inequalities and conflict: Understanding group violence in multiethnic societies.* Basingstoke, UK: Palgrave.

Stoddard, A., Harmer, A., et al. (2006). Providing aid in insecure environments: Trends in policy and operations. *Overseas Development Institute, Humanitarian Policy Group Report* 23, 1–66.

Stoddard, A., Harmer, A., et al. (2009). Providing aid in insecure environments: 2009 update: Trends in violence against aid workers and the operational response. ODI, *HPG Policy Brief,* 34.

Sullivan-Owomoyela, J., & Brannelly, L. (2009). *Promoting participation: Community contributions in conflict situations.* IIEP/CfBT.

Tanada, K. (2001, Winter). Mindanao: Trail of conflict: Paths to peace. *SangSaeng 2,* 25–29.

Tawil, S., & Harley, A. (Eds.). (2004). *Education, conflict, and social cohesion.* Geneva: International Bureau of Education (IBE).

Tenenbaum, S. (2004). *History and lessons learned, IRC Guinea: 1991–2004.* New York: International Rescue Committee.

Theron, L., Mitchell, C., Smith, A., & Stuart, J. (Eds.). (in press). *Picturing research: Drawing(s) as visual methodology.* Rotterdam, the Netherlands: Sense.

Thompson, J. (2009). How we see this place: An intergenerational dialogue about conservation around Tiwai Island, Sierra Leone. Unpublished masters's thesis, McGill University, Montreal.

Torrente, N. (2004). Humanitarian action under attack: Reflections on the Iraq war. *Harvard Human Rights Journal, 17,* 1–29.

Transparency International. (2004). *Corruption fighters' toolkit.* Berlin: Author.

Turrent, V. (2009). *Expanding support for education in fragile states: What role for the Education for All—Fast Track Initiative?* Brighton, UK: Consortium for Research on Educational Access, Transitions, and Equity (CREATE), University of Sussex.

Turrent, V., & Oketch, M. (2009). Financing universal primary education: An analysis of official development assistance in fragile states. *International Journal of Educational Development, 29,* 357–365.

Umurungi, J. P., Mitchell, C., Gervais, M., Ubalijoro, E., & Kabarenzi, V. (2008). Photovoice as a methodological tool for working with girls on the street in Rwanda to address HIV & AIDS and gender violence. *Journal of Psychology in Africa, 18*(3), 413–420.

UNDP (United Nations Development Programme). (2004). *Human development report, 2004.* New York: Author.

UNDP. (2005). *Human development report 2005: International cooperation at a crossroads: Aid, trade and security in an unequal world.* New York: Author. Retrieved from http://hdr.undp.org/reports/global/2005

UNDP. (2007). *Turning vision 2020 into reality: From recovery to sustainable human development.* Kigali, Rwanda: Author.

UNDP. (2009). *HDI rankings.* New York: Author.

UNESCO. (1990). *World Declaration on Education for All and Framework for Action to Meet Basic Learning Needs.* Paris: UNESCO.

UNESCO. (1996). *The Amman Affirmation: Mid-Decade Meeting of the International Consultative Forum on Education for All Amman, Jordan, 16-19 June.* Paris: UNESCO.

UNESCO. (2000). *The Dakar Framework for Action: Meeting our collective commitments resolution adopted by the World Education Forum, Dakar, April 2000.* Paris: UNESCO.

UNESCO. (2004). *Education for All: The quality imperative.* Paris: Author.

UNESCO. (2005). *Education for All—Global Monitoring Report: Education for All The Quality Imperative.* Paris: UNESCO

UNESCO. (2010). *Protecting education from attack.* Paris: Author.

UNESCO. (2011). *UNESCO Education for All global monitoring report: The hidden crisis: Armed conflict.* Paris: Author.

UNESCO & UNHCR. (2007). Educational responses to HIV and AIDS for refugees and internally displaced persons (Discussion paper for decision-makers). Paris & Geneva: Author.

UNHCR (UN High Commissioner for Refugees). (2002). *2002 UNHCR statistical yearbook.* Geneva:Author.

UNHCR. (2005). *2005 UNHCR Statistical Yearbook.* Geneva: Author.

UNHCR. (2006). *State of the world's refugees 2006.* Oxford: Oxford University Press.

UNHCR. (2009a). *Education strategy: 2010–2012.* Geneva: Author.

UNHCR. (2009b). *2008 global trends: Refugees, asylum-seekers, returnees, internally displaced and stateless persons.* Geneva: Author.

UNHCR. (2010). *2009 global trends: Refugees, asylum-seekers, returnees, internally displaced and stateless persons.* Geneva: Author.

UNHCR & Save the Children. (2002). *Note for implementing and operational partners on sexual violence and exploitation: The experience of refugee children in Guinea, Liberia and Sierra Leone.* Geneva: UNHCR.

UNICEF. (2000). *From survival to thrival: Children and women in the southern part of Sudan.* Nairobi, Kenya: Author.

UNICEF. (2001). *Corporal punishment in schools in South Asia.* Kathmandu, Nepal: UNICEF Regional Office for South Asia.

UNICEF Somalia. (2005). *Education: Issue.* Retrieved from www.unicef.org/somalia/

UNICEF. (2006). Rwanda: Facts and figures. Retrieved from http://www.unicef.org/infobycountry/23867_20292.html

UNICEF. (2010a). *Child protection from violence, exploitation and abuse: Children in conflict and emergencies.* New York: Author. Retrieved from www.unicef.org/protection/index_armedconflict.html

UNICEF. (2010b). *Learning Plus research study: Mapping care and support for quality education.* New York: Author.

UNICEF Somalia. (2005). *Education: Issue.* Retrieved from www.unicef.org/somalia/education_56.html

United Nations. (1948). *Universal Declaration of Human Rights.* New York: United Nations.

United Nations. (1989). Convention on the rights of the child (61st plenary meeting ed., Vol. A/RES/44/25). Retrieved from http://www2.ohchr.org/english/law/crc.htm

United Nations. (2001). *Strengthening the coordination of emergency humanitarian assistance of the United Nations* (Report of the Secretary-General No. A-56-95-E-2001-85). Retrieved from http://www.reliefweb.int/rw/lib.nsf/db900SID/LGEL-5D9CJ4?OpenDocument

United Nations. (2003). The Monterrey Consensus of the International Conference on Financing for Development: The final text of agreements and commitments adopted at the International Conference on Financing for Development, Monterrey, Mexico, 18-22 March 2002. New York: United Nations.

United Nations. (2005). Humanitarian response review. An independent report commissioned by the United Nations Emergency Relief Coordinator and Under-Secretary-General for Humanitarian Affairs, Office for the Coordination of Humanitarian Affairs. New York & Geneva: Author.

United Nations. (2008). UN and NGOs condemn attacks on Somali students, teachers and schools. Retrieved from: http://www.hiiraan.com/comments2-news-2008-Sept-un_and_ngos_condemn_attacks_on_somali_students_teachers_and_schools.aspx

United Nations Office for Coordination of Humanitarian Affairs (UN OCHA). (2007). *Appeal for improving humanitarian response capacity: 1 April 2007–31 March 2008.* New York & Geneva: Author.

United Nations Security Council. (2000). Resolution 1325 on women, peace and security. New York: United Nations.

USAID (U.S. Agency for International Development). (2005a). *Education strategy.* Washington, DC: Author.

USAID. (2005b). *Fragile states strategy.* Washington, DC: Author.

USAID. (2005c). *Youth and conflict.* Washington, DC: USAID Office of Conflict Management and Mitigation.

USAID. (2006). *Education and fragility: An assessment tool.* Washington, DC: Author.

USAID. (2008). *Civil military cooperation policy.* Washington, DC: Author.

USAID. (2009). *Liberia youth fragility assessment.* Washington, DC: Equip 1, Aguire.

USAID Africa Bureau. (2005). *Fragile states matrix* (Draft). Nairobi, Kenya: USAID.

U.S. Department of State. (2008). *Country reports on terrorism 2007.* Washington, DC: U.S. Department of State, Publication Office of the Coordinator for Counterterrorism.

U.S. Department of State. (2009). *Cambodia: Adjustment or instability?* Interagency conflict assessment. Washington, DC: U.S. Department of State.

Volavkova, H. (1978). *"I never saw another butterfly": Children's drawings and poems of Terezin concentration camp, 1942–1944.* New York: Schocken Books.

Vongalis-Macrow, A. (2006). Rebuilding regimes or rebuilding community? Teachers' agency for social reconstruction in Iraq. *Journal of Peace Education, 3*(1), 99–113.

Wahrman, H. (2003). Is silencing conflicts a peace education strategy? The case of the "Jewish state" topic in Israeli civics textbooks. In Y. Iram (Ed.), *Education of minorities and peace education in pluralistic societies* (pp. 219–254). Westport, CT: Praeger.

Wakefield, S. (2004a). *Gender and local level decision-making: Findings from a case study in Mazar-e Sharif.* Kabul: Afghan Research and Evaluation Unit.

Wakefield, S. (2004b). *Gender and local level decision making: Findings from a case study in Panjao.* Kabul: Afghan Research and Evaluation Unit.

Waldman, M. (2009, April 3–4). *Caught in the conflict: Civilians and the international security strategy in Afghanistan: A briefing paper by eleven NGOs operating in Afghanistan for the NATO Heads of State and Government Summit.* London: Oxfam.

Walker, G., Millar Wood, J., Allemano, E. (2009). *Liberia Youth Fragility Assessment.* Washington, DC: USAID.

Walters, P., & Lareau, A. (2009). Introduction. In P. Walters, A. Lareau, & S. Ranis (Eds.), *Educational research on trial* (pp. 1–13). New York: Routledge.

Wang, C., & Burris, M. (1994). Empowerment through photo novella: Portraits of participation. *Health Education Quarterly, 2*(2), 171–186.

Wang, C., Burris, M., & Xiang, Y. (1996). Chinese village women as visual anthropologists: A participatory approach to reaching policymakers. *Social Science & Medicine, 42*(10), 1391–1400.

Wang, L. (2007). *Education in Sierra Leone: Present challenges, future opportunities,* (Africa Human Development Series). Washington, DC: World Bank.

Wang, T. Y. (1999). US foreign aid and UN voting: An analysis of important issues. *International Studies Quarterly 43,* 199–210.

Wessells, M. (2006). *Child soliders: From violence to protection.* Cambridge, MA: Harvard University Press.

Whitworth, S. (2004). *Men, militarism and UN peacekeeping: A gendered analysis.* Boulder, CO: Lynne Rienner.

Williams, J. (2004). Civil conflict, education, and the work of schools: Twelve propositions. *Conflict Resolution Quarterly, 21*(4), 471–481.

Winthrop, R. (2008). *Armed conflict, schooling, and children's wellbeing.* Unpublished doctoral dissertation, Teachers College, New York.

Winthrop, R. (2010). *Education, conflict and fragility: Past development and future challenges* (Background paper prepared for the UNESCO *Education for All global monitoring report 2011, The hidden crisis: Armed conflict and education*). Paris: UNESCO.

Winthrop, R., & Kirk, J. (2008). Learning for a bright future: Schooling, armed conflict, and children's well-being. *Comparative Education Review, 52*(4), 639–661.

Women's Refugee Commission. (2009). *Building livelihoods: A field manual for practitioners in humanitarian settings.* New York: Author.

Woodhead, M., & Faulkner, D. (2008). Subjects, objects or participants? Dilemmas of psychological research with children. In P. Christensen & A. James (Eds.), *Research with children: Perspectives and practices* (2nd ed., pp. 10–39). New York & London: Routledge.

Woods, N. (2005). The shifting politics of foreign aid. *International Affairs, 81*(2), 393–409.

World Bank. (2003). *Breaking the conflict trap: Civil war and development policy.* Washington, DC: Author.

World Bank. (2005). *Reshaping the future: Education and postconflict reconstruction.* Washington, DC: Author.

World Bank. (2006). *Engaging with fragile states.* Washington, DC: Author.

World Bank. (2009). *Fragile and conflict-affected countries.* Retrieved from http://go.worldbank.org/BNFOS8V3S0

World Bank. (2011). *Harmonized list of fragile situations FY 2011.* Retrieved from http://siteresources.worldbank.org/EXTLICUS/Resources/511777-1269623894864/Fragile_Situations_List_FY11_(Oct_19_2010).pdf

World Children's Museum. (2009). *About.* Retrieved from http://www.worldchildrensmuseum.org/Pages/about.html

World Vision International. (2001). *Every girl counts: Development, justice and gender.* Ontario: Author.

Yi, W. K., Li, V. C., Tao, Z. W., Lin, Y. K., Burris, M. A., Ming, W. Y., Yun, X. Y., & Wang C. (1995). *Visual voices: 100 photographs of village China by the women of Yunnan Province.* Yunnan: Yunnan's People's Publishing House.

Yin, R. K. (2003). *Case study research: Design and methods* (3rd ed.). Thousand Oaks, CA: Sage.

Zambernardi, L. (2010). Counterinsurgency's impossible trilemma. *Washington Quarterly, 33*(3), 21–34.

About the Contributors

Lesley Bartlett is associate professor in the Programs in International and Comparative Education and Anthropology at Teachers College, Columbia University. Her research and teaching interests include qualitative research methods, teacher education, migration and education, education in post-conflict settings, literacy, and bilingual education.

Stephanie Bengtsson is a doctoral candidate in International Educational Development at Teachers College, Columbia University. She works as an independent education consultant and researcher, specializing in African issues, inclusive education, and aid policy. She holds an MPhil in International Perspectives on Special and Inclusive Education from the University of Cambridge.

Lyndsay Bird is a Program Specialist at the UNESCO International Institute for Educational Planning. She has 20 years of experience with education in emergencies and is Chair of the INEE Working Group on Education and Fragility. She holds a doctorate from the Institute of Education, University of London.

Peter Buckland is an independent consultant specializing in education policy and management in fragile and conflict-affected countries. From 2002 to 2010 he was Lead Education Specialist at the World Bank, following 5 years at UNICEF as focal point for education and emergencies. His background is in education policy and administration.

Dana Burde is an Assistant Professor of International Education at New York University and a research affiliate at the Saltzman Institute of War and Peace Studies, Columbia University. Her research and teaching focus on education in emergencies, political violence, international organizations, and humanitarian action in countries at war.

Lynn Davies is Professor of International Education at the Center for International Education and Research, University of Birmingham. Her current research and consultancy interests include the role of education in conflict, extremism, and deradicalization; capacity development in fragile contexts; Islamophobia; and violence in schools.

Sarah Dryden-Peterson is a postdoctoral fellow at the University of Toronto affiliated with the Comparative, International and Development Education Centre. Her research and teaching focus on the intersections between education and community development in conflict-affected countries in Sub-Saharan Africa and in African Diasporas in the United States and Canada.

Dorian Gay is an Assistant Program Specialist at the UNESCO International Institute for Educational Planning. He manages technical partnerships with education ministries, focusing on capacity development for education sector planning. He has been especially involved in such cooperation in Afghanistan and Angola where national and provincial sector development plans are developed.

Elisabeth King is a postdoctoral research fellow at Columbia University associated with the Earth Institute and the Center for the Study of Development Strategies. She works on issues at the intersection of conflict, peace building, and development in Sub-Saharan Africa and has written widely on education in Rwanda.

Jackie Kirk was a specialist in education in emergencies, post-emergency and fragile states, with a particular focus on gender, and on teacher-related issues. She was an Education Advisor to the International Rescue Committee (IRC), and an Adjunct Professor at McGill University. Jackie was the convener of the Gender Task Team of the Inter-Agency Network for Education in Emergencies (INEE) and co-founder of *Girlhood Studies: An Interdisciplinary Journal*.

Claudia Mitchell is a James McGill Professor at McGill Univerity and an Honorary Professor at the University of KwaZulu Natal where she is a co-founder of the Centre for Visual Methodologies for Social Change. She is the co-editor of *Girlhood Studies: An Interdisciplinary Journal*.

Karen Mundy is an Associate Professor and Canada Research Chair at the Ontario Institute for Studies in Education of the University of Toronto, where she directs the Comparative, International and Development Education Centre. Her research has focused on the politics of educational assistance in the developing world, educational reform in Africa, and the role of civil society in the reform of educational systems.

Mario Novelli is Senior Lecturer in Education and International Development at the University of Sussex. His research currently focuses on the intersections between globalization, education, and international development. He has published recently on several issues relating to the area of education and conflict: the merging of security and development in the education sector and its implications; political violence against educators in Colombia; and critical approaches to the subfield of education and conflict.

Susan Shepler is an Assistant Professor of International Peace and Conflict Resolution in the School of International Service at American University in Washington, DC. Her interests include youth and conflict, reintegration of former child soldiers, and the localization of children's rights in African settings.

Morten Sigsgaard is an Assistant Programme Specialist at the UNESCO International Institute for Educational Planning. He has edited the forthcoming IIEP publication *On the Road to Resilience: Capacity Development with the Ministry of Education in Afghanistan* and has 5 years of field experience, mainly in South East Europe.

Victoria Turrent is a Ph.D. student at the Institute of Education, University of London, researching modes of financing education in fragile states. Her research interests include issues of economics and governance in developing countries, international aid policy and practice, and the financial barriers to achieving universal access to primary education.

Charlotte Wilson completed a master's degree in Education, Gender and International Development at the Institute of Education, University of London, in 2009. After an internship at the UNESCO International Institute for Educational Planning, she currently is interning as a communications and research assistant at the Gender and Development Network.

Rebecca Winthrop is a senior fellow and director of the Center for Universal Education. She is the former head of education for the International Rescue Committee, a humanitarian aid NGO. Her research focuses on education in the developing world, with special attention to fragile states and contexts of armed conflict, forced migration, and violent extremism.

Index

NAMES

Aguilar, P., 53, 177
Akresh, R., 142
Akyeampong, K., 216n, 217n
Al-Haj, M., 149
Alderson, P., 241
Allemano, E., 36
Allport, G. W., 146
Amaziah (refugee child), 89, 93–98
Anastacio, A., 186, 194
Anderson, M., 170
Angrist, J., 256
Annette (refugee child), 89–91, 95–98
Apfel, Roberta, 102, 103
Appadurai, A., 109
Arafat, C., 102
Arefee, M. A., 190
Atmar, Hanif, 185, 190
Avery, P. G., 149

Bagoyoko, N., 50
Baines, E., 151n
Bamusanire, E., 147, 149
Banerjee, A., 263
Barakat, B., 36
Baranyi, S., 16, 24, 29, 30
Barker, J., 245
Bartlett, Lesley, 12, 87, 235–253
Bartulovic, A., 36
Bengtsson, Stephanie, 12, 87, 235–253

Bennell, P., 216n, 217n
Bernard, C., 37
Betancourt, T., 110
Betts, A., 86
Bird, Lyndsay, 7, 11, 35, 103, 183–197, 197n
Bishai, L., 43
Bloom, A., 108
Bonham Carter, R., 62
Boothby, N., 102
Boyden, J., 119
Bradbury, M., 51
Bragin, M., 102, 103
Brandeis, Friedl Dicker, 231, 233
Brannelly, L., 37, 43
Bray, M., 258
Bridgeland, J., 142, 145
Brigety, R. E., 62
Brouwer, A. M., 138
Brown, Gordon, 3, 5, 6, 60–61
Brown, S., 151n
Bruce, B., 102
Buckland, Peter, 8, 9, 11, 35, 52, 102, 155–167, 176
Buckley-Zistel, S., 139
Bulír, A., 179
Burde, Dana, 12, 186, 255–271, 271n
Burnside, C., 178
Burr, R., 237, 252
Burris, M., 222, 225

Bush, K. D., 6, 15, 22, 26–27, 35, 53, 101, 137–138, 140
Byiringiro, I., 147

Carroll, P., 231
Castagno, R., 125
Cerecina, Mila, 48n
Chambers, R., 86
Chauvet, L., 177
Cheney, K. E., 87
Chisholm, L., 225
Choudhuri, S., 184
Christensen, P., 235, 239
Christians, C. G., 241
Clacherty, Glenys, 231
Clark, A., 238, 241, 242, 247, 248, 249
Clark-Kazak, C. R., 87, 88, 98n
Clegg, J. W., 257
Clemens, M., 178
Cole, A., 227
Cole, E. A., 148
Cole, S., 263
Colenso, P., 170
Collier, Paul, 5, 50, 55, 57, 177, 178, 180
Conway, G. R., 86
Cook, T. D., 256
Craig, D., 59
Cranton, P., 124
Crisp, J., 86
Crombe, X., 61

Das, Veena, 117
Davies, Lynn: chapter by,
    10, 33–48; references to
    works by, 3, 6, 7, 25–26,
    30, 34, 35, 40, 42, 46,
    47, 48, 53, 101, 140,
    183
Davis, J. H., 88
De Berry, J., 102, 103
De Grauwe, A., 184,
    188–189
de Lange, N., 222, 223, 225,
    227, 232
De Vriese, M., 86
De Walque, D., 142
Delap, E., 103
Des Forges, A., 138
Dollar, D., 171, 173, 176,
    178, 179
Dryden-Peterson, Sarah:
    chapters by, 1–12, 85–99;
    references to works by, 7,
    87, 90, 93
Duerr, A., 98n
Duffield, M., 50, 51, 53, 55,
    56, 57
Duflo, Esther, 255, 256, 263
Dunn, G., 110

Easterley, W., 177
Edwards, S., 179
Elder, G. H. Jr., 87
English, R., 50
Enloe, C. H., 70, 78
Erikson, E. H., 87
Eyber, C., 102

Falkner, D., 235, 238
Fayolle, A., 180
Fearon, J. D., 5, 51
Fraser, S., 239, 241
Fredriksen, B., 87
Freedman, S. W., 150
Fuhrer, H., 181n
Fuller, B., 109
Furth, H., 124

Gahima, M., 139
Gale, L., 98n
Garrow, Stephanie, 29,
    221–222, 232
Gathu, K., 251
Gay, Dorian, 183–197
Geist, A., 231
Geltman, P., 143
Gervais, M., 223
Ghani, A., 42
Gibert, M. V., 50
Gilbert, M., 98n
Glad, M., 186
Gourevitch, P., 139, 144
Greeley, M., 174
Greenberg, M. T., 103
Greene, S., 242
Gregory, D., 50, 53
Greig, A., 235, 238, 245, 252
Gubrium, A., 222

Habermas, J., 124
Hamann, A., 179
Hansen, H., 178
Harber, C., 22, 35, 144
Harley, A., 140
Harmer, A., 55, 63–64
Hart, J., 119, 120, 235, 238,
    241, 242
Hart, R. A., 87
Hayden, T., 50, 53
He, F., 263
Henig, J., 257
Hess, F., 257
Hill, M., 242
Hoeffler, A., 5
Hoffman, B., 50
Hofmaener, J., 222
Horst, C., 86
Hossain, F., 238
Hovil, L., 88
Hromadzic, A., 37, 41
Huitt, W., 238
Huntington, Samuel,
    55–56, 57
Huvilo, I., 232

Jacobsen, K., 86–87
James, A., 235, 239
Jebb, Eglantyne, 237
Johnson, D. W., 149
Johnson, R. T., 149
Jones, D., 202
Jones, P., 237
Julie (refugee child), 89,
    91–93, 95–98
Jung, D., 55

Kaag, M., 86
Kabarenzi, V., 223
Kaldor, M., 50
Kanyangara, P., 223
Kanyarukiga, S., 139, 150
Karam, A., 20, 73
Karegeya, C., 139
Karpinska, Z., 36
Karzai, Hamid, 190
Keenan, J., 52
Kellett, M., 237–238, 239,
    241, 244, 252
King, Elisabeth: Burde
    study and, 271; chapter
    by, 137–151; references
    to works by, 6, 11, 87,
    139, 140, 150, 151n, 183
King, K., 59
Kirk, Jackie: Afghanistan
    workshops of, 192–193;
    chapters by, 6, 9,
    10–11, 15–31, 67–81,
    101–121; commitment
    to education in conflict
    zones of, 1, 10; goals of,
    167; IRC Guinea refugee
    program and, 199; MSE
    and, 9; murder of, 10,
    64–65n, 269; PACE-A
    work of, 269; references
    to works by, 3, 10, 28, 29,
    37, 69, 70, 71, 72, 73, 78,
    80, 88, 95, 97, 110, 123,
    124, 146, 147, 166, 185,
    192–193, 199, 200, 201,

217*n*, 221–222, 223, 232, 238, 239, 269; stages of conflict and, 8
Klees, S., 257
Knowles, G., 227
Kos, A. M., 102, 103
Kremer, M., 256
Kunder, James, 56

Laitin, D., 5
Lareau, A., 256, 257
Lather, P., 256
Lawrence-Lightfoot, S., 88
Leach, Fiona, 22, 25, 35, 103, 230
Leader, N., 170
Lefoka, P., 251
Levin, V., 171, 173, 176, 179
Levine, D., 43
Lewis, M., 87
Linden, L. L., 186, 263, 267, 271*n*
Lockhart, C., 42
Lockheed, M., 87
Longman, T., 150
Longwe, S., 25
Lopes-Cardoso, T. M., 36, 53
Lopez, A. M., 50
Loughry, M., 102
Lundborg, P., 58
Lykes, Mary Brinton, 225

MacEwen, L., 184
Machel, Graça, 20, 29, 31, 71, 102, 103, 141, 259
MacKay, T., 235
MacLeod, M., 263
Magill, Clare, 48*n*
Magno, Catherine, 222
Mahbub, T., 247, 248
Mahmoodi, Saeed, 271*n*
Mak, M., 230
Manchanda, R., 31, 71
Marcus, T., 222
Marshall, D., 119
Martone, G., 238

Mathews, D., 41
Mazibuko, E. Z., 251
McClure, K. R., 62
McKay, Susan, 73
McNaught, M., 142
McQuail, S., 241, 242
Menocal, A., 170
Messiou, K., 247
Mezirow, Jack, 124
Mezran, K., 50
Miles, M., 238
Millar Wood, J., 36
Miller, D., 50
Mills, T., 50
Minow, M., 148
Mirembe, R., 25
Mitchell, Claudia: chapter by, 12, 221–233; references to works by, 35, 103, 222, 223, 225, 227, 229, 230, 232
Mitchell, J. M., 149
Mnisi, T., 232
Moletsane, R., 223, 225
Molyneux, M., 81*n*
Moran, M., 36
Moreno Torres, M., 170
Moser, C., 81*n*
Moss, P., 238, 241, 242
Mukarugomwa, V., 144
Mundy, Karen: chapter by, 1–12; references to works by, 59
Münkler, H., 55
Munyakazi, A., 147
Muramila, G., 139
Murphy, K., 150

Ndurahutse, S., 43
Neighbor, H., 238
Nicolai, Susan, 102, 103–104, 109, 259
Nishimuko, M., 217*n*
Novelli, Mario: chapter by, 6, 9, 10, 49–64; references to works by, 49, 53

Ntagaramba, J., 147
Nyabanaba, T., 251
Nyamwasa, G., 139

Obura, Anna, 27, 69, 102, 142–143, 187, 239
Ogango, M., 28
Oketch, M., 169, 171, 173, 175, 176, 179, 180
O'Malley, B., 62, 144
Osman, R., 200, 201
Othieno, T., 170
Ottaway, D. B., 59

Paalman, M., 139
Park, E., 232
Parker, I., 255, 256
Pasalic–Kreso, A., 36
Patch, J., 40
Paulson, J., 36
Pettigrew, T. F., 146
Phillips, D. C., 256
Pia, P., 28
Picciotto, R., 55
Pigozzi, M.J., 102, 103
Pinheiro, P. S., 22
Poate, D., 139
Posner, S. F., 98*n*
Postman, N., 33
Powell, Colin, 49–50, 60
Powell, K., 16, 24, 29, 30

Qahir, K., 71
Quinn, D., 40

Radelet, S., 178
Ranis, S., 256, 257
Ratcliffe, M., 40
Retamal, G., 53, 177
Reyntjens, F., 139
Richards, P., 37, 114
Rigaud, C., 43
Roberts, A., 51
Robinson, C., 237, 239, 241, 244, 252
Rogers, W., 98*n*

Rose, G., 227
Rose, P., 174, 178, 179, 258
Ross, M. H., 149
Rubin, H., 269
Rubin, I., 269
Rudasingwa, D., 139
Rutayisire, Paul, 200
Rwezaura, B., 238, 252

Sachs, J., 177
Said, E., 56
Saigol, Rubina, 25, 70
Salomon, G., 148
Saltarelli, D., 6, 15, 22, 26–
	27, 35, 53, 101, 138, 140
Schleicher, A., 119
Schrader, T., 139
Scott, J., 139
Sebatane, E., 251
Seitz, K., 15, 26, 27, 35
Sen, A., 56
Shah, S. M., 190
Shepler, Susan, 8, 11,
	199–217
Shilton, K., 232
Shriberg, J., 216n, 217n
Sigsgaard, Morten, 36, 37,
	42, 48n, 183–197, 197n
Simon, Bennett, 102, 103
Sinclair, M., 102, 103, 259
Slife, B. D., 257
Slim, H., 51
Smith, A., 15, 22, 36, 53,
	140, 201, 202, 222, 225,
	227
Smith, W., 110
Solomon, J., 225
Sommer, M., 80
Sontag, Susan, 223, 228
Spence, J., 225

Spink, J., 23, 26, 30, 36
Srinivasan, R., 232
Stannard, H., 186, 194
Steiner-Khamsi, G., 257
Stephens, J., 59
Stewart, F., 6
Stoddard, A., 55, 63–64
Stover, E., 143
Stuart, J., 222, 225, 227
Sullivan-Owomoyela, J., 37

Tanada, K., 41
Tarp, F., 178
Tawil, S., 140
Taylor, J., 235
Taylor, S., 73
Tenenbaum, S., 202
Teng, Nina, 48n
Theron, L., 222, 227
Thompson, J., 230
Thomson, S. M., 151n
Toomer, Chris, 48n
Torrente, N., 62–63, 64
Triplehorn, Carl, 102,
	103–104, 109, 259
Tryer, B., 120
Turrent, Victoria: chapter
	by, 3, 8, 9, 11, 169–181;
	references to works by,
	169, 171, 173, 175, 176,
	179, 180
Tyrer, B., 235, 238, 242

Ubalijoro, E., 223
Umurungi, J. P., 223

van de Walle, D., 87
van der Meer, E., 139
van Wijnberg, S., 179
Vaux, T., 15, 22, 36, 53, 140

Volavkova, H., 231
Vongalis-Macrow, A., 200,
	201

Wahrman, H., 149
Wakefield, S., 25
Waldman, M., 63
Walker, G., 36
Walsh, S., 225
Walters, P., 257
Wang, C., 222, 225
Wang, L., 212, 216n
Wang, T. Y., 58
Weingartner, C., 33
Weinstein, H. M., 150
Weller, S., 245
Wessells, M., 87
Whitworth, S., 70, 78
Williams, James, 48n, 140
Wilson, Charlotte: chapter
	by, 183–197
Winthrop, Rebecca:
	chapters by, 11, 101–121,
	123–136; references to
	works by, 4, 7, 29, 37,
	72, 78, 88, 95, 97, 98,
	110, 124, 146, 147, 1
	85, 199, 201, 202, 238,
	239
Woodhead, M., 235, 238
Woods, N., 61
Wulsin, S., 142

Xiang, Y., 222, 225
Xixhi Liu, 48n

Yi, W. K., 225
Yin, R. K., 88

Zambernardi, L, 50

SUBJECTS

Absorptive capacity, 178–179
Accelerated learning programs, 39, 41
Access to education: aid and education in
    fragile states and, 177, 180; architecture
    of aid to education and, 155, 156;
    community schools in Afghanistan
    and, 261, 270; dangers of securitization
    of education and conflict and, 62;
    education in fragile states and, 19, 23,
    25, 30; education as an interruption to
    fragility and, 36, 37, 38, 39, 40, 45, 46, 47;
    future aspirations of refugees and, 89,
    92, 93–94, 98; gender issues and, 67, 68–
    69, 71, 74, 75, 79; out-of-school children
    in conflict zones and, 2; participatory
    visual methodologies and, 232; policy
    recommendations concerning, 16;
    randomized research methods and, 260,
    270; relationships between education
    and conflict in Rwanda and, 140, 145;
    well-being of children and, 104, 111
Accountability, 38, 40, 44, 161, 175, 178
Activism, 29, 39, 43, 73. *See also* Change,
    educational
Adaptability, state: education as an
    interruption to fragility and, 34, 38, 43–46
Administrators. *See* leadership, educational
Adult education, 38, 41, 45
Afghan Research and Evaluation Unit
    (AREU), 191–192, 197*n*, 260
Afghanistan: aid and education in fragile
    states and, 169, 174; Brown speech
    about, 60; child-friendly research
    methods and, 239; in Cold War, 58–59;
    community-based schools in, 12, 255–
    271; complexity of education in fragile
    states and, 30; as conflict zone country,
    2, 3; context of education in, 185–188;
    curriculum and textbooks in, 30, 36;
    dangers of securitization of education
    and conflict in, 50, 51, 52, 53, 57, 58–59,
    60, 61, 62, 63, 64; definition of fragile
    state and, 170; developing trust and
    mutual respect in, 194–195; economy

of, 41–42; education as an interruption
    to fragility and, 34, 36, 37, 40, 41–42,
    43, 46, 48; gender issues in, 24, 25, 37,
    59, 71, 72, 186, 192–193, 196, 201, 259,
    261, 262, 264, 267–268, 269, 270; IIEP
    capacity development for educational
    planning study in, 8, 11, 183–197; INEE
    report about, 34, 48*n*; Kirk's death
    in, 10, 64–65*n*, 269; learning valued
    by children in, 124, 125–136; lessons
    learned from, 195–197; ministries of
    education in, 11, 183–197, 260, 261, 262,
    266, 270; national education planning
    in, 40; out-of-school children estimates
    for, 4; randomized research methods
    in, 255–271; refugees in/from, 11, 58,
    71, 101–102, 105, 107–108, 109–110,
    112–114, 115–121, 124, 125–136; rural
    areas in, 253–271; school-building
    initiatives in, 53; Soviet invasion of, 58;
    tarbia teaching in, 113, 131, 132; teachers
    in, 72, 105, 107, 109–110, 185, 187, 260,
    261–262, 264, 265, 266, 267; two faces
    of education and, 23; U.S. invasion of,
    59; well-being of children study in, 11,
    101–102, 105, 107–108, 109–110, 112–
    114, 115–121. *See also* PACE-A; Taliban;
    specific agency or project
Africa. *See specific nation*
African Development Bank, 170
Aga Khan Foundation, 48*n*, 197*n*
Agency for Co-operation and Research in
    Development (ACORD), 223
Agenda for Action, Accra, 162
"Agenda for All" (EFA Jomtien
    Conference), 155
Aid/assistance, international: allocation of,
    169–181; architecture of, 11, 155–167,
    175–176; dangers of securitization of
    education and conflict and, 49–50,
    58–64, 64–65*n*; dependency on, 36;
    education as an interruption to fragility
    and, 36; effectiveness of, 177–180;
    flows to fragile states of, 11, 169–181;

fragile states in globalized world and,
18; misuse of, 172; and violence against
aid workers, 63, 64–65n. *See also*
Development/development agencies;
Humanitarianism; *specific agency*
Al Qaeda, 60
Alphabet Soup, Education in Emergencies,
157, 159
Altruism, 111, 126, 133, 135
Angola, 3, 181n, 184
Asian Development Bank, 170
Asociación de la Mujer Maya Ixil, 225
Australia, 18, 50, 52

Babies, disposal of, 228–229
Back to School campaign (Afghanistan), 36
Beijing Platform for Action, 74
Bosnia-Herzegovina: architecture of aid to
education and, 156; Dayton agreement
about, 48n; definition of fragile state
and, 181n; education as an interruption
to fragility and, 34, 36, 37, 40, 41, 43, 48;
INEE report about, 34, 48n
Burundi, 3, 88, 143, 170
Bush (George W.) administration, 56, 60

Cambodia, 12n, 20, 34, 36, 37, 40, 42, 43,
48n, 184
Canada, 18, 50
Canadian International Development
Agency (CIDA), 24, 52, 222, 259
Canadian International Policy Statement
(IPS), 17, 19–20, 31n
Capacity development/building:
architecture of aid to education and,
161, 162; education as an interruption
to fragility and, 38, 43, 46, 48; for
educational planning in Afghanistan, 11,
183–197
CARE, 48n, 197n, 260
Catholic Relief Services (CRS), 48n, 197n,
258–271
Central African Republic, 3, 169, 170, 175
Chad, 3, 170, 184
Change, educational, 11, 138, 145–146, 150,
200–201, 211, 213, 216

Child-Friendly Schools (CFS), 12, 43,
235–253
Child-headed households, 223–224
Child-soldiers, 2, 5, 8, 21, 38, 41, 53
Children/students: distress in school of,
115–117; reflections of Rwandan, 137–
151; as shaping school experience, 117–
118, 120; teachers interactions with, 36,
75, 135. *See also specific person or topic*
Chronic Poverty Research Center, 240, 242
CIDA. *See* Canadian International
Development Agency
Civilians, 3, 7, 64, 72
"Clash of civilizations" theory, 55–56
Community: community schools in
Afghanistan and, 258–271; education
in fragile states and, 31; education as an
interruption to fragility and, 38, 40, 46,
48; gender issues and, 68, 75; learning
valued by children and, 132, 134;
randomized research methods and, 261,
262, 266; teachers as employees of, 213;
well-being of children and, 110, 111,
113–114, 115, 120. *See also* Community-
based education/schools
Community Based Education Management
Information System, Norway, 40
Community-based education/schools:
in Afghanistan, 12, 255–271; capacity
development for educational planning
in Afghanistan and, 186, 194; education
as an interruption to fragility and, 37;
emergencies research methods in, 255–
271; repatriated refugee teachers and,
210; stages of conflict and, 8; well-being
of children and, 120
Concern Worldwide, 213
Conflict Analysis Framework (CAF)
(World Bank), 21, 27
Conflict/conflict states: after-effects of, 3;
architecture of aid to education and,
155–167; dangers of securitization of
education and, 49–65; definitions of, 2,
3, 4, 6, 7–8, 12n, 139; education as root
cause of, 15; grievance/inequality theories
of, 6; homo-economicus and rational

choice theories of, 57; learning valued by children in, 123–136; lists of, 3, 4; motivations for, 5–6; multiple relations between education and, 137–151; "opportunity theories" of, 5, 6; out-of-school children in, 2–5; prevention of, 148–149, 184; re-envisioning education in, 134–136; stages/phases of, 6–8; understanding linkages between education and, 5–6. *See also specific nation*

Confliction resolution workshops (IRC), 215

Congo, Democratic Republic of: aid and education in fragile states and, 169; as conflict zone country, 3; definition of fragile state and, 170–171, 181*n*; IIEP work in, 184; out of school children in, 5; refugees in/from, 88, 89–91, 93–95, 96, 142, 143, 144

Consent forms, 105, 230, 241–242, 244–245, 260, 271*n*

Consolidated Emergency Relief Fund, 156

Convention on the Elimination of All Forms of Discrimination against Women, 74

Convention on the Rights of the Child (CRC) (UN), 9, 74, 98*n*, 237–238

Coping and hoping, 102, 103, 108, 138, 147–148

Corruption: aid and education in fragile states and, 173, 179, 180; capacity development for educational planning in Afghanistan and, 195; dangers of securitization of education and conflict and, 57; domains of fragility and, 34; education in fragile states and, 19, 23, 30; education as an interruption to fragility and, 38, 42, 44, 45, 46; repatriated refugee teachers and, 216; teachers' reasons for leaving teaching profession and, 208–209

Country Policy and Institutional Assessment (CPIA) (World Bank), 3–4, 16, 170, 178

Creditor Reporting System (CRS), 171, 172

Crisis/crises: aid and education in fragile states and, 176, 177; child-friendly research methods and, 235–253; education in fragile states and, 17; gender issues and, 73–75, 79, 81

Culture: child-friendly research methods and, 242, 244, 250, 252, 253; community schools in Afghanistan and, 267–268, 269; dangers of securitization of education and conflict and, 56, 57; as domain of fragility, 34, 35; education in fragile states and, 27; education as an interruption to fragility and, 35, 37, 39, 42–43, 44–45, 47, 48; gender issues and, 78, 79; politics of visual, 231–232; randomized research methods and, 267–268, 269; well-being of children and, 104

Curriculum: community schools in Afghanistan and, 262; dangers of securitization of education and conflict and, 59; education in fragile states and, 28, 30, 31; education as an interruption to fragility and, 36, 38, 39, 41, 42, 47, 48; gender issues and, 69, 70, 75, 80; Pakistan/Afghanistan conflict and, 59; randomized research methods and, 262; relationships between education and conflict in Rwanda and, 140, 141, 149, 150; stages of conflict and, 7, 8; use of conflict analysis and, 7; well-being of children and, 101, 103

DAC. *See* OECD-Development Assistance Committee

Dakar: World Education Forum in (2000), 157

Dakar Framework for Action, 160, 161

Danish Refugee Council, 213

Dayton agreement, 36, 48*n*

De-escalation and negotiation stage, 6

Declaration of the Rights of the Child (1924), 237

Development/development agencies: aid and education in fragile states and, 10, 169, 171–172, 174, 177; and amount of assistance, 51; architecture of aid to education and, 155–156, 157, 159–160, 161, 162, 164, 166, 167; capacity

development for educational planning
in Afghanistan and, 183, 195; dangers of
securitization of education and conflict
and, 10, 50–52, 53, 55, 58–64; definition
of fragile state and, 170; distribution of
assistance and, 51; future aspirations
of refugees and, 86; purposes of, 61;
relationships between education and
conflict in Rwanda and, 139; "3D"
approach and, 52. *See also specific agency
or nation*
Displaced persons. *See* Refugees/displaced
persons
"Donor orphan" countries, 18
Drawings, 225, 227–229, 230, 231, 248, 250
DRC. *See* Congo, Democratic Republic of
Dropouts, 4, 24, 67, 185
Drugs, 40, 42, 43, 181

Economic Development and Poverty
Reduction Strategy, Rwanda, 224
Education: benefits of, 20–21; as
commission, 22–23; content of, 28;
functions of, 102–104; multiple relations
between conflict and, 137–151; as
omission, 16, 20–21; as priority, 26, 27,
180; as stabilizing force, 26–30; student
distress in school and, 115–117; and
students as shaping school experience,
117–118; "two faces" of, 6, 11, 16, 20–23,
27, 35, 137–138;understanding linkages
between conflict and, 5–6. *See also
specific nation, organization, or topic*
Education for All (EFA): "Action Plan" for,
161; aid and education in fragile states
and, 174, 175–176, 178, 180; "Amman
Affirmation" of, 156; architecture of
aid to education and, 11, 155, 156, 157,
158, 159, 160–163, 165, 167; children's
rights and, 74; Dakar promise and, 160;
dangers of securitization of education
and conflict and, 49, 52, 59; development
of, 9, 59; education in fragile states
and, 20, 22, 29–30; education as an
interruption to fragility and, 33; Fast
Track Initiative of, 160–163, 165, 167,

174, 175–176, 178; gender issues and, 71;
goals of, 2, 165, 167; High-Level Group
of, 157; Jomtien World Conference for
(1990), 155, 156–157, 167*n*; out-of-
school children in conflict zones and, 2,
5; relationships between education and
conflict in Rwanda and, 148; Secretariat
for, 157, 161
Education for All Global Monitoring Report
(UNESCO), 157
Education Cluster, 9, 68, 76–77, 165, 166.
See also specific cluster
Education Cluster Working Group, 166
Education Development Board (EDB)
(Afghanistan), 191, 194
Education Development Forum (EDF)
(Afghanistan), 190, 194, 197*n*
Education and Fragility Working Group,
28, 31
Education Strategy (USAID), 21
Emancipatory learning, 124–127, 133, 134
Emergency, state of: aid and education
in fragile states and, 172, 176, 177;
architecture of aid to education
and, 155; capacity development for
educational planning in Afghanistan
and, 184; child-friendly research
methods and, 235–253; as conflict
stage, 6; dangers of securitization of
education and conflict and, 51, 53;
definition of education in, 4; education
in fragile states and, 31; education as an
interruption to fragility and, 43; future
aspirations of refugees and, 85, 89, 90;
gender issues and, 68–72, 73–75, 76, 77,
79, 80; research methods for, 255–271;
well-being of children and, 102, 103,
108
EMIS (Education Management
Information Systems) (Afghanistan), 38,
45–46, 187, 188, 192
Employment: domains of fragility and,
35; education in fragile states and, 21;
education as an interruption to fragility
and, 36, 37, 39, 41, 42, 45; learning
valued by children and, 128–129;

relationships between education and
conflict in Rwanda and, 148; repatriated
refugee teachers and, 213–214, 215–216;
teachers' motivation and, 205–206; and
teachers' reasons for leaving teaching
profession, 207; understanding conflict-
education linkages and, 5, 6; well-being
of children and, 115
Environment: architecture of aid to
education and, 160; degradation of, 34,
35, 39, 43; as domain of fragility, 34, 35;
education as an interruption to fragility
and, 34, 35, 39, 43, 48; as priority, 43
Eritrea: as conflict-affected country, 3;
definition of fragile state and, 171; gender
issues and, 72; refugees from, 101–2, 105,
106, 107, 110–112, 124, 125–136
Ethics, 12, 229–230, 232, 233, 239, 241–242,
257, 258, 262, 268, 270
Ethiopia: child-friendly research methods
and, 239; as conflict zone country, 3;
dangers of securitization of education
and conflict and, 52; gender issues and,
70, 72; IIEP work in, 184; learning valued
by children in, 124, 125–136; out-of-
school children in, 5; refugees in, 11, 70,
72, 101–102, 105, 106, 107–108, 109, 110–
112, 114–121, 124, 125–136; well-being of
children study in, 11, 101–102, 105, 106,
107–108, 109, 110–112, 114–121
Ethnicity: domains of fragility and, 34;
education in fragile states and, 22, 23,
27; education as an interruption to
fragility and, 35, 36, 38, 40, 41, 47; future
aspirations of refugees and, 87; gender
issues and, 67, 69, 70, 72; out-of-school
children in conflict zones and, 2; in
Rwanda, 139, 140, 141, 143; security and,
72; understanding conflict-education
linkages and, 6
European Development Fund, 60
European Union, 17–18, 37, 60
Eurotrends, 36, 37, 46

Failed States Index (Fund for Peace), 186
Family: future aspirations of refugee

children and relationships with, 87, 89–
98, 108–109; learning valued by children
and, 133, 135; well-being of children
and, 108–109, 112, 114, 120
Fast Track Initiative (FTI): aid and
education in fragile states and, 174,
175–176, 178; architecture of aid to
education and, 160–163, 165, 166, 167;
Catalytic Fund of, 161, 176; Education
for All (EFA) and, 160–163, 165, 167,
174, 175–176, 178; Education Program
Development Fund of, 161; Indicative
Framework, 161, 162–163, 165, 176;
as program to support education in
conflict zones, 9; Progressive Framework
for Fragile States and, 34, 162, 165, 176;
Steering Committee/Board of, 165
Fragile states/fragility: aid and education
in, 169–181; architecture of aid to
education and, 155–167; conflict stages
and, 6, 7; definition and characteristics
of, 3–4, 16–17, 23, 169, 170–171, 181n;
domains of, 34–39; education as an
interruption to, 33–48; education
policies in, 18–20; education as priority
in, 26, 27; education as stabilizing force
in, 26–30; gender issues in, 15–16, 19,
20, 22, 24–26, 27–30, 31, 35, 36, 37,
39, 42, 46, 68–72, 73–75, 77, 81; policy
papers about, 15, 16; recommendations
for future policy in, 16, 30–31; role
of education in, 10, 15–31; school
enrollment in, 20; as urgent concern in
globalized world, 16–18
Framework for Action (Dakar), 160, 161
FTI. *See* Fast Track Initiative
Fund for Peace, 186
Funding, educational: education in
fragile states and, 30; education as
an interruption to fragility and, 46,
47; gender issues and, 68; military
purposes and, 9; priorities for, 9; for
randomized research methods, 257, 262;
stages of conflict and, 7. *See also* Aid/
assistance, international; Development/
development agencies; Humanitarianism

Future: aspirations of refugees/displaced persons for, 85–99; dimensions of education and, 138; learning valued by children and, 124, 130; participatory visual methodologies and, 232–233; relationships between education and conflict in Rwanda and, 147–148; stages of conflict and, 7; teachers' motivation and, 205; well-being of children and, 103, 108–121

Gender issues: architecture of aid to education and, 159, 160; capacity development for educational planning in Afghanistan and, 186, 192–193, 196; challenges and opportunities concerning, 68–72; child-friendly research methods and, 236, 244, 252; community schools in Afghanistan and, 259, 261, 262, 264, 267–268, 269, 270; dangers of securitization of education and conflict and, 59, 61, 62; domains of power and, 35; education in fragile states and, 19, 20, 22, 24–26, 27, 28–30, 31; education as an interruption to fragility and, 35, 36, 37, 39, 42, 46; educational leadership and, 78, 80–81, 193, 196; emergencies and, 68–72, 73–75, 76, 77; fragile states and, 15–16, 19, 20, 22, 24–26, 27–30, 31, 35, 36, 37, 39, 42, 46, 68–72, 73–75, 77, 81; future aspirations of refugees and, 87, 95–96; health and, 78–80, 159; international commitment to, 15–16; learning valued by children and, 130; Minimum Standards (INEE) and, 11; out-of-school children in conflict zones and, 2, 5; participatory visual methodologies and, 221–233; randomized research methods and, 259, 261, 264, 267–268, 269, 270; reconstruction and, 69, 73–75; relationships between education and conflict in Rwanda and, 144, 145, 146; rights and, 70, 73–74; stability and, 28–30; stages of conflict and, 8; strategic versus practical interests and,

81*n*; student distress in school and, 116; teachers and, 69, 70, 71–72, 74, 75, 78–79, 80–81, 107, 116–117, 144, 187, 201, 215, 251, 252; violence and, 67, 68, 69–70, 72–73, 74, 78, 79, 80, 138, 144, 227, 229–230, 231–232; well-being of children and, 104, 107, 115, 116–117, 119. *See also specific nation*

Gender Task Team (GTT) (INEE), 75, 77, 81

German Development Agency (GTZ), 26, 27, 213, 214

Girls Education Initiative (AGEI) (Afghanistan), 193

Girls/women: as activists, 73; as heads of families, 223–224; menstruating, 79–80. *See also* Gender issues

Global Campaign for Education, 59

Global Consultations (INEE), 75

Global Education Cluster, 52, 76, 81

Global Monitoring Report (UNESCO), 3

Government/governance: accountability of, 40, 42, 44; aid and education in fragile states and, 169, 174; challenges facing post-conflict, 8; definition of fragile state and, 170; as domain of fragility, 34; education in fragile states and, 28; education as an interruption to fragility and, 38, 40, 42, 44, 46, 47, 48; NGOs as threat to, 202; trust in, 38, 40, 46, 47

Grievance/inequality theories of conflict, 6

GTZ. *See* German Development Agency

Guinea: aid flows and, 175; as conflict zone country, 3; definition of fragile state and, 171; gender issues and, 78; IRC Refugee Education Program in, 11, 201–217; IRC teacher tracer study and, 203–212

Haiti, 3, 12*n*, 24, 171, 175

Handicap International, 213

Healing Classrooms Initiative (HCI) (IRC), 43, 101–102, 104–120, 239

Health issues: architecture of aid to education and, 159, 160; child-friendly research methods and, 250; education as an interruption to fragility and, 35; education policies in fragile states and,

19; future aspirations of refugees and, 91, 93; gender issues and, 78–80, 159; holistic approaches to, 79–80; learning valued by children and, 125, 127–128; relationships between education and conflict in Rwanda and, 147; well-being of children and, 104, 111–112

"Hearts and minds" strategies, 50, 53, 57, 60, 61, 62, 63, 64

Herzegovina. *See* Bosnia-Herzegovina

Home-based education, 107, 110, 113, 132

Homo-economicus theory of conflict, 57

Human Resource Development Board (HRDB) (Afghanistan), 191, 194–195, 196

Human resources: capacity development for educational planning in Afghanistan and, 191–193

Human rights. *See* Rights

Human Rights Watch, 62

Humanitarianism: aid and education in fragile states and, 169, 171–172, 176–177; architecture of aid to education and, 11, 155, 156, 157, 158, 159–160, 165, 166, 167; community schools in Afghanistan and, 258, 270, 271; dangers of securitization of education and conflict and, 51, 52, 53, 55, 58, 61, 62, 63, 64, 64–65*n*; future aspirations of refugees and, 86, 87, 88, 98; gender issues and, 76, 77, 81; and programs to support education in conflict zones, 9; randomized research methods and, 257, 258, 270, 271; well-being of children and, 103, 119. *See also specific agency*

IASC (Inter-Agency Standing Committee), 52, 73, 76, 77, 156, 165–166

Ibis, 213

Identity/identities, 6, 38, 41, 48, 70, 78, 79, 113–114, 119, 132

INEE (Inter-Agency Network for Education in Emergencies): aid and education in fragile states and, 177; alternative research methodologies and, 12; architecture of aid to education and, 157, 159, 162, 165, 166, 167; and

conflict as disruption to education, 141; dangers of securitization of education and conflict and, 52–53; education in fragile states and, 28, 31; education as an interruption to fragility and, 34, 36, 41, 42, 46; expansion of, 166; formation of, 9, 53, 159; functions and role of, 53, 159, 166; gender issues and, 68, 73–76, 77, 81; Global Consultation of, 157; impact of, 9; relationships between education and conflict in Rwanda and, 141; Steering Group of, 166. *See also* Minimum Standards for Education in Emergencies, Chronic Crisis, And Early Reconstruction

Instrumental action: learning valued by children and, 126, 127–129

Inter-Agency Standing Committee. *See* IASC

International Bureau of Education (IBE), 26

International Committee of the Red Cross, 213

International Crisis Group, 58

International Institute for Educational Planning (IIEP): capacity development for educational planning in Afghanistan and, 11, 184–197; future aspirations of refugee children and, 88; typology of needs in conflict situations and, 8; well-being of children and, 102

International Medical Corps, 214

International Organization for Migration, 213

International programs/interventions, 8–10. *See also* Aid/assistance, international; Development/development agencies; *specific organization or program*

International Rescue Committee (IRC): education in fragile states and, 24–25; founding of, 104; gender issues and, 70, 71; Healing Classrooms Initiative of, 43, 101–102, 104–120, 239; LEGACY initiative of, 200, 216*n*; Liberia research and, 24–25; mission and functions of, 103; and murder of Kirk and colleagues,

64–65n; PACE-A and, 48n, 197n, 269; randomized assessment methods and, 255; Refugee Education Program of, 201–217; teacher training in Guinea and, 199; teachers as employees of, 213; well-being of children study and, 101–102, 104–120, 124, 125–136

International Save the Children Alliance, 52

Iraq: as conflict zone country, 2, 3; dangers of securitization of education and conflict and, 50, 51, 52, 53, 57, 61, 62, 63, 64; definition of fragile state and, 181n; education in fragile states and, 24; education as an interruption to fragility and, 43; gender issues in, 24; IIEP work in, 184

Islam, 56, 59, 62

Ivory Coast, 3, 181n, 184

Jobs. See Employment

Jomtien World Conference for (1990): Education for All (EFA), 155, 156–157, 167n

The Key to Peace (Inter-agency paper), 25

Knowledge; three modes of, 124–125

Latent/build-up conflict stage, 6, 7

Leadership, educational: capacity building of, 80–81; capacity development for educational planning in Afghanistan and, 185; child-friendly research methods and, 251, 252; community schools in Afghanistan and, 265, 266, 267; education in fragile states and, 28; gender issues and, 78, 80–81, 193, 196; randomized research methods and, 265, 266, 267; relationships between education and conflict in Rwanda and, 140, 141; repatriated refugee teachers and, 212–214; shortages of, 8; stages of conflict and, 8; teachers as change agents and, 201; well-being of children and, 103

Learning: benefits of, 109; as central to educational programming, 119; definition of, 103; emancipatory,

124–127, 133, 134; future aspirations of refugees and, 98; gender issues and, 68, 69, 74, 75; official certification of, 109; valued by children, 123–136; well-being of children and, 103, 108, 109, 110–121, 123. See also type of learning

Learning Plus Initiative (UNICEF), 235–253

LEGACY Initiative (IRC), 200, 216n

Lesotho, 236, 249

Liberia: Accelerated Learning Programme in, 41; aid and education in fragile states and, 175; community-based education in, 37; as conflict zone country, 3; definition of fragile state and, 171; education in fragile states and, 24–25; education as an interruption to fragility and, 34, 36, 37, 40, 41, 46; gender issues in, 24–25, 37; INEE report about, 34, 41, 48n; international organizations/programs and, 9; refugees in/from, 101–102, 105, 114–115, 124, 125–136, 199–217; teachers in, 199–217

Literacy: learning valued by children and, 125, 127, 128, 130, 134; out-of-school children and, 4

Livelihoods: defining refugee, 86–87; of refugees/displaced persons, 11, 85–99

Médecins Sans Frontières, 61, 209

Military: capacity development for educational planning in Afghanistan and, 195, 197n; dangers of securitization of education and conflict and, 49, 51, 52, 53–54, 56, 57, 58, 60, 61, 62, 63–64, 65, 65n; education as interrupting fragility and, 36, 43; out-of-school children in conflict zones and, 2; and programs to support education in conflict zones, 9

Millennium Development Goals (MDG): aid and education in fragile states and, 172, 174, 179, 180, 181; architecture of aid to education and, 160–161; capacity development for educational planning in Afghanistan and, 183; dangers of securitization of education and conflict

and, 59; development of, 9, 59; education
in fragile states and, 15, 17, 18–19, 29–
30; fragile states in globalized world and,
17; gender issues and, 15, 71; out-of-
school children in conflict zones and, 2;
participatory visual methodologies and,
232; relationships between education
and conflict in Rwanda and, 148; rights
and, 74

Minimum Standards for Education in
Emergencies, Chronic Crisis, And Early
Reconstruction (INEE), 9, 11, 31, 68,
73–75, 76, 77, 79, 81, 253*n*

Ministries of education, 183–184, 216. *See
also specific nation*

Monterrey Consensus on Financing for
Development (UN), 160, 175

Moral education, 40, 113

Mosaic approach, 238, 244

Muslims, 61–62, 64, 107, 260. *See also*
Islam; *specific nation*

National Education Strategic Plans
(NESP-I), Afghanistan, 185, 186, 187, 188,
189, 190–191, 192, 193, 194, 196, 197*n*

National Education Strategic Plans (NESP-
II), Afghanistan, 187, 188, 191, 192, 193,
195

National University of Rwanda, 142

Natural disasters, 4, 35, 39, 43, 155, 183,
236

Needs, educational: typology of, 6–8

Nepal, 3, 36, 40, 71, 171, 175

New student activity: child-friendly
research methods and, 249, 251, 252–253

NGOs (non-governmental organizations):
aid and education in fragile states
and, 172, 179; architecture of aid to
education and, 155–156, 159–160, 165,
166, 167; capacity development for
educational planning in Afghanistan
and, 186, 194, 197*n*; certification of
learning by, 109; community schools in
Afghanistan study and, 258, 259, 260,
261, 268, 270; dangers of securitization
of education and conflict and, 49, 50, 55,

63; education in fragile states and, 20;
education as an interruption to fragility
and, 43; future aspirations of refugees
and, 86; gender issues and, 68, 70, 71, 72,
76; participatory visual methodologies
and, 227, 229; randomized research
methods and, 255, 257, 258, 259, 261,
268, 270; repatriated refugee teachers
and, 202; teachers as change agents and,
201; teachers as employees of, 207–208,
213, 214, 215; as threat to governments,
202; well-being of children and, 109; and
workers as role models for children, 108.
See also specific organization

Nigeria, 3, 5, 21, 236

9/11, 49, 50, 53, 60

Normalcy, 102, 119, 126, 130–132, 135, 137,
146, 200

North Atlantic Treaty Organization
(NATO), 17–18

Norwegian Ministry of Foreign Affairs, 189

Norwegian Refugee Council, 214

Nurturing environment, 27, 102, 103, 112,
119, 138, 147, 185

Obama (Barack) administration, 60

Office for the Coordination of
Humanitarian Affairs (OCHA), 156,
165–166, 171, 172, 176

"Opportunity theories" of conflict, 5, 6

Organisation for Economic Co-Operation
and Development—Development
Assistance Committee (OECD-DAC),
21, 28, 51, 52, 54, 161–162, 170, 171, 173,
181*n*, 183

Organisation for Economic Co-Operation
and Development (OECD), 4, 21, 170,
172

Orphans, 142–143, 223–224

Out-of-school children: aid and education
in fragile states and, 169, 174;
characteristics of, 2; community schools
in Afghanistan and, 260; in conflict
zones, 2–5; dangers of securitization
of education and conflict and, 53;
education as an interruption to fragility

and, 40; future aspirations of refugees
and, 88; number of, 2, 4; randomized
research methods and, 260; well-being of
children and, 120
Overseas Development Institute (ODI), 178

Paintbrush Diplomacy, 231
Pakistan: adolescents in, 21; anti-U.S.
feeling in, 59; in Cold War, 58–59; as
conflict zone country, 3; dangers of
securitization of education and conflict
and, 52, 58–59; education in fragile states
and, 25; gender issues in, 25, 71; out-of-
school children in, 5; refugees/displaced
persons in, 58, 61; teachers in, 71
Palestinian Territories, 3, 24, 102
Parent-teacher associations, 28, 31, 38, 213,
259, 261
Parents: child-friendly research methods
and, 252; community schools in
Afghanistan and, 261, 266, 267, 268;
as killers, 224; learning valued by
children and, 132; randomized research
methods and, 260, 261, 266, 267, 268;
relationships between education and
conflict in Rwanda and, 142–143, 144,
145; teachers interactions with, 80–81;
trust of teachers by, 113, 132; well-being
of children and, 110, 113
Paris Declaration on Aid Effectiveness
(OECD), 59, 161–162, 196
Participatory visual research
methodologies (PVRM), 12, 221–233
Partnership for Advancing Community
Education (PACE-A), 43, 48*n*, 186, 194,
197*n*, 261, 266, 269, 270
Peace-building/keeping: capacity
development for educational planning in
Afghanistan and, 185; as conflict stage,
6; dangers of securitization of education
and conflict and, 51, 55; definition
of fragile state and, 170; education in
fragile states and, 25, 26, 27, 29, 30, 31;
education as an interruption to fragility
and, 33, 35; in fragile states, 16; future
aspirations of refugees and, 85; gender

issues and, 73, 75, 77–81; international
organizations/programs and, 9–10;
relationships between education and
conflict in Rwanda and, 137, 141, 148–
149, 150; youth engagement in, 29
"Peace dividends," 8
Peace Research Institute Oslo, 12*n*
Peers/friends: child-friendly research
methods and, 251, 252; learning
valued by children and, 131, 133, 135;
relationships between education and
conflict in Rwanda and, 144, 146;
student distress in school and, 115–117;
well-being of children and, 112, 115–
117, 121*n*
Persona dolls, 249, 250, 253
Photovoice, 12, 225–227, 230
Planning, educational: architecture of aid
to education and, 162; and capacity
development for educational planning
in Afghanistan, 183–197; education as an
interruption to fragility and, 38, 40, 45,
46; stages of conflict and, 8
Politics: dangers of securitization of
education and conflict and, 58, 63,
65*n*; education as an interruption to
fragility and, 37, 38, 39; of visual culture,
231–232
Portsmouth Ethnic Minority Achievement
Service, 249
Poverty: aid and education in fragile states
and, 174, 178, 179, 180; architecture
of aid to education and, 160; capacity
development for educational planning
in Afghanistan and, 183; dangers
of securitization of education and
conflict and, 53, 56–57; education as
an interruption to fragility and, 39, 42,
44; in fragile states, 17, 21, 23; future
aspirations of refugees and, 86, 90,
96; out-of-school children in conflict
zones and, 2, 5; participatory visual
methodologies and, 230; relationships
between education and conflict in
Rwanda and, 138, 139, 146, 148
Poverty Action Lab, 255

Poverty Reduction Strategy, Rwanda, 148
Practical learning: as valued by children, 124–127, 130–133, 135
Project Ploughshares, 12*n*
Protection: child-friendly research methods and, 236; cognitive, 104; community schools in Afghanistan and, 259, 261; education as an interruption to fragility and, 35, 38; in fragile states, 17, 26, 29, 30; future aspirations of refugees and, 98; gender issues and, 69, 73, 74, 75, 78–80; holistic approaches to, 79–80; Kirk's views about education in fragile states and, 10; participatory visual methodologies and, 230; randomized research methods and, 259, 261; relationships between education and conflict in Rwanda and, 147; stages of conflict and, 7; strategic, 78–79; well-being of children and, 102, 103, 104. *See also* Security/safety
Public Expenditure Tracking Surveys (PETS), 38, 45

Quality of education: aid and education in fragile states and, 177; child-friendly research methods and, 236, 237; community schools in Afghanistan and, 261; dangers of securitization of education and conflict and, 62; education in fragile states and, 20, 23, 30, 31; future aspirations of refugees and, 94, 98; gender issues and, 67, 69–70, 71, 80; learning valued by children and, 123–136; out-of-school children in conflict zones and, 2; randomized research methods and, 261; re-envisioning, 134–136; relationships between education and conflict in Rwanda and, 141, 146, 148; teachers role in, 199; well-being of children and, 104, 120

Randomized research methods: benefits of, 257–258; community schools in Afghanistan and, 12, 257–271; criticisms of, 256–258, 270; ethics and, 257, 262,

268, 270; funding for, 257, 262; increase in use of, 255–256
Rational choice theory, 57
Reconstruction: architecture of aid to education and, 166; capacity development for educational planning in Afghanistan and, 185, 188; characteristics of, 8; as conflict stage, 6, 8; education in fragile states and, 31; funding of education by international organizations/programs and, 9; gender issues and, 69, 73–75, 79; repatriated refugee teachers in Sierra Leone and Liberia and, 11, 199–217; well-being of children and, 102
Red Cross Movement, 76
Red Cross/Red Crescent, 172
Refugees/displaced persons: durable solutions for, 121*n*; education in fragile states and, 21; education as an interruption to fragility and, 37, 41; future aspirations of, 85–99; gender issues and, 70, 71, 72, 80; integration and repatriation of, 11, 96–97, 203; international organizations/programs and, 10; IRC strategy and, 103; livelihoods of, 11, 85–99; out-of-school children in conflict zones as, 3, 5; participatory visual methodologies and, 231; relationships between education and conflict in Rwanda and, 11, 142, 143; resettlement of, 94, 95, 96–97;stages of conflict and, 7; teachers as, 199–217; well-being of children and, 11, 101–121. *See also specific nation*
Religion: dangers of securitization of education and conflict and, 56, 58; domains of fragility and, 34; education as an interruption to fragility and, 38, 40, 41, 47; gender issues and, 69, 70; Pakistan/Afghanistan wars and, 58; understanding linkages between conflict and education and, 6
Resilience: capacity development for educational planning in Afghanistan and, 183–197; education in fragile states

and, 10, 20, 27, 31; education as an
interruption to fragility and, 34, 36–37,
38, 40, 44, 45–46, 48; use of conflict
analysis and culture of, 7
Rights: aid and education in fragile
states and, 177; architecture of aid
to education and, 155; capacity
development for educational planning
in Afghanistan and, 193; child-friendly
research methods and, 235, 237–239,
251, 253; conflict stages and, 7; dangers
of securitization of education and
conflict and, 51, 52; education in
fragile states and, 30; education as
an interruption to fragility and, 35,
36, 39, 42, 43, 45, 47, 48; as frame for
understanding educational needs of
children affected by conflict, 1; gender
issues and, 70, 73–74; international
organizations/programs and, 9; out-of-
school children in conflict zones and,
5; participatory visual methodologies
and, 230; prioritizing of, 238–239;
relationships between education and
conflict in Rwanda and, 147, 149;
teachers as change agents and, 201; use
of conflict analysis and, 7; well-being of
children and, 119–120
Rural areas; randomized research methods
and, 257–271
Rwanda: architecture of aid to education
and, 156; child-friendly research
methods in, 236, 239, 244, 245, 246, 248,
249, 250, 252; as conflict zone country,
3; dangers of securitization of education
and conflict in, 51; development in,
139; education in fragile states and, 22,
27, 30; education as an interruption to
fragility in, 35, 47; ethnicity in, 139, 140,
141, 143; gender issues in, 30, 138, 139,
144, 145, 146, 221–233; genocide in,
27, 35, 47, 137, 138, 142, 143–144, 145,
149, 156, 224, 233; goal of schooling
in post-genocide, 149; Ministry of
Finance and Economic Planning of, 223;
participatory visual methodologies and,

12, 221–233; population of, 138; poverty
in, 138, 139, 146, 148; reconstruction
in, 102; reflections on relationships
between education and conflict in, 6, 8,
11, 137–151; refugees in/from, 11, 88,
91–93, 142, 143, 150, 200; relationships
between education and conflict in,
137–151; repatriated refugee teachers
and, 200; Sector Wide Approach (SWAp)
in, 187; stages of conflict and, 8; teachers
in, 6, 8, 137–151, 200, 249; teaching
methodologies in, 35; UMWALI
Center in, 225; understanding conflict-
education linkages and, 6; Vision 2020
for, 148; well-being of children and, 102

Safety. *See* Protection; Security/safety
Save the Children: aid and education
in fragile states and, 171, 174, 177,
181*n*; architecture of aid to education
and, 166; capacity development for
educational planning in Afghanistan
and, 186; child-friendly research
methods and, 249; dangers of
securitization of education and conflict
and, 52, 53; education in fragile states
and, 22, 24; education as an interruption
to fragility and, 40, 43; founding of, 237;
gender issues and, 67, 107, 116; and
impact of conflict on education, 4; list
of fragile and conflict-affected countries
compiled by 3, 4, 12*n*; moral education
in Afghanistan and, 113; out-of-school
children in conflict zones and, 4–5;
participatory visual methodologies and,
231; and stages of conflict, 7; teachers as
employees of, 207; well-being of children
and, 113, 116
Security/safety: aid and education in
fragile states and, 174; architecture of
aid to education and, 162; capacity
development for educational planning
in Afghanistan and, 186; child-friendly
research methods and, 250, 251, 252;
community schools in Afghanistan
and, 260, 261, 263, 265, 266, 267–268,

269; and dangers of securitization of education and conflict, 49–64; dangers of securitization of education and conflict and, 57; definition of fragile state and, 170; as domain of fragility, 44; education as an interruption to fragility and, 38, 40–41, 42, 43, 44, 47, 48; in fragile states, 17, 19, 20, 24, 26, 30; future aspirations of refugees and, 11, 88, 89, 90, 91, 92, 93, 94, 95–96, 97; gender issues and, 68, 69, 70, 72–73, 74, 78, 96; learning valued by children and, 135; out-of-school children in conflict zones and, 5; participatory visual methodologies and, 223, 224, 226; randomized research methods and, 257, 260, 261, 263, 265, 266, 267–268, 269; relationships between education and conflict in Rwanda and, 147; and rise of security agenda in international development and education, 50–52; theories about nexus of education and, 55–57; well-being of children and, 103, 104

Sending a Message: drawing activity, 248; writing activity, 247–248

Senegal: World Education Forum in (2000), 160

Sierra Leone: aid and education in fragile states and, 175, 176; child-friendly research methods and, 239; as conflict zone country, 3; definition of fragile state and, 171; Distance Education Program in, 203; gender issues and, 70, 78; learning valued by children and, 124, 125–136; refugees in/from, 11, 70, 101–102, 105, 107–108, 109, 114–121, 124, 125–136, 199–217; repatriated refugee teachers in, 199–217; well-being of children study in, 11, 101–102, 105, 107–108, 109, 114–121

Social consciousness: learning valued by children and, 125, 127, 134

Socialization/social learning: community schools in Afghanistan and, 263; education as an interruption to fragility and, 35; learning valued by children and,

125, 126, 130–132, 135; randomized research methods and, 263; relationships between education and conflict in Rwanda and, 146; social, 103–104; well-being of children and, 102–104, 111, 112–113, 115, 119

Socioeconomic issues, 6, 30, 36, 39, 56, 150

Somalia, 2, 3, 20, 24, 51, 62, 64, 88, 171, 237

Sphere Project, 253*n*

Sports heroes, 226, 229, 230

Sri Lanka, 3, 34, 36, 41, 47

Stability: aid and education in fragile states and, 169, 174, 177; definition of fragile state and, 170; education as force for, 26–30; education in fragile states and, 19, 22–23, 26–30, 31; education as an interruption to fragility and, 33; future aspirations of refugees and, 85, 98; gender issues and, 28–30; relationships between education and conflict in Rwanda and, 138; well-being of children and, 102

State Department, U.S., 36, 61–62

Status: learning valued by children and, 126, 132–133

Stone Soup Museum of Children's Art, 231

Strategic Planning and Capacity Development Project (Afghanistan), 189, 193

Students. *See Children/students*

Sudan: adolescents in, 21; Basic Education Program in, 28; as conflict zone country, 3; dangers of securitization of education and conflict and, 51, 52; definition of fragile state and, 181*n*; education in fragile states and, 24, 25, 28; education as an interruption to fragility and, 43; gender issues in, 24, 25, 69, 70, 80; out-of-school children in, 5; refugees from, 88

Survival, 2, 38, 43, 69

Swaziland, 236, 247, 250–252

Tajikistan, 171, 175

Taliban, 10, 36, 37, 42, 59, 61, 62, 64–65*n*, 189, 269

Tanzania, 142, 143, 236

Tarbia, 113, 131, 132

Teacher Registration System, 187, 192

Teachers: bribes for, 38, 209; capacity building of, 80–81; capacity development for educational planning in Afghanistan and, 185; career trajectories of, 213–214; certification of, 11, 202–203, 209, 210, 211, 216; as change agents, 11, 200–201; child-friendly research methods and, 251, 252, 253; code of conduct for, 39, 42, 74, 79; community schools in Afghanistan and, 260, 261–262, 264, 265, 266, 267; education as an interruption to fragility and, 36, 38, 39, 42, 43, 46, 48; evaluation of, 120; fears of, 143; in fragile states, 15–16, 24–25, 28, 30, 31; future aspirations of refugees and, 92; gender issues and, 69, 70, 71–72, 74, 75, 78–79, 80–81, 107, 116–117, 144, 187, 201, 215, 251, 252; inexperienced/underqualified, 70; learning valued by children and, 128–129, 130–131, 132, 134, 135–136; as male dominated profession, 70, 80; mistreatment of students by, 116–117, 224, 249, 251, 252; motivations for teaching of, 204–206, 212; parents and, 80–81, 113, 132; perspective on own teaching of, 134; randomized research methods and, 260, 261–262, 264, 265, 266, 267; reasons for leaving profession of, 207–211, 216; recruitment of, 8, 31, 61, 80, 92, 202, 210–211, 216; reflections of, 6, 8, 137–151; as refugees/displaced persons, 199–217; respect for, 118; as role models, 70, 80, 108, 109, 128; role of, 30; rural, 211–212; salaries/compensation for, 24–25, 39, 43, 128–129, 136, 146, 207, 208, 216, 261–262; securitization of education and conflict and, 61; shortages of, 8, 216; stages of conflict and, 7, 8; and students as shaping their own school experience, 118; supervision of, 15–16, 31; training and development of, 4, 8, 15, 28, 30, 31, 46, 48, 69, 70, 72, 79, 80, 81, 104, 111, 136, 142, 146, 185, 199–217, 253, 261,

262, 264;urban, 211–212; violence and, 69, 70, 142, 144; volunteerism of, 110; well-being of children and, 101, 103, 104–105, 107, 108, 109–110, 111–112, 113, 115, 116–117, 118, 120; women as, 80–81, 201, 261; working conditions of, 208, 216. *See also specific nation*

Teachers College, 252

Teaching/pedagogy: education in fragile states and, 28; education as an interruption to fragility and, 35; gender issues and, 70; impact of conflict on, 4; learning valued by children and, 134, 135; relationships between education and conflict in Rwanda and, 141; as stepping stone to other jobs, 205–206; as subversive activity, 33; teachers perspective on own, 134; use of conflict analysis and, 7; well-being of children and, 103, 104, 111, 112

Technical and vocational learning, 36, 39, 41, 42, 48, 124–130

Teddy Bear Activity, 249–252

Terezin Concentration Camp (Prague Museum), 231, 233

Terrorism, 18, 50, 53, 57, 60, 61–62, 64, 181

Textbooks, 23, 30, 36, 47, 58–59, 147, 149, 185

"3D" approach, 52, 60

Tour/Camera Activity, 244, 245–247

Tour/Paper Plate Activity, 247

Transparency: aid and education in fragile states and, 178, 179; capacity development for educational planning in Afghanistan and, 187; education in fragile states and, 30; education as an interruption to fragility and, 38, 40, 42, 44, 45, 48; teacher hiring and, 216

Transparency International, 42

Uganda, 3, 11, 85, 86–99, 150

UNDP (United Nations Development Programme), 56–57, 106, 138, 139, 145

UNESCO (United Nations Education, Scientific, And Cultural Organisation): aid and education in fragile states and,

181n; architecture of aid to education and, 156, 157, 160, 161; definition of conflict-affected states of, 3, 12n; education in fragile states and, 15, 26; EFA and, 157, 161; functions of, 9–10; and funding of education by international organizations/programs, 9; gender issues and, 15, 68; and impact of conflict on education, 4–5; list of conflict-affected countries of, 3, 4; and out-of-school children in conflict zones, 4–5; participatory visual methodologies and, 222; relationships between education and conflict in Rwanda and, 148; stages of conflict and, 7, 8; violence in schools and, 144; well-being of children and, 102

UNHCR (United Nations High Commissioner for Refugees): architecture of aid to education and, 157; definition of child by, 98n; durable solutions for refugees and, 121n; future aspirations of refugees and, 86, 87, 88, 89, 91, 92, 94, 96, 97, 98; gender issues and, 68, 107, 116; typology of needs in conflict situations and, 7; UNICEF coordination with, 10; well-being of children and, 116

UNICEF (United Nations International Children's Fund): architecture of aid to education and, 165, 166; capacity development for educational planning in Afghanistan and, 186; Child-Friendly Schools initiative of, 12, 43; and children as disabled or casualties in conflict zones, 2–3; community schools in Afghanistan and, 260; dangers of securitization of education and conflict and, 52, 53, 59; Education Clusters and, 9; education in fragile states and, 20, 22, 24; education as an interruption to fragility and, 43; functions of, 9–10; Learning Plus Initiative of, 235–253; participatory visual methodologies and, 222, 231; randomized research methods and, 260; relationships between

education and conflict in Rwanda and, 142, 143; UNHCR coordination with, 10; U.S. invasion of Afghanistan and, 59

Union Carbide/Bhopal disaster, 43

United Kingdom: Afghanistan and, 60; child-friendly research methods in, 238; dangers of securitization of education and conflict and, 50, 52, 53, 56, 60; Department for International Development (DfID) in, 16–17, 18–19, 20, 23, 26, 52, 53, 56, 60, 187; education as priority for, 18

United Nations: aid and education in fragile states and, 171, 179; architecture of aid to education and, 155, 157, 160, 167; dangers of securitization of education and conflict and, 52, 62, 63; definition of fragile state and, 170; education in fragile states and, 20; fragile states in globalized world and, 17–18; gender issues and, 73, 76–77; Global Education Cluster of, 76–77; peace-keeping expenditures of, 51; Security Council of, 51; Security Resolution 1325 of, 29; and workers as role models for children, 108. *See also specific organization/agency*

United Nations Development Group (UNDG), 156, 157, 158, 159

United Nations Humanitarian Response, 9

United Nations Millennium Summit, 160

United Nations Peace-Building Fund, 10

United States: dangers of securitization of education and conflict and, 50, 51, 57, 63; education as priority for, 18

Universal Declaration of Human Rights (UN), 155

University of Nebraska-Omaha, 23, 58

USAID (U.S. Agency for International Development): Africa Bureau of, 28; community schools in Afghanistan and, 260, 261; dangers of securitization of education and conflict and, 52, 56, 58–59, 60, 61–62; domains of fragility and, 34; domains of power and, 35; education in fragile states and, 17, 19, 21, 23, 24,

26, 28; fragile states in globalized world and, 18; PACE-A and, 261; Pakistan/Afghanistan in Cold War and, 58–59; randomized research methods and, 260

Violence: against aid workers, 63; capacity development for educational planning in Afghanistan and, 184; child-friendly research methods and, 236; community schools in Afghanistan and, 261, 269; culture of, 4; dangers of securitization of education and conflict and, 55, 56, 63; descriptions of conflict zones and, 3; dimensions of education and, 138; domains of fragility and, 34; domains of power and, 35; education in fragile states and, 19, 22, 23, 24, 25–26, 27, 29, 30; education as an interruption to fragility and, 35, 36, 37, 38, 39, 40, 41, 42, 44, 46, 47, 48; gender issues and, 67, 68, 69–70, 72–73, 74, 78, 79, 80, 138, 144, 227, 229–230, 231–232;international organizations/programs and, 9; participatory visual methodologies and, 221–233; randomized research methods and, 261, 269; relationships between education and conflict in Rwanda and, 139, 140, 141, 142, 144, 147; schools as sites of, 144; stages of conflict and, 7; teachers as change agents and, 201; teachers as perpetuating, 69, 70
Vision 2020, Rwandan, 148
Vocational education. See Technical and vocational learning
Vulnerability: capacity development for educational planning in Afghanistan and, 184, 187, 195; child-friendly research methods and, 237, 238, 243, 249; definition of fragile state and, 170; education in fragile states and, 17, 29; future aspirations of refugees and, 87, 95; gender issues and, 69, 74, 75, 78, 107; well-being of children and, 107

Well-being of children: concepts related to, 102–104; gender issues and, 104, 107, 115, 116–117, 119; learning for a bright future and, 11, 101–121; learning valued by children and, 123, 124, 125–136; relationships between education and conflict in Rwanda and, 146–148; student distress in school and, 115–117; and students as shaping school experience, 117–118
West African Examinations Council, 217n
Women's Commission for Refugee Women and Children, 24, 86
World Awareness Children's Museum, 231
World Bank: aid and education in fragile states and, 171, 175, 178; architecture of aid to education and, 157–158, 161, 166; capacity development for educational planning in Afghanistan and, 183; classification of economies by, 181n; Conflict Analysis Framework (CAF) of, 21, 27; Country Policy and Institutional Assessment (CPIA) of, 3–4, 16, 170; dangers of securitization of education and conflict and, 57; definition/concept of fragile state and, 3, 170, 171; education in fragile states and, 20, 21, 22, 24, 27; list of conflict-affected countries compiled by, 4, 12n; randomized assessment methods and, 255; relationships between education and conflict in Rwanda and, 145; Sierra Leone urban-rural teacher report of, 211–212; teacher motivation study for, 216n
World Child Welfare Charter (1924), 237
World Education Forums, 53, 157, 160
World Vision International, 69, 222

Yemen, 3, 62, 181n
Youth: activism of, 39, 43
"Youth bulge," 34–35, 41

Zimbabwe, 44, 169, 171